The Royal Navy

An Illustrated Social History 1870–1982

VE Day, 1945. Lieutenant Douglas Ford RNVR, officers and men of HMS *Acacia* at Fountain Lake Jetty, Portsmouth

The Royal Navy

An Illustrated Social History 1870–1982

CAPTAIN JOHN WELLS

With a foreword by
Admiral of the Fleet
The Lord Lewin of Greenwich

A Sutton Publishing Book

First published in the United Kingdom in 1994 by Alan Sutton Publishing Limited, an imprint of Sutton Publishing Limited · Phoenix Mill · Thrupp · Stroud · Gloucestershire in association with The Royal Naval Museum, Portsmouth

This edition published in 1999 by Wrens Park Publishing, an imprint of W.J. Williams & Son Ltd

A catalogue record for this book is available from the British Library

ISBN 0-905-778-308

Jacket illustrations: front: carpenters, HMS Antrim, c. *1903; back: dinner hour, fo'c's'le deck, HMS* Queen, *Malta, 1904 (reproduced by kind permission of the Royal Naval Museum, Portsmouth).*

Typeset in 10/13 Baskerville.
Typesetting and origination by
Sutton Publishing Limited.
Printed in Great Britain by
Redwood Books Limited,
Trowbridge, Wiltshire.

Contents

Foreword

The Royal Navy, with its record of service reaching back for some four hundred years, has a reputation for conservatism, an in-built resistance to innovation. While this criticism might have been well deserved at some periods in the past, it is certainly not true of the last half of the century, a period that has seen the Navy adapting to the ever increasing pace of both social and technical change. Let me give a personal illustration. When I and my contemporaries joined our first ship, the training cruiser HMS *Frobisher*, in January 1939, our very first lesson was how to sling, lash up and stow a hammock. As cadets and midshipmen it was in hammocks that we slept, as did everyone in every ship except the officers, who had cabins. Since Columbus and his men discovered the Caribbean natives sleeping in this comfortable device in 1492, sailors had slung hammocks to sleep in the messdecks where they also ate and lived. By the time I left the Navy – if one ever does – there was not a hammock to be seen; all had been replaced by bunks, with separate dining halls for meals and recreation.

After centuries of stability, in the period encompassed by this book change has affected virtually every aspect of naval life. Officers used to be drawn from a limited section of society and at an early age. Now anyone who can meet the required high standard, man or woman, may join or be promoted from the lower deck; all have equal opportunity. The advent of complex machinery for both ship propulsion and weapons required a new artificer branch whose recruits had to be of a higher level of education if they were to cope with their long specialized training; later the electronic revolution posed a similar challenge. Some improvements to conditions of service were adopted to keep pace with the higher standard of living in the country as a whole. The existence of sailors' wives and families, long ignored, was recognized by the introduction of marriage allowance. Married quarters, recognized in the other two services, were provided in increasing numbers. Once embarked on this caring course further improvement was steady; the Navy's support for its families is now second to none.

John Wells has researched and recorded the wide-ranging and dramatic changes in the social structure of the Royal Navy in the last hundred years, set against the circumstances and events that have stimulated them. Some reforms have been a reflection of changing patterns in our society, while others have been born of a closer understanding and a growing mutual respect between officers and men. Is the Navy better for them? The Falklands Campaign gives the answer: never before in its long history has the Navy been so immediately ready to answer the nation's call and seldom has it met its task with such success.

This book is a major contribution to our maritime history and one that has been long awaited.

Terence Lewin

The Lord Lewin of Greenwich
Suffolk, 1994

Preface and Acknowledgements

Wearing sailor suits from an early age, collecting cap ribbons and experiencing the thrill of going aboard warships for children's parties undoubtedly nudged my destiny towards the Royal Navy. Barely thirteen and a half I was roused one night from the captain's spare cabin of the battleship *Royal Sovereign* to be told of passing into Dartmouth; next day brought a summons to the flagship to meet an awe-inspiring but kindly admiral called Howard Kelly who offered his good wishes and a glass of sherry. Then followed thirty-five happy and rewarding years that generated a deep, abiding love for the Service, so much so that when the time came to say goodbye I felt very sad, a sentiment not unknown among sailors of every generation. Looking back I would not have chosen any other career, and given the choice today would almost certainly do so again.

Research and restoration of the Victorian ironclad HMS *Warrior* awakened a latent interest in the lifestyle and administration of nineteenth- and twentieth-century naval people, a subject ably covered by Professor Michael Lewis in the second of two volumes terminating in 1864; other writers confined their studies to the lower deck, though no later than the 1930s. Because the lives of officers and men are totally interrelated I decided to combine both in a work that started in 1870 when national education and social awareness within the Navy had become a reality. Less easy to determine was when to stop. The closer one gets to the present day the more difficult it is to grasp essentials and put them in a proper perspective. Because of its importance as an assessment of human endeavour everything pointed to the South Atlantic campaign 112 years later.

Social history is a complex but fascinating subject, hard to define in precise terms, especially in its application to the Royal Navy. It is found in a mixture of books and periodicals, official documents and publications, and in private memoirs, letters and recordings of officers and men. Fortunately there was a wealth of material for the groundwork of earlier chapters and from the 1930s I was able to supplement research with my own experience, supported by individual recollections of people, many of whom I knew personally. A recurring problem in tracing the course of history was impartiality to all branches of the Service; for any serious omissions I extend my apologies.

While it can be said that history seldom if ever repeats itself it is equally true that the circumstances of history frequently repeat themselves. From being a highly conservative institution the modern Navy has become hardened to constant change; perhaps future problems that may arise among naval people have their counterparts in the recorded experience of the past.

My acknowledgements for assistance are numerous. First I must thank most warmly Captain Hugh Owen and Mr Alan McGowan who read the manuscript chapter by chapter, kept me on course and acted as a sounding board. For their advice I am also indebted to Admirals of the Fleet the Lord Hill-Norton and Sir Henry Leach, Admirals Sir Frank Twiss, Sir Louis Le Bailly and Sir

Brian Brown, Vice-Admirals Sir John Forbes and Sir Peter Ashmore, Rear Admiral Colin Dunlop, Captains Michael Barrow, Christopher Burne and Richard Kirkby and Lieutenant Geoffrey Mason. Response to a notice in *Navy News* seeking contributions led to abundant correspondence with many retired ratings and I am sincerely grateful for the immense trouble they took to give me the benefit of their service impressions.

Three libraries yielded the bulk of research material, and my thanks go to Andrew Trotman of the King Alfred Library of the Royal Naval Museum, Portsmouth, Fred Lake and Bridget Spiers of the MOD Whitehall Library in London and to Alan King of Portsmouth Central Library. I am also grateful to the Department of Sound Records of the Imperial War Museum for permission to work on their material and to the Directorate of Naval Manpower and Training in MOD (Navy) for permission to study their historical records.

In selecting illustrations Andrew Trotman and Nicola Scadding of the Royal Naval Museum, Portsmouth, made available their unique collection of photographs and photograph books, besides giving me every assistance, in conjunction with the facilities provided by Alan Sutton Publishing. Permission to reproduce other illustrations is gratefully acknowledged to the following: Royal Marines Museum, Eastney, pp. 22, 51, 113, 123, 127, 184, 215, 258, 260, 261, 262, 263; Commander J.R. Phillimore, p. 4; Captain, Britannia Royal Naval College, Dartmouth, pp. 6, 235; Messrs A. & C. Black Ltd, pp. 15, 128, 149, 244, 252; Mrs Jacqui Davis, p. 21; Victoria and Albert Museum, p. 34; Mr Ashton, p. 52; Mr David Gieve, pp. 93, 104; *Navy News*, p. 217; Lieutenant Commander John Cooper, p. 218; RN Photographic Unit, Portsmouth, pp. 259, 262.

Mrs Gaye Briscoe has typed the whole manuscript with great care and accuracy and I should also like to thank Mrs Chris Grover and Mrs Kathy Carline for work in the earlier stages.

Finally, my appreciation to Roger Thorp and Simon Fletcher at Alan Sutton Publishing for their helping hands.

John Wells
Liss
Hampshire

CHAPTER ONE

The Community of the mid-Victorian Navy

Engines and machinery are liable to many accidents, may fail at any moment, and there is no greater fallacy than to suppose that ships can be navigated on long voyages without masts and sails, or safely commanded by officers who have not a sound knowledge of seamanship.

Preface to Seamanship *by Commander G.S. Nares, 1865*

One month after his fifteenth birthday Naval Cadet Lord Charles Beresford was appointed to HMS *Marlborough* at Portsmouth: 'As I climbed up her side by the hand rungs I perceived two huge men looking down upon me, and I heard one say to the other: "That white-faced little beggar ain't long for this world."'

Marlborough differed from Nelson's *Victory* only in her greater dimensions and the addition of a single screw driven by a steam reciprocating engine. In the early 1860s she was flagship of the Mediterranean fleet and in Beresford's words:

> Her efficiency was shown the night before sailing for Malta. Newly commissioned we carried large numbers of supernumeraries for passage, 1,500 all told. A fire broke out on the orlop deck; the drum beat to quarters; every man went instantly to his station and the fire was speedily extinguished. That was my first experience of discipline in a big ship.

In his memoirs Beresford, who commanded the same fleet forty-four years later, asserted that:

> A sailor's offences were seldom crimes against honour; they arose from the character of his calling which was hard, dangerous and often intensely exciting. The sailor was devil-may-care, free with his language, handy with his fists and afraid of nothing. Granted very little leave they remained there until the last penny had been spent; and they returned either drunk or shamming drunk, for drunkenness was the fashion then. Excess was the rule in many ships; I remember one man who ate and drank himself to death on Christmas Day.
>
> The ordinary rations were so meagre that hunger induced men to chew tobacco and I cannot understand how they were so hardy on such an insufficient diet. They used to go aloft when a gale was blowing with snow and sleet and remain there for hours reefing sails, clad only in flannel vest, serge frock and trousers. Then they would go below to find the decks awash in a foot of water, the galley fire extinguished, nothing to eat until next meal time but a biscuit and nothing to drink but water. The sanitary appliances were placed right forward in the open air; if the sea was rough they could not be used and the state of the lower deck may be better imagined than described. Our sail drill was a miracle of smartness and speed. The

men would go aloft so quickly that their bare feet were nearly indistinguishable. They would run along the yards when the ship was rolling; sometimes they would fall, saving themselves by catching the yard.

To young Beresford *Marlborough* was a 'ship of the happiest memory', a survival of the old Navy described by a contemporary as a 'hardfisted, freeliving, implacable, tragic, jovial, splendid Service; it was England at her valorous best'.[1]

❖❖❖

The Royal Navy's character has always been reflected in the social life of the nation, which in 1870 could look back with pride on a wealth of achievement. The industrial revolution had reached its apogee and Britain was the foremost trading nation in the world. Gradually the whole basis of English life was changing, the focus of employment shifting from agriculture to industry and from the country to the towns. A different society had emerged, eager to learn about machinery, how to produce energy and how to expand national resources. Benefits of industrialism were felt in everyday life, not so much among the aristocracy but by the middle classes, whose higher standard of living had given them a new vitality and with it social aspirations. At the same time the majority of urban lower classes paid the price of overcrowding, living in disease-ridden squalor, eating frugally and working under backbreaking conditions. However, the combination of communal reforms and cheaper food was starting to have an effect; trade unions were recognized and those people who did not emigrate to the colonies or America could nearly always find work. Life expectancy was approximately forty-six years and despite urbanization the crime rate was falling: prison life was highly regimented and corporal punishment commonly administered. The observance of religion played an influential role in family life.

Because it made primary education available to the masses the passing of the Education Act (1870) was a turning point in social history; until then the advantage of schooling was largely confined to the upper and middle classes. And as more people learnt to write letters and read books improvements in printing technology led to massive growth in newspaper circulation by the end of the century. Meanwhile, independent (public) schools taught classics and ancient history, their aim to develop character, manliness and self discipline through organized team games like cricket and football. The aura of the country house, London society and clubland was matched by the growth of working men's clubs, enthusiasm for football and the appeal of the pub and music hall. Immoderate drinking and gambling prevailed in a male dominated society, smoking was fashionable and the image of the typical Victorian of all classes was a man with a beard and a pipe.

The year 1870 was also mid-term in the period between Waterloo and the First World War in which British power politics played a significant role in preventing widespread conflict. The wars that occurred were of short duration and successfully contained, piracy was all but ended and the slave trade suppressed. The chief instrument of *Pax Britannica* was the Royal Navy, unchallenged at sea and able to exercise a greater influence on global affairs than at any other time in its history.

The state of the mid-Victorian Navy owed its roots to the aftermath of the Great War with France that ended in 1815. After twenty years of almost uninterrupted sea warfare the Royal Navy suddenly found itself at peace, having to seek a new role and having to face drastic reductions in manpower and ships. At that time the Navy only employed its personnel for the duration of a ship's commission, about four years. When not so engaged, officers were placed on a retainer of half pay while the crews were left to their own devices. Post-war economy dictated immediate demobilization by paying off ships into reserve; to the hardship and unemployment caused among men the Admiralty were unsympathetic.

The officers suffered as well. Traditionally separated into two distinct branches, military and civil, the former were the executives who fought and commanded warships – and virtually ran the Navy – while the civil branch were non executive specialists. Officers were either commissioned or warranted by the Admiralty and their names shown in the official Navy List in order of seniority. By 1870 all civil branch warrant officers had been transferred to commissioned rank by which time a new branch had emerged of engineers, initially as warrant and subsequently commissioned, as is shown in the following table.[2]

COMMISSIONED OFFICERS		*WARRANT OFFICERS*	
Military	*Civil*	*Military*	*Civil*
Admirals	Surgeons	Boatswains	Carpenters
Commodores	Engineers	Gunners (from 1878)	
Captains	Pursers	Carpenters (until 1878)	
Commanders	Chaplains		
Masters	Naval Instructors		
Lieutenants			
Sub-Lieutenants			

Distinguished by the flags or pennants hoisted to denote their presence, rear, vice- and (full) admirals, as well as commodores, were known collectively as flag officers. The rank of captain, until 1860 'post captain', was the most senior below flag rank and eligible to command a major warship; the term 'senior officers' comprised admirals and captains. Officers below captain and above sub-lieutenant lived in the wardroom while subordinate officers (sub-lieutenants and below) together with assistant surgeons and assistant clerks lived in the gunroom. The courtesy title of captain was also given to commanders and lieutenants in command of minor warships and to members of the crew holding certain jobs, such as 'Captain of the Hold'.

When peace was declared in 1815 there were 833 captains, 70 commanders and 394 lieutenants competing for jobs in a fleet that quickly shrank to thirteen major and eighty-nine minor warships. Unlike the Army the Navy required professional skill in its officers long before Victoria's reign and all had entered the service on a long-term career basis. Promotion to flag rank lay in attainment of seniority, and having no retirement scheme those unable to obtain a sea appointment remained ashore on half pay, a bleak outlook for lieutenants but ruinous for the senior ranks. In no time lists became swollen with ageing officers having scant prospects of seagoing or promotion or, in the long run, remaining employable.

Initially the Admiralty did little to make amends and it is remarkable that the professional corps of officers survived under such unfavourable conditions. Some sat back and lost touch while others kept their hands in by serving the Merchant Navy or the revenue service; the more enterprising

Captain Augustus Phillimore and officers on board one of the early ironclads, HMS *Defence*, 1863

volunteered for sponsored voyages of Arctic exploration or else joined foreign navies, inspired by men like Thomas Cochrane and Charles Napier. Several took up the offer of free land by emigrating to Australia, and a few like Captain Marryat turned to writing. But survive they did though recovery from the 'great slump' took a long time, excessive numbers diminishing through disability, deaths and compulsory retirement schemes. In the civil list pursers and surgeons were less affected because their professions enabled them to find employment ashore more readily.

The test came when the Navy mobilized for the Anglo-French war against Russia (1854–5). In this largely land-fought campaign the average age of senior naval officers was well over sixty which, when added to physical defects and years of stagnation, explained the instances of intransigent outlook and incompetency in the Baltic and Black Sea fleets. Not before time the blockage at the top was eased by the compulsory retirements of flag officers until the number employed reached more reasonable proportions. By 1870 the situation had further improved, the average age of lieutenants down to twenty-eight, commanders thirty-seven, captains forty-four and rear admirals fifty-six, personnel being the responsibility of the Second Naval or Sea Lord and his department.

Fortunately the Admiralty did not restrict the flow of officer recruitment; new entrants aged twelve and thirteen, initially called first class volunteers, could only be nominated by captains, flag officers and the Admiralty, who insisted on approving all nominations. That naval officers had faith in the system and in the future is substantiated by statistics showing that the majority (33 per cent) of applicants continued to be the sons of naval families; the rest were from the aristocracy, the landed gentry, the clergy, the Army and other professions. Geographically most officers originated from those English counties south of a line from the Humber to the Mersey and nearest to naval ports.

Because business and working classes were not represented it could be argued that the Navy's stock suffered from the influx of youngsters with high breeding, which made the caste of executive officers unduly upper class. During the Napoleonic wars men had risen from the lower deck to become captains and admirals but this type of entry was abandoned. As a lord commissioner of the Admiralty who did much for the welfare of naval ratings Admiral Milne wrote in 1859: 'As regards promotion from the forecastle to the quarterdeck, I have no desire to see anyone but a *gentleman by birth* decorated in a Post Captain's uniform.'[3] Officer-like qualities in the Victorian Navy were based on the character of the English gentry, a social order held in respect throughout the country. Leadership, education, acceptance of responsibility and a sense of fair play were also attributes expected of an officer by men on the lower deck.

Qualifications to join were minimal, as young John Moresby found in 1842 when he presented himself with his father at the guardship *Caledonia* in Devonport:

> The examination paper was not an alarming one, consisting of 'rule of three' sums – 'If 50 pounds of salt pork cost £2 10*s* what is the price of one pound?' This accomplished, my name and that of the ship written, and having been found sound in mind and limb, Mr Gossman (the Master and a Trafalgar veteran) reported that I had passed an excellent examination and signed my certificate.[4]

Successful volunteers went directly to sea or, if Admiralty nominated, received a two-year theoretical course at the Royal Naval College, Portsmouth. On joining their first ships the superior education of the collegians clashed with the unpolished but more practical exponents of seamanship. When the College was closed to midshipmen in 1837 training was transferred afloat, but the atmosphere of a warship was hardly conducive to study and academic pursuit made little headway.

Renamed naval cadets and rated midshipmen after one or two years the 'young gentlemen' learnt their seamanship the hard way, as Cyprian Bridge found when he joined the line-of-battleship *Cumberland* in 1853 at the age of fourteen. 'With twenty in the gunroom mess who had nothing but their chests to contain their clothing and washing apparatus' he slung his hammock in 'the after cockpit below the lower deck'. Appointed for duties in the mizzen top Bridge raced aloft daily with the seamen but in his first experience of doing so barefooted, 'the sensation of stepping from rattlin to rattlin, especially after the feet had been made tender by ascent, was decidedly painful'. Another aspect of practical instruction was that:

> nearly all midshipmen whom I knew could make all the knots and splices; could point, graft and make mats; could strop a block, put on all the different seizings and use the palm and needle of the sailmakers. Also we had to take the helm and actually steer the ship, and take

> soundings by heaving the lead . . . it was expected in those days, when there was no continuous service afloat and large sections of the ship's company were newly raised, that we should, as sub-lieutenants, be able to show with our own hands untrained men how to do the work.[5]

This tradition continued well into the twentieth century.

Although cadets and midshipmen missed the wider education of their civilian contemporaries, 'catch 'em young' remained Admiralty policy, the only point at issue being the nature of training. Should they be sent straight to sea or first given a broader education ashore? The Admiralty compromised with the old hulk *Illustrious* as a harbour training ship where cadets would study mathematics, navigation, French and seamanship. When a larger ship was needed *Britannia* was selected, and in 1863 the Dartmouth tradition was founded when she dropped anchor in the River Dart.

After a year or so in *Britannia*, four years at sea and having studied the manuals of Captain Alston or Commander Nares, the nineteen-year-old midshipman took the first and most important

Britannia and *Hindostan* moored off Sandquay, River Dart, 1875

of his examinations for lieutenant – seamanship. At Portsmouth, in the rank of acting sub-lieutenant, he joined the RN College where he took courses in navigation, steam engines and gunnery. Rejoining the fleet his promotion to lieutenant depended mainly on seniority gained from examination results; some had to wait three or four years. Keeping watch at sea and in harbour on an exposed deck, as well as supervising the well-being of a fair-sized division of seamen, the average lieutenant led a strenuous existence during long passages under sail. In contrast most stations assured him of an agreeable social and sporting life ashore, as Lieutenant Fitzgerald experienced when serving in the Channel squadron visiting Portugal in the 1860s:

> There were so many sportsmen in the squadron that when one discovered anything fresh it was necessary to exercise some selfishness and protect one's vested interests and sporting rights by secrecy. . . . During one visit to Vigo I found a very nice little trout stream a few miles from the town and managed to keep it to myself and my shipmates for some time; but it was eventually unearthed by the whole fleet and its placid waters soon lashed into foam like bottled beer. At Gibraltar during the winter months we had the Calpe hounds and many a good gallop I had with them on a hired screw at one guinea a day and cheap at the price, as the hardy little Barb horses were very good goers.[6]

After eight years a lieutenant acquired a half stripe between the two rings on his sleeve; advancement to commander, later to captain, depended partly on merit but mainly on the patronage or interest of a flag officer to ask for an officer's appointment to give him the necessary sea time and secure his promotion. Even so an enterprising officer, without family or political connections, could also be promoted by catching the eye of a superior or perhaps by acquiring steam experience, like Admiral Cooper Key. As always luck was a major factor and although nepotism was overdone and had to be curbed, it was not altogether a bad system. Regulations required a commanding officer to render annual confidential reports on the character and ability of his officers – with particular reference to sobriety – on forms known as 'flimsies'.

Another way to get ahead was to specialize in gunnery. In 1830 the old three-decker *Excellent* was commissioned as a gunnery school in Portsmouth harbour to train officers and men to fight guns more professionally and evaluate their performance. From the school emerged the Navy's first weapon specialists, and by 1875 there were 240 qualified gunnery lieutenants. Besides carrying extra pay and responsibility the branch was popular because it brought an officer into the limelight when being seen and heard was an asset.

As deputy to the captain the commander – first lieutenant in small ships – was the senior executive officer, president of the wardroom mess and responsible for the organization or 'internal economy' of the ship and its company. This influential assignment was a stepping stone to higher rank.

In every warship navigation was performed by a qualified master who evolved as a professional seaman through warrant and commissioned rank to progress as navigating midshipman, sub-lieutenant or lieutenant and then staff commander or captain. In 1879 lieutenants (N) were introduced, but as executive lieutenants took on more pilotage responsibilities so the old specialist Navigation Branch faded out from 1883. The title Master of the Fleet was in force until 1947.

The executive warrant officers – gunners, boatswains and carpenters – were named after the warrant they received on promotion from the lower deck, being descendants of the standing officers who managed the ship while the gentlemen fought the sea battle. Although eligible for commissioned rank – almost none reached it before 1900 – and keeping officer of the watch in small ships, gunners and boatswains were relegated to humbler positions than their ability deserved. And so feelings of frustration and discontent sprang up as they witnessed masters, pursers, chaplains, surgeons and, as a last straw, engineers pass through warrant to commissioned grade and into the wardroom. Unfortunately their parochial outlook and departmental petty jealousies did little to promote their standing.

As well as suffering from the 'great slump' the evolution of the civil list of specialist officers became a struggle against the unbending attitude of the much larger executive branch. The surgeon was a case in point. Well educated and professionally qualified after hospital training an assistant surgeon must have found it galling to join the gunroom and share the company of younger, less responsible officers. Despite surgeons being commissioned promotion prospects remained poor, pay and status compared unfavourably with Army equivalents and at the outbreak of the Russian war the fleet's medical strength was seriously undermanned. However, the standard of those serving in the Crimean campaign, whose care of the wounded saved innumerable lives, had risen appreciably and by 1875 pay had been improved, the rank of fleet surgeon introduced, and every operational warship carried at least one medical officer.

The purser was another long established character in naval hierarchy, who was the official storekeeper and dispensed the victuals. Soon after the branch received commissioned status, pursers were given a proper rate of pay and made responsible for officers' and ship's company wages; in 1852 they were re-classified to become paymasters, assistant paymasters, clerks and assistant clerks. The more senior were secretaries to flag officers or paymasters of major warships; the more junior were secretaries to captains and lived in the gunroom. Mr Nipcheese, the fictional embezzler too often mirrored in the real life purser, was on the way out and a brighter future lay ahead.

The chaplain has always occupied an anomalous position in the Navy and, like the surgeon, was not specifically trained for life afloat. His background and university education entitled him to a seat at the wardroom table, although of warrant rank, and opportunity for extra payment in the dual role of naval instructor. When commissioned it was unclear how he ranked with other officers since he wore no uniform or marks of distinction. By 1870 there were ninety chaplains in the fleet serving in major warships and training ships; wearing contemporary clerical dress they held divine service to suit the ship's routine, administering their flock in much the same way as the parish parson.

Education in the Navy originated with schoolmasters of warrant rank, their job to teach young officers and seamen. From them evolved the naval instructor (with better pay and conditions) specifically to train subordinate officers, and the introduction of a petty officer schoolmaster to teach the crew, a job that later achieved warrant rank. Shortly after naval instructors were commissioned in 1861 the Admiralty appointed an inspector of education to co-ordinate the schooling of the fleet at a time when the need for a better educated sailor was pressing. In 1870 there were sixty-five naval instructors, the majority university graduates and half of whom were chaplains.

When engines were fitted in warships engineers or mechanics came with their installation in the form of a package deal. Possessing little education, rough and ready in approach and under no obligation to authority these men got off to a bad start. But because they were indispensable the Admiralty recruited them as first, second and third class engineers, gave them warrant rank, an outfit of uniform and substantially increased pay; this did not go far enough and there were recruitment shortages for some years. What they lacked was better status. Opposition centred on the military branch officer who hated the idea of steam propulsion usurping the motive power of sails over which he had paramount control, who objected to the embarkation of coal that deposited funnel soot on *his* deck and who regarded the engineer as socially unacceptable. Ignoring such antagonism the Admiralty reorganized the branch, created an inspector of machinery afloat, commissioned the senior engineers into the wardroom and increased pay all round. Yet junior (assistant) engineers continued to be segregated in a separate mess and the branch remained civil and non-combatant, a role that rankled after service in the Russian war. Nevertheless, the campaign proved beyond all doubt the value of steam ships in maritime wars and as machinery plants grew larger so naval artificers were recruited to replace junior engineer officers. The entry of qualified tradesmen as engine-fitters, boilermakers, smiths or coppersmiths was a major feature in the evolution of artificer engineers.

Below the officers were the crew, officially described as the ship's company – or the men – and colloquially as the lower deck, in contradistinction to the quarterdeck. Captains often referred to them as 'my people', an epithet that sometimes included officers. The generic title bluejackets or 'blues' was popular until the 1930s; aboard ship men were called 'hands' when ordered for work, a Victorian expression.

Except for the marines all were ratings in the sense of being rated by higher authority to a position in the ship that was both rank and job. Divided into military and civil branches the former comprised chief petty officers, petty officers (first and second class), leading, able and ordinary seamen, and boys. With jobs related to sailing the ship they held meaningful titles like captain of the maintop, quartermaster and sailmaker's mate. The civil branch held corresponding positions such as blacksmith (petty officer), cooper, leading stoker and 'stoker and coal trimmer'. As with the officers so it was that the seamen who fought the ship took precedence over the non-combatant civil branch. Paradoxically the latter included the master-at-arms, the senior lower deck rating, who, with the ship's corporals, was responsible for internal discipline. A detachment of marines formed about a quarter of the complement in almost every warship; although good fighting material they could not assume naval command and did not fall into either category. What role did they play?

The uniform of a chief petty officer, 1870

Raised in the seventeenth century as soldiers trained and adapted for maritime warfare, the Royal Marines were designated a light infantry corps in 1859 with a marine artillery division established a little later. A typical ship's detachment, comprising two-thirds artillerymen and one-third infantrymen, provided guards and sentries throughout the ship and manned guns and fighting tops; their most important role in war was to land by boat with field guns and rifles to spearhead the ship's task force ashore. In contrast to seamen and stokers marine recruitment found little difficulty in maintaining an official strength of 18,000 and, because volunteers were drawn right across the nation, the corps contained a high proportion of robust, solidly built countrymen. Unlike the seamen they were sworn in for seven or ten years' service and were to undergo stringent barracks training before going to sea, where they messed traditionally between the wardroom and the ship's company. Their reliability, discipline and steady performance earned them respect, spiced with many a leg pull on the lower deck. In common with their naval contemporaries marine officers found progress up the promotion ladder sluggish.

Less popular were the ratings of the steam department. Ranking with able seamen and petty officers (second class), stokers and leading stokers were recruited with the inducement of higher pay. In common with engineers, 'the poor stokers', wrote an able seaman, 'did not lead a very pleasant life. The seamen looked on them with contempt and for one to show himself on deck in his stokehold garb, was to court certain punishment'.[7] Nonetheless, many volunteers preferred stoking to going aloft.

By 1830 British imperial policy had created a new role for the Royal Navy with a wide variety of tasks for a comparatively small fleet. For ratings the prospect of battle with its chance of prize money was exchanged for the perpetual chores of a lengthy foreign commission. Hydrographic surveys and related chartmaking rendered an invaluable contribution to international navigation but gave little pleasure to the humble seaman. Patrolling to stop the slave trade in the South Atlantic area known as the White Man's Grave was a worthy cause but at considerable cost in men's lives. The best chance of a scrap and a welcome change of atmosphere lay in being selected to form part of a naval brigade to fight a minor war alongside the soldiers. Unquestionably the Navy had lost much of its glamour and with it a major incentive to recruitment and retention.

The majority of unemployed seamen continued to follow the sea by joining the mercantile marine or a foreign flag, particularly the American navy with its attractive rates of pay; and since old style impressment, last employed in 1815, the captain's job of commissioning a ship with volunteers became tedious. With the build-up of the fleet the Admiralty tried to induce a better quality of volunteer, directing the *Excellent* to enlist men for five or seven years, with incentives to re-engage. Extra money was given to seaman gunners and men awarded a good conduct badge after five years' exemplary service. But the plan failed, and worse still there was no prospect of calling on the merchant service in emergency.

By 1852 the situation was sufficiently serious for the Admiralty to set up a Commission on Manning. Its principal recommendation was to establish continuous service in which young seamen, stokers and boys could enter for a ten-year engagement from eighteen with opportunity to re-engage before service in the reserve. When the Continuous Service Act was passed pay was increased all round, long-service pensions were instituted and the rates of chief petty officer, shipwright and leading seaman introduced. Lower deck response was encouraging but reforms came too late for the Russian war and the Baltic and Black Sea fleets were desperately short of men. Despite war fever that swept the country ships were delayed, their complements topped up with any men that could be found. Captain Lord Clarence Paget of *Princess Royal* reported:

there was a scarcity, indeed almost an absence, of seamen. However, with the assistance of several valuable officers who were appointed to the ship, and by dint of handbills and touting of all sorts, we managed to enter at an average of 20 or 30 a week, such as they were. Scarcely any of them had been in a man-o-war, and consequently were entirely ignorant of the management of great guns and muskets.[8]

After the war Parliament was sufficiently alarmed to appoint a Royal Commission to enquire how best to man the Navy and create a reserve force; its report made a tremendous impact throughout the social structure of the lower deck. Far-reaching recommendations included the improvement of boy training arrangements, signing on young recruits for twelve years with option of a further ten, and then additional periods of five years. Pensions were to be payable after twenty-two years' continual service and were boosted for further engagements, and both basic and badge pay increased. In future hammocks and bedding would be issued free, as would uniform for continuous service boys; and there were improvements to the sailors' diet. It was at once an indictment of the haphazard methods of the past and a charter for a more enlightened approach to service conditions.

Manning the Navy was strengthened by the passing of the Royal Naval Reserve (Volunteers) Act, followed by the Royal Naval Reserve Officers Act, which established a permanent force of trained seamen from the mercantile marine. Through Thomas Brassey MP, later Earl Brassey, the Royal Naval Artillery Volunteers were set up in 1873, the forerunner of the RNVR.

For more than a century it had been recognized in the Royal Navy that a code of behaviour and discipline had to be understood and implemented by officers and men in the close and complex confines of a warship. Discipline was closely allied to the development of leadership, as well to the divisional system whereby large bodies of men were divided and subdivided into smaller groups so that officers and petty officers could teach the importance of obedience to orders – not blind observance but willing and intelligent co-operation in carrying out work in the highly dangerous circumstances that so often occurred at sea. For the minority who failed to live up to the mainly self-imposed standards of conduct there was punishment in its various forms.

Equally important to the Royal Commission recommendations because of its association with discipline, was the long overdue penal reform. For years punishments in the fleet had been based on the individual interpretation of outdated Articles of War by commanding officers. Since flogging with a cat o' nine tails was the sole penalty for serious crime it is hardly surprising that its use had got out of hand.

As late as 1852 Midshipman Cyril Rockleigh of the line-of-battleship *Albion* was able to write:

A week rarely passed at this period without some man receiving his three or four dozen lashes at the gangway. The first time I witnessed corporal punishment I was horror struck and, after the first minute or so, averted my eyes to avoid the ghastly sight; but after a time I became so used to seeing what was called 'scratching a man's back' that I could contemplate the spectacle from beginning to end without shrinking. Flogging was usually inflicted for crimes of insubordination or drunkenness and more often for the latter. That the punishment was not considered degrading by the great majority of men I am quite certain. Indeed the young

> and plucky ones used to consider it a feather in their caps to be able to undergo their flogging without uttering a cry, advancing themselves considerably in the eyes of their shipmates if they took their 'four bag' (forty-eight lashes) like a man.[9]

Alive to public and parliamentary protests the Admiralty tightened up the procedure for flogging and ordered ships to send in quarterly punishment returns for scrutiny and comment. To shift the balance towards detention punishment, cells were introduced in major warships and a naval prison established at Lewes in Sussex. Supervised by a Board of Visitors and run on naval lines, with classes for conduct wearing different coloured uniforms, an observer was struck by 'the good order and dead silence of its occupants'.[10]

In 1857 fate played its hand once more because no sooner had the fleet reduced to peacetime strength than there was a general recall to meet operational emergencies. Complements had to be made up hurriedly with the bounty system of inducement – £10 for an able seaman or stoker and £5 for an ordinary seaman – opening the door to undesirable characters, precisely what the Navy was trying to avoid. The desertion rate soared, leave-breaking increased and as well as fluctuations in the manning level there was an acute shortage of petty and warrant officers. Over fifteen months discipline deteriorated through riots and demonstrations to the point of mutiny in certain warships of the Mediterranean and Channel fleets, precipitating considerable alarm in Whitehall.

Defined as a combination of two or more persons to defy authority with or without violence and ranging from passive refusal of duty to wholesale usurping of power, mutiny is the ultimate crime in an armed service. Cases of mutiny in the Army or Navy were almost invariably tried by court martial and the maximum naval penalty up to the early nineteenth century was death by hanging at the yard arm. While the source of unrest could usually be traced to pay, food, leave or harsh treatment from the quarterdeck, the root of dissatisfaction was almost always the lack of trust between officers, petty officers and other ratings. Men, who would put up with any hardship if they believed higher authority was doing its best, lost patience with muddle and indifference. This happened in 1859–60 when the primary complaint was about ship's company leave, then regarded as a privilege but undergoing transition from an occasional forty-eight hours' general liberty to regular leave for men of good conduct. Lacking Admiralty guidance it was left to individual captains to adopt their own policy, resulting in misunderstandings and inconsistencies, even between ships of the same squadron. After the disturbances when ringleaders were punished, petty officers admonished and officers dismissed their ships, captains were directed to grant leave on a more reasonable basis. As well as being graded for conduct men were also classified for leave, and in 1890 leave became a right, not a privilege, for ratings of good character.

Meanwhile, the first Naval Discipline Act was passed in 1860 and a Table of Summary Punishments distributed to standardize the method of dealing with defaulters.[11] Judging by the tone of official letters criticizing punishment returns, the Admiralty had become totally authoritarian in matters of discipline as well as adopting a positive approach towards creating better conditions on the lower deck. Flogging was significantly limited, monthly pay instituted, eligibility for good conduct badge and pay reduced to three years and authority of ship's police overhauled. Unusual sensitivity and clemency was shown in the mitigation and remission of punishments on the grounds of former conduct, heroism and medical disabilities.[12] In 1871 flogging was suspended in peacetime, but was not suspended in wartime until 1879. It was finally removed from the list of punishments in 1948.

Officially the Navy claimed a close relationship between discipline and religion. Besides directing captains to suppress 'all cursing and swearing, drunkenness, gaming, rioting and quarrelling', Queen's Regulations required him to 'discountenance everything tending to the disparagement of religion' and make compulsory the attendance of officers and men at Sunday matins and weekday morning prayers. Throughout nineteenth-century Britain there ran strong evangelical currents, reinforcing the view held by some commanding officers that a sense of religion was valuable in a close-knit warship community because it helped keep men on a straight and narrow path. Other captains attached little importance to the Church's contribution, nor did they see eye to eye with the behaviour of some chaplains. When an obvious misfit in one ship refused to read prayers on the upper deck because ship's company washing was on the lines he was reported for insubordination, lacking in common sense, and left the service. Another chaplain capitalized on the display of laundry in his ship with the observation: 'everybody tells me that cleanliness is next to godliness; so let us have a little godliness to put it next to!'

Sailors have always groused about the food they received, which often had to sustain them throughout twenty-four hours of great physical effort in cold and wet conditions. Compared with English working-class fare, naval rations appeared ample, the daily entitlement being 1½ lb of biscuit, a liberal quantity of sugar, chocolate and tea, 1 lb of fresh meat and ½ lb of vegetables. At sea the fresh meat was substituted by an equivalent amount of preserved meat, alternating with salt pork or salt beef, together with flour, suet, raisins, split peas and preserved potatoes. Traditionally the main meal was dinner, cooked in the coal-fired galley amidships; breakfast consisted of cocoa and biscuits. For tea or supper there might be dinner left-overs, with biscuits and strong sweetened tea that had stewed for hours in a copper. The trouble was that many ingredients suffered from inefficient stowage and dinners were not only badly prepared but appallingly cooked, usually through boiling, by 'cook' ratings who did not start to be trained until 1873. Furthermore menus seldom altered between tropical and temperate latitudes. The best feature was that men could be credited with money savings for rations not taken up, which enabled them to buy delicacies ashore or from a ship's canteen; this made for some variety in a barely adequate and monotonous diet.

Although their food was cooked in the same galley wardroom officers could afford to supplement their victualling allowance with extra provisions, such as eggs, fish or poultry, for two or three daily cooked meals. Being less wealthy gunroom officers did not fare so well and the average midshipman, like the average young seaman, was always hungry.

Included in the daily rations for officers and men over eighteen was an allowance of half a gill (an eighth of a pint) of rum. Imported from the West Indies at a strength of 4.5 under proof, rum had displaced brandy, wine or beer to become an indispensable item of the Navy's diet; yet it caused more tribulation, more crime and more punishment than almost any other factor. Drunkenness on board by a minority persisted in many ships of the fleet despite reforms that stopped the evening issue, halved the ration and paid a compensating allowance to teetotallers. In 1870 rum was issued neat to officers and senior ratings while the remainder drank it mixed with three parts water as grog. Brought up from the spirit room in casks and mixed with water in a tub as part of a daily ritual it was either issued individually or carried to the mess in a container. For those that drank it, that is the majority, the tot was the supreme moment of the day; hardships were momentarily forgotten, dinner became more palatable and for those coming off watch it was the prelude to peaceful slumber. In the wardroom officers preferred wines and brandy to rum, although the latter was popular with warrant officers.

Until well after the arrival of distilling machinery the supply of water was still a precious commodity and served out sparingly. Stored in large iron tanks sited below to protect the magazines, water was pumped up daily to smaller tanks for consumption and washing, those on the messdecks watched by a marine sentry to prevent waste.

In matters of clothing military branch officers could claim to be the first to wear uniform in the Navy. Whatever the climate full dress blue uniform with cocked hat, epaulettes, sword and gold lace denoting rank were obligatory for ceremonial occasions, amended to frock coat and cap for daily wear. When the executive curl on gold lace was introduced in 1856 to single out military branch officers the civil branch were authorized to wear colour cloth between stripes – scarlet for surgeons, white for paymasters, purple for engineers and blue, initially for navigators but subsequently for the instructor branch. The woollen cloth cut for uniform had the suppleness of cardboard and the typical Victorian officer was a picture of sartorial inelegance with ill-fitting frock coat, wrinkled trousers and a variety of black ties influenced by civilian fashion. Relaxation from formality with unofficial garments was only permitted at sea; the monkey jacket worn later in the century being a frock coat with the skirt removed. In hot weather the only concession allowed to blue uniform was white duck trousers.

At their own expense ratings contrived to dress more functionally yet prided themselves on looking smart when the occasion demanded. Promulgation of uniform regulations merely confirmed what was becoming the accepted pattern, soon to be copied by the seamen of every other navy.[13] The essential feature was suitability for work aloft or on deck; thus frocks (shirts) in white duck or blue cloth were loose fitting yet could be worn under blue jackets, with trousers wide enough to roll up above the knee. Pockets being dangerous, men kept small personal belongings in soft blue caps, clasp knives were worn round the waist on a lanyard and sheath knives forbidden. One good suit in blue or white was kept for weekly inspections and going ashore. Badges of rank and good conduct on the left arm, gunnery proficiency on the right, black silk under a blue collar and a straw hat plaited sennit fashion and tied with the ship's hat ribbon completed the picture. Only ashore did men wear boots or shoes, bare feet being the universal custom afloat. While dress material and several articles of uniform could be bought from the paymaster, most of the ship's company wore clothes made on board, including tarred jackets that kept men reasonably warm and dry. Folded and 'stopped' with tape to make them compact, clothes were neatly stowed in canvas kit bags while letters, sewing materials and trinkets were kept in a small wooden 'ditty' box. This was always kept unlocked with implicit confidence in its sanctity. Messdeck theft was rare.

After the day's work men found little difficulty in providing their own entertainment:

> Generally in the evenings at sea and very often in harbour the men sang [remembers Midshipman Henry Fleet serving aboard the frigate *Constance*]. We had quite a melodious crowd and some of the songs were excellently rendered. It was before the days of music hall ditties and many of the favourite ones were written by Dibdin, the sailor's poet. Jack was sentimentally inclined and the songs that appealed most were of that class – of Mother and Home. In harbour with other ships present a regular concert would often take place, each

Badges in 1870: chief petty officer (top left), 1st class petty officer (top right), 2nd class petty officer (bottom left), leading seaman (bottom right)

> man giving a turn in rotation, the ditty rendered receiving so much applause as the audience considered it merited, and they were impartial critics. The effect on a fine, still night was most pleasing. Sometimes in harbour the hands were piped to 'dance and skylark'. Then – if in the mood – the men would dance and play games such as Sling the Monkey, Baste the Bear or Able Whackets. A favourite was Follow the Leader, when all sorts of pranks were indulged in and some daring feats performed on the masts and yards.[14]

By the 1870s it was apparent that a better Navy had been created. In recovering from the 'great slump' the executive officer had been forced to accept the advance of the engineer, paymaster, surgeon and instructor into justifiable positions within his own hierarchy; yet the pay and perquisites of civil branch officers remained less than their executive counterparts and their advancement tied to the attainment of seniority, in other words 'the dead hand of promotion'.

Unquestionably the lower deck had been the main beneficiary of recent reforms. For the first time in her history Britain possessed a standing Navy of trained men engaged for a long term of service. As well as being fed and housed the sailor had gained permanent job security, a reasonable salary of which part could be allotted to his family or put into a savings bank, the opportunity for promotion within an enlarged rating structure and the certainty of a pension if he stayed the course. Family separation being an inevitable burden for everyone serving a foreign commission it was a comfort for married men in the Channel squadron to expect regular leave in home ports over Christmas. Above all the sailor could look forward to a more just and dignified way of life.

As promising youngsters joined the service there is evidence that captains were becoming aware of the growing potential of men in the fleet. One such boy was Patrick Riley who entered in 1872 to serve in the training ship *Impregnable* (hulk) at Devonport. His first seagoing ship was the corvette *Amethyst* on the Pacific station. Spending Christmas at Montevideo the ship called at Rio de Janeiro where, on 14 September 1875:

Able Seaman Patrick Riley, 1876: '. . . strong, able bodied and physically fit for Her Majesty's Service', *Circular 290/1857/*

> I passed for Ordinary Seaman, the bo'sun taking me on the fo'c'sle, where I was questioned about the fittings of the spars and sails that had been carried away and was also examined by questions about other parts of the ship. I then had to appear before the Captain to be rated. What a change from the present day! My pay was increased from seven pence to one shilling and a penny per day. Shortly afterwards I passed for trained man in gunnery, making my pay one shilling and two pence per day. Shall I ever forget the feeling of shyness that came over me when I arrived in my mess for dinner as a 'man'? I had finished with the drudgery of a mess-boy . . . in future I would have more time to myself. I was entitled to all the privileges of a Man in Her Majesty's Navy; being allowed to take up one pound of tobacco each month from the purser. I never smoked until I was thirty, so I had no use for it. I was also allowed half a gill of rum each day, I had that! Although rated as a man in the service, my real age at the time was only sixteen years and six months. I was gradually overcoming my handicap of age, and was growing a fine, upstanding youth.[15]

Riley mentions smoking, about which current regulations were strict. To avoid fire only officers were allowed to smoke below decks at certain times, the remainder limited to the upper deck. Most men chewed tobacco, a mild vice encouraged in preference to smoking but naturally forbidden when addressing an officer. This necessitated saluting by 'touching the hat or cap or taking it off' and if chewing at the time a man took off his cap 'into which he threw his quid of tobacco, having smartly removed it from his mouth. When conversation ended cap and quid were

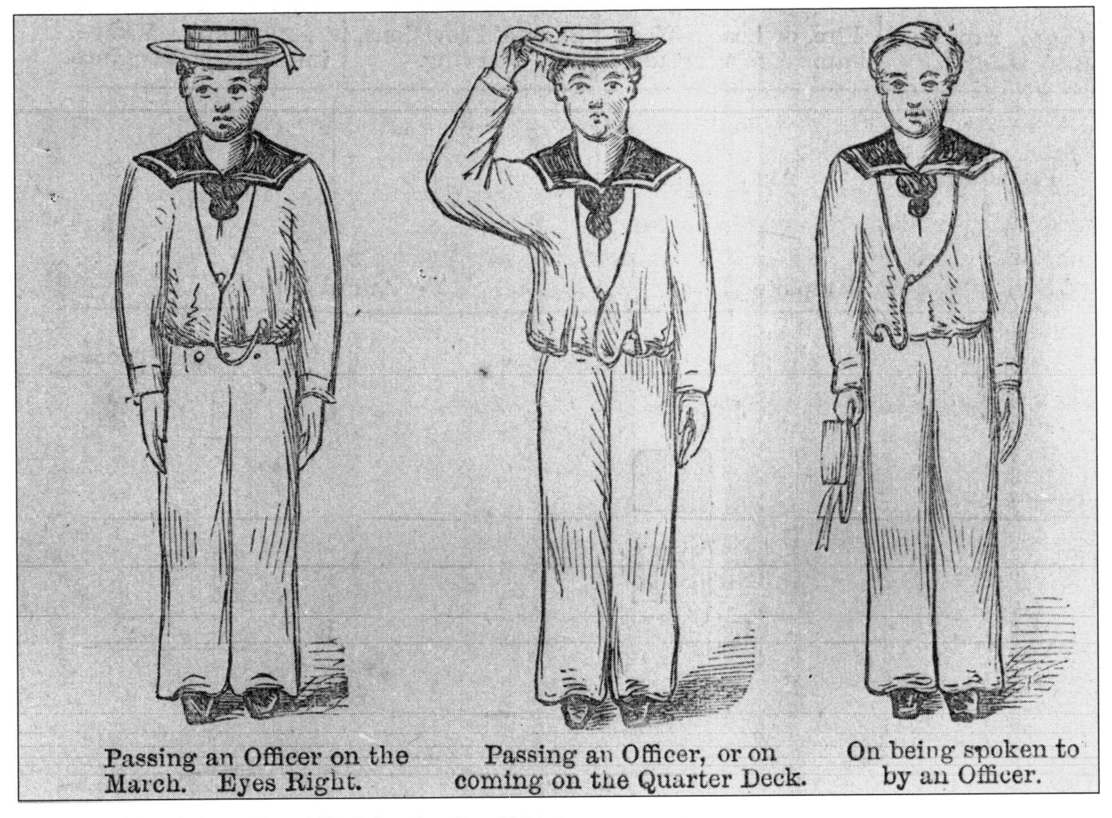

Instructions for Salutes: Boys' Training Service, 1874

returned to their rightful places with one and the same movement'.[16] Riley saluted on coming aboard or stepping on the quarterdeck and in 1890, with the rest of the Navy, changed to what is now recognized as the hand salute. In keeping with fashion he probably cultivated side-whiskers which he trimmed while shaving on Sundays and Thursdays, when ship and company were inspected by the captain. In 1869 Admiralty Circular 36 permitted the growing of beards and moustaches as 'conducive to health and comfort'. But no moustaches were permitted without beards, this concession allowed only (Circular 67) to Royal Marines when embarked.

Living on board for long periods and working in a manner unique to seafarers a naval rating spoke a language peculiar to the sea. From the moment of stepping aboard his first ship he acquired a jargon handed down from generations that was both vigorous and extensive, characteristic of people who were as resourceful in speech as they were in action, masters of repartee and gifted with wit as well as humour. Officers' vocabulary was similarly affected but theirs was more educated, more formal, almost as humorous but less earthy and exuberant in style. Going ashore the sailor would take his world with him and although his salty expressions were unintelligible to landsmen many were sufficiently meaningful to find a permanent home in English prose and conversation.

Besides learning the conventions of naval phraseology the young rating or officer became familiar with bawdy language. When aloft in a gale of wind furling and reefing sails Beresford was adamant that, though seamen cursed and swore, they never blasphemed because the elemental forces of nature emphasized the mere insignificance of man. It could also be argued that lower deck language was the only form of speech that could never sink to indecency for the simple reason that indecent words were rendered innocuous by repetitive misuse. Others contended that because sailors were inarticulate they made up for a lack of fluency with a range of four letter words. At any rate matters got worse because the Admiralty issued a fleet memorandum in 1902 deprecating the use of bad language and urging commanding officers to discourage the practice. It seems to have had little effect.

CHAPTER TWO

The Fleet in which they Served

If I want a thing done well in a distant part of the world, if I require a man with a good head, a good heart, lots of pluck and plenty of common sense, I always send for a captain in the Royal Navy.

Lord Palmerston (1784–1865), Foreign Secretary and Prime Minister

The battlefleet of the 1870s reflected the recent introduction of ironclads. HMS *Warrior* embodied most of the technological advances available to the world's leading industrial power by combining an iron hull with powerful armament, armour protection and 14 knots under steam. The timing of her arrival in 1861 had been accelerated by the advent of the French ironclad *La Gloire*, built to challenge naval supremacy in the sensitive area of the English Channel. Although designed as a forty-gun super-frigate with single gun deck and sails on three masts, *Warrior* was essentially the first true armoured battleship, displacing over 9,000 tons and manned by 700 officers and men. Her place in history is firmly stamped as the watershed between the wooden three-deckers that she made obsolete and the battle squadrons that fought at Jutland.

A naval arms race with France had already begun in which the Royal Navy, ever confident of superiority, believed in experimentation. And so the battlefleet consisted of thirty armoured warships of twenty different designs and almost as many armament layouts; only in sails did ships conform to a standard pattern. The rest of the active fleet under naval command included wooden-hulled frigates, corvettes, sloops, gunboats, tenders, tugs, storeships and troop transports, all equipped with sails and steam machinery. To promote and protect British interests more than half of the 150 seagoing ships were deployed overseas where flag officers commanded squadrons in the Mediterranean, North America and the West Indies, the Pacific, China, East Indies, Australia and both South and West Africa. Base facilities and coaling stations had to be regularly supplied and it seems incredible that so much was achieved by so few ships, especially as an ironclad Channel squadron was retained to inspire public confidence at home.

Because the Navy regarded shore barracks as wasteful in money and injurious to discipline and training, almost all the 55,000 officers and men were accommodated afloat. Those not in seagoing ships were based in old wooden two- and three-deckers used as receiving ships (floating barracks), training ships or flagships for commanders-in-chief at the Nore, Portsmouth, Devonport and Queenstown (Ireland), traditional dockyard towns from whose areas the majority of seamen were recruited. The fleet's worldwide commitments were administered by the Lords Commissioners of the Admiralty and some 550 civil servants in Whitehall; home dockyards employed over 11,000 civilians maintaining the fleet and building new ships; victualling yards at Deptford, Gosport and Plymouth supplied food, rum and clothing while hospitals at Haslar and Plymouth cared for the sick. A pattern of infrastructure had evolved that was to serve the Navy until after the Second World War.

Warship characteristics had changed little since the eighteenth century; design continued to be a compromise between guns, protection and speed, all of which took priority over habitability, a term then unknown. Internally all ironclads were similar in having three decks – upper, main and lower – and traditionally the captain's quarters were right aft on the maindeck. Further forward on the half deck were senior officers' cabins, the remainder berthed on the lower deck in a row of cabins either side and opening out to the wardroom, whose only furniture was a dining table, chairs and a sideboard near the pantry. Apart from daylight that came through hatches in both decks above the wardroom tallow candles and oil lamps were the only illumination.

In smaller ships cabin space was proportionately restricted but anyone visiting *Warrior*, now restored to 1860 and berthed at Portsmouth, will be amazed at the generous size of a lieutenant's cabin, fitted with bunk frame over a nest of drawers, a washstand, bookshelves, table or desk, and a portable tin bath that was tended daily by the officer's servant. Despite poor lighting and ventilation there were redeeming features as 'A Naval Officer' later wrote:

> The cabin of an officer is what a man's library or study or den is to a man ashore. It is his one place of privacy, and even that only partially, for often it is just divided from the mess by a curtain – there is certainly a door but that is seldom shut – and there some men make their home. There they amuse themselves with their hobbies – painting, carving and the like; or a man of musical tastes will perhaps agonize his messmates by his breathings on the flute or his playing of the 'bumblejar', a generic term for all instruments. Home letters are written in the cabins, the mess is open to many interruptions but when the curtain is drawn across the cabin door . . . one is only interrupted when absolutely necessary and it is here too that the tired man retires to think. On an afternoon in warm weather nearly everyone thinks deeply; it is known in service slang as 'taking a caulk'.[1]

For 200 years the wide open gundecks running almost the length of wooden ships provided the living and sleeping quarters of the ship's company, mess tables positioned between guns and hammocks slung overhead. Each morning hammocks were lashed up tightly and stowed in nettings on the upper deck; each evening they were taken below and slung from deckhead hooks. At sea natural light and fresh air were minimal, although absence of bulkheads provided some measure of through deck ventilation. But in steam-powered ironclads the rising heat from boilers and engines on uninsulated iron surfaces led to condensation in cold weather and almost unbearable conditions in hot sun; attempts to reduce moisture with windsails and experimental air pumps made little headway against the continued passion for scrubbing decks. In the earlier broadside-firing ironclads all 650 of the ship's company were berthed on the maindeck, with curtained-off messes for chief and senior petty officers. When central batteries and turrets arrived in later ships the crew were accommodated in separate messdecks, a system already popular in frigates where the hands were less disturbed by gunnery drills and firings. Hygiene was basic and traditionally the latrines, known as heads and consisting of wooden planks with holes to sit over, were positioned behind a canvas screen on a platform either side of the bow and exposed to the wind and sea. Since only ironclads had additional heads fitted each side of the upper deck amidships, the effect of steep swells must have caused some discomfort in smaller vessels.

Describing life on the lower deck of a typical ironclad Admiral Ballard paints a gloomy but realistic picture:

> The bare bleakness of the mess deck with its long range of plank tables and stools had as little suggestion of physical ease as a prison cell. It was damp and chilly in a cold climate, and damp and hot in the tropics. It was swept by searching draughts if the ports were open, and nearly pitch dark if they were closed, glass scuttles not having been invented. It was dimly lit at night by tallow candles inside lamps at long intervals; and as there were no drying rooms it reeked of wet serge and flannel in rainy weather. In short the living quarters of the mid-Victorian bluejacket, stoker or marine were as widely dissociated from any ideal of a home in the usual sense as could well be imagined. Moreover, he was always in a crowd by day or night. His work and his leisure, his eating, drinking, washing and sleeping were all in crowded surroundings. He swallowed his bully beef and hard tack (biscuit), his pea soup and rum at a mess table so congested that he had absolutely no elbow room and scarce space to sit. He washed himself twice a week on deck at the same time as he washed his clothes, in the two tubfuls of cold water which formed the allowance for the whole twenty-three men in his mess. And he slung his hammock at night among hundreds of others so tightly packed that they had

Starboard side maindeck of HMS *Warrior*, showing mess tables interspaced with 68-pounder guns

no swinging room however much the ship rolled. Even in the heads he had no individual privacy. All this doubtless had compensations of a kind; for human nature is strongly gregarious by inclination; and this crowd were all of his own breed, mainly drawn from his own native district without any alien element. He knew nothing of the lonely solitude of the shepherd or farm hand, and whatever else he may have lacked he never lacked company of a kind which he thoroughly understood.[2]

In its widest sense seamanship can be defined as the art of moving and working a vessel at sea, affecting every member of her company and embracing every aspect of ship life. The cornerstone of the Victorian Navy's ability to maintain an effective international peace-keeping force lay in the superb seamanship displayed by its ships. Because wind was always available as motive power, inexhaustible in quantity and immune from enemy interference, sails were used whenever possible to present an image of expertise and dependability. Thus seamen were organized around three masts to handle spars, ropes, boats and anchors; whether aloft, on deck or below, the *modus operandi* was highly detailed and uniform throughout the fleet. On commissioning a warship the ship's company was divided into port and starboard watches, each man being given a number and a specific duty in the station bill. Comprising more than half the complement, seamen were allocated to forecastle, foretop, maintop and quarterdeck divisions, their age around twenty-four and their height about 5 ft 6 in.

Maintopmen of the port watch, HMS *Victoria*, 1867. Note hammocks in nets on the bulwarks

Forecastlemen were selected from the best seamen because, as well as working on the bowsprit, they handled the massive anchors and cables, jobs that entitled them to wear their hats a little differently. In contrast the quarterdeckmen were a mixture of older, steady men past their best for going aloft, working alongside inexperienced youngsters known as 'lambies'. The most agile seamen were picked to man the topgallant and royal yards – often 150 ft above the upper deck – and called upper yardmen. Because the ship's reputation in competitive sail drill would rest on their shoulders they became an élite group: 'the spoilt darlings of the crew, their leave breaking, drunkenness and other offences leniently dealt with and in some ships they were allowed to wear fancy stitching on their collars. They were fine specimens of manhood . . . and had to be in the pink of condition; the race from deck to the upper yards caused terrible heart disease, even though an Admiralty order insisted on a one and a half minute rest in the tops before the further stage aloft to the masthead'.[3] In the steam department the more capable stokers were found in the stokeholds where each man shovelled as much as a ton of coal an hour into the furnaces.

Since it was man's muscle that hoisted boats, weighed anchors, made sail and braced yards the immense physical effort often required the support of marines, stokers and idlers. Idlers were anything but idle; being mainly artisans they worked as daymen to be called out in emergency. At sea, seamen and marines worked continuously in two watches – four hours on and four hours off – but, due to punishing conditions caused by excessive heat and poor ventilation, engineers and stokers worked in three watches. Except for lieutenants and midshipmen keeping bridge watch day and night all officers were designated daymen, although the executive element could be, and frequently were, called on deck at any time. For eating and sleeping messes of up to twenty-five men were split into port and starboard watches, so that everyone had an opposite number with whom to share duties. Hammocks were slung so that each watch berthed alternately, to balance the number of men in and out of their hammocks.

The artisans, who comprised about 5 per cent of the ship's company, were indispensable to Admiralty policy that the fleet should be able to keep the sea for a commission of three years or more in an efficient state and ready to fight. Every trade necessary to maintain the ship, its weapons and equipment was represented in the rate of chief petty officer, petty officer or able seaman – boilermaker, founder, shipwright, armourer, blacksmith, plumber, ropemaker, sailmaker, carpenter, caulker, cooper, lamptrimmer, tinsmith and painter – each entered as a tradesman direct from shore practice or at apprentice level. Storm damage, action damage, defective machinery and hull faults were all made good on board, engendering a spirit of self-reliance and pride in work that have always been distinctive features of artisans and artificers in the Royal Navy.

The remainder of idlers or daymen included a barber, shoemakers, cooks, stewards, domestic servants, tailors and sick berth attendants, to complete an amalgam of talent comparable with that found in a typical English village. Personal details and qualifications of every man in the ship were recorded in his parchment certificate of service.

When the bugle or drum sounded General Quarters every officer and man scrambled to his action station as directed by the quarterbill. The majority of seamen and some marines manned the guns, with officers of quarters in charge of groups; other seamen went to the powder magazines or to steer the ship. With the tradition that sea battles were fought at close range marine marksmen still went aloft to the fighting tops, the steam department raised full power, surgeons prepared first aid posts and a fire brigade of stokers and carpenters connected up the hoses. Supported by the navigator, officer of the watch and signalman the captain fought his ship from the bridge, constructed across and above the upper deck, with voice pipe communications to the engine room.

So many systems to operate a warship may appear over-complicated but they were standard practice and readily understood by a partly illiterate ship's company. A man's watch bill number, stencilled on his kitbag and hammock, became more important than his name; seamen were further identified by wearing distinctive watch stripes on their sleeves – starboard watch right arms, port watch left arms. The Navy's professional man management left nothing to chance.

Equally important was the ship's routine described by Master-at-Arms George Crowe as 'the punctilious regimen of a man-o'-war, without which life would be near intolerable. It provides for individual comfort, is essential to procure efficiency and conduces towards the proper care and maintenance of the ship'.[4] Pretentious as this may sound there was a lot of sense in the programme of work, drill and relaxation, adjusted to sea or harbour requirements and the latitude of the station, its purpose to make best possible use of daylight hours. Able Seaman Thomas Holman wrote this revealing description of routine aboard a frigate in the tropics in the late 1870s:

> We start at 4 a.m. when the stillness is broken by the shrill pipe and hoarse voice of the Bosun's Mate calling all the Starboard Watch and Idlers, who have to 'rouse-out – rouse-out – and lash up' and take their hammocks around the capstan, where the Midshipman of the Watch calls out their names in turn. They walk or stumble past the Officer of the Watch, according to their degree of wakefulness, and stow their hammocks in the netting. The Idlers man the pumps below and supply the water, while the sailors with their trousers rolled up to their knees scrub and wash most thoroughly every plank and corner of the upper deck. Idlers come on deck again and assist in drying up the decks, coiling down the ropes and resetting sails, if there are any set. The sun by this time has appeared above the horizon and the fresh morning air is most enjoyable. A huge canvas bath is generally got up and filled; at 6.15 the other watch is again turned out and all hammocks lashed up and stowed. Then the hands are piped to bathe, and those who choose can revel in a salt water bath to their hearts' content. At a quarter to seven the hands are piped to breakfast, usually consisting of cocoa and bread or biscuit or such other luxury in the way of butter etc. the individual may care to treat himself to. At 7.15 the watch coming on deck at 8 for the forenoon dress themselves in white duck clothing, the watch remaining below starts to scrub the mess deck.

During the forenoon and afternoon men would be employed on maintenance work and:

> at 5 the bugle sounds 'evening quarters'. The guns are seen secure for the night, the men inspected and half an hour's smart drill often follows. Between 7 and 8 o'clock the men usually have their supper. As this meal is not recognized by the Admiralty, unless something remains from dinner, the men have to provide it from the canteen at their own expense. At 8 o'clock the first watch goes on deck, musters around the capstan and remains until midnight.[5]

Thomas Holman was patently happy in his work, as were most ships' companies of small warships operating independently from their admiral. Such opportunities were less feasible in the

Mediterranean or Channel squadrons linked more closely with their commander-in-chief, when the only way to add zest to a humdrum routine was through competition. Daily in harbour royal yards or top gallant masts were sent up smartly at 8 a.m., to be replaced on deck at sunset. On Mondays a heavy evolution took place such as sending away both kedge anchors and at sea it was usual to have a watch drill twice a day, in addition to making, shortening or trimming sails to meet wind and weather conditions. 'Every new ship's company had their reputation to establish against every old one that had their reputation to maintain,' wrote Ballard:

> Unfortunately in both cases a tragic price had sometimes to be paid in a form leading to half-masted colours and three volleys with blank. The men often grew reckless under the stimulus of competition and needed constant watching for their own safety; but no vigilance could prevent accidents . . . as many as half a dozen or more fatalities often occurred in a single commission, nor were top midshipmen exempt. A signal from the admiral 'evolution well executed' was enough to elate a ship for days – the more so as all the fleet saw it – and a signal 'repeat the evolution' brought a proportionate sense of public humiliation.[6]

Although insanitary conditions below decks caused infectious diseases and bronchial disorders, while heavy manual labour contributed to ruptures and muscular strains, ships' companies were generally fit and healthy. Regular work aloft developed men's arms and shoulders to the build of acrobats, a physique well suited for pulling (rowing) in boats. Since ships rarely came alongside harbour jetties but anchored well offshore, such as Plymouth Sound or Spithead, the transport of stores and personnel was carried out by boats of all sizes. Crews of twelve-oared cutters thought nothing of covering four or five miles at a stretch and were always game to challenge the crews of other ships to unofficial races involving money stakes. Whether sailing or pulling drill and formality in boats was strictly enforced. To sum up, it is easy to criticize a routine which exacted so much activity by so many to achieve what would appear to be so little, but in the age of *Pax Britannica* smartness and silence aloft and in boats remained the criteria of an efficient ship. Although overdone it did teach officers and men to be disciplined, resourceful and team spirited, its true value realized when ships encountered heavy weather.

For a new ship's company a shake-down cruise was incomplete without a gale to test equipment and assess human reaction. Many suffered from sea sickness and overcame it; for a few it became a chronic handicap. 'The naval remedy was to ignore it,' was the view of Admiral Cresswell. 'On the whole I think this was the best treatment, even if it was rather spartan.'[7] Tempestuous weather was often difficult to predict as the frigate *Newcastle* found in the Pacific one evening early in 1880. Arriving on the bridge soon after 9 p.m. Midshipman Mark Kerr remembers:

> I was the captain's ADC at the time and stood beside him. Strips of canvas were streaming out to leeward and cracking in the wind with reports loud enough to awaken the jealousy of a cowboy giving an exhibition with his whip. We had been caught by a storm when unprepared for it and the hurricane blew sails from the bolt ropes in quick succession. As each one split it made a sound like the firing of a large gun. No orders could be heard; everything had to be conveyed by messenger to the officer concerned and then only by putting the lips of one against the ear of the other and yelling loudly.

Hands loosening sails aboard the seagoing training ship *Calliope* in the 1880s

Kerr was sent forward with a message for the first lieutenant and as *Newcastle* carried an extra complement of young seamen boys:

> they were naturally terrified at the babel of sound and the jumping, pounding and shaking of the ship as she plunged into the sea or was struck by a heavy wave. . . . I had to fight my way through but eventually reached the forecastle and yelled my message. The storm having forcibly reduced sail the whole ship's company, with the exception of the youngsters, spent four hours aloft in furling some sails, gathering up bits of others and close reefing the main topsail as she lay to and bowed and climbed over the great waves on her bow.

Kerr concludes: 'The hurricane made the ship's company. To those for whom it was a new experience it gave a feeling of security for the future and in many cases a young midshipman found himself a leader and not a follower.'[8] Similar sentiments were echoed by that great seaman Lord Charles Beresford, who noticed: 'It is a curious fact that the spirits of both officers and men rose whenever it came on to blow; and the harder it blew the more cheery everyone became.'

By the 1870s the quality of seamen had been upgraded by the regular intake of sixteen and a half-year-old boys – as many as seventy in an ironclad – from the five training ships in south coast ports. As recruiters widened their net youngsters were drawn from all over the United Kingdom, the pattern of entries relevant to industrial cycles, as Sam Noble recorded: 'In 1875 when trade was bad in Dundee a few youths in our locality, millworkers like myself, took it in their heads to join the navy and I went along with them.' Once an inquisitive youth fell into the hands of a Royal Marine recruiting sergeant there was no turning back from silken tongued stories about the marvellous life afloat and how there was 'nothing to do but sit and let the wind blow them along whilst they fed off the roast beef of England'.[9] Parents' written permission was required before the sergeant could collect his 10*s* reward.

Hoisting boats on board, HMS *Calliope*

Boys underwent a fifteen-month intensive programme aboard a training ship, which started by teaching them to read, write and understand basic arithmetic. Active service instructors introduced them to gunnery, small arms and seamanship with proficiency badges awarded for 'diligence, assiduity and good conduct'. Above all they learnt to swim, go aloft, keep themselves clean, dress uniformly in a free issue of kit, prepare meals and to share them out equitably. 'The social life of a training ship', wrote James Woods about *Impregnable*, 'was similar to any other congregation of boys. There was the usual bullying and fagging . . . which could only be resisted by an appeal to the fists. I think it impossible for anyone to have passed through the Naval Training Service without benefiting morally, mentally and physically.'[10]

In an age when the rod was an accepted element in

youth education, training ship discipline was rigorously enforced. As well as 'official cuts' for serious misdemeanours the ship's police used their canes while instructors were equally free with 'stonnickeys' (knotted ropes' ends), not for sadistic reasons but simply because it was the tradition to which they had been brought up. Public and parliamentary outcry against such treatment did sow the seeds for later reform; even so, apart from unjust chastisement, James Woods 'cannot remember any instructors or corporals who were other than kind and thoughtful of those in their charge'.[11]

Joining the fleet, the crux came when a boy was rated ordinary seaman and began his twelve years' service, a situation summed up by Tom Holman:

> It is from eighteen to twenty-one that all the dangers of a young man's career in the navy confront him. Recently let loose from close supervision . . . and becoming entitled to be rated as a man on the ship's books, together with receiving different treatment from all the men around him, and being allowed grog, it is seldom indeed that a young man has sufficient ballast on board to steady him in such a seam of excitement. If a lad can but tide over his first two or three years of manhood without getting into serious trouble, his position is comparatively safe.[12]

It must have been discouraging to find that the liberal attitude towards the granting of leave and the gradual phasing out of corporal punishment led to an alarming increase in disciplinary offences and a desertion rate in excess of 12,000 seamen and marines in a year. In January 1875, as related by Patrick Riley in *Amethyst*, 'the ship received instructions that revolutionized the whole system of punishment. Men who had broken their leave, instead of losing a day's pay for every twenty-four hours adrift had a day's pay stopped for every three hours' absence or part thereof', a scale that remained in force for nearly a hundred years. 'The drastic punishment known as 10A was introduced at the same time and men so punished had an awful time.'[13] For improperly performing his duty as look-out in HMS *Swallow* Able Seaman Sam Noble was sentenced to seven days of No. 10A, which in his words meant: 'Eat your grub under that 7-inch gun and woe betide if you left a mark on the deck. Grog stopped, leave stopped, holystoning, blacking down (rigging) and all sorts of dirty work to do in the dog watches and spare time.'[14] When offences continued to rise after the last man was flogged there were universal complaints that discipline had fallen apart, reinforced by pleas from the lower deck to re-introduce the cat. Wisely the Admiralty stood firm; the Navy had become accustomed to the suspension of flogging and offences gradually declined.

During the latter half of the nineteenth century the foremost social problem in the Navy was alcohol. No respecter of class, rank or status, drunkenness was just as bad in the Army; throughout the United Kingdom the *per capita* consumption of alcohol reached its peak in 1876, much more than in the present day. The Navy, of course, enjoyed duty-free privileges.

Regarded as a fashionable pastime the habit of heavy drinking by officers, often in private, was widespread. Attacks of *delirium tremens* were not uncommon, as well as chronic disease of the liver, the worst cases being invalided from the service. When serving as a lieutenant Prince Louis of Battenburg recollected the stupefied bodies of midshipmen being laid out in rows on the flagship's upper deck after a gunroom guest night, each batch marked with chalk so that they could be collected by a boat's crew from their ship.

As early as 1863 the Admiralty ordered incidents of excessive drinking on board to be treated as disciplinary offences, going as far as to censure a commander-in-chief for allowing an alcoholic commander to resign before being charged. Between 1870 and 1885 Admiralty returns indicate that 800 officers (16 per cent of total officer strength) were tried by court martial, of whom the majority were charged with drunkenness or associated offences. The accused were a cross section of younger officers of all branches, plus a proportion of older warrant officers. The punishments ranged from dismissal from the service to severe reprimands with reductions of pay. In 1881 the wardroom rum ration ceased, although warrant officers, with their roots on the lower deck, were allowed to draw it until 1918. Though the situation had improved by 1890 the problem remained.

The lower deck was even less restrained. 'The bluejacket of the period, a splendid man in most ways,' wrote an officer, 'was unfortunately possessed with the idea that he owed it to his reputation to get outside the greatest amount of drink he could stagger under.'[15] Older men often managed to contrive an extra tot, and in ships where spirit room security was lax there was always some way of broaching a cask of rum. As a form of currency it stood up well. Going ashore James Woods remembers: 'The men were in a state of mental excitement at the glorious freedom of the moment and before the meal was finished the foundation had been laid for a good drunk from which the majority did not emerge until they found themselves on board or their money exhausted and their leave broken.'[16] Provided libertymen could climb up the gangway and go below to sleep it off a lenient attitude was taken; fighting drunks, on the other hand, had to be handled carefully. But in ships where discipline was harsh and petty restrictions numerous the crew's reaction on going ashore, even without a drink, was to go on the rampage, causing havoc with the local populace.

For many years the evils of drink in Britain had been opposed by temperance campaigns, in which the Royal Navy became a major target. Concern for the sailors' well-being had also been expressed by privately sponsored sailors' rest homes, but until the advent of Miss Agnes Weston, these steps made little progress. A woman of remarkable personality, 'Aggie' Weston's purpose was to spread evangelical Christianity and encourage temperance among sailors. She started by writing letters to men at sea; very soon monthly newsletters called *Ashore and Afloat* were reaching the fleet, to be followed by *Blue Backs*, a short religious pamphlet, which proved equally popular. She was present at the inaugural meeting of the Royal Naval Temperance Society in 1873; within ten years there were over 200 branches with 8,000 pledged abstainers. Her real triumph was the raising of funds to build a number of temperance hostels. Receiving a deputation of seamen from the gunboat *Dryad* in Plymouth she was asked 'to open a house for bluejackets close to the dockyard gates to which they could resort and from which intoxicating drinks would be excluded'. In 1876 the first Royal Sailors' Rest opened in Fore Street, Devonport, setting a new standard in comfort with a reading room and restaurant, features that impressed Petty Officer Henry Capper: 'To men accustomed to eat from tables covered with tarpaulin cloths, with their own knives and never a two pronged fork in the mess – that change was startling indeed. Many of the waitresses were unpaid volunteer ladies and the rule was to avoid familiarity, so that whereas in their own haunts they were called "Jack" "Tom" or "Bill" here each customer was "Mr . . .", "Yes, sir" and "No, sir". What wonder that a new atmosphere created new desires and in some measure what they had experienced on shore began to be the rule afloat.'[17] Like most crusaders Aggie Weston had her critics, yet she did untold good in keeping young men away from pubs and brothels in her unofficial role as 'Mother of the Navy' and its first welfare officer.

Dame Agnes Weston and members of the Royal Naval Temperance Society, Devonport, *c.* 1890

Apart from drink the desire of many libertymen was to find a woman – readily available in home and foreign ports – which often resulted in syphilis, known in lower deck jargon as 'lady's fever'. Standard treatment consisted of internal or external applications of mercury, illustrated by the maxim: 'one night with Venus and a lifetime with Mercury'. Apprehension at the high incidence of venereal disease induced concerted efforts by the Admiralty and War Office to press for the passing of the Contagious Diseases Acts of the 1860s, which allowed protected districts to be set up round naval ports in which prostitutes had to undergo medical examination and treatment. These brought VD cases per 1,500 men down from 104 in 1863 to 48 in 1874. However, opposition to this policy on the grounds of state recognition of prostitution grew into a public campaign, and when in 1882 a Liberal government eased enforcement and then repealed the acts, a horrified Admiralty had to face dramatic increases. In due course its prevalence gradually declined thanks to education, propaganda and the issue of prophylactics until the disease became controllable. It was by no means eliminated, and in every big ship was a mess for CDA cases, usually known as 'Rose Cottage'.

In common with the whole seafaring profession occasional incidents of homosexuality were inevitable. Commissions of three to four years' duration, long sea passages, little or no privacy, the proximity of older men to boys and the exclusion of women on board were all conducive to immoral acts, not necessarily confined to ratings. Intimacies between males were held to be anathema in a fighting service and homosexual acts were made the subject of a court martial or a court of enquiry with powers to punish or recommend punishment with extreme severity. Regarded by the great majority with repugnance, official findings showed no evidence that the evil was widespread nor does it seem to have affected discipline. Less serious but often very painful was dental disease, which the medical staff could do little about except extract offending teeth.

It was during these years that the technical age arrived in battleships with the mounting of enormous guns in turrets fired by electricity, their turret machinery maintained by engineers and the operation of loading and aiming controlled by a seaman 'captain of turret'. The gunnery branch continued to attract a new breed of scientifically trained officers, and when the Whitehead torpedo emerged to become a naval weapon of much promise it was logical that the *Vernon* torpedo school should work under the wing of *Excellent* to train torpedo lieutenants and ratings. It was also fortunate that its development should be handled by Commander John Fisher, whose reforming drive and powerful personality were to dominate the navy and its people in later years.

Born of an impecunious army family in Ceylon without naval or political connections, Fisher won the navigation prize in his lieutenant's exam and specialized in gunnery. Promoted commander at twenty-eight he threw himself wholeheartedly into the development of torpedo warfare, to which was added mining and electricity. When instructing an officers' class he roused them with

> If you are a gunnery man you must believe and teach that the world must be saved by gunnery. If you are a torpedo man you must lecture and teach the same thing about torpedoes. But be earnest, terribly in earnest. The man who doubts, or who is half-hearted, never does anything for himself or his country. You are missionaries; show the earnestness, if need be the fanaticism of missionaries.[18]

Fisher was commanding the battleship *Inflexible* when the Mediterranean fleet was faced with a crisis in Egypt. Defiantly manning batteries and fortifications at Alexandria, where anti-European feeling was running high, the Egyptian commander, Arabi Pasha, disregarded the commander-in-chief's ultimatum to withdraw. The ensuing nine-hour bombardment silenced the forts – although the fleet suffered casualties – and Fisher was put in charge of the naval brigade to occupy the city, restore order and clear up the mess. Included in one of the detachments was Lieutenant Percy Scott of *Inconstant*, who recalls overhearing this example of the sardonic humour that characterized the lower deck when serving ashore in a foreign country:

> While gathering up unexploded naval projectiles in the town we found a gigantic 16-inch shell outside the door of a baker's shop, that had penetrated the roof, wrecked the inside but without causing apparent external damage. A sailor remarked 'wonder how this ....ing thing came here; there is no hole anywhere'. His mate looked round and seeing one of the extremely narrow alleys of Alexandria behind him replied 'I suppose it must have made this ....ing street.'[19]

Apart from weapon specialists it was evident that technical advances had not been matched by a better educated officer. Arguments over junior officers' training led to the establishment in 1873 of the Royal Naval College at Greenwich to replace its predecessor at Portsmouth. Run on university lines under its first president, Admiral Cooper Key, with a director of studies and an erudite staff, it brought together under one roof the training of executive and later engineer officers above the rank of midshipman. The curriculum covered theoretical and scientific subjects, languages, naval history, naval architecture and engineering. Acting sub-lieutenants sat a short course to stimulate their intellect after four years at sea, while gunnery and torpedo lieutenants required pre-qualification courses with a deep study of ballistics, hydraulics and electricity. Regular nine-month courses on general subjects were offered to captains, commanders and lieutenants to fill in time while awaiting a new appointment.

At first not everything worked out as expected and an early course scarcely impressed Lieutenant Henry Fleet:

> We Half Pays arrived full of zeal, but in most cases it soon oozed out. Nobody seemed to mind whether we attended lectures or not. We were under obligation of a very limited kind to the Admiralty who only provided quarters and contributed toward our messing. We did not even wear uniform, messed in evening dress . . . and finished off the term in a blaze of glorious hospitality by giving a big ball that was attended by over a thousand people. We had a good football team . . . held an athletic meeting and one of the lieutenants sportingly provided a pack of beagles.[20]

Regardless of the fact that steam was rapidly displacing sail, engineer officers continued to face resistance from the executive branch in their attempts to achieve better standing in the service. One sore point lay in the rule that only the executive officer besides the captain had the power to punish engineering branch defaulters; in consequence stokers and their petty officers felt less respect for their officers and discipline suffered. Another was their accommodation:

> The engineer officer was somewhat of a fish out of water [records Assistant Clerk Henry Willis of *Invincible*]. Only the chief engineer was a wardroom officer, the remainder formed a mess by themselves, not even the young ones being allowed to join the gunroom. Neither was there any exchange of courtesies; indeed quite the reverse, a barrier of stupid prejudice preventing any intercourse. Still many were real good fellows and it was a good day for the naval service when the standard of education and upbringing of engineer officers was raised.[21]

The first stage of reform was marked by the move of young engineers to Greenwich; the breakthrough came in 1876 in the shape of recommendations by a carefully chosen committee chaired by Admiral Cooper Key, a great supporter of the branch. These included pay, promotion, rank and status in line with executive officers, the abolition of separate messing and setting up the hulk *Marlborough* to accommodate engineer students under training at Portsmouth. Although only the last two proposals were accepted – the remainder took years to be realized – the report had many beneficial results, including a later decision to move officers training to Devonport on a far more ambitious scale. Above all it made for better inter-departmental relations, especially in the fleet where commanding officers were able to use their influence on behalf of the engineers.

A feature of the 1880s that aggravated commanders-in-chief was the growing lack of uniformity in dress. Officers were addicted to overcoats, mackintoshes, cloaks and capes of different styles and shades, besides carrying umbrellas. Some had frock coats with 'grotesquely long skirts' while black satin ties were 'passed through gold rings' or secured with highly ornamental pins, the mode typical of the splendid individuality of the Victorian naval officer. No wonder the bluejacket was also partial to personal decoration including tattoos on various parts of his body, a custom not unknown in the modern Navy. To be well turned out when ashore entailed embroidery of flannels, trousers and black silks with fancy designs cunningly concealed for inspections, abnormally large collars and, as a *pièce de resistance*, the button taken out of a straw hat crown and a gold sovereign inserted in lieu. Its patience exhausted, the Admiralty convened committees in the 1890s to introduce new regulations, complete with illustration and precise measurements. Those for officers dictated the pattern of uniform until 1939; instead of dealing rank by rank, instructions appeared under the title of a particular dress, with a table indicating how and when each 'rig' should be worn. For everyday wear officers adopted monkey jacket and trousers known as No. 5s, and though hats were mandatory most commanders-in-chief allowed officers to land in plain clothes for recreation. Ratings' dresses were also overhauled and numbered from one to eight in blue and white uniform.[22] Those worn by seamen were known as 'square rig'.

❖❖❖

For an ambitious executive commander the crowning moment came with promotion to captain. Having attained what many considered the pinnacle of a naval career it seems strange by modern standards that a newly selected captain had to kick his heels for up to four years doing virtually nothing before his first command; some even took steps to broaden their mind in civilian life by farming or serving as magistrates. How qualified were these men and what sort of leaders did they turn out to be?

In the 1879 Navy List there were 170 captains, aged between thirty-four and fifty-four, of whom three-quarters were actively employed. The majority held seagoing commands, four were commodores of squadrons, a few were employed in harbour service, one was a naval attaché and another private secretary to the First Lord. The remainder were unemployed on half pay, which was customary not only on promotion but between their first ship and a harbour service or coastguard job and, if they were lucky, a second command. By that time their seventeen years were up and promotion to rear admiral was in the offing.

Almost all possessed medals for war service in the Baltic, Crimea, India or China; one held a VC, four were Companions of the Order of the Bath, nine wore one or more Humane Society's Medals on their right breasts for saving life and two had a pension for wounds suffered in action. Only a quarter had previously obtained a certificate in steam machinery, a third were qualified in gunnery and rather more had received brief torpedo training in the *Vernon*. All had been brought up in sail. Two were earls, one was knighted and four were sons of barons.[23] Many had been elected to the 'Senior' United Service Club in London and an unknown number were members of the Royal Navy Club of 1765 and 1785, exclusive to the executive branch, that dined periodically to celebrate the anniversaries of important naval victories. It is likely that the majority had married in their late thirties and lived within their means on an annual pay of £420 rising to £602; despite additional command money their emoluments were not over generous.

Wearing No. 5s, the executive officer of HMS *Blenheim* in conversation with his captain of marines

Joining his first command and accustomed to wardrooms teeming with good fellowship, the new captain found himself overnight a remote and solitary figure with status little below that of God. As he came up on the quarterdeck everyone would vanish quietly and nobody, not even his second in command, could speak to him except on service matters. The captain kept his distance and made sure others kept theirs, not from deliberate arrogance, although some captains were pompous snobs, but because tradition demanded that there should be a gulf; moreover, the ship's company liked it that way. Treated with deference and ceremony not always accorded to a head of state he was an autocrat pure and simple, with powers of punishment to influence the careers and welfare of a large body of people. There is a story that when the Sultan of Morocco paid a visit to the Navy's latest battleship he was asked what impressed him most – the 16-in gun turret, the 8,000-hp engines, the two torpedo boats carried on board or perhaps the electric light throughout? 'The captain's face' was his reply.[24]

There is plenty of evidence that the late nineteenth-century captain was competent in his job, paternally austere but just in his dealings, unhesitatingly conservative in outlook, idiosyncratic and unlikely to suffer fools gladly. The majority had the good of the service at heart, such as Captain John Borlase Warren whom Able Seaman Sam Noble considered one of the finest:

> Strict on duty but an honest, fair minded gentleman for all that. He never punished a man on the day he was taken up before him but always delayed sentence till the day following so he could think the crime over and give the man fair play. If you happened to be at the wheel, or in the chains or on lookout you would sense him going the rounds unseen and speaking to nobody. But you knew he was there, watchful and vigilant, and felt that the safety of the ship was in his capable hands; God was in his heaven and all was right with the world. And the thought bucked you up tremendously and made you stick to your guns for all you were worth. We all liked him.[25]

In the opinion of Commander Penrose Fitzgerald, executive officer of *Agincourt*:

> Undoubtedly the art of keeping all hands in good humour is of exceeding value to the captain of a ship. It is a personal gift, like genius. It cannot be acquired. It may not be imitated. It is not gained by relaxing discipline, by undue familiarity, by seeking popularity or by any of the devices with which the unhappy imitator seeks to attain it. Captain Hopkins . . . was the most popular captain I ever served with.[26]

John Hopkins possessed that indefinable charisma that helped promote him to flag rank and ultimately to the Board of Admiralty.

Not all captains were held in such affection and in some ships the power at the captain's disposal proved a corruptive influence leading to an unhappy ship; in a few cases the loneliness of command caused addiction to the bottle that was always handy. Stories abound of eccentricity to the verge of madness during four or five years on distant foreign stations. Midshipman Chambers remembered the Pacific Squadron in 1885 when 'Captain Thomas Branch of the flagship *Swiftsure* had ridden down to the landing (at Esquimalt) and called for his boat; he was seated on a great coal-black horse and he was without a stitch of clothing.'[27] A whimsical skipper was Captain

Frederic Doughty of *Constance* who walked the poop in a tall white hat, otherwise in orthodox uniform, while the senior officer on the West Coast of Africa always took off his coat before reading the Bible since when in uniform he could not recognize any superior power. Some possessed high intellectual qualities, and the majority enjoyed a strength of personality tempered by good judgement that made them natural leaders and proud to represent the acknowledged power of their country in keeping the peace of the world.

Life for the captain of an ironclad in the crack Mediterranean squadron was somewhat different. From December 1879 the battleship *Invincible* was commanded by Captain the Hon. E.R. Fremantle, who at forty-three had everything going for him. An enthusiastic and expert swimmer he held several awards for lifesaving, exploits that did not always turn out as expected. Assistant Clerk Willis recounted what happened when Fremantle had commanded the frigate *Doris* some years previously:

> [He] was in his bath when the shout 'Man overboard' was raised; without a moment's hesitation he leapt overboard from the stern gallery. Meanwhile his ship had shortened sail, backed foretopsail, lowered the lifeboat and having picked up the man, proceeded to get under way again, not knowing that the captain was overboard. But at the signal 'Man overboard' the ship astern had stopped, lowered a boat and was able to pick up Fremantle who, on reaching the quarterdeck, explained what had happened. The officer of the watch, who had never before dealt with a captain not only out of uniform but in a state of nature, sent for a bath towel. Meanwhile a signal was made to his ship 'we have your captain on board' and a much underclad officer was restored to his astonished command.[28]

In those days the average cruising speed underway was about 4 knots.

During 1880 the ironclad squadron cruised the Mediterranean with a programme that entailed foreign visits, steam manoeuvring, target practice, competitive evolutions and on one occasion making all plain sail from Nice to Palermo. Fremantle was lucky when *Invincible* was detached on three occasions – to rescue a British colonel captured by Greek brigands, to liaise with a Russian squadron in Alexandria and to salvage an Austro-Hungarian barque. On return to Malta's Grand Harbour Fremantle was informed that early in 1881 his next job would be Senior Naval Officer Gibraltar; from the pages of his journal one gains a vivid picture of a captain's social and service life as he prepares to hand over command.

A keen sportsman and aspiring linguist, Fremantle records lawn tennis matches as well as regular Italian lessons from a local teacher. Eagerly awaited was the mail steamer with letters from his wife in England, who shared his concern about Gibraltar by being 'rather low about the expenses' of running a second house and 'the arrangements for children's schooling'. Then comes his joy at the news that his son 'had passed into the Navy first' and the next day a proud father 'brought him a set of silver links and studs to send home by the Admiralty bag'. Attendance at balls and dinners ashore, added to the inevitable calls on hostesses that social etiquette demanded, are mixed with courts martial, seamanship examinations, surveys, inspections and an enquiry into 'shameful bullying in the midshipmen's berth of *Invincible* when 4 youngsters had a broad arrow marked on their noses'. After church on Christmas Day, Fremantle and his guests walked round the decorated messdecks 'which were rather good on the whole'. In addition to grog the 'men were allowed two quarts of beer each'. In the evening he had '5 youngsters and 3 wardroom officers to dinner and regaled them with regular Xmas fare. After dinner we played whist and had songs in the wardroom. I retired when one of the songs seemed to verge on the improper'.[29]

Fremantle was promoted to rear admiral and second-in-command of the Channel squadron, eventually retiring as commander-in-chief at Plymouth. Being a man of substance it is probable that Fremantle aligned himself with that select body of active and retired elder statesmen referred to as the Establishment. In common with other professional bodies the Navy's Establishment regarded themselves as the guardians of all that was – in their opinion – right for the Service. Though willing to move things along a little or make small adjustments they were strongly opposed to radical change. During the long years of peace their influence prospered.

CHAPTER THREE

Thou shalt not Criticize but Obey

A genuine man-o'-war's man . . . was always in good humour and if you understand how to manage him, would do anything he was asked to do – whether he could or not!

He would make brooms, milk the cows, play at cricket, march, fight, run, dance, sing, play the fiddle, smoke a pipe, drink a glass of grog and mind the baby. That he had his weaknesses and shortcomings cannot be denied, but take him all in all he was a splendid fellow – and I expect we shall never see his like again.

Martello Tower

Nobody would dispute that England possessed the world's largest navy. Few were aware that France was rapidly catching up, that Italy and Russia were increasing their fleets and that even German warship construction was beginning to match her colonial ambitions. When tension with France in 1884 focused attention on the country's first line of defence, public opinion was severely jolted by a series of articles entitled 'The truth about the Navy' in the influential *Pall Mall Gazette* edited by W.T. Stead. Supported by an array of statistics – inspired leaks from knowledgeable sources – their purpose was to expose the inadequate and unprepared state of the fleet and demand an immediate heavy increase in naval expenditure.

Much of the blame for this outburst stemmed from the long-standing struggle in the Navy between the far-seeing technicians and conservatively minded senior officers over future warship design. Coupled with a succession of weak Boards of Admiralty the controversy was used by politicians of both parties to keep naval budgets low. Concern was keenly felt by younger officers, noticeably Lieutenant Reginald Bacon, who considered that:

> the fleet possessed the lowest level of efficiency of material since the middle of the 18th century. The officers and men were just as zealous, the love of their profession just as great, but they were imbued with ideas that had not altered with the times. Sail drill still occupied a place in the scale by which efficiency was measured. Gun range was too short to evoke any real interest in gunnery as an art and coupled with slow ships it was clear that tactics had not advanced beyond ideas of a close range mêlée. Fleet manoeuvres – the practice of altering the formation of ships – were exercised but no one appreciated whether these gyrations would be of use in fighting or not![1]

The Channel squadron then consisted of four twenty-year-old ironclads, the new breech-loading guns had run into serious trouble and there were lengthy delays in big gun manufacture. Coincident with war scares and encouraged by Captain Fisher of the *Excellent*, the *Pall Mall Gazette* articles were widely quoted; every newspaper and periodical began discussing the state of the Navy and the government became uneasy. At Queen Victoria's review of the fleet in 1887 obsolete ships were much in evidence, causing Vice-Admiral Sir William Hewett, flying his flag in the old *Minotaur*, to remark: 'Most of what you see here is mere ullage.' In March 1889 the first Naval Defence Act was passed to restore efficiency, augment personnel, accelerate warship construction and make the navy as powerful as that of any two other nations – the Two Power Standard.

As well as increasing active service recruitment to man seventy new warships, additional reserves were needed to top up the fleet in event of mobilization. Here the situation was quite promising; the Royal Naval Reserve possessed a growing number of volunteers from the Merchant Navy and fishing fleets, supplemented by coastguards and RN and RM pensioners. In 1873 the post of Admiral Superintendent of Naval Reserves had been created to command the reserve squadron of ironclads and co-ordinate the activities of coastguard and reserve districts round Britain. Besides training in drill ships reservists and coastguards went to sea for six weeks every summer in the reserve squadron, sometimes taking part in manoeuvres and war scares. According to Able Seaman James Woods, who served in the coastguards, 'these embarkations were thoroughly detested by the men' who lost subsistence money and resented leaving their 'cushy' jobs ashore; nevertheless the experience did them a world of good. Further improvements followed recommendations from a Committee on Reserves, and in 1898 the men were allowed to wear uniform at all times when ashore.

For the first time since Trafalgar the British public started to take a more intelligent but critical interest in their Navy, that had hitherto shunned publicity. Following an army pageant at Chelsea in 1891 a Naval Exhibition was held on the same site with displays by seamen and marines, mock battles on a lake and numerous exhibits by shipbuilding and engineering firms. In five months it was visited by two and a half million people. Fired by this blaze of promotion the Admiralty revived the programme for 'meet the people' cruises round Britain and supported the inception of the Navy League in 1895, its purpose to create awareness by the man in the street of the need for a strong fleet. Through their own journal *The Navy*, articles in the press, lectures and influential contacts within Parliament such as Lord Brassey, the Navy League aimed especially at the younger generation. All of this did much to stimulate recruiting and make the country more sympathetic to a naval cause when it came to spending taxpayers' money.

Prominent among the Navy League's supporters was Captain Lord Charles Beresford, probably the most talked about figure in the late Victorian Navy. Good looking and well connected he was elected MP for his Irish constituency at twenty-eight. Promoted commander at twenty-nine, his speeches in the House were mainly confined to naval affairs, about which he spoke with authority and vehemence, irritating their Lordships who could do nothing to prevent a naval officer from being an eloquent member of Parliament. As a junior Naval Lord in 1887, he persuaded the Admiralty to establish a Naval Intelligence department, then resigned after his colleagues refused to form a Naval Staff. The ships he commanded were disciplined and happy; with his Tory aristocratic background he was more liberal minded than most of his contemporaries, refusing to accept the enormous difference in lifestyle between officers and men. And in an age when the slightest fault was harshly condemned and praise for good performance rarely given he was quick to recognize a deserved compliment. Known as 'Charley B' in the Fleet and a prime favourite with the public, Beresford did much to educate British people to the realities of sea power and the need for a strong navy.

Further moulding of public opinion stemmed from a spate of naval literature and a remarkable change in press attitude. Among the former the writings of Captain Alfred T. Mahan of the US Navy stood out as of supreme importance, not only in Britain where they became a naval bible but among foreign navies. Novels, verse and theatrical melodramas about the sea flourished and the staunchly pro-Navy *Daily Mail* was launched in 1896 as the first mass circulation newspaper. For keen historians the Navy Records Society was founded to introduce rare or unpublished works of naval interest while development of photography was no better exemplified than in the pages of *Navy and Army Illustrated.* Naval biographies also became popular reading and from the youthful memories of retired admirals emerged a down-to-earth picture of gunrooms and life at sea under sail.

Captain The Rt Hon. Lord Charles Beresford

For some years the training of cadets in *Britannia* had received a bad press, with unfavourable comparison with public school education. Matters reached a head in 1882 when an article in *The Times* claimed that subjects taught were inappropriate, age entry was too low and the entrance examination all wrong. Admiralty response was a hands-off attitude, to the extent of regarding criticism as impertinent. Even when a high powered committee was appointed in 1885 to review the system not one of its recommendations was accepted. When about to relinquish command of *Britannia* a similar reaction confronted Captain Nathaniel Bowden Smith, who sought permission from the Admiralty 'to submit a memorandum on the training system, proposing alterations to the curriculum and bringing seamanship instruction up to date'. Bowden Smith was also one of those who felt strongly it was wrong to impose the thirteen-year-old age limit on boys who were slow developers or did not know their own minds, because 'we want the best men we can get to officer the navy and by cutting off the supply at such an early age we may be losing valuable services'.[2] His proposals fell on deaf ears.

Admiral Tweedie recollected in 1890 that 'conditions were at a low ebb and the ship was virtually run by the cadet sergeant major. . . . The captain and commander were seldom seen, neither were the two lieutenants who kept day on and day off and were reputed to turn over to each other at Paddington Station'. Bullying and fagging had evidently got beyond a joke while 'the punishment system for trivial offences was inhuman'.[3] Much of this changed with the arrival of Captain Moore in 1894 who started the term lieutenant system, abolished ship's corporals and put discipline in the hands of a gunner and four gunner's mates. Training was improved and in 1897 the Admiralty altered the age of entry by stages to between fourteen and a half and fifteen and a

Britannia naval cadets at seamanship instruction on shore model, *c.* 1880

half years old. Because the old hulks were wearing out, Captain Moore's final effort was to persuade the Admiralty to build the college on the hill above the Dart to plans drawn up by one of his staff. Aston Webb was the selected architect; the go ahead was given in 1898.

Entrants to the paymaster branch went straight to sea where the regime was equally tough, as William Martin found when he joined the Mediterranean flagship *Alexandra* as a sixteen-year-old assistant clerk:

> My duties were to keep the ship's ledger *without previous instruction.* My boss, Paymaster Silas Winter Parker, had rough ways with him, but on looking back I realize that I needed discipline, and he proved a good friend. For every mistake that I made he assured me he would stop my leave for a day and see that I received a cut with a horsewhip. He was a man of his word; I had a year's leave stopped and received over three hundred cuts. This system of tuition had the effect of compelling me to take a personal interest in my work so that at the end of another three months I was sent for on the quarterdeck where, to my pleased astonishment, I was complimented by the captain on progress made.[4]

Martin was certainly a courageous officer because ten years later he took the almost unprecedented step of matrimony under the age of thirty while secretary to Flag Officer, Sheerness: 'We were married at Forest Hill, before returning to Sheerness immediately as I could not get long leave. It was a rash experiment marrying on my pay alone of seven shillings a day, even with lodging allowance and subsistence amounting to £90 per year but liable to be stopped at any time. It was only due to my wife that I was able to win through those hard times.'[5]

Mr Hugh Childers may not have been the most popular First Lord of the Admiralty in 1870 but his reform of the executive officer structure earned praise from the committee convened in 1894 to review progress.[6] Broadly speaking Childers' intentions had been to establish the number of officers in each rank to ensure sufficiency for war mobilization; to maintain a healthy flow of promotion – by seniority to lieutenant and flag officer and by selection to commander and captain; to enforce compulsory retirement at certain ages and to allow optional retirement, whenever possible, with appropriate pension. Not everything worked out as expected but the scheme did achieve a 40 per cent promotion factor to commander, with relatively better chances to captain.

Lieutenants (there were no lieutenant commanders in those days) could expect twelve to seventeen years in the rank before promotion to commander at an average age of thirty-five. Similarly commanders were about forty-one on promotion to captain; but the latter would now spend eleven years in the rank before getting a flag at fifty-two. The worst aspect was the inordinate time spent on half pay in the rank of captain, which induced a soporific effect on mental outlook. 'I don't think we thought very much about war with a large W,' commented Admiral Humphrey Smith. 'We looked upon the Navy more as a world police force than as a warlike institution. Our job was to safeguard law and order, put out fires on shore and act as guide, philosopher and friend to the merchant ships of all nations.'[7]

Not until the late 1880s did the fleet engage in more realistic exercises and because press comment fired public interest, fleet commanders began to think seriously about future sea battles at a time when a rigid inflexibility of command was stifling the individual initiative so encouraged by Nelson a century before. Delegation of authority was rare and the practice of following or imitating the movements of senior officers' ships in the fleet was cultivated to an absurd degree, contributing to the belief that the admiral could do no wrong. Inevitably this led to disasters such as when the battleship *Camperdown* rammed *Victoria* off Tripoli in 1893. On receiving the signal for the manoeuvre to approach the anchorage, the second-in-command and eleven captains realized the order to reverse the course of two parallel columns of ships by turning inwards was impossible to execute. Yet they carried it out all the same, resulting in the loss of a fine warship and the lives of 350 officers and men, including Vice-Admiral Sir George Tryon, the commander-in-chief. More startling was the verdict of the court martial: 'It would be fatal to the best interests of the service to say that he (the rear admiral second-in-command) was to blame for carrying out the directions of the commander-in-chief, present and in person.' In other words officers should obey orders even if they knew them to be incorrect. Prominent among *The Laws of the Navy* – approved reading for wardroom officers – ran the lines of the verse 'Every law is as naught besides this one – "Thou shalt not criticize, but obey."'

As a petty officer in charge of one of the boats rescuing survivors of the disaster, Thomas Lyne observed:

> [there was] absolutely no panic or rushing about. Officers went quickly to their stations and the men to their various positions at the watertight compartments, hoisting out boats and performing other duties. In the case of men working below there was evidence of their

> coolness; and when the order was passed down for everyone to go on deck there was no undue haste . . . and . . . as the list increased it must have passed through their minds to look out for themselves.[8]

The display of discipline and self control by officers and men was the only redeeming feature of a shocking and avoidable tragedy.

Thomas Lyne rose to the rank of gunner and in 1901 was specially promoted to lieutenant when in command of HM Torpedo Boat No. 60 during the Boer War; his ship sustained a fractured propeller shaft so he sailed her back to harbour under jury rig. After a distinguished career he retired as a rear admiral with a knighthood.

Lyne was almost the sole rating to reach the wardroom for over fifty years and the story of warrant officers was one long fight to gain better recognition. Though the Admiralty declined further advancement on the grounds of their lack of education, it is difficult not to believe that a deeper reason lay in social status.

For Queen Victoria's Jubilee celebrations in 1887 the cruiser *Canada* on the North America and West Indies station was berthed off Prince Edward Island. The gunner, Henry Capper, discovered from friends ashore that he was expected to join them at an official reception. Not receiving an invitation card he sought advice from the first lieutenant, who referred him to the captain. 'You and your messmates (boatswain and carpenter)', said Captain Beaumont, 'are not included in the term "officers" in the social matters; I regard you, Mr Capper, as one of my most responsible professional officers, but in social affairs you must not consider yourself an officer.'[9] Naturally Capper was deeply offended at this discrimination, not realizing that Beaumont, in all probability, wanted to spare him the inevitable snub from his hosts whose class consciousness was every bit as, if not more, rigid as that of the Royal Navy. Many years were to elapse before warrant officers and their wives were able to find a level in service social hierarchy that satisfied all parties.

By tradition the warrant officers lived forward on the lower deck adjacent to their stores. As a rule they had no mess of their own and were served meals in their cabins, attended by a servant and cook in isolation from the wardroom and ship's company. The great majority did their job well, so much so that first lieutenants and commanders were known to owe them their promotion. And midshipmen did not forget their fatherly advice or the spirit of camaraderie that sprang up, as happened in *Invincible* when:

> the boatswain, carpenter and gunner occasionally dined in the gunroom. Now and again hospitality was given when, having missed our breakfast, we got cocoa, biscuit and perhaps fried salt pork in their mess. Occasionally a bottle of whisky was exchanged for a bottle of rum, the WOs not being allowed the former, though they could save up their daily tots of the latter till a full bottle was obtained for exchange.[10]

Relations between warrant officers and lower deck varied. In the gunboat *Swallow*, relates Sam Noble:

> the bosun, Tommy Freedie, was a big man, muscular and hairy, with a hand like a deck bucket and a voice like the Archangel Gabriel. Nobody could say they couldn't hear him. And

Gunner, boatswain and carpenter discuss the day's programme

> swear! We used to say he made the ship's candles burn blue. But it was done in such a cheery, hearty fashion and with such honest goodwill that we rather admired this special gift of his. The best of it was he didn't know he was swearing. I remember one day Tommy was conducting operations to men on the fore yard when the first lieutenant remonstrated 'Oh Mr Freedie, don't use such abominable language.' Tommy pulled up as if he had been shot. 'Beg pardon, sir, what language?' 'Why, the language you are using. It's enough to sink the ship.' 'Why bless ye, sir, they don't mind. They knows all about that, sir. It ain't nothing.' 'Ah, but you must not use such language' retorted the first lieutenant and walked aft. 'Aye, Aye, sir' said Tommy; then, after a pause, addressed the men aloft. 'Now then you Saltash fishwives' he roared, almost choking with restraint; 'D'ye hear that? you d..d..darlings. Come on, you d..d..doddering dockyard maties! I'll teach you, you b..b..beauties! Just you wait!' For all that Tommy Freedie was a fine officer that we all admired.[11]

In another ship it was the lower deck that displayed their own form of class prejudice. In the frigate *Newcastle* Midshipman Mark Kerr remembers:

> One morning the boatswain came aft and reproved the petty officer in front of his men over some laxity of duty performed as captain of top. The petty officer listened without comment and when the warrant officer had passed on remarked 'I don't mind being sworn at or told off by an officer what is a gentleman, but it makes me mad when one comes along who has worn blue serge like myself and hurls all that abuse at me. That's the difference and you know it, sir, and we all know it on the lower deck.'[12]

Pay and promotion prospects for warrant officers had long been insufficient to attract the best petty officers and when Capper joined the Naval Ordnance Department in Whitehall under Captain Fisher in 1888 he started to campaign for a better deal. After founding the *Warrant Officers Journal*, full of propaganda for the cause, he enlisted support from MPs and the press, in particular for granting commissions 'for selected (warrant) officers who could pass the same tests as Lieutenants'. Eventually a Committee on Manning was set up whose recommendations succeeded in raising the pay, trebling the number of 'chief' grades and later extending warrant rank to artificer engineers with the expectation that other branches would soon follow. Proper warrant officers' messes were established and formal full dress uniform approved. But recommendations fell short of selective promotion to lieutenant and it was a bitter disappointment to the branch when an increase in the establishment of lieutenants in 1895 was achieved by recruiting a hundred Royal Naval Reserve officers (The Hungry Hundred) followed by a further fifty (The Famished Fifty).

On return from five years in an ordnance appointment in Australia, where he had been banished for too much political wire pulling, Capper was promoted chief gunner and appointed to Sheerness Gunnery School to preside over a large warrant officers' mess. Keen as ever on promotions to the wardroom he had to admit that 'the undoubted unsuitability of some of those about me for holding higher rank became very apparent and this to some extent shattered my ideals. There were those with professional ability and service experience, yet quite unfit for, nor desired, any social advance'. Visiting some of their homes he was shocked by 'disgraceful conduct' brought about by early and unsuitable marriages. Not until 1903, when Admiral Fisher was Second Sea Lord, did the Admiralty establish the rank of lieutenant for 'long and meritorious service for 4 per cent of commissioned (chief) warrant officers of both military and civil branches'. A year later congratulations poured in when Capper himself was so promoted.

The medical branch had also fallen into the doldrums, principally due to the mediocre quality of its surgeons. Although some rose to the top of their profession the majority were not regarded highly in the fleet, sufficient proof to convince the Admiralty that pay, prestige and prospects would have to be improved to engage medical officers of a higher standard. This happened in 1881, coinciding with the abandonment of the preliminary course with the Army at Netley hospital and setting up a Naval Medical School at Haslar. As well as being allowed to specialize, doctors were introduced to the peculiarities of naval hygiene, food and clothing. When reviewed some years later opinion was expressed that the 'service was in a satisfied and contented condition . . . with only one examination for promotion – from surgeon to staff surgeon'.

Economy of administration being the hallmark of naval hospitals, reforms took time to permeate, especially in Haslar hospital at Gosport where Mr Bishop, a former foreman of labourers, recollected that:

> the garden was a vast shrubbery surrounded by an iron railing and the place looked more like a prison than a hospital. 'Abandon hope, all ye that enter here' would have been a good inscription over the gate. In 1888 the inside of the hospital was like a workhouse. The walls were lime washed, the plain white decks were seldom dry from constant scrubbing, the windows were shuttered on the inside and the sanitary arrangements primitive. The operating table and the duty cabins were all in one, and it was a common thing for a wardmaster to be writing at his desk whilst a surgeon was operating. They were not apparently troubled about the question of germs. As duty labourer I have often been called out at night to hold a man down whilst the medical officer inserted stitches in a wound.[13]

Although a handful of female naval nurses supported Florence Nightingale in the Crimea it was not until 1884 that the Navy agreed to introduce them to Haslar and Plymouth hospitals. In an expression of male chauvinism their arrival was deeply resented by medical officers and pensioner male nurses – but instantly popular with the patients. Gradually the forbearance and determination of the nursing sisters overcame objections and soon medical officers began to realize their value; above all the women helped to train young sick berth attendants, who later replaced the pensioners. In 1906 civilian dental surgeons were first engaged in naval hospitals and later at shore establishments.

As the fleet developed with bigger, more powerful steam machinery so the engineer branch increased from under 6,000 in 1880 to nearly 26,000 at the turn of the century. This put considerable strain on the chief engineers, shortfalls lower down the list being made up by chief engine room artificers. With the gradual closing down of *Marlborough* in Portsmouth students transferred to what later became the Royal Naval Engineering College at Keyham in Devonport. Aged between fourteen and sixteen the engineer cadet was accepted into the service with proper uniform, ranking with an assistant clerk and equivalent to a naval cadet. Instruction being mainly of a practical nature the college was liberally equipped with sports grounds, and rugby football and cricket were popular among cadets who spent four to five years under training. Academic results were initially disappointing as there was a lack of suitable candidates and very soon the number of junior engineer officers had fallen so alarmingly that standards in general had to be lowered. Numbers were made up with the introduction of the artificer engineer of warrant rank and by other means to stimulate recruiting. To improve the standing of the branch in 1900 the most senior engineer officer was given the title of engineer-in-chief, equivalent in rank to rear admiral. Simultaneously the relative ranking of engineers was tidied up so that fleet engineers, chief engineers and engineers ranked with commanders, senior lieutenants, and lieutenants. There remained the hotly debated 'Engineer Question' of how responsibilities should be divided between the professionally trained supervisor and the skilled manual worker, more simply the engineer officer and the artificer. With the current acute shortages in mind there were those who felt the engineer officer should disappear, his place taken by an executive lieutenant trained in engineering; at the other end of the scale were those who wanted engineers to be given similar responsibilities and status to that held by the executive officer. A solution was not long in coming.

For too long the contribution of the engineer, the artificer and the stoker towards fighting efficiency had remained unrecognized as they performed unseen among coal-fired boilers and triple expansion compound engines. This description of a battleship raising steam to proceed on manoeuvres brings home the punishing conditions below decks:

Stoker feeding the furnace in a battleship's stokehold

> And already the blackened smoke rolls quicker from the funnels, fed from the four great stokeholds below. In each are men, black from head to foot, hard at it with pick and hammer and shovel, waking up the fires. In one corner some are scratching coal out of the bunker doors and loading it on trollies, which others haul with a thundering roar across the plating to the furnace doors and tip up on to the plates in front, ready for the specialists who work the fires. There are sixteen fires in this one stoke-hold; each must be kept clean and blazing for the next three days and nights.
>
> The door of the farthest fire is thrown open and a splendid glare sweeps the black iron walls, showing up the implements all slung overhead, the pitchy openings to the bunkers and the grim faces of the blackened men sweating in the dust. And then the stoker of that fire, standing a little back, sends shovel after shovelful of coal flying cleanly through the little opening and landing in appointed places round and behind the fire. Nothing drops in the middle, nothing hits the side of the little oval door; but with splendid straight strokes from the shoulder he drives each helping clean into its place with absolute certainty. Stopping an instant, he peers his black devil face into the flaming six foot horror of the fire, then wraps a rag round hand and shovel, clears the blazing ashes and clangs the door shut again across the hole. The trollies rattle to and fro and a man slides, boots first, from a bunker at the other end shining black all over, his hair glistening with tiny particles, literally soaked in coal-dust. He has been in there for half an hour. Steadying himself a minute, he walks to the air-trunk and breathes hard at the pumped-down air, spitting to clear his throat.

Unlike the seaman branch stokers were not trained as boys but enlisted from eighteen up to twenty-five as stokers second class. They came from a wide background, many in the 1890s being ex-Army or ex-marines. That they resented discipline was plainly demonstrated at the defaulters' table; furthermore stokers rarely went ashore with the seamen, though in some ships they had an affinity with the marines. Their rate of pay was higher than their seamen counterparts and as their numbers grew so they became an influential component of a ship's company:

> . . . the engine rooms behind are warming in the haze. All round their huge joints crawl ant-like men with oil-cans, feeling, tapping, oiling, easing and sweating in the cruel heat while on the platform by the log desk is the Engineer of the Watch in shirt-sleeves, humming a little

In the engine room of a battleship

> tune and rolling a cigarette. He climbs up to the cylinders to see that the indicators are ready; here the heat is worst of all. It shimmers off and up through the bars of the armoured hatches – which remind men that the engine-room is a death trap in war, cut off from light and air for the safety of the rest.
>
> Presently a sharp whistle calls from the clustered voice tubes overhead; immediately an ominous mighty hissing answers in one corner, filling the whole place. Then with a sudden heave and roar the great beast moves – but only just – turns once round and once back, groans, hisses and is still. This is the little Engineer of the Watch seeing all correct, cigarette in mouth. The other monster next door – for we have twin screws here – moves as well and the whirring bells ring up 'Ready' to the bridges above. Then indeed he throws away his cigarette stump, and walking to the platform stands ready by the telegraph for orders. Above his head is a row of glittering gauges; all around are wheels and rods and levers in bunches at his hand. The mist has gone now, the time has come and the great engine stands out in all its triple strength ready to be played upon like an organ by the little man beneath it.[14]

When the *Vernon* torpedo school, moored off Portsmouth dockyard, became an independent command in 1876 the executive officer was Commander A.K. Wilson, a contemporary and close colleague of Fisher. *Excellent* could then concentrate on gunnery leaving *Vernon* to compete with torpedoes, torpedo nets, mines, demolitions, electric generators, lighting and searchlights. The two branches were already attracting different types of officer, one observer describing the torpedo lieutenant as 'exceedingly, painfully, and boringly scientific' while his opposite number, 'the Gunnery Jack, is addicted to military customs in methods of drill and saluting', referring to the recent adoption in the Navy of the Army-style hand salute. The critic concluded: 'Not a bad fellow but too conservative in these days for rapid advancement.'[15] Whatever their differences the two branches rubbed along together in developing their respective schools, petty officer instructors of both skills wearing distinguishing badges for a short time on which a torpedo and gun were crossed below a crown. As outlets grew for young ratings to acquire technical expertise so an able seaman's answer in an examination bore witness to the co-operation, when he wrote: 'Electricity is a suttle and impondrous fluid invented by Captain Fisher and perfected by Captain Wilson.'

In 1884 Fisher commanded the *Excellent*, living in the old Royal Naval College and going aboard to start work before breakfast. His secretary, Assistant Paymaster Willis, tactfully preceded his master by taking the routine liberty boat which gave him opportunities to study the change that had come over the sailor in the last decade:

> To begin with they were all sober and showed few signs of overnight drinking. They were nearly all bundlemen, i.e. married men, carrying the inevitable blue handkerchief bundle. Whether raining or not the bluejackets were always in oilskins and the petty officers in dark blue mackintoshes with neat little black bags. Bags and bundles usually took ashore a flannel (white front) 'to be run out' and 'my bit o'meat'. This requires an explanation. Any fresh meat ration not 'taken up' was only credited to the messes at the 'savings' price of four pence per lb; thus the married men naturally took all they could ashore to their families. So prevalent was this habit that it was thought the married men underfed themselves and the quantity each man was allowed to take ashore strictly limited.
>
> Sailors make good husbands; the little home up Fratton way was a luxurious abode compared to the hammock, open mess place and absence of privacy on board. These men coming off seldom spoke; the married men had been up early to do the grate and put the kettle on 'to save the missus'; they had already walked or bicycled a long distance on an empty stomach and must have loathed leaving so early. The elder men were tired, while the younger men, in their first home billets and recently married, had troubles connected with their small pay to ruminate on during that damp, foggy journey. The petty officers looked anxious. Somehow an examination was always ahead and the tortuous drill learnt parrot fashion was not always digested and had been left too long in the hopes that it might be picked up in the 'rezoom' [resumé] over three days prior to examination. Failure or success and consequent promotion meant much with a growing family.[16]

A relic of the old Navy was the administration of increasingly large numbers of ratings awaiting fleet service aboard the depot ships (hulks) at Portsmouth, Chatham and Devonport. Conditions were anything but comfortable and corruption was rife, as Able Seaman Woods found on arrival in the old three-decker *Duke of Wellington*, where:

> I was met at the gangway by one of the Ship's Police, who told me to put my bag down between the guns and fall in, and the 'Jonty' [master-at-arms] would see me. After waiting about ten minutes he came over to me, and after a few questions about the ship I had paid off etc., finished off with 'Let me see, did I understand that you would like another seven days' leave?' This, naturally, somewhat took me aback and while hesitating what to reply he broke

in with 'Ah! that's all right, I daresay we can manage that. I'll see Mr ——' mentioning another Master-at-Arms known as the Pay Jonty, 'and see if he can manage to get your pay back for you, but we shall have to look slippy if you want to get ashore again tonight.' He was just turning away to go to Mr (we will call him Jones) when he said 'By the by, you had better tell him you are going on a week's leave, and that Mr (we will call him Smith) sent you down.'

This treatment seemed very extraordinary to me, and the only conclusion I could come to was that I had either fallen among angels, or that I was being mistaken for another man.

After a time I found the Captain of the Hold just about to indulge in siesta, but like everyone else in this wonderful craft he was also obliging, and instead of the string of curses I was expecting to receive (I had had some experience of his class), he simply said, 'Come on, sonny, let's stow it away.' And stow it away we did. Whilst engaged in this task I remarked 'Jonty Smith is a very nice man'. He looked at me, stuck his tongue in his cheek, winked one eye with a very expressive wink and at last replied 'Yes, a werry nice man to such young strops as you, and so is I.' Of course, I agreed, and after thanking him profusely for his kindness in stowing my bag safely, I was about to leave for the main deck, when he broke in with 'Ere, chuck it, I don't want no thanks, half a dollar [half a crown] is my charge for this little job, so hand it over.' I handed it over. 'And' he continued, 'don't you go up to Jonty Smith or Jonty Jones, with that boarding-school miss yarn of *Thank you, sir*, or blast me you won't go ashore tonight, but'll go in the rattle like one man and don't you forget it. Half a thick 'un [10*s*] is the charge for little jobs, and see that you dub up. Anyone would fancy we ran this ——ing show for fun.'

Then all the strange stories I had heard of the ways of the *Duke* came back to me. When I arrived on the main deck the two Masters-at-Arms were there. One took me to the pay office, where I drew my back pay to date – about nine weeks – from which he deducted ten shillings. From there I went to the main deck, where my other friend received me. To him I paid ten shillings, was handed a liberty ticket, a waterman's boat was called alongside and I went ashore for seven days.

That was my introduction to the old *Duke of Wellington*.[17]

An able seaman's pay at that time was only 1*s* 7*d* per day, yet for a matter of 2*s* paid to the ship's corporal known as the Clothing Crusher, a uniform kit list could be signed as correct without the owner having to lay out his clothes. More serious were the constant allegations of unfairness in the sea service rosters controlled by the drafting masters-at-arms who, for a deposit of 10*s*, would arrange a draft ashore. The majority of these were 'married men anxious for a home billet of which the great number existed in various boat's crews for different dockyard officials. These men were "on compensation" i.e. they lived permanently on shore, and in lieu of victuals they would have received on board, were allowed 1*s* 7*d* per day. Once obtained these billets were held for as long as they could pay for the privilege'.

Blame lay squarely on the depot ship officers who must have been aware of the rackets yet took no action against the mafia. Criticism could also be levelled at the system of recruiting the ship's corporals from marines and able seamen who, according to Woods, 'were more or less failures in their own profession' and, referring to the seamen, 'could never hope to become petty officers or whose temperament did not fit them for strenuous deck life. . . . A fair proportion of the police are

Royal Marines at Flathouse Quay in Portsmouth Dockyard by the accommodation hulks *Duke of Wellington* and *Asia, c.* 1890

composed of the type of man who jumped straight from AB to PO 1st class and immediately commenced to lord it over those who had hitherto treated them with contempt'. Leave arrangements, clothing, victualling, requests to the commanding officer and punishments were all under the control of the ship's police.[18]

Woods was prone to exaggerating sharp practices but undoubtedly they did occur, and when a suspicious commander-in-chief ordered an investigation the repercussions were widespread; included was the discovery of a nest of engine room artificers in the Torpedo Boat Slip at Haslar who had not been to sea for ten years. Appointed to tighten up discipline in *Duke of Wellington*, Captain Robert Woodward was an officer of the old school whose unorthodox methods of dealing with recalcitrant ordinary seamen were effective at a time when an officer going rounds had to take with him a file of Marines. Admiralty approval was speedily obtained to discharge ashore a number of insubordinate and worthless characters as 'objectionable', which seemed to gain the desired result.

A rather different state of affairs prevailed in the active fleet where a bond of companionship was common between officers and men, particularly on overseas stations. In September 1891 the battleship *Colossus* was anchored off Port Sigri, near Rhodes in the Mediterranean, when Chief Petty Officer George Ashton was sent down as the ship's most experienced diver to search for a lost mine. Not a great deal was known then about the dangers of deep diving and in his determination to find the mine Ashton did not take precautions that are now standard practice. After some time below he came up suffering from the 'bends', from which he never recovered. On the following day he was buried at sea and his widow in Portsmouth was informed officially by letter from the captain of her husband's death. This was followed by a personal letter to Mrs Ashton from Captain Jackson expressing deep sympathy and assuring her that there would be no difficulty about her pension. Another was sent by the chaplain in *Colossus* in similar terms, enclosing £10 subscribed by wardroom officers. A month later the president of Ashton's mess wrote enclosing the sum of £58 subscribed by the captain, officers and men of *Colossus*. George Ashton was evidently 'very much liked by all with whom he came in contact'.[19] These gestures of humanity were symbolic of the Victorian way of life and might have occurred in almost any ship of that era.

Chief Petty Officer George Ashton, HMS *Colossus*

In 1893 all ratings were given official numbers and allocated to one of the three home ports, or port divisions as they were later called, men being allowed to express their choice. This reform went some way towards enhancing the security of home life, as more married men wanted to settle near their depots where drafting offices were set up. More important to welfare was the long overdue replacement of depot ships by shore barracks, the plans for Portsmouth having been drawn up as early as 1862. First to move ashore was the depot ship *Royal Adelaide* at Devonport in 1890 and a year later the *Excellent* decided that a gunnery school was better situated on land. This idea sprang from Commander Percy Scott, who realized that students would benefit from learning their skills ashore rather than in cramped conditions afloat.

For some years soil excavated from the construction of the docks in Portsmouth yard had been transferred by railway trucks across a viaduct and dumped by convict labour on a mud flat called Whale Island. By 1880 the area had increased to nearly 80 acres, by which time it was evident that the school with 1,000 officers and men under training was too big for the wooden hulks. Against opposition Scott persisted in his plan and finally the Admiralty agreed. After further draining and levelling to provide sports grounds HMS *Excellent* was transferred to Whale Island early in 1891, the Navy's first shore training establishment and the home of the gunnery branch until 1974.

It was during Scott's command of the *Excellent* (1903–5) that Whale Island was called upon to stage large-scale displays on the cricket ground in front of the wardroom block, firstly for the

Coronation of Edward VII and then to cement the *Entente Cordiale.* Percy Scott's showmanship was much in evidence, and on the latter occasion the story goes that the grand finale comprised a number of sailors dressed in white positioned on the grounds to form the words VIVE LA FRANCE – to vociferous applause from the French visitors. After it was all over a rating wiped the short grass from his knees and exclaimed to his mate: 'I've been a steward, I've been a cook, I've been a signalman – but that's the first time I've been part of a bloody French letter.'[20]

From the mid-nineteenth century, training in small arms and land fighting for marines, seamen and stokers was of paramount importance as naval brigades became involved in more military operations all over the world than at any other period in naval history. One example from the South African war of 1899–1900 must suffice to illustrate the versatility and stamina of those taking part. The heavy cruisers *Terrible* and *Powerful* arrived in Simonstown in the nick of time to dispatch a brigade under Captain Hedworth Lambton to defend Ladysmith. The contingent of 300 men were mainly seamen and stokers, but included ERAs, armourers, blacksmiths, carpenters, signalmen, cooks and sick berth staff. Ammunition for the *Terrible*'s two 4.7-in guns on hastily improvised mountings was limited, but the Boers did not know this and naval counter-battery fire was almost always successful. When the enemy cut off the water supply, leaving only muddy water from the local river, Engineer Sheen constructed a distilling apparatus from railway engine boilers, supplying the whole defence force with clean water until the coal ran out; but for this the ravages of enteric and dysentery would have been even worse. Victuals were soon in short supply so horses were slaughtered and at the end of the four months, with relief imminent, the daily ration for each man was reduced to one and a half biscuits and three-quarters of a pound of horseflesh. Foreseeing a long siege the Fleet Paymaster had bought up the entire stock of Ladysmith beer for the naval canteen soon after arrival, which kept the brigade going for some time. Six weeks after the siege was raised and the brigade re-embarked in *Powerful,* they were publicly welcomed in London and inspected by the Queen at Windsor.

With no decks to holystone, no brightwork to polish and no irksome routine to perform, campaigning on land was a welcome diversion to which officers and men adjusted with conspicuous success, as borne out by numerous medals gained for gallantry and general service. First presented in 1856 the Victoria Cross was awarded to officers and ratings for exceptional valour; thirty years later the Distinguished Service Order was awarded to officers too junior to receive the CB (Companionship of the Bath), while the Conspicuous Gallantry Medal was re-instituted for ratings.

By the early 1890s sail propulsion had disappeared from the active fleet; the training squadron with young seamen continued until the end of the century leaving a few sailing brigs and sloops as tenders to training hulks. To keep men fit and active the Admiralty introduced compulsory physical 'jerks' as part of the daily routine which was initially far from popular in the fleet, instructors being trained at Whale Island and subsequently by the Army. In 1900 physical training became a specialist branch with a commander appointed as Superintendent of Gymnasia, while commanders-in-chief were instructed to encourage all forms of physical exercise and sport, a policy that has continued ever since.

As the nineteenth century drew to a close there were older officers in positions of responsibility who had joined the service when sailing comprised the whole knowledge of a seaman. They did not want to learn about engines or the latest guns and hated the mine and torpedo:

> These fine old seamen were the last who could call all hands on deck and see every petty officer and man aloft. The voice of such a one needed no voice pipe or telephone. His word might save or lose a ship. He had the responsibility of fighting the constant daily battle with the wind and sea . . .[21]

Regrettably these officers could not easily forget their early years when ships were manned by rough and poorly schooled men who needed stiff discipline. They did not appreciate that training ships were turning out ratings who could understand weapons and that technical branches included well-educated artificers. As one petty officer pointed out, on joining the training staff of *Britannia*:

> the customs of the nineteenth and twentieth centuries could not run side by side and there was no question which should give way. So far as the education of the lower deck was concerned the country was beginning to get its value for money. The men's outlook was widened and officers' lectures, books, newspapers etc. enabled them to develop individual ideas. Men began to exhibit a keen impatience with the delay and laxness underlying many of the restrictions then in force and to criticize the inability of their superiors to create the reforms necessary to ensure contentment.[22]

A remarkable pioneer of lower deck reform was Petty Officer James Woods, of whom mention has been made. After nineteen years' service he purchased his discharge in 1898, changed his name to Lionel Yexley and became editor of a newspaper called *The Bluejacket*. For the next twenty-five years Yexley's aim was to publicize lower deck grievances and campaign for improvements in promotion prospects, the punishment system and victualling. An early example concerned the failure of the daily standard ration to provide more than one proper meal, which led to ship's companies supplementing their diet with purchases from the ship's canteen. Publicity generated by *The Bluejacket* attracted MPs who claimed that sailors were being exploited. In May 1900 an investigatory committee under Vice-Admiral Rice recommended the adoption of two new official meals, one at 'stand easy' in the forenoon and the other at 7.30 in the evening. Even so, the marginal increase in rations did not silence grumblings and the problem of the canteens remained.[23]

Providentially a hard core of enlightened officers was emerging that had the conviction and moral courage to shock the Navy out of its obsolete methods. Their leaders included Beresford, Wilson, Scott, Battenberg, and above all Fisher, the genius with the vision and ruthless determination to prepare the Navy for war that seemed inevitable. Support for their cause also came from younger officers, impatient with blimpish attitudes and eager to grasp what the future had to offer. There were exciting times ahead and the introduction of torpedo boats and destroyers commanded by lieutenants to take an active part in annual fleet manoeuvres did much to arouse enthusiasm and initiative. About 125 ft in length and capable of 19 knots, torpedo boats carried one or two sub-lieutenants, a warrant officer, signalman and minimal deck and engine room complement. 'Life in a torpedo boat was no joy,' remarked Bacon, 'and the crews suffered equal if not greater discomfort than the officers; but they had their regular rest and liked the free and easy way of life away from the more monotonous routine of a large man-of-war.'

When Queen Victoria died in 1901 her death was compared with the passing of the Old World. There was not a single officer or man who had served under any other monarch, and there were very few officers on the retired list who had ever drunk the health of a king. At her funeral fate decreed that the hundred-strong Royal Naval Guard, assembled at Windsor Station to await the coffin from London, should take over the Royal Horse Artillery gun carriage and limber when the horses became so restive as to threaten disaster. In no time drag ropes were improvised from harness and even the Royal Train communication cord was called into service. Quick thinking by Prince Louis of Battenberg and Lieutenant Percy Noble saved the day, creating a precedent whereby the Royal Navy was granted the great privilege of drawing the gun carriage at the Sovereign's funeral.[24]

As Britain entered the twentieth century Paymaster George Willis was one who felt the turning point had been reached when:

> the modern Navy, with vigour, impatience and self-confidence of youth, diverges from the old. It is no longer the 'Silent Service' mysteriously hidden from public eye by a barrier of reserve. The Annual Manoeuvres, Press Correspondents, speeches, letters and controversies . . . have torn the veil from the life that officers and men lived apart from their fellows in the days of long commissions and slow communications. Changes in personnel, the granting of home leave, marriage and its amenities, all contribute to a ship being regarded less as a home and one's messmates less as a family than in the old days – all changes that, to my mind, make the modern Navy far less interesting than before.
>
> Increased comfort, higher standards of conduct and efficiency as well as improvements to service conditions may have been gained; but the numerous examinations for promotion, the increased desire to 'get on', stimulated by competition and personal ambition have brought in their train restlessness and a desire to press forward into the highest posts at all costs. All this may really be for the good . . . but personally I cannot help thinking that something of the old time whole-hearted devotion to Service and self-obligation of that ideal has been dimmed.[25]

CHAPTER FOUR

The Fisher Revolution

I thought it would be a good thing to be a missionary, but I thought it would be better to be First Sea Lord.
Admiral of the Fleet Lord Fisher

In January 1901 Naval Cadet A.L. Fletcher left school to join HMS *Britannia*, which:

compared with Marlborough, seemed a most civilized existence. Excellent food, boat sailing to one's heart's content, hammocks very comfortable but washing arrangements primitive in the extreme. We had no trouser pockets – this to prevent 'slouching' – and in the spring and winter terms we wore long woollen drawers, or were supposed to. Occasionally when ready to go ashore in pinnaces there would be a shout from the petty officer ''ave we all got our drawers on in the outside pinnace? Mr Fletcher, show your drawers'. It was 3 days' punishment drill if Mr F. was caught without them.

As in a public school the Lords of Creation were the cricket and football kings; from that tribe the cadet captains who ruled the terms were drawn. Those mighty gentlemen in special blazers despised those who found pleasure in boat sailing; but soon after we joined the fleet it was they who got their bottoms tanned for breaking up ships' cutters and gangways.

Then follows first impressions of the easy going China Station as seen by Midshipman Fletcher in the cruiser *Amphitrite*:

Admirals were almost without exception bearded and so were most of the captains, but as ranks descended so the clean shaven face predominated. The lower deck were also bewhiskered with fine well trimmed beards . . . they were all much tougher than the men of the post '14–'18 war. Booze and girls their main recreation. How they boozed and, in a sense, what gentlemen they were; I never heard a drunken sailor of that period be rude or insolent to an officer, not even to the wretched snotty (midshipman) trying to control 50 or more libertymen he was bringing off under sail. They staggered somehow up the gangway and with tremendous effort stood to attention for inspection on the quarterdeck. Unless a man fell flat on his face and passed out – all was well.

Periodically midshipmen carried out engine room training, where Fletcher found that:

The Chief Engineers were nearly all rugged survivors of a past era – 'I mind the time we need to bind a broken pipe with tow' they used to say. Crude in their language, demons for work and not ashamed of being seen in overalls with a sweat rag round their necks they showed little love for young gentlemen in the gunroom. The younger members of the engine room staff were classy in inverse ratio to their seniority and affected white collars up to 3 inches in height. In *Amphitrite* they also pretended to despise the dear old Chief because, tropics or below zero, he always went ashore in a bowler hat and had left all his aitches somewhere on Tyneside.

As far as the rest of the wardroom was concerned:

> The surgeons were about 75 per cent ex-Trinity College, Dublin, 20 per cent Scottish universities and the odd 5 per cent English. Perfect dears but very thirsty when young. Their medicine may have been crude but they knew a lot about malaria and VD. My chief memories of the sick bay were No. 9 pills, almost atomic in action, for internal disorders; santonin for worms – very prevalent in the East – and vats of zinc ointment for everything else. The paymasters, kindly humans with hours of time to spare, generally kept the mess wine books and organized ship's concert parties; but they had 50 times more to do than the marine officer. After daily inspection of the detachment he would sleep peacefully in a wardroom chair till time for a shore boat, while the chaplain (unless a naval instructor) slept opposite him.[1]

Within the Admiralty Secretariat at Whitehall the scene was also one of undemanding composure. There were four branches – Civil Establishments, Naval (which dealt with officers and ratings), Legal (later known as Naval Law) and Military. Joining as a clerk in the middle 1890s Charles Walker came direct from university; he was soon placed in the Military Branch, 'the hub round which the rest of the Admiralty turned. There was, of course, no semblance of naval staff in those days, such advice as there was being supplied to the Board by the Naval Intelligence Department, which included a section dealing with manpower and mobilization'.

Walker discovered that:

> The thing that struck me most on settling down was the leisurely way in which things were done. In most departments papers took weeks, even months to deal with and if one had chosen not to work there was little incentive to do so. Hours were nominally 10.30 to 5.30 but these were more honoured in the breach than in observance. The second (clerk) in my Branch was quite incompetent, in fact even seniority could not get him promoted. . . . However, the volume of work was a mere fraction of what it became later. Wireless was not then in existence and little business was conducted by telegram: the arrival of a cypher telegram caused quite a flutter in the Military Branch where it had to be decoded.[2]

The accession of King Edward VII in 1901 coincided with a new social era in the country; it also gave much satisfaction to the Royal Navy. For the first time the sovereign decided to associate himself with the Senior Service by appearing in the *Navy List* as its head, together with his various aides-de-camp. Furthermore, he counter-signed naval officers' commissions: those issued to sub-lieutenants carried them up to the rank of captain. Subsequent commissions were given to rear admirals and admirals-of-the-fleet.

As Britain entered the twentieth century times had changed perceptibly since 1870. Trains were running faster though the motor car was restricted to 20 mph, the motor bus was competing with the electric underground railway, and in most towns electricity and gas were commonplace. Hospitals possessed X-ray apparatus, anaesthetics and antiseptic surgery, the first telephones were being installed and the cinematograph was starting to replace the magic lantern. Balloons had grown into airships, the Wright brothers had achieved powered, sustained and controlled flight and in 1901 Marconi had sent the first wireless signal 2,170 miles across the Atlantic to Cornwall. Half the population lived in towns, slum clearance was under way, local education authorities were established, secondary education prospered and new universities were opening their doors. Spurred on by the newly formed Labour party the Liberal Government of 1906–14 initiated a programme of social reforms; the Trades Union Congress of 1910 represented 2.5 million workers. Although they had yet to get the vote women were fighting for their rights, some even smoked, and the idea that it was a woman's business merely to marry and breed children was widely discredited by their protagonists.

The Navy had changed too. At the 1902 Coronation Review in Spithead there were 15 miles of British warships to give the public their money's worth, the *Naval and Military Record* stating: 'The fleet is a good fleet and, as Mr Kipling says, "Men live there". It is not a perfect fleet nor is it as strong as we would like to see it; but it is, we believe, a good deal better as a fighting machine than any two navies in this world.' From the inventions of Captain Percy Scott came a renaissance in naval gunnery with greatly improved loading and aiming performance. At long last a faster and more determined fleet began to shake off the lethargy of interminable peace routine as captains took an interest in 'heavy gun shooting', and seaman gunlayers – like the upper yardmen of old – became a race apart while working up for the next competitive prize firing. Yet in its life-style the Navy remained staunchly uncompromising; the mental and practical training of senior officers was almost non-existent, that of junior officers in need of overhaul. And because the number of seamen required to fight the new armaments exceeded those required for ship maintenance, tradition demanded that men should be kept happy by performing questionably useful evolutions originating from the sailing era. It was still customary to make ships into objects of beauty, for which commanders and first lieutenants would willingly dip into their pockets. Arising from the new Dress Regulations the meticulous inspection of uniform had become a fetish with captains armed with tape measures, as well as a source of irritation and needless expense to the lower deck. Discipline remained overly strict, food was adequate but indifferently served up and in an era of national prosperity and stable prices the rates of pay had remained unchanged. There were murmurs, but nothing serious.

When Admiral Sir John Fisher became Second Sea Lord and responsible for naval personnel in June 1902 – a post normally reserved for a rear admiral – no-one was in doubt that sensational changes were imminent. And although his reputation as a weapon specialist had led him to important technical appointments he knew that it was the human element and not ships that won battles.

A feature in his early career was an instinct for handling subordinates. In the battleship *Ocean* a contemporary remembered Commander Fisher as 'really the Warrant Officers' and Seamen's friend; no officer I have ever met better understood human nature'. On taking command of the battleship *Bellerophon* 'the ship's company had not at first known how to take their new captain but soon learned his forcible ways and how he wished things done. His style appealed to them, for the bluejacket loves a strong man in command'. When invalided home with dysentery after the bombardment of Alexandria in 1882 the men of *Inflexible* addressed a letter that concluded: 'May you receive your share of rewards and laurels and your ship's company will feel as proud and prouder than if it was bestowed on themselves.' This unusual tribute touched him deeply.[3]

In shore appointments Fisher's dynamism was inexhaustible. On arrival in the *Excellent* he blew away the cobwebs of twenty years of established interests; promoted rear admiral he administered a similar shock to his staff when Director of Naval Ordnance and Torpedoes. Besides accelerating the mounting of breech-loading and quick-firing guns and declaring, believe it or not, boarding pikes obsolete, he successfully fought for the supply of naval weapons and ammunition to be transferred from the Army to the Admiralty. As Third Sea Lord and the Navy's Controller in Whitehall he wrestled with the problem of modernizing an ageing fleet, introduced water tube boilers and built fast, well-armed destroyers to counter French torpedo boats. Hoisting his flag briefly as a fifty-seven-year-old vice-admiral on the North America and West Indies station, he found time to admire the professionalism and training methods of the United States Navy.

Admiral Sir John Fisher KCB

In 1899 came command of the Mediterranean fleet, transforming it from mediocrity to a faster, more battleworthy force. But it was unfortunate for the Navy that a feud was started with Beresford, his second-in-command, over a ship handling incident that blew up out of all proportions. Happily Fisher could count on the personal support of the King whose considerable influence was behind his sweeping reforms. Without the sovereign's backing it is doubtful if Fisher could have survived the later opposition from Beresford and the society that he represented.

In the Mediterranean Fisher became aware that some engineer officers were pressing for executive rank and to wear executive branch uniform. Indeed the extremists went as far as to demand that when a ship was in harbour its engineer officer, if senior to the second-in-command when the captain was ashore, should take over command of the ship. Fisher was not unreceptive to these views, noting that although the social standing of engineers had improved there was a stigma attached to the branch, as this story illustrates. It was one that Fisher was fond of telling, although he disliked the implications:

> A chief engineer called Brown worried the first lieutenant of a ship to exasperation by telling him that he ranked before him when on shore or when going in to dinner. 'Look here, Brown'

said the first lieutenant, 'it don't matter what rank the Admiralty like to give you and I don't care a damn whether you walk into dinner before or after me. But all I know, Brown, is that my ma will never ask your ma over to tea.'[4]

In the training of junior officers Fisher was convinced that a naval cadet should complete his theoretical studies ashore before gaining practical experience at sea; furthermore, that every executive officer should have a more expert knowledge of marine engineering. He was also determined to break down the social barriers surrounding the executive branch. These started to go up as soon as an aspiring cadet had applied for nomination from the First Lord, who had to be satisfied that his parents were of suitable background and sufficiently well-off to support him while a subordinate officer. Traditionally the Navy had always been officered by sons of gentlemen – whether middle class, upper class or aristocracy – and those in authority saw no reason to change this policy, particularly as it found favour on the lower deck. Additional argument lay in the importance of diplomatic and social duties which, it was alleged, could only be properly conducted by officers of polite upbringing.

Fisher had no time for these sentiments. With his unpretentious, impoverished background he was a democrat at heart who hated class distinction, declaring it inefficient and wasteful of talent in a navy preparing for war. In his endeavour to create greater equality of opportunity he insisted that 'brains, character and manners were not the exclusive endowment of those whose parents can afford to spend £1,000 on their education'. Moreover he flatly disagreed with the widely held opinion that if the social status of those entering was greatly lowered then the prestige attached to the executive branch would be similarly reduced, and men of social position would no longer send their sons into the navy. Conviction that he was on the right track could be traced to the United States Navy, which in 1899 had adopted the policy of integrating the officers of the deck (executive) and engineering branches. This meant that an officer might find himself a deck officer in one commission and an engineer in the next. Although this system did not appeal to Fisher, he was attracted by the American lack of class distinction.

Within hours of arrival at the Admiralty as Second Sea Lord Fisher briefed Lord Selborne, the First Lord and Board on his intentions; six months later on Christmas Day 1902 the revolution started. His scheme was launched as the Selborne Memorandum, which started by explaining that: 'In the old days it sufficed if a naval officer was a seaman. Now he must be a seaman, gunner, a soldier, an engineer and a man of science as well. . . . Now as always the highest type of naval officer is that wherein great professional knowledge is added to force of character. . . . The Executive, the Engineer and the Marine officers are all necessary for the efficiency of the fleet . . . yet they all enter the service under different regulations and have nothing in common in early training.'

Fisher's solution was simple and straightforward. Enter all executive, engineer and marine officers as cadets between the ages of twelve-and-a-half to thirteen (instead of fourteen to fifteen-and-a-half). Train all cadets and midshipmen under a common system ashore and afloat until passing for sub-lieutenant at about twenty. Finally, distribute lieutenants to specialize in the three main branches; on attaining rank of commander most, but not all, officers would drop their speciality. 'The cardinal feature of the scheme is homogeneous training of the executive, engineer and marine officers. . . . The result aimed at is, to a certain point, community of knowledge and lifelong community of sentiment. The only machinery which can produce this is early companionship and similarity of instruction.'[5]

The rapid increase in the strength of the Navy had outpaced the supply of officers, making it necessary to have two naval colleges, the junior at Osborne in the Isle of Wight and the senior at Dartmouth, already nearing completion. Cadets would spend two years at each for general education before six months in a training cruiser. Joining gunrooms as midshipmen they would learn practical navigation, engineering and seamanship, supervised by a lieutenant, later known as the 'snotty's nurse'. After examinations in seamanship and other subjects each sub-lieutenant would 'choose the branch he would join, subject to proviso that all branches are satisfactorily filled'. To improve chances of obtaining sufficient engineer volunteers this choice was later deferred until sub-lieutenants had completed a further spell of engine room watchkeeping. The memorandum continued:

> The ranks of engineer officers will be assimilated to the corresponding ranks of executive officers and engineer officers will wear the same uniform and bear the same titles – sub-lieutenants (E), lieutenants (E) . . . rear admiral (E). The engineer branch will receive additional pay . . . and every endeavour to provide those who enter the branch with opportunities equal to those of the executive branch including . . . rising to flag rank.[6]

In sea and shore appointments interchangeability between the two branches was clearly intended at commander level and above. Behind the decision to include Royal Marines was Fisher's well-grounded conviction that seagoing marine officers were grossly underemployed. His solution was to turn them into lieutenants (M), who would incidentally help to make up the current officer shortage.

Hailed warmly by the press the scheme was received in the fleet with a mixture of apprehension, opposition and acclaim. Serving officers protested that it would make 'plumbers and greasers of us all' while from the armchairs of the 'Senior' United Service Club in Pall Mall retired admirals denounced it as 'a hazardous experiment' and a 'great naval blunder'. Bulk of approval centred on certain flag officers, captains and commanders who formed an entourage round Fisher, colloquially known as 'the Fishpond'. It must have surprised the Second Sea Lord to receive early and enthusiastic support from Beresford.

The stumbling block was interchangeability. The idea of a commander without an executive background commanding a ship or even being second-in-command was anathema to the Establishment. More convincing were those who insisted that only through deeper specialization by lieutenants in engineering, gunnery and torpedo could the Navy master the increasing complexity of machinery and weapons, to say nothing of electricity and wireless telegraphy still in their infancy. Such views infuriated Fisher, and his intolerance fell on Captain Egerton of *Vernon* who did not accept that 'a torpedo lieutenant could be made in three months'. Fisher dragged him out of a committee meeting on training into his room, where he 'shook his fist and almost spat at him saying: "If you oppose my Education Scheme I will crush you"'. A diplomatic illness was conjured up and 'Captain Egerton was precluded by ill health from attending subsequent meetings of the committee.' Nonetheless he stood his ground – and survived.[7]

In 1914 the fact that there were only sixteen lieutenants (E) in the *Navy List* must have been galling to Fisher. From Osborne Captain Rosslyn Wemyss reported that: 'I have observed a tendency on the part of the parents of some cadets . . . to hope at least that their sons might never become lieutenants (E), with no chance of commanding ships or fleets and I have a suspicion that . . . they have in some cases even discouraged their sons in their engineering studies.'[8] Even the 'old entry' engineer officers were disconcerted because, having no military status themselves, they disliked the idea of subordinates becoming executive officers. In 1903 the granting of military titles by the prefix of 'Engineer' to their ranks went some way towards appeasement and their grudging approval.

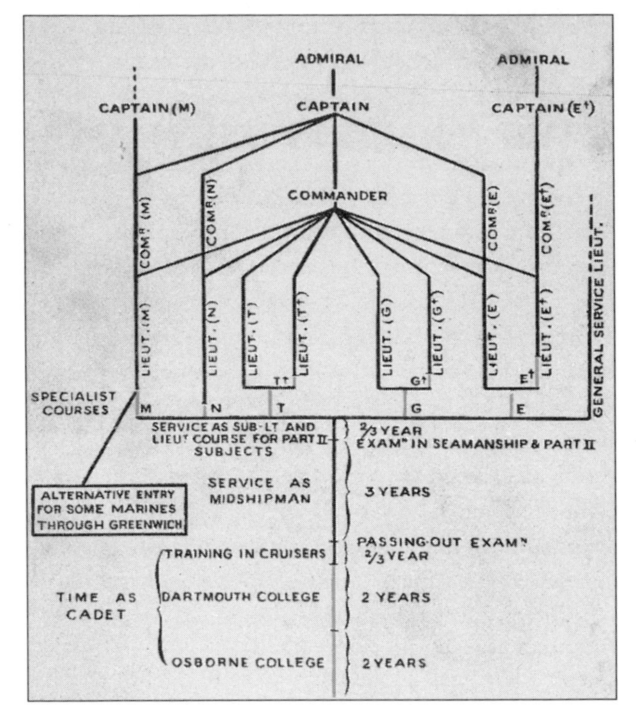

Diagram illustrating promotion ladder in the Selborne–Fisher Scheme

As far as the Royal Marines were concerned cadets and midshipmen could see little future in becoming 'substitute sailors'. In the face of stiff opposition from the Corps, Fisher's intention of making seaman officers out of marines was abandoned in 1912 and never repeated, although many Royal Marine officers later specialized in aviation, physical training and gunnery.

Despite the contentious issues it generated and the need to adjust original intentions, Fisher's scheme of common entry and training was an unequivocal success. It produced a better educated, more capable officer just in time to fight the First World War and remained in force until past the Second. But it did not bring about interchangeability between the executive and engineering branches. Had it transpired then a radically new dimension would have been created in officers' careers, with benefits felt on the lower deck. It failed, partly because war intervened too soon after the scheme was started, partly because the executive branch was too big, too powerful and too reactionary to accept its implications, and partly because Fisher never really gained the total confidence of the Navy. Unsociable feeling between executives and engineers gradually dwindled, although some would claim that it was never wholly eradicated.

Equally important to Fisher's plans for putting new heart into the fleet lay in the promotion of senior officers. 'The increasing average age of our admirals is appalling,' he wrote to the Private Secretary to the First Lord when Commander-in-Chief Mediterranean. 'In a few years you'll see them all going about with gouty shoes and hot water bottles.' Based on the recommendations of a committee under Lord Goschen, a former First Lord, to examine Executive Lists, the Admiralty announced decisions in 1903 which effectively lowered the age limits of promotion, increased the number of commanders, captains and admirals and pensioned off other officers earlier than previously stipulated. The next few years were a golden era for officers in the promotion zone, advancement being so rapid that promising officers could reach commander's rank at thirty, captain's rank at thirty-five and become a rear admiral ten years later, instead of having to wait fifteen or more. Prince Louis of Battenberg received his flag at fifty but Jellicoe got his at forty-seven and Beatty, quite exceptionally, at thirty-nine. And when Fisher wrote 'Favouritism is the secret of efficiency' he did not mean rewards for yes-men but selection based on merit and ability, measuring standards by his own exacting yardstick. Younger officers like Bacon, Madden, Oliver, Richmond and Jackson were among his assistants, all of whom were put into the fast stream and successfully occupied responsible positions in the First World War.

Evidently Fisher had little opinion of the paymaster branch, to the extent that Paymaster Martin alleged in 1904: 'Fisher tried to abolish the branch. He failed because the Treasury told him they could not get anyone else to do the work as well or as cheaply. Fisher then said he would break our hearts and make us cry to go.'[9] At the back of Fisher's mind was the unorthodox belief that he could make savings by combining separate duties in the person of one officer, for example, by employing unpromoted lieutenants on accountant officers' duties. This led to the remark of a well-known secretary to many flag officers that 'what he really wanted was a medical missionary with a good knowledge of accounts'.[10]

Fisher was equally active in his reforms of the lower deck, a task not made easier by the rapid expansion of the fleet. To man additional ships the boy seaman entry had to be supplemented by slightly older youth entry who received six months' training in cruisers; additionally men about to take their pension at forty were encouraged to re-engage up to the age of fifty. In 1900 the continuous service system was broken by entering ordinary seamen and stokers between eighteen and twenty-three for Short Service of five years in the fleet, followed by seven years in the Royal Fleet Reserve. Soon the combined entries approached 5,000 per year, of which more than half came from boys' training ships at Portsmouth, Devonport, Portland, Queensferry and Falmouth. In the ten years from 1892 naval strength increased by two-thirds to 105,000 officers and men.

Certainly more than most, Fisher was conscious that fleet expansion and recruiting of more enlightened, better-type youngsters caused human problems. His perception was revealed to Lord Selborne in 1902 when he wrote: 'There has been a vast change in the bluejacket of late years, which our older officers have failed, I fear, fully to recognise. They are far more discriminating and far more susceptible to want of fairness and far more critical of the qualities of those above them than they used to be. Consequently are more sensitive to the whip and spur of discipline than they were. . . . I am personally convinced that for these reasons you can nowadays maintain discipline more easily.' Action by the Admiralty in 1907 led to a reduction in severity of court martial sentences.[11]

First in a series of Admiralty directives was the abolition of the Masted Training Squadron for young seamen in favour of organized physical and mechanical training, the latter undertaken in the engine room. To qualify for able rate, ordinary seamen in future had to learn the use of tools in the stokehold, the idea being to make seamen interchangeable so they could help out during high speed steaming. Not all youngsters were convinced of its value, as William Lovell complained: 'We did 6 weeks seamanship, gunnery, torpedoes and stokehold, though what you went to the stokehold for I shall never know; hulking coal out of bunkers for someone else to sling in the fire.'[12] After abolishing the rate of petty officer, second class, the standing of all petty officers was raised, as well as more emphasis being given to the responsibilities of leading rates. Then in 1903 was announced the promotion of 100 warrant officers, gunners, boatswains, carpenters and engineers to lieutenant, as well as increased pensions for chief petty officers.

Although the Navy's engineering personnel had increased to 1,400 officers and 37,000 men by 1910 there was still a shortage of engine room artificers (ERAs), a branch enlisted from outside the service. One of Fisher's priorities was to launch a training scheme for boy artificers in the hulk *Fisgard*, improve the promotion prospects for ERAs and introduce the rate of Chief Engineering Artificer.

Since their inception in 1868 as skilled engineering tradesmen ERAs had taken their cue from the original steam engineers. W.A. Leggatt, an ex-Chief ERA, reckoned:

> they were the best paid people on the lower deck, by far. They had to pay to get them, and they had a charter that if, for example, there were two or more ERAs in a ship they had a mess of their own with a stoker to look after them. They were good men in the sense that they were well trained engineers and they were very conscientious; there were some ne'er-do-wells and drunks amongst them although in the main they were good chaps. But they formed a society which was hated by the Admiralty – the Royal Naval Engineers Benevolent Society.[13]

Thus ERAs became very union minded and when warrant rank was conferred to them in 1898 the attitude of many was that they preferred more pay to promotion.

After the Boy Artificer scheme had got under way the young fifth class ERAs were well received in some ships by the older artificers. Joining the cruiser *Venus* in 1911 Leggatt found:

> we were in the Chief ERAs' mess and the chief put the Jaunty up to telling us to take off the red badges, the official ones, and put on the gold, chief's badges. He wanted us to have full privileges. . . . But things were very different in *Essex*. The old chiefs in the mess were anti-boy artificers. They'd had a succession of young men, ex-boys, in the previous two or three years who had not been the best samples. The Jaunty, a bitter man – I think some ERA had seduced his wife – anyway he didn't like us at all . . . and he said 'You might have been alright in the *Venus* but you'll be bloody miserable here.'

According to Leggatt *Essex* was an unhappy ship. As one of the 4th Cruiser Squadron for seaman's training and based at Portsmouth she was:

> a hot bed of sodomy. When we used to go ashore up Queen Street, if a seaman or stoker went along with *Essex* on his cap, the harlots used to put their aprons over their sterns as a sign of disgust. I'm not going to blame the captain, the Honourable somebody or other who was God. He knew his lieutenant and his watch keeping officers and he probably knew his chief engineer and the doctor but I doubt if he knew by name anybody else. I don't know who to blame for this homo business but it was rife and it was new to me – us boys just couldn't understand it. An unpleasant ship that was – very unpleasant.'

Another ERA, H.W. Wright, was quick to notice the change when engineer officers from the Selborne Scheme brought together two types in the engine room: 'The Engineers and the monied people who had taken up engineering. They weren't really very practical engineers and they relied on us greatly. The old Engineers were the ones you respected and often they were hard nuts to crack.'[14]

Lionel Yexley (1860–1933)

Meanwhile lower deck grievances continued. To investigate complaints about uniform Captain Stopford's committee managed to reduce clothing expenses.[15] Then Commodore Spencer Login's committee looked into the poor standard of naval cooking where the obvious solution was to provide more and better trained cooks and ensure a lieutenant visited the messdecks daily at dinner time to ascertain if there were any complaints.[16] Login's committee also recommended equipping major warships with bakeries and refrigerators. And it seems astonishing that until then the lower deck had had to provide their own mess utensils and that their replacement by an Admiralty issue of fork, knife, china basin and plate was the result of a question in the House raised by an MP through Yexley. By now Yexley was determined to crusade on behalf of the lower deck for better conditions. He started another newspaper, *The Fleet*, sending a copy to Fisher who responded with a personal message of congratulation to be printed in the next issue. Informal liaison developed between the two, leading to Yexley being invited to inform the Second Sea Lord about the iniquities of the tenant canteen system; as a result Login was appointed to investigate the whole problem of feeding sailors. He recommended that the standard ration comprising basic necessities of diet should become an automatic issue, supplemented by a messing allowance in cash that would enable a sailor to vary his menu by purchases of service stocks, canteen or shore supplies. As well as being better fed many bluejackets actually made financial gains on the deal, all of which marked an improvement in the quality of life. Login's insistence that canteens be let only to responsible tenants brought prices down and ended many a nefarious privilege enjoyed by canteen committees.

Having re-organized standard ration messing Login advocated trial of a system used by the US Navy, which became known in the RN as general messing. In this the paymaster catered for the whole ship's company, his staff taking over from mess 'cooks' the preparation and cooking of food and providing a weekly menu with three daily meals to suit all tastes. Particularly applicable to large numbers the system took time to be installed in major warships; in 1910 it was the wish of the lower deck to have general messing in all naval barracks.

In 1905 Selborne was succeeded as First Lord by Earl Cawdor and jointly with Fisher produced the Cawdor Memorandum, which included a review – and minor revision – of recent personnel reforms. One of its recommendations reinforced the need to improve the prospects of the stoker by instituting the new rate of mechanician, to which up and coming leading stokers could aspire, with eventual advancement to warrant rank. Mechanicians would also be able to relieve the hard-

Corporal RM, butcher and bugler at the beef screen, HMS *Suffolk*, at the turn of the century

pressed ERAs of some of their watchkeeping duties. The scheme prospered and in the First World War seventy-two were promoted to warrant mechanician.

Meanwhile the programme of building naval barracks ashore continued, following the move into Devonport in 1890. In 1903 the *Hampshire Telegraph* reported that in Portsmouth some four thousand officers, chief petty officers, seamen, marines and stokers marched in four companies 'to take possession of the new naval barracks'. Accompanied by marine and seaman bands 'it had the appearance of a triumphal procession. Immense crowds lined the route and . . . the bluejackets were cheered loudly as they passed along'. In their new accommodation blocks were long rooms in which hammocks were slung in four rows and 'when seen with the men sitting at messtables in the rooms . . . had the appearance of the deck of an old fashioned line-of-battle ship'. Compared with the old *Duke* the quarters were a perfect palace, with electric light, lavatories on each floor and water taps in each room. Warrant officers and chief petty officers had separate blocks, as did the officers across the (*Edinburgh*) road in their wardroom building, which contained cabins and bathrooms on the upper floors. On the ground floors were capacious rooms for dining, smoking and billiards, designed in the style of a London club with a uniformed hall porter at the entrance. To match service tradition establishments on shore had to bear a ship name and very soon the first issue of HMS *Victory* cap ribbons was made. The barracks at Devonport and Chatham were called *Vivid* and *Pembroke* after the old hulks they replaced.

Early in 1904 King Edward VII arrived by royal train alongside the barracks for the first official inspection. This visit was closely followed by that of the Prince of Wales, recently promoted to vice-admiral, such occasions endorsing widespread approval of the benefits of shore accommodation. All this seemed far removed from the events that took place two years later.

On Sunday 4 November 1906 Portsmouth Naval Barracks lay in its usual state of quiescence as seamen, signalmen and stokers paraded for 4 p.m. Evening Quarters, when heavy rain began to fall. As officer in command Lieutenant Collard hurriedly completed the inspection and gave the order to dismiss. Because of the noise as they left the parade ground – mainly created by stokers – he ordered everyone to reassemble in the gymnasium where the seamen and signalmen were soon dismissed. Because of their attitude he decided to speak severely to the stokers; and to enable everyone to see him – Collard was about 5 ft 4 in – he gave the order to the front rank 'on the knee', a command often used in gunnery instruction with which he was familiar. Anyhow, the order was greeted with indignation by the stokers and shouts of 'Don't obey'. The order was repeated, the men obeyed reluctantly and were duly reprimanded. Collard reported the incident to the commodore, assuring him that, though the matter was serious, all was now well.

He was mistaken. About three hundred stokers were drinking quietly in the canteen that evening; at 9.40 p.m. the canteen was being cleared when pent-up feelings boiled over and men began smashing glasses, tables and windows. Word was sent to the guardhouse, 'General Mobilization' was sounded, a guard turned out and the barrack gates locked. By this time an angry mob of stokers had poured out on to the parade ground and three were arrested at the moment the commodore arrived. Amid booing and shouting he had a difficult job of addressing the men, but managed to calm them down.

On Monday evening the barracks' gates were again locked and extra guards mounted. Returning libertymen were refused admittance without explanation; congregating in the road outside they mixed with civilians and the mood of the crowd became ugly. As the road was under repair, with heaps of rubble handy, the air became thick with stones hurled towards the barracks' buildings and into the wardroom block opposite. Inside the barracks a group of excited stokers tried to overpower the guard, while others started tearing their quarters apart. Matters became so serious at midnight that men were mobilized from ships in harbour and two companies of Royal Marine Artillery arrived from Eastney. Gradually the crowd of about a thousand sailors and civilians was forced to disperse and twelve rioters were put in the barracks' cells.

Actual violence had ended but repercussions were considerable. Public and naval opinion was shocked, Fisher informing the King that the press had exaggerated the incident and that 'the men concerned are young stokers who have recently joined the Navy and are unaccustomed to discipline, but it is of course possible that want of judgement was shown'. The court of enquiry found that Fisher's qualms of mishandling were justified; the commodore and two commanders were sacked from their jobs. Collard was tried by court martial, acquitted of the order 'on the knee' in the gymnasium but found guilty and reprimanded for improper use of a similar order a year earlier. Pilloried by a large section of the press he subsequently obtained heavy damages from the *Daily Mail* in a libel action; and went on to reach flag rank. Eleven stokers were also tried, being charged with making a mutinous assembly and inciting others. The ringleader, Stoker Moody, was sentenced to five years' penal servitude, later reduced to three following a fierce debate in Parliament and lengthy press coverage.

Collard's legitimate but tactless order was not the sole cause for the disturbances. Recent personnel reforms had not yet become effective and discontent had built up over the stoker's terms of Short Service. As if to play it down *The Fleet* reported: 'The incident has been largely referred to as a "naval mutiny": we think it would be just as reasonable to refer to a riot in Trafalgar Square as "civil war in England".' Writing about the lower deck Stephen Reynolds pointed out: 'The older type of happy-go-lucky, devil-may-care sailor, who made his money fly on land and then went to sea for more, had been giving place in the Navy to a man bent on making a career for himself. The Admiralty has demanded intelligence, a steadier, brainier type and in the main has got it. But the Admiralty has not paid for it.'[17]

Final word came from Commodore John Eustace of Portsmouth Barracks in 1913, who remarked:

> we had trouble in the barracks some time ago and we aren't having it again. There are some 7,000 men here. About 6,000 are Short Service 2nd class Stokers, with five year engagements. Their only qualification is strength and ability to shovel coal into the ships' furnaces. Some day we may have oil fuel but we haven't got it yet. The recruiting officers don't ask too many questions as to their past. They're a tough lot and discipline has to be strict accordingly.[18]

The opening of Portsmouth barracks accelerated the evolution of two hitherto homeless branches, signals and physical training. The latter was now sufficiently important for lieutenants RN and RM to specialize in PT. Among the first batch was Hugh Tweedie, who took the Army course at Aldershot:

> conducted by a sergeant major and four staff sergeants, all first class gymnasts of the old school. The effect on most of my colleagues was a severe attack of muscular rheumatism. We spent the morning on the horizontal bar hanging like a row of carcasses in a butcher's shop listening to the monotonous order 'To the breast pull, lower; pull, lower", until there wasn't any pull left. However, nine months later we were properly tuned up.

The group was then sent to Portsmouth for a course under Professor Broman, a Swedish expert. 'The first thing we were taught was that all the stuff we had learnt at Aldershot was entirely wrong and we were quite remarkable to be alive.' After six months 'we were asked to say which method was appropriate for the navy; the verdict was unanimous for the Swedish system'. Appointed to join *Britannia* at Dartmouth in 1903, as inspector of the gymnasia, Tweedie was greeted by the commander: 'What do you suppose you are going to do here? I can tell you that there is no time for this new fangled business. The cadets have a full day as it is.' However, common sense prevailed and very soon excellent facilities were provided for the college.[19]

In 1908 the PT school moved to a separate building in Pitt Street, between the barracks and Portsmouth dockyard, to become the headquarters of an emergent branch. With gymnasium, swimming pool and classrooms it could claim to be the most modern and best equipped in the country, able to teach gymnastics, swimming, boxing, wrestling, fencing and even ju-jitsu. Physical training instructors, first and second class, were trained for battleships, cruisers and depot ships to improve the general fitness of officers and ratings and create a more positive approach to life in the fleet. The era had arrived, too, when sailing, boatpulling and boxing were augmented by naval teams playing soccer, rugby, cricket and hockey in countries all over the world, indirectly spreading their popularity throughout the Empire. While the gunroom and wardroom featured

Gymnastic class aboard the cruiser *Hermes*, 1909

predominantly in most teams it gave the lower deck a chance to learn new sports and above all for officers and ratings to mix together informally.

Signals was another branch that had been handled almost entirely by specialist ratings, in this case for far longer. In view of the growing dependence of the fleet on inter-ship and ship-shore communications, visual signalling by flags, semaphore, heliograph and finally electric light was pushed to its utmost limits in the Victorian Navy. At sea watchkeeping officers had a good knowledge of signals, one being detailed as signals officer; in a flagship responsibility lay with the flag lieutenant. Signal ratings were chosen from the more intelligent boy entries, rising through signal boy to chief yeoman of signals and, in 1890, to signal boatswain. 'The signalman's is a nice, clean job but a very responsible one, for a mistake in making or receiving a signal may easily lead to trouble or even disaster' wrote Chaplain George Goodenough. 'It takes a smart man to "smack it about" with the flags when the admiral is doing a little conversation with his squadron.'[20] Yet there was no shortage of quick-witted volunteers to join the branch, the prestige of being able to master the morse code and work on the bridge directly with officers more than outweighing the hazards and hardships of the signal deck. Training was mainly on the job, until in 1888 the Admiralty introduced a Higher Standard Qualification and better pay, as well as setting up signal schools in depot ships in Portsmouth and Devonport. The Portsmouth school was moved to *Victory* and in 1895 Commander Lionel Tufnell was appointed as Superintendent of Signals Schools.

Shortly afterwards Tufnell commanded the cruiser *Astraea* in the Mediterranean, his arrival coinciding with the unpopular introduction of new signal books, for which he had to suffer unjust criticism and remarks like 'I am not going to be taught my job by that fellow'. When the admiral joined the critics, making some highly offensive signals to *Astraea*, Tufnell decided he had had enough and confronted the admiral who apologized.[21] In 1906 the main Signal School moved to the Portsmouth Barracks, where it remained until the Second World War.

Jointly pioneered by Signor Marconi and Captain Henry Jackson, wireless telegraphy was used successfully out to 30 miles during the 1899 fleet manoeuvres. Two years later a separate wireless experimental section was established in HMS *Vernon*, where instruction was given to torpedo lieutenants and marine officers. The Telegraphist Branch was formed from selected signalmen in 1908, one being Charles Cutler who recollected:

Signalmen on flag deck, *c.* 1905

> Wireless telegraphy was just beginning and wireless was looked after by the torpedo party, although the signalmen manned the sets. I decided to try the wireless and the Admiralty gave all of us a step up to open the branch. Then they offered it to the whole fleet to anyone who . . . would like to join and they were formed into classes to teach them the morse code . . . then they went on to wireless training proper. That was how the wireless branch was formed in the Navy – from nothing.[22]

The iron-hulled hulk *Warrior* – as W/T trials ship she was known as *Vernon II* – was full of Marconi gear, Leyden jars, coherers and magnetic detectors. Here Cutler qualified as leading telegraphist and found: 'the early sets were rough and exposed; if you touched them the shock would throw you off your chair'. Conditions were much the same for Telegraphist Bottle who joined the Nore Defence Flotilla of older reserve destroyers that had wireless aerials but no equipment:

> We budding sparkers, as we were generally known, were allocated one to each boat from Monday to Friday for exercises. These boats were built before wireless was thought of and we were allocated any old space; in one boat I was allotted an old lavatory and had to rig up my apparatus and spent best part of four days in it. Still we were young and got a good deal of fun out of it.[23]

Although restricted and erratic in operation wireless telegraphy had arrived with immense potential for naval communications. In 1910 the Signal School at Portsmouth completed its first course of signal officers, who qualified in flags and W/T.

In contrast to signals the long-established navigation branch was wholly composed of officers; by the 1880s there were signs that it was in trouble. The navigator's status and authority in the ship was open to dispute, promotion to commander was stagnant and volunteers to specialize were falling off. Known by his contemporaries as 'the pilot' the average navigator had not kept up with the times and the popular view was:

> in harbour they led a detached life in some quiet nook carefully correcting charts with Admiralty Notices to Mariners. . . . They even escaped Daily Divisions by arranging to wind chronometers at that time. Tankie, the midshipman attached as his assistant, having collected the key from the keyboard sentry, would report to the Pilot, generally in the middle of his breakfast, and the two would descend to the gloomy depths where the chronometers lay in state.
>
> Most pilots wound their clocks in profound silence but some of the old school made quite a ritual of the daily occasion . . . Every day the Pilot would turn to his Tankie and ask 'Who are the salt of the earth?' The Tankie was obliged to respond 'the Navigating Branch, sir', the short ceremony being brought to a close by the Pilot's response '. . . And the princes amongst men'. In fact the sergeant of marines, being the least concerned with the ritual, was made responsible for checking and for reporting to the captain 'Chronometers wound, sir'.[24]

The man with the initiative and drive to restore the branch to its former prestigious position was Commander H.F. Oliver, who rose to Admiral of the Fleet and was known as 'Dummy Oliver'. With Fisher's support a committee was convened that recommended setting up a school to train navigating officers, Oliver being promoted captain to take command. Initially the school was afloat in the old cruiser *Mercury*, but it was soon apparent that a shore establishment with seagoing tenders afforded a better solution. It so happened that Fisher's intention of setting up a War Course for captains and commanders was temporarily thwarted, because Greenwich was found unsuitable. In a consequent move to site the War College in Portsmouth dockyard Oliver managed to get the Navigation School included, to be established in the old Naval College adjacent to Admiralty House, the commander-in-chief's residence. The school was formally opened on 1 January 1906, taking its name from HMS *Dryad*, one of its tenders. Thus re-invigorated the navigators joined torpedo, gunnery, physical training and signals officers to form the team of executive specialists, all with shore-based alma maters, all earning extra pay for their particular skills and all essential to the development of a service preparing for war.

Fisher's fourteen months as Second Sea Lord 'witnessed an activity at the Admiralty which had never before occurred in times of peace', wrote Charles Walker. 'Reform after reform was brought about with bewildering rapidity.'[25] There was still much to do and on appointment as Commander-in-Chief, Portsmouth in September 1903 Fisher was able to supervise the building of the college at Osborne, as well as setting up the committee to interview candidates for cadetships. Hitherto only a medical test and a written exam were needed but now applicants had to appear before an Interview Board consisting of an admiral as president, a public school headmaster, a prominent civilian and an assistant Admiralty secretary.

Many years later a senior officer, who had served with Fisher in the Mediterranean fleet, wrote:

> Fisher had a practice of consulting young officers which was proper enough in itself. But regrettably he spoke to them in a derogatory way about their superiors. It was his ruthless character and scorn of tact that led to violent criticism and enmities that shook the Service, reducing the value of his great work. Fisher's greatness was not then realised. His was not the method of leading smoothly but driving relentlessly and remorselessly. He prided himself on this policy . . . and of his scorn of opposition.
>
> Whether the Navy could ever have emerged from its old ways in time for the Great War without his forceful acts is difficult to estimate; but in my opinion it could not. He was the leader the young technicians wanted.[26]

On 21 October 1904, ninety-nine years after his greatest hero had fought the Battle of Trafalgar, Fisher became First Sea Lord. The revolution was far from over.

CHAPTER FIVE

Prelude to War

Wooden walls are obsolete, long and long ago
All their fighting sailormen are dead and gone below
Fortresses of steel and steam now command the sea
Bearing men of different stamp from those that used to be.
Anon.

The First Lord introduced the 1901 Naval Estimates with the announcement that 'five submarines of a type invented by Mr Holland have been ordered. . . . What the future value of these boats may be in naval warfare can only be conjecture, but experiments with them will assist the Admiralty in assessing their true value.' Captain Reginald Bacon was appointed to mastermind their development at a time when 'the submarine was looked upon as a low class of weapon, underhand, unfair and un-English . . . a risky occupation'. Although there is no evidence that collective prejudice curbed its adoption submarines were feared and distrusted by many naval authorities, including the Director of Naval Construction and the Engineer-in-Chief who refused to have anything to do with them. And as Controller of the Navy Admiral Sir A.K. Wilson ordered the submarine boats but advocated 'treating captured submarine crews as pirates' as if to warn off other navies with similar ideas.

From the start Fisher was an ardent supporter, declaring 'the immense impending revolution which the submarines will effect as offensive weapons of war'. When Commander-in-Chief Portsmouth he took personal interest in their development and their appeal was such that Bacon had no difficulty in recruiting young lieutenants, engineers, ERAs and seamen ratings into the branch. A base was established at Fort Blockhouse on the Gosport side of Portsmouth harbour where the old hulk *Dolphin* gave her name to the headquarters. William Halter volunteered for submarines after qualifying telegraphist in HMS *Defiance*, the torpedo and wireless school ship at Devonport – mainly because his instructing officer hated telegraphists and made their lives miserable:

> It was an exclusive service because nobody but a submarine rating was allowed in a submarine. We got more pay and had a very stiff medical exam. Your character had to be perfect to get in and we were regarded as something a bit special. We went to *Dolphin* for training, messed in the hulk and slept in the Fort. Discipline was quite comfortable and after instruction you could lie in the sun on the ramparts, a very different Navy altogether. When we got in the boats we were so near to the officers . . . everyone was close to each other. No red tape, no falling in and out.[1]

After three weeks' sea training volunteers were examined before qualifying for submarine pay; and because his first boat D4 had no wireless Halter was employed as an AB. Until the war most submarine crews slept in the parent ship and worked in the boat (which had no sleeping or cooking arrangements) by day; when on passage or during exercises crew members dossed down where they could find a billet and subsisted on tinned food. But these handicaps, as well as primitive sanitary arrangements and strictly rationed fresh water, did little to offset the youthful enthusiasm and early responsibility that infused the branch.

Courage and determination also characterized the executive officer volunteers facing criticism from a surface navy that called them 'unwashed chauffeurs' and mocked their shortcomings. Training took place in the depot ship *Thames* in Portsmouth harbour, the first parent ship for submarines, but without formal instruction. New officers and ratings picked up what they could from existing crews who had learnt their trade from the building yard or by trial and error when commissioning their boats. As well as their other duties officers had to understand nuts and bolts and second captains (first lieutenants) found themselves maintaining engines and motors, as well as looking after torpedoes and auxiliary electrics.

An early volunteer was Sub-Lieutenant Max Horton. 'In those days', recalled Bernard Acworth, First Lieutenant to Horton in his command of C8:

> the submarine service was, in many respects, a . . . nest of pirates in the eyes of the old established and austerely disciplined Navy. Perhaps because life in the early submarines was exceptionally risky, and pay extremely high, gambling for modest stakes was popular with many of those who did not invest their extra pay in early marriage. Max H's reputation as a poker player was second only to his credit for coolness and sobriety as a submarine commander. As an executive officer he was a perfect exponent and to some extent a founder of that form of discipline which has characterised the Submarine Service for fifty years – a combination of ruthlessness towards any form of incompetence or slackness in the performance of duty, and a warm hearted and very real fraternity amongst all ranks and ratings.[2]

Not all submariners were gamblers and when Captain Roger Keyes took command of submarines in 1910 he found officers who were to distinguish themselves in the First World War and in high rank in 1939. The Navy, however, had to be convinced that submarines had made the grade and with his extrovert qualities Keyes succeeded. In 1914 Britain started the war with seventy-four submarines.

❖❖❖

After the 1903 flight of the Wright brothers at Kill Devil Hill in USA an offer of patents was dispatched to the American, French and British governments. All were turned down, the Admiralty writing in 1908: 'Their Lordships are of the opinion that they [aeroplanes] would not be of any practical use to the Naval Service.'[3] Within three years the first four naval officers were on their way to becoming pilots. The Navy's initial reluctance to take aviation seriously was understandable since it reflected the mood of a country that regarded flying as a dangerous sport practised by a few eccentrics. Much of this changed with the realization that technical developments could lead to the submarine playing a dominant role in the North Sea for which a counter-measure had to be found. Although an airship project failed enthusiasm for aviation flourished, and when a Mr Frank McLean offered to provide aeroplanes and an aerodrome to teach naval officers to fly the Admiralty gratefully accepted. Eastchurch in the Isle of Sheppey was established in 1911, the Admiralty acquiring further land for air stations in the Isle of Grain, Calshot, Felixstowe and Dundee. One of the first senior officers to give serious encouragement to flying was Captain Murray Sueter, originally a submariner, who told the Committee of Imperial Defence that Britain might well be forced to command the air as well as the sea.

From 200 volunteers Lieutenants Samson, Gregory and Longmore with Captain Gerrard RMLI were selected for training at Eastchurch, bringing a party of ratings to push the machines about and marine servants to look after their needs in the bungalows. Within six months they had gained pilots' certificates, the most outstanding being Charles ('Sammy') Samson, described as 'a stocky, explosive little man with a privateer's beard and sharp blue eyes who was a natural aviator and just the kind of character this new and irregular arm needed'.[4] Due to their short endurance it was soon evident that shore-based aircraft must be launched by ships. So Samson persuaded Sueter and the First Lord, then Winston Churchill and himself an aspiring airman, to carry out trials from the old cruiser *Africa* anchored in Sheerness. On 12 January 1912 the intrepid Samson was seated in his Short S27 Box Kite, and in the words of the *Sheerness Guardian*: 'When all was ready the pilot gave word to "Let go all" and with his engine working perfectly he shot down the sloping rails clear of the ship's stern and was borne upon the air with the grace of some winged creature.

Hoisting in a Short seaplane, 1912

. . . Cheer after cheer echoed from the ship.'[5] From that moment Churchill gave naval aviation every possible support.

Just after this epic event the Royal Flying Corps was constituted with a naval and military wing; a year later Captain Sueter – the father of naval aviation – was appointed to head the Admiralty's Air Department and Captain Godfrey Paine to command the Central Flying School at Upavon to train all service pilots.

The role of military aircraft was reconnaissance and gunfire spotting, which presented few problems for the Army; conditions for the naval wing operating with the fleet were vastly different, and successful co-operation did not occur until after the First World War. For some time Longmore and the Short Brothers experimented with aircraft floats to produce a seaplane that could take off and land on a calm sea. By 1913 seaplanes were spotting the wake of a submarine's periscope and Longmore (later Air Chief Marshal RAF) always regarded this feat as the real beginning of the Navy's interest in flying.

With their open cockpits and rudimentary instruments naval pilots had to be content with unreliable engines and fuselages that had to accommodate W/T sets, rifles, cameras, bomb racks, gun mountings and even a 14-in torpedo. The establishment for a squadron included thirteen sailmakers and six blacksmiths, since aeroplanes were considered 'easy to bend, easy to mend and the very devil to rig'. It was nothing for a squadron to endure 50 per cent unserviceability and with one death for every 500 flights well might the Navy regard aviators as a reckless lot with a dubious future.

On 1 July 1914 the naval wing of the RFC became the Royal Naval Air Service with a strength of 128 officers and 700 ratings, mostly petty officers. Adopting its own officer ranks, ranging from Wing Captain to Flight Sub-Lieutenant, the RNAS possessed fifty-two seaplanes, thirty-nine aeroplanes and seven airships, with a chain of naval air stations and the seaplane carrier *Hermes*.

❖❖❖

On becoming First Sea Lord Fisher ordered a major redistribution of the Royal Navy's fleets and squadrons. Since France was no longer an enemy, Japan had become an ally and Anglo-American relations were cordial, the way was open to oppose the threat from Germany across the North Sea. Fisher's policy was to pay off some 150 obsolete ships on foreign stations, a move that brought a howl of protests but, as one journalist put it: 'Though the old system of [worldwide] distribution was popular there was one fatal mistake in it. For lawn tennis, waltzing, relief of distress or ambulance work after an earthquake it was admirable; for war purposes it was useless, because the force was divided and sub-divided and largely composed of ships that could neither fight an enemy nor escape him.'[6]

Reductions overseas made it possible to create, in addition to the Channel Fleet, a new force to be known as the Atlantic Fleet based at Gibraltar but able to give leave in home ports. Furthermore Fisher determined to make reserve ships nearly as efficient as the active fleet, by keeping on board nucleus crews; these included an executive officer, gunnery and torpedo lieutenants, key engineers, medical and accountant officers, together with sufficient watchkeepers and crew to take the ship to sea at short notice and fight for a limited period. Supported by fully manned battleships and cruisers the three-fifths complement ships were based on port divisions to form the Home Fleet.

Redistribution of the fleet was not popular among older officers. Many overseas commands were cut down in size and a number of sought-after appointments – where life was one long holiday – ceased to exist. On the other hand the return of warships to the United Kingdom was welcomed by the young married officers and men, especially when followed by the announcement that the length of foreign service commissions would be cut back. For reasons of economy and to suit dockyard refits commissions of three to five years had jeopardized family life for far too long. Bacon recalls a lieutenant 'who, within three months of marriage, was sent abroad for five years; six months after return to England he went overseas again for another four years'. Prolonged separation must have caused even greater heartache to men on the lower deck. But now the chance of being able to set up home in the United Kingdom and take on family responsibilities became a reassuring prospect.

An adequate reserve of manpower to sustain an expanded fleet was now of vital importance. Officers and men of the Royal Naval Reserve, augmented by seasoned veterans of the Royal Fleet Reserve, amounted to a sizeable force. In the event of sudden mobilization would they be ready to join in sufficient numbers? Following the ill-advised disbandment of the Royal Naval Artillery Volunteers in 1891 and despite Establishment prejudice against 'landsmen volunteers' the Admiralty decided to investigate how best the regular Navy could be complemented by additional reservists. A year later the Naval Forces Act of 1903 authorized the Admiralty to 'raise and maintain a force to be known as the Royal Naval Volunteer Reserve' and another to comprise the Royal Marine Volunteers.

All over the country young men rolled up in hundreds to enlist, their purpose to serve their country at sea. Almost entirely self financed these true volunteers were entitled to wear the same uniform as the Royal Navy, except that officers' stripes were wavy and their buttons embossed RNV, while ratings' blue jean collars had wavy stripes. Organized in divisions round the country they had to find and maintain their own headquarters, weapons and drill sheds. Public and press regarded them with 'a mixture of admiration, envy . . . and amusement'. *Punch* showed pictures of London RNVR carrying their nautical ways into the City with the chief clerk dancing a hornpipe to the office boy's mouth organ and a bare-footed junior clerk swabbing down the office floor with a long-handled mop and bucket. New language was reported on the Stock Exchange, which included 'Belay there with that telegram' and 'Rands are a trifle choppy this morning'. All good clean fun, though the humour was not shared by their professional brothers. Nevertheless they trained hard, gave up their holidays to go afloat and paraded impressively with army volunteers. By 1914 the RNVRs had convinced the Admiralty that they meant business and that youthful enthusiasm more than made up for lack of seamanlike expertise.[7]

Fisher's name will always be associated with the construction of the first all big-gun fast battleship, followed by the battle-cruiser. HMS *Dreadnought* was laid down in October 1905 and started trials a year later: with an armament of ten 12-in guns, a displacement of nearly 18,000 tons and top speed of 21 knots her superiority over existing battleships was such that no naval power could afford to build to any other design. Until *Dreadnought* the inherent defects of reciprocating engines limited effective fleet speed to 14 knots, since no major warship could maintain full power for more than eight hours. Only by the adoption of Parsons' turbines, then in experimental stage, could full steaming efficiency be assured:

When at full speed . . . with reciprocating engines [wrote Bacon about the older ships] the engine room was a glorified snipe marsh; water lay on the floor plates and was splashed about everywhere to keep the bearings cool; even oilskins were worn to avoid being wetted to the skin. Noise was deafening . . . telephones useless . . . voice pipes of doubtful value. In *Dreadnought* at full speed it was only possible to tell that engines were working . . . by looking at certain gauges. The whole engine room was clean and dry.'[8]

After *Dreadnought* came *Invincible*, the first battle-cruiser, of comparable displacement and armament but with less armour. To reach a top speed of 26 knots demanded prodigious boiler power, thus nearly half her lower deck complement were engine room ratings.

Although the superiority of oil as a fuel to fire boiler furnaces had been recognized its supply was not assured until 1912 and the vast majority of warships burnt coal, its replenishment a major bugbear. 'The evolution of coal ship was a periodical misery and a filthy occupation,' recalled Assistant Clerk Noel Wright:

All officers and men taking part would be as black as Christy minstrels within a hour of the start and although portholes were invariably kept tightly closed the coal dust descended through the hatchways and ventilation trunks into the messdecks, officers' messes and cabins.

Filling bags in the collier, *c.* 1910

It was also a backbreaking job. I remember how weary I felt in *Invincible* when, with only one watch on board, we had to take in 2,700 tons – a task that took over twenty hours.[9]

Coal ship was also a competitive affair demanding meticulous organization and split-second timing. Everyone on board took part and because coaling was an irksome chore it brought officers and men together in a way that no other evolution could achieve. Hands were piped to 'clean into coaling rig', which meant any costumes or fanciful dress and headgear that covered the body. As soon as the collier was alongside seamen scrambled into the holds to fill the bags held up by boys. Hoisted aboard by derrick a load of bags was dumped on deck, transferred to barrows by marines and transported to the chutes. Coal was tipped into chutes down to bunkers below, where it was trimmed by stokers. Until ships were fitted with permanent metal shafts the canvas chutes leaked coal dust everywhere. Half an hour was allowed for meals – thick slices of bread and butter with slabs of bacon washed down with a basin of tea. In big ships the band played, although in the cruiser *Good Hope* Bandsman Whacker Payne remembered the bandmaster telling the band to get into coaling rig: 'We went up on deck. The commander came along and said "Put that tin gear away and get hold of some bloody shovels. You'll be more good than making that bloody noise."'[10]

The worst part was after coaling when the whole ship had to be hosed down from truck to keel to the commander's satisfaction, before officers and men could go away to clean. There was an inevitable scrum in the bathrooms and Signal Boy Broadwater in the battle-cruiser *Queen Mary* complained:

Coaling party, cruiser *Birmingham*, 1914

> You had to go and have a bath and there was absolutely no room as everyone wanted one at the same time. There wasn't enough water to go round and your coaling rig you used to bundle up and stow away somewhere and then wash it whenever you could. Even in those days some of the instructors wanted to muster you and see if you had washed the coal out of your ears.[11]

❖❖❖

Beyond ensuring a high freeboard, that enabled natural ventilation through ships' side scuttles, the living accommodation in Fisher's new ships was unconventional. Due to their great length officers' quarters were moved forward so as to be near the bridge superstructure; the ship's company of 900 were accommodated aft. Quite apart from making commanders apoplectic with rage when they observed seamen and stokers lounging on the quarterdeck the arrangements were unpopular with officers, chiefly because of the departure from tradition, despite a light and airy wardroom on the upper deck forward. Lionel Dawson, a junior lieutenant, complained: 'Cabins were small and distributed wherever room could be found for them. My cabin was in one of the messdecks aft, and a horrible place it was to live in. From it one had to walk half the length of the ship to the officers' bathroom.'[12]

Nor did the ship's company approve the new layout. In the battle-cruiser *Lion* Captain Chatfield commented that the men were mostly accommodated two decks down behind the main armour and thus had no light from portholes or scuttles, except in a few messdecks right aft and right forward to which the armour did not fully extend. The advantage of this arrangement in war was obvious but it was largely offset by the great discomfort caused to the ship's company. During a visit to *Lion* an MP 'was amazed to find . . . there was not room for the men to live in, much less sleep in. Hammocks were slung quite close together; some of the men slept on the floor and some on the tables'. A young seaman went as far as to complain: 'You can't get into your hammock without disturbing the men each side of you; and when they cough – there's any amount of coughing aboard ship – the spit comes right into your face.'[13] Probably untypical, but the Design Committee had evidently ignored habitability aspects; in later classes accommodation reverted to traditional locations. As Chatfield remarked: 'The fact that this trial should have been made in the *Dreadnought* and her variants is symbolical of the priority given in those days to war efficiency over every other consideration.'[14]

Even so, by 1910 heavy ships possessed steam and diesel generators providing a wide range of services. As well as electric lighting below decks, forced draught ventilation made conditions in the engine room more tolerable and living spaces more comfortable, especially as the air could be heated. Large capacity refrigerators guaranteed a source of fresh meat while fresh water could be pumped direct to messdeck drinking tanks, bathrooms, galley and sickbay. Similarly the salt water pressure main supplied WCs, as well as washplaces fitted with showers and a row of basins in galvanized troughs. Admittedly the actual messdecks had not changed since ironclad days but there were metal racks for stowing cap and hat boxes, ditty boxes and boots, the last item increasingly but by no means universally worn by seamen. Clothing was still kept in kitbags and hammocks stowed in messdeck bins. Wardrooms had leather-upholstered easy chairs and a club fender round the heating stove; officers' cabins were better ventilated with ample space for occupants to wash their bodies in 3 ft diameter metal baths. Alternatively they could venture to a communal bathroom where waiting time was in order of seniority.

At the other end of the scale service in torpedo craft was acknowledged to be rugged, and the Admiralty accepted the hardships incurred by paying a common compensatory 'hard lying' allowance. 'The first torpedo boats were no palaces' claimed Lionel Dawson:

> Picture yourself in a compartment about the size of a railway carriage with similar seats on either side. There were no scuttles and entrance was effected through a hatch on the upper deck. The small amount of floor space was occupied by another hatch leading to the bilges below, in which were stored officially the small arms ammunition and fireworks and unofficially the contents of the officers' cellar. In this lodging were supposed to sleep, eat and live four officers, although two, or at the most three, were the usual complement. Add to the luxury of this housing the constant movement of the ship in the smallest sea and it will be agreed that 'hard lying' was no misnomer; the origin of the term being that wooden planks were considered an admirable foundation on which to sleep at night and sit upon by day.

Ratings' accommodation forward was similar to the officers'. Dawson continued:

> The only electric light in the ship was in the engine room; in living spaces we had . . . oil lamps and candles. There was little stowage for food, water was none too plentiful and was

Lieutenant Dawson and his ship's company – HM Torpedo Boat 045

> used more for drinking than for washing. One's kit was kept in tin cases in preference to the very damp lockers provided; cooking in calm weather was difficult and, with any sea running, impossible. The early destroyers were little better, although a small cabin for the captain was added right aft and there were scuttles in the wardroom.[15]

Like submarines, destroyer life appealed to young officers and ratings and there was no lack of volunteers.

After a propitious start as First Sea Lord, Fisher found the going increasingly hard through becoming embroiled in bitter dissensions, mostly of his own making. His feud with Beresford, which divided the Navy down to junior officer level, went from bad to worse when the latter's appointment as Commander-in-Chief Channel Fleet was cut by a year. On his retirement early in 1909 Beresford mounted a major assault on Fisher's handling of naval affairs, resulting in a Cabinet Committee of investigation. One of its proposals was the institution of a war staff. Although a War College had been established at Portsmouth with Fisher's blessing there was no Admiralty naval staff for the very good reason that Fisher did not want one. Another recommendation highlighted the lack of understanding and co-ordination between the Admiralty and War Office over the future direction of war. Such criticism was overwhelming and on 25 January 1910 – his sixty-ninth birthday – Lord Fisher of Kilverstone retired reluctantly from the Admiralty. Needless to add, his influence was far from ended.

Since the turn of the century few could deny that the Navy was now stronger, more efficient and imbued with a greater sense of purpose. But regardless of reforms and changes it remained very much the Senior Service, jealous of its traditions of pomp and ceremony. When the fleet was in harbour – the only occasion when it was seen by the public – it generated an air of imperious self-importance which early in February 1910 inspired the notorious 'Dreadnought Hoax', a practical joke of classic status. Though the basic idea was suggested by a naval officer acquaintance it was Horace de Vere Cole who planned and executed the scheme with great verve and skill. First of all a telegram was sent to Admiral Sir William May, commanding the Home Fleet in his flagship *Dreadnought* anchored in Weymouth Bay, purporting to come from Sir Charles Hardinge, the Permanent Under-Secretary of State for Foreign Affairs. This warned the Navy of the arrival later that day of the Emperor of Abyssinia and suite on an official visit.

When this was accepted as genuine there remained but to produce the visiting party, which consisted of Anthony Buxton as the Emperor, Duncan Grant and Guy Ridley as bodyguards, Virginia Woolf as an Abyssinian prince, Adrian Stephen as Herr Kaufman, the German interpreter, and in frock coat and top hat, Cole himself as Mr Herbert Cholmondeley of the Foreign Office. Dressed and made up by Willy Clarkson of theatrical fame they arrived at Weymouth station to find a guard of honour drawn up by a red carpet. They knew the ruse had worked so far; there was no turning back. The admiral's brass funnelled barge took them to *Dreadnought* where they were received by a ceremonial guard and band, with the admiral, flag captain (Herbert Richmond) and flag commander (W.W. Fisher), all wearing full dress uniform. Introducing his party Cole added that they had been unable to bring the court coffee-maker who was to have brewed up on deck, and that Abyssinians were forbidden to take food or drink from alien hands. With that Cole disappeared to the wardroom for refreshment leaving Herr Kaufman, looking (in his own words) 'like a seedy commercial traveller', to interpret when the admiral proudly pointed out the differences in the naval and marine uniforms. 'I'm afraid that will be hard to put into Abyssinian, sir, but I will try.' He did so in a gibberish of Swahili mixed with 'a fine repertory of nonsense from remembered lines of Virgil and Homer'.

Fortunately Buxton picked up bits of the mumbo-jumbo which carried the day while the wonders of the great ship were explained. At each new sight they raised their eyes heavenwards, chanting '*Bunga Bunga*', soon to become a national catchword. The make-up miraculously survived even on the train journey back to London. When Cole revealed the truth to the press a few days later the country rolled about with laughter. It was quickly exploited by cartoonists, music hall comedians and urchins, all of whom took up the cry of *Bunga Bunga* – the urchins to such an extent that shore visits by the admiral and staff became intolerable. No official punishment was ever meted out to anyone involved.[16]

It was Horace de Vere Cole's salvo against pomposity and for every reason its like will never be seen again. An echo was heard in 1914 when *Dreadnought*, having rammed a U-boat, received a signal from a sister ship – '*Bunga Bunga*'.

In May 1910 King Edward VII died; the close links that he had forged between the Navy and the monarchy were more than maintained by King George V, a professional naval officer who was deeply interested in Service affairs. In 1911 Germany precipitated the Agadir crisis which caught the Navy totally unprepared. When it broke, the First Sea Lord (A.K. Wilson), together with most of the Board, were on leave and on return to Whitehall were found to have no coherent plan for war of any kind. In fact Wilson stated his case so ineffectively that Haldane, the Secretary for War, threatened to resign unless the Admiralty appointed a naval staff that could and would plan for war in collaboration with the War Office.

In a government reshuffle Winston Churchill, aged thirty-seven, was moved from the Home Office to become First Lord. He sacked Wilson, appointed Admiral Sir Francis Bridgeman as First Sea Lord and set out to familiarize himself with every aspect of service life with intense fervour. His abrupt visits to the fleet earned him little popularity with senior officers, such as when he arrived on board *Invincible* on a Sunday afternoon to find ratings staging down the ship's side prior to painting. According to Able Seaman Minchin: 'the gunnery officer met him at the gangway and Winston wanted to know why the men were working on a Sunday. He was told: "On orders from the Commander".

'"Where is the Commander?" demanded Winston.

'"Ashore, sir".

'"Where is the Captain?"

'"Ashore, sir".

'Anyway they brought us in out of it and the Skipper had to go to the Admiral's quarters the following day and he made a report.'[17]

On occasions his passionate enthusiasm and curiosity about the service for which he was responsible struck a rapport with younger officers. So much so that when invited to a battle-cruiser's wardroom after night firings and becoming involved in a technical discussion he entranced his listeners. But the Establishment chose to snub him; when he dined as guest of honour with the Royal Navy Club and asked the president 'Would I have done well in the Service?', the admiral replied that he might have got as far as commander if he had not been court martialled first.[18]

Despite criticism for currying favour with the men at the expense of officers, Churchill was a leading social reformer who was genuinely concerned over the rumbling unrest now prevalent on the lower deck. A low rate of re-engagement for further service, continual requests for discharge by purchase, desertions approaching an annual figure of 2,000, gunsights being thrown overboard and sporadic refusals of duty were all symptomatic of storm clouds ahead. There were unusual circumstances in that 60 per cent of the active fleet was in home waters and very much alive to countrywide labour strife, to say nothing of lower deck societies and 'unions'. Except for isolated incidents in the China and East Indies stations nearly all cases of serious indiscipline occurred among seamen and stokers in Home Fleet battleships and cruisers. It seemed that the misbehaviour was a protest against the unacceptable features of service life, more specifically the administration of captains' summary punishments, the absence of promotion prospects from lower deck to wardroom and the inadequacy of naval pay. Ratings were beginning to question and reject the *status quo*, especially chief and petty officers who were behind the distribution of a series of pamphlets entitled *Loyal Appeal from the Lower Deck* described as 'A Naval Magna Carta' and aimed at sympathetic MPs and receptive media. Besides pleas for better pay and pensions was one seeking the privilege of forwarding petitions to the Admiralty on conditions of service. Complaints included the awards of unauthorized punishments, the disrating of petty officers without recourse to court martial, having to pay for the issue and maintenance of uniform clothing and the discomfort of messing and sleeping accommodation.

Churchill sought advice from Fisher who, as the Navy's *éminence grise*, put him in touch with Yexley, editor of *The Fleet* and author of *Our Fighting Seamen*, an indictment of the inequitable nature

Kit muster on the quarterdeck was not a popular evolution

of life on the lower deck. Early in 1912 Churchill told the House that he had set up a committee under Rear Admiral Brock to enquire into the system of summary punishments, in particular the 'consequential effects as regards to pay, position, badges and status'. Having wide terms of reference the committee received many written statements and the verbal evidence of over ninety officers and men. Many officers agreed with Captain Fremantle of *Dreadnought* who wrote: 'I do not consider there is much wrong with discipline of the service at the present day . . . the situation is certainly not one which calls for drastic revision of the regulations,' but he did concede that 'administration has tended to become unsympathetic'. Concerning cell punishment Captain Vaughan Lee of the battleship *Collingwood* complained that prisoners were so well treated in the (recently instituted) detention quarters that they came back looking as if 'they had been on holiday . . . by contrast prisoners looked very broken down at the end of 14 days' cells'. There was much censure of 10A punishment, known as being on the 'black list'; in addition to extra work and various deprivations it involved 'standing on the upper deck in the place appointed' for over two hours, an act described by a stoker as 'keeping the flies off the paintwork'. Questioned on 10A it seems scarcely credible that Captain Leveson of *Indefatigable* should remark: 'men must learn to stand still. . . . Sailors are simply childish men, and must be treated as children'. Brock took exception to these and other opinions reminiscent of the mid-nineteenth century.

Younger officers held different views. Commander Dewar wrote: 'Although ships differ widely the discipline is not good in the Navy at present . . . administration does not get as willing and cheerful work out of the men as it should.' Lieutenant Nicholson hit the nail when he stated: 'My first point is that officers are very much out of touch with the men and if there were sympathy between them . . . the personal influence of officers would tend to reduce the number of small breaches of discipline which are so numerous.' Evidence given pointed to over-centralized administration and a deep-seated dislike of the ships' police, described as *agents provocateurs*. In the questioning of rating witnesses Brock did not subscribe to lower deck reform campaigners and tried to obtain an admission that Yexley and *The Fleet* were to blame for the unrest. 'Do the men agree with him [Yexley]?' 'Is there much socialism in the Navy?' Yexley himself was interrogated exhaustively about his *Fleet* articles, but would not budge. Several ratings confirmed the exasperating nature of discipline enforcement, the marines pointing out that punishment afloat was approximately twelve times as much as that inflicted on shore. It must have been reassuring for the committee to receive a letter from Captain Sydney Hall of the cruiser *Diana* in the Mediterranean who recommended: 'no cleaning or polishing in best clothes; voluntary church and no parades of any kind on Sundays; and reducing time spent on cleaning ship in favour of useful instruction'.

Submitted in July the Brock Report was cautiously worded. Recommendations included the substitution of extra work and drill for 'paintwork watching' in 10A punishment, standardization of scales of punishment for leave-breaking, abolishing injustices in classification of men for leave, re-assertion of the right of appeal against unjust or severe sentences, institution of a procedure for stating complaints and the removal of the ban on messdeck card playing. The report advised restraint of police powers, sharply attacked the rigidity of fleet routine and the interference to training caused by surprise evolutions. 'The routine and work of the ship must be closely connected with discipline. Unnecessary work should be eliminated, so that to a man who uses his brains there should be a substantial reason for the work on which he is employed. Uncertainty of

Holystoning the deck. After wetting and sanding, decks were rubbed with sandstone to make them almost white

what is going to happen is the greatest evil that any organization has to contend with.' Brave words, yet they were heard.

Brock's recommendations of the report were accepted but Churchill wanted to go further, insisting that 'cell punishment is more severe and less beneficial than detention and should not be used in harbour for more than 3 days', also 'that every petty officer should be safeguarded as that of NCOs in the Army with the right to trial by court martial'. In both cases he got his way and the final report was loudly acclaimed by the reformers. The *Daily Express* declared: 'We have treated you like naughty boys, while demanding from you the best work of a man. In future we will treat you like self respecting men.'[19] The system of summary punishments introduced by Churchill in 1912 lasted, with minor amendments, until 1950 when an overhaul by the Pilcher Committee found little to criticize.

Lest it be thought that all senior captains were archetypal 'drive and punish' characters it is worth recounting this story. Before Captain Reginald Hall commissioned the new battle-cruiser *Queen Mary* in 1913 the Admiralty asked him to evaluate running a ship without a master-at-arms or ship's corporals. Because the quality and number of recruits for the regulating branch had fallen off a trial was needed to investigate if selected chief and petty officers could do the job instead. At heart a strict disciplinarian 'Blinker' Hall realized the possibilities of this radical departure; the experiment was a total success. And in anticipation of war when ships would be at sea with all guns manned, only to return to harbour to embark vast quantities of coal, Hall organized his ship in three watches instead of two, because he knew that the latter would not cope with the strain of war. At the outbreak of war all major warships adopted this system. That was not all. A deeply religious man, he felt the need for a proper place of worship on board so he built a chapel, the first ever in a warship and an example followed in other large ships. Turning to chief and petty officers, whose prestige in the ship's company required a boost, he decided they deserved more comfortably fitted messes; a call for volunteers to rebuild them met with instant response to become another reform adopted by the Admiralty. Later he established a laundry with a commercial washing machine specifically for chief and petty officers. Perhaps his most popular innovations were setting up a bookstall and a cinematograph projector, the first ever seen in the fleet; a few years later every major warship had them installed. Hall was one of the few enlightened senior officers of that era who realized that unless officers led the way towards improving service conditions the men would react by compelling the Admiralty to do so.[20]

Having dealt with punishments the second unresolved grievance concerned promotion from the lower deck to wardroom, something better than making 'old and bold' warrant officers into lieutenants towards the end of their active career. Just before his resignation Fisher wrote to Yexley: 'Unfortunately for them [the lower deck] my departure has been precipitated by political events and I cannot expect my successors to have quite the same enthusiasm as I sincerely felt on their behalf. The lower deck richly deserves all we can do . . . our warrant . . . and petty officers are competent for much higher positions . . . and for the good of the Service their status must be raised.'[21] In 1910 came a proposal before Parliament for youngsters from deprived families to be awarded scholarships to join the naval entry to Osborne and Dartmouth. This suggestion proved as unpopular to those advocating lower deck promotions as it did to the officers, the *Naval and Military Record* stating: 'The British Navy has long obtained an ample supply of capable officers, also a fair proportion of the most able Admirals and Captains in the world, without recruiting from the Democracy . . . we should view with grave apprehension any attempt to officer the fleet at all largely with men of humble birth.'

As far back as 1910 *The Fleet* had published a scheme drafted by Lieutenant N.F. Usborne for young leading seamen and petty officers to be promoted acting warrant officer, undertake courses with sub-lieutenants and later be promoted to lieutenant. As soon as Churchill became First Lord he was urged by Fisher to look into his unfinished programme of personnel reforms that included lower deck commissions. In March 1912 Churchill's scheme of promotion was accepted on both sides of the House, almost before the Board had fully approved the details. This emerged as the Mate Scheme by which selected warrant officers and qualified petty officers were given a round of specialist courses, with subsequent promotion to the wardroom as mates before becoming lieutenants. Keeping the candidate's age below thirty was the stumbling block and with only lukewarm Admiralty support the scheme was not an unqualified success. But it was a breakthrough and by 1914 some forty-four mates were on their way and 200 young warrant officers had been promoted to chief warrant officer after fifteen years' service.[22]

Finally, pay. Healthy recruitment at the turn of the century suggests that pay was considered adequate by the lower deck, in line with the security of a paid job that included food and lodging. Incentives in the shape of proficiency qualifications and good conduct badges were an integral part of naval pay strategy that offered the carrot to ambitious men to achieve higher responsibility.

At the same time badges could be deprived for misconduct and seamen could lose proficiency pay for poor weapon performance. And although the basic pay of an able seaman was still 1*s* 7*d* per day his proficiency allowances brought earnings in line with slightly better-paid stokers, signalmen and telegraphists. Over the years some ninety different rates and allowances had grown up on the lower deck, all of which were overhauled in 1906 by a Pay Revision Committee; there was no attempt to alter basic pay.[23] With the rise in inflation after 1900 money started to get tight and Telegraphist Ives recalls:

> The life was a good one but we were very short of money. Now for instance, I lived in Southampton before I was married and went home to Mum every weekend. Well, it cost me two shillings Southampton to Portsmouth return. I couldn't afford to go ashore during the week. But I would say this much – there were more young fellows made [monthly] allotments to their mothers than did not.[24]

Churchill's arrival at the Admiralty coincided with a Parliamentary campaign for a better deal on sailors' pay, in which both Fisher and Yexley played their parts. The First Lord was quick to grasp the essential features of a rating's daily life, his service conditions and domestic problems, sufficient to address an eloquent appeal to the Treasury, spelling out the hardships of a man at sea, whose lot compared unfavourably with the industrial worker or the soldier. Churchill proposed that any increase in pay should not be spread overall but concentrated so as to give substantial improvements (4*d* per day) to fully grown men of twenty-two and twenty-three as they were approaching marriageable age, with a similar increase of 6*d* per day for senior ratings.

After a long and bitter dispute the Chancellor of the Exchequer, Lloyd George, conceded 3*d* for junior ratings after six years' service (i.e. aged twenty-four) and 4*d* for senior ratings, as a temporary settlement. As the first increase in basic wages for sixty years this minimal rise was surprisingly well received, both in the fleet and by the public. Churchill was bitterly disappointed. *The Navy* commented in January 1913 that the increase of pay probably represented the best that could be done with the money available.

Hard-lying money of 6*d* a day for small ships was also under fire by Lloyd George who, according to Ives:

> wanted to cut down the services costs. At the time he was reported to be a pacifist. So Winston said 'Well, before I agree to cutting down hard-lying money I must go and see for myself.' So he went up to the Orkneys and Shetlands and came out on the boat I was serving in. He vomited for three days. And he went back and made Lloyd George give us seven pence halfpenny.[25]

The First Lord's proposal for a separation or marriage allowance was turned down by the Treasury, despite the fact that considerable numbers in the Army and Royal Marines had the use of marriage quarters or drew separation allowances. Due to the rise in the cost of food and accommodation in dockyard ports Churchill was anxious to do something for men with a family to support, since 60 per cent of petty officers and 10 per cent of junior ratings were married. But nothing happened until just after war was declared a year later when approval was obtained for the immediate introduction of separation allowances of 6*s* per week for married men below petty officer, plus children's allowances, equivalent for some recipients of a near 50 per cent pay rise. Younger married men had never been so well off and in retrospect it was providential that lower deck grievances were tackled successfully before the end of 1914.

After Fisher's wide-ranging officer reforms there was little need for further action other than to apply fine tuning and maintain momentum. Since the first cadets to enter under the Selborne Scheme were now about to become lieutenants it was timely to appoint a committee to take stock. Fisher had been obsessed with the idea of young entry but twelve and a half years did not match the educational pattern of preparatory schools; furthermore, in an increasingly democratic age it was an anachronism to put such young boys into uniform and call them officers. To the delight of prep. school headmasters the age was raised to thirteen and a half, and to accelerate training flow sea time for midshipmen was cut by eight months and engineering training reduced.

Further steps were needed in 1912 when the rapid growth of the fleet caused an acute shortage of lieutenants. Against some opposition the Admiralty, keenly backed by Churchill, decided to recruit cadets from public schools at ages seventeen and a half to eighteen and a half and give them eighteen months' instruction in the training cruiser *Highflyer* before joining the fleet as midshipmen. Thus the Special Entry system was born in the autumn of 1913; to reassure the traditionalists who feared it would not mould boys into the right type of naval officer the Admiralty described it as a temporary measure to meet expansion. Not only did it regulate entries more easily with an eye to the future but produced a commissioned officer in three and a half years less time than from Dartmouth. In fact the scheme prospered for the next forty-two years, producing many first-class officers in all branches. In the long run there was little if anything to choose between the two forms of entry.

In parallel with negotiations for the lower deck Churchill secured small increases in half pay for officers. Half pay, when unemployed between appointments, was half pay less allowances and Charles Walker (Admiralty principal clerk) in remarking on the increase of 3*s* 6*d* for captains, wrote: 'The half pay of a junior captain on promotion was then 12*s* 6*d* a day, a pitiful sum for a successful officer of nearly 40 years, especially when he ran the risk of two years half pay before getting a ship.'[26] Another improvement affected officers' appointments. By custom captains were still allowed to hand pick their own commanders and first lieutenants, appointments subsequently confirmed by the Second Sea Lord's office where the less fortunate were handled by a civilian secretary with no feel for their outlook or suitability. On becoming Second Sea Lord Prince Louis of Battenburg arranged for a senior commander to supervise appointments for executive officers, likewise a fleet paymaster for accountant officers. Finally, on 1 April 1914 the rank of lieutenant commander was officially introduced for all lieutenants on attaining eight years' seniority.

Further up the scale it was Churchill's wish to upgrade the calibre of senior officers, whose ages had been noticeably rising. Early in 1914 regulations decreed that rear admirals who had not hoisted their flags and captains not selected for promotion would be compulsorily retired. In his belief that merit and not seniority should govern appointments Churchill had already passed over several flag officers to make Rear Admiral David Beatty his Naval Secretary; later on and urged by Fisher, he moved Vice-Admiral Sir John Jellicoe up several places to be appointed second-in-command of the Home Fleet. But in setting up a War Staff Churchill was less successful. Because the idea of a staff was still regarded by many with indifference, if not with distrust, the War Staff was treated as purely advisory, the chief of the staff did not sit on the Board and nobody in authority paid much attention to what they said. Although a staff course was established in 1912 at the War College to train commanders and lieutenants there was no great rush to get the course filled with suitable officers. It was said that 'officers who made any real study of war from the point of view of staff work were regarded as cranks or lunatics, hunters of soft jobs. . . . The gin-and-bitters school were quite content to be left to the guidance of their splendid, but not always highly trained, instincts'.[27] Among the lecturers at the first Staff Course was Captain Herbert Richmond, a rare combination of an outstanding naval officer and an erudite historian. Largely on his initiative a small group of younger officers boldly founded *The Naval Review* in 1913 in the form of an unofficial quarterly journal, with the approval of the First Sea Lord and First Lord. Its purpose was to 'encourage thought and discussion by naval officers on strategy, tactics, organisation, command, discipline . . . and any other subject affecting fighting efficiency'. It continues to flourish today.

As events moved inexorably towards war with Germany, what was the state of the Royal Navy in 1914? In capital ships and cruisers Britain possessed a marked numerical superiority; in gun armament, gunnery skill and communications the two navies were about equal. What was not recognized until later was the German superiority in mines, torpedoes, shells, armour and watertight sub-division in major warships.

Lacking war experience senior officers had no clear idea of how the Navy would fight at sea; it was left to annual manoeuvres and major exercises to simulate fleet action, most of which were conducted under set-piece conditions in which both sides wanted to fight. The tactical effects of developments in high-speed ships, long-range guns, torpedoes, submarines, aircraft and communications remained largely unknown. As flag officers jockeyed for position to gain sea command in the run up for war there was a serious dearth of impressive admirals. Churchill complained that we had 'competent administrators, brilliant experts . . . unequalled navigators, good disciplinarians, fine sea officers, brave and devoted hearts; but at the outset of the conflict we had more captains of ships than captains of war. In this will be found the explanation of some untoward events'.[28]

Officers continued to stem from the middle class of society, from service families, country gentlemen and professional men. As cadets and midshipmen they were brought up to a strenuous way of life, a high sense of duty and a readiness to accept challenge. In most ships there was much to commend their training which allowed them to make mistakes and gain an understanding of the men they would lead. Among 1,500 executive lieutenants about half had qualified in navigation, torpedo, gunnery, signals, submarine boats and physical training, the remainder being 'salt horses'; there were 500 engineer lieutenants, the most junior being Selborne Scheme. Lack of decentralization and the curbing of initiative shown at higher level tended to make the average lieutenant somewhat unimaginative and conformist in outlook, with few outside interests apart from sport. Based on tradition and faith in their ships, their weaponry and their seamanship executive officers assumed a sense of superiority over the German Navy that verged on complacency.

To meet an expanding fleet Churchill stepped up ratings recruitment in the immediate pre-war years and where the Navy gained most was in the quality of its lower deck, which in 1914 amounted to more than 90 per cent of the 146,000 officers and men in the fleet. Entering in the main as long-service volunteers, trained to high standards and filled with supreme confidence the British bluejacket compared favourably with his short-service opposite numbers in the High Seas Fleet.

The test mobilization of three-fifths of the Third Fleet in mid-July 1914 had been first mooted by Churchill in the previous year. It was timed to commence two days before the Grand Review of the fleets in Spithead by the King, described by Churchill as 'incomparably the greatest assemblage of naval power ever witnessed in the world'. Thus the whole Navy was on a war footing and when war appeared imminent Battenberg, as First Sea Lord, stopped demobilization on his own initiative. At the end of July the First Fleet – renamed the Grand Fleet – sailed north to Scapa Flow and Cromarty where Admiral Sir John Jellicoe succeeded Sir George Callaghan as commander-in-chief. At 11 p.m. on 4 August the Admiralty signalled to all HM ships and naval establishments: 'Commence hostilities against Germany.'

CHAPTER SIX

Action Stations

Oh what avails the classic bent
And what the cultured word
Against the undoctored incident
That actually occurred.
Rudyard Kipling

At the Royal Naval College, Dartmouth, Saturday 1 August 1914 was a day when the English countryside looked its best. A cricket match was in progress when a messenger with a telegram was seen hurrying along towards the captain: 'All eyes were on him as he broke the seal. When he stood up, we knew it was the real thing: "Mobilize!" In a matter of minutes the visiting team found themselves alone in the field. Bugles sounded the "retire". Officers and masters set off on bicycles to pass the word around. Cadet captains ran about shouting "Pick up the double there! Shake up, will you".'

Aged fourteen and three-quarters and standing 4 ft 9 in tall in his socks, Cadet Eric Bush also remembers:

> cadets swarmed out of the canteen still eating as they ran. We cleared our lockers and . . . packed everything into our sea chests. Then followed pay and a final meal. At 6.30 p.m., less than three hours after the telegram had been received, all terms [420 cadets] were ready to proceed. When our term, the Blakes, crossed the river and boarded a waiting train I could hardly believe that only three months had passed since our first arrival. It was not until the train started that we realised how tightly we had been packed in. I climbed onto the luggage rack and rested. At 3.30 a.m. the train stopped with a jerk . . . at the Royal Naval Barracks, Chatham. We clambered out and were herded into the gym. In spite of early hours the barracks was alive with sailors. After breakfast someone came along to say we were not to take our sea chests with us but seamen's kit bags instead. Propping the kit bag against my sea chest I began to fill it, then hesitated not knowing how much to put in. 'Enough for six weeks' war' we were told.[1]

Keen as mustard Bush joined the cruiser *Bacchante*, part of the 7th Cruiser Squadron.

❖❖❖

At the end of July 1914 Stoker (Clinker) Knocker landed for night leave in Portsmouth from the destroyer *Hind*:

> I was struck by the total absence of bluejackets who at this hour usually crowded the vicinity of Portsmouth Hard. A naval patrol petty officer approached me: 'Go aboard your ship

Midshipman's chest, 1914 – used by generations of young officers until after the First World War

immediately.' 'What for?' I asked with surprise. 'Go on board or else come along with us to the guardroom.' Having no wish to renew my acquaintance with any guardroom I turned about and noticed great black type placards outside the newsagent's shop: 'GRAVE WAR NEWS – SIR EDWARD GREY'S SPEECH.' 'Well,' I said to myself aloud, 'I'm going to spend what money I have before I go on board, for if there's going to be a war I won't have the chance to spend it.'

After a couple of pints Knocker decided to try his luck in Gosport:

'All ships are putting to sea, Jack' said a policeman as I walked towards the Ha'penny ferry. Stepping off I called in at the Hoy Hotel for what I intended to be my final drink. An old shipmate was bewailing his luck. 'I finish my twelve years tomorrow an' expected to be discharged as a time expired man, but now it looks as if we're going to have a bloody war.' I felt sorry for him. Tears were in his eyes, he looked the picture of abject misery. Suddenly he began to laugh and said: 'You and me is going to get drunk tonight, Clinker, and when I go aboard the *Prince of Wales* they can't say much when they know I'm time expired.' 'Drink up fellars,' said a marine, 'we're all in the same boat tonight and I'm going to get as drunk as a fiddler's bitch.' We did get drunk and after much shaking of hands wended our wobbly way to our respective homes.'[2]

After the battleship *Prince of Wales* arrived in Portland Commander K.G.B. Dewar, the executive officer, takes up the story:

Few of my generation will ever forget the circumstances attending the actual declaration of war. It came to me in the noise and dirt of coal ship. It was nearly dark on the 4th August when the bugle sounded the 'Still'. The collier's winches suddenly stopped and the bosun's mate piped 'Hostilities will commence against Germany at midnight'. The loud cheers which followed were soon silenced by the renewed clatter of winches and the thud of coal bags as they came in with increased speed and more clearly defined purpose.[3]

❖❖❖

In HMS *Excellent* general hostilities became imminent as Commander A.J. Davies took over as executive officer; in fact the first bugle call he ordered to be sounded was 'Mobilize'. The effect was startling. Within a few days he was left with a deserted Whale Island. His captain had gone, his staff had gone, his long course and forty-six sub-lieutenants had gone and every active service rating in the place had vanished to sea. The doctors from Haslar hospital came to look, anxious to get all their convalescents away to make room for the wounded, following the general fleet action which was expected to take place. But not only were they horrified by the sanitation arrangements, they also found that nothing could be done until the belongings of some two hundred officers had been sorted and stored. For such had been the speed of mobilization and the certainty of a short war that everyone had packed seagoing clothes and left everything else in their cabins. The doctors duly returned to Haslar.[4]

❖❖❖

Flight Lieutenant Geoffrey Bromet, an RN Air Service Intelligence Officer, en route to join his seaplane base, wrote in his diary:

This is what we have been looking forward to and working up for, ever since we put on the King's uniform – this is the real thing and thank God I've had the luck to be alive and in the Navy on 'The Day'. The average Englishman and certainly nine out of ten servicemen have no bitter feelings against Germany; but Germany has sinned and must be made to pay for it and you can depend on the Navy . . . to give them a good hiding in the straightforward humane and thorough fashion that is one of the features of our race.[5]

And so the Great War had come at last, almost to the month that Fisher had predicted and barely six weeks after a British squadron had assembled at Kiel for festivities marking the opening of vital improvement to the canal that linked Kiel to the North Sea. Expectation of major action was shared by the whole Navy who believed that German warships would break out and the two fleets would fight a second Trafalgar.

Mobilization was conducted ashore and afloat with great efficiency, ships' complements being topped up with reservists before the Grand Fleet sailed for its war base in Scapa Flow. After coaling frenetic steps were taken to prepare for battle, and a midshipman in the battleship *Monarch* recalled: 'The beach near Scapa Pier was piled high with boats, accommodation ladders, cabin and mess furniture, pianos, in fact any superfluous woodwork as would be likely to cause fire in action. This was even carried to the extent of ripping up wooden deck planking which, when the likelihood of immediate action had passed, had to be replaced.'[6]

Lieutenant Lionel Dawson was serving in the battleship *Dreadnought*, which he regarded as:

> another 'blood and iron' ship where officers and men with blow lamps and chipping hammers removed layers of the best enamel paint that had been the pride of successive commanders' hearts. There was also the surreptitious sharpening of swords – my own weapon still bears the marks of *Dreadnought*'s armourer. Finally, the beard complex. Everyone tried them, whether they could actually grow them or not!
>
> The first few months saw the Grand Fleet constantly at sea. The menace of the submarine was upon us and the U-boats were seen in imagination everywhere. The weather was very bad and constant watchkeeping very wearying. And although we were usually within a day's post from London for the first six months of the war we in *Dreadnought* never saw a tree, a train or a woman. Scapa Flow possessed no trees to all intents and purposes, no trains at all and opportunities for going ashore were remote.[7]

Censorship came into force immediately, and the chaplain, doctor and non-watchkeeping officers were told off in rota for the unenviable task of reading everyone's personal correspondence, cutting out offending sections with scissors. In keeping with national susceptibilities the Navy became paranoid about security, to the extent of secrecy existing for secrecy's sake; when at sea only those on the bridge – the captain and his immediate staff – knew what was happening. The remainder asked no questions and simply did as they were told. And under protests from its editor, Admiral W.H. Henderson, publication of *The Naval Review* was suspended in 1915 for the rest of the war by order of the Admiralty, because 'some numbers have contained statements which might be of serious detriment to our interest if they became known to the enemy', despite the fact that *The Naval Review* was already officially censored.

❖❖❖

A cross section of personal experience in the first two years of war portrays the contrasting reactions of officers and men to the then unknown conditions of sea warfare.

Less than a month after war started, and initiated by the resourceful Commodores Keyes and Tyrwhitt, the light cruisers *Arethusa* and *Fearless*, each with a flotilla of destroyers left Harwich to attack enemy light forces off the Heligoland Bight. The sheer exhilaration and audacity of the Navy's first ever high speed destroyer action is vividly described by Commander Lennon Goldsmith in *Laertes*, when the third flotilla in line ahead encountered the cruiser *Mainz*:

> At 4,000 yards our good little guns were sending bursts of flame all over her and I yelled down to stand by for a torpedo. Her shooting was really admirable. As *Laurel* turned after firing torpedoes she got a broadside . . . and lurched away in a dense cloud of black smoke. . . . Next came *Liberty* – as she turned a salvo struck her. I saw her mast disappear and feared for her captain – he was killed together with everyone on the bridge, except the coxswain who was badly wounded but nobly hung on to the wheel. *Lysander* miraculously escaped absolutely untouched. With relief I saw our torpedo plunge on its way and put the helm over to follow in *Lysander*'s wake.
>
> Then a great wave of stinging spray hit me in the face and a deafening crack shook the ship. I was watching *Mainz* – saw her broadside flash out – and knew what was coming. One shell burst in the water just below the bridge – gave me my bath, wounded a man on the fo'c'sle and nearly cut the topmast in half. Another entered the ship's side, burst inside a boiler and scalded four men tending it. A third went through the base of the centre funnel, killing two men, wounding a third and shattering the two boats. The fourth entered and passed through my cabin, went on through two more bulkheads and exploded in the officers' quarters. It blew the next bulkhead to bits and sent some spare parts through the engine room bulkhead beyond. The ship had stopped. I looked at *Mainz* and saw a great explosion under her quarter – 'our fish' I thought, and felt happy.[8]

Able Seaman Stokes was gunlayer at a 4-in gun mounting in *Fearless*, which sank German destroyer V187:

> [My] next impression was seeing *Mainz* blazing and crew jumping overboard. I then saw *Laertes* and she caught an enemy broadside and was disabled. *Fearless* was holed along the starboard side mostly in the bunkers, 1st Lieutenant's cabin and spirit room while another two exploded on the fore messdeck and busted a steam pipe. Well, I was beginning to think we'd had it as the Germans seemed to outnumber us. And then we saw some big ships loom up. We cheered our heads off when they shouted from the bridge that they were our cruisers. It was a very cheering sight too when they opened fire . . . we could proceed back and they would finish the job.[9]

Fearless took *Laertes* in tow and headed for Harwich. On return to harbour there was much rejoicing in the destroyers who had come through their baptism of fire in brilliant style. *Laertes* gave leave to as many as possible. Goldsmith concluded his letter: 'The men were splendid. I've sent them away to see their best girls – and took those onboard to a nice service in the Dockyard Church this morning.'

The Heligoland Bight action was a fortuitous success that boosted naval and national morale. Few of our ships were badly damaged and casualties were light; whereas the Germans lost three light cruisers, a destroyer and over 1,000 officers and men. Above all it brought to notice the fighting ability of our destroyers, whose youthful captains had not hesitated to tackle light cruisers.

To check the German advance along the Channel coast a number of small craft, including horse boats, were converted into gunboats and transported to the mouth of the Yser river. One former horse boat was commissioned by a lieutenant, petty officer coxswain and eight men, their job indirect bombardment with a 4.7-in gun as directed by an Army observer in telephonic communication. Living in close quarters with his crew the lieutenant wrote after the war his observations, of which: 'The most striking feature was that we seemed to be always eating. Just before daylight when hands turned out – a bowl of cocoa and biscuits; then a breakfast of eggs and bacon collected from a farm behind the lines. Mid-forenoon we had a "snack". Dinner was always ready at noon even if the air was full of shrapnel. How sacred is the dinner hour to the sailor.'

The 'cook' was an AB of a type popularly known as a 'bird'. Drink had been his downfall but as he liked the job he was an exceptional working hand. After dinner there were more meals before turning in:

> The conduct of the bluejacket in the mess impressed me more than anything. His table manners are good and his general demeanour most gentlemanly. His references to home life are particularly tender and every man seems to take a delight in unburdening his life history and private affairs to his officer . . . confirming the spirit of comradeship between officers and men, which virtually won the war. In a big ship . . . opportunity seldom permits its demonstration, except perhaps in games and sing songs. But in stress of action it is bound to come out and is a great asset to our service.
>
> To the man, the officer, on account of his education, is a person of vast knowledge . . . the officer was expected to know the exact state of affairs along the whole front, what we were doing at sea, how long the war would last and when there would be the chance of a drop of leave.
>
> In contrast, the most striking feature of the bluejacket is his lack of imagination. This deficiency becomes a valuable quality in a fighting man because it permits him to sleep when he can, eat when he can and gives him a real fearlessness and self confidence in most dangerous situations.

There were casualties among the crews of gunboats and when it came to funerals they seemed to envy the pomp and circumstance of laying their departed messmates to rest. Indeed 'the service custom of slow marching to the grave to the tune of *Dead March* and returning at the quick to that of *It's a different girl again* was typical of the bluejacket's character'.[10]

❖❖❖

The arguable decision to send all 420 Dartmouth cadets to sea at the outbreak of war had been taken at high level a year previously. Junior officers were in short supply so what better than to continue their training in the fleet. As less likely to encounter battle they were distributed among older ships, including a dozen to each unit of the 7th Cruiser Squadron, responsible for patrolling off the Dutch coast. On 22 September 1914 the cruisers *Aboukir*, *Hogue*, and *Cressy*, recently commissioned from reserve, were steaming in line abreast at 9 knots without destroyer escort and seemingly oblivious of danger. No wonder they were called the 'live bait squadron'.

Shortly after 6 a.m. *Aboukir* was torpedoed by submarine *U–9*. Cadet Hereward Hook in *Hogue* 'was rudely awakened by someone violently shaking my hammock . . . and a voice saying that *Aboukir* was sinking. I jumped out, put on a great coat and sea boots over my pyjamas and dashed up to the after bridge'. In response to a call for assistance the captains of the other two cruisers – with misplaced chivalry – stood by and at 6.45 a.m. *Hogue* was struck amidships by two torpedoes so that 'poor old *Hogue* was almost cut in two. No. 3 funnel collapsed like a pack of cards.' There was little panic or excitement, several men going below to fetch their hammocks which, if tightly lashed, were a good substitute for lifejackets not easily obtainable. After the explosion Hook discarded his coat and seaboots, went down to the quarterdeck already awash and jumped in to make for a fogbuoy about 50 yards away. 'As I reached the buoy', continued Hook, 'I saw *Hogue* slowly turn over and disappear.' Rescued by the ship's launch 'we were rounding *Cressy*'s stern when . . . a torpedo struck her starboard side . . . then another torpedo which exploded her 9.2-in magazine and she went down almost at once. The time was 8 a.m.'.[11]

Chaplain Wilfred Ellis of *Hogue* had a narrow escape from death when going down with the ship:

> I remember wondering that I was not afraid. Humanly speaking there was little chance of being saved, yet strangely enough I never contemplated the possibility of being drowned. I went down a long way and came back up breathless with a spar under my arm . . . I got another and on these I kept afloat for about twenty minutes until I was picked up by . . . our pinnace. . . . My prayer book with hymns had remained in my pocket and we spent hours of waiting, singing all manner of songs and hymns . . . until picked up by a Dutch vessel *Flora*.[12]

Hook was among 180 survivors that transferred to a passing fishing smack and on arrival in Harwich 'was taken to the Great Eastern Hotel which had been turned into a military hospital. Next day Messrs Gieves' representative arrived betimes and we were soon in uniform again'. In this wholly unnecessary disaster sixty officers, including thirteen cadets, and 1,400 men out of a total of 2,200 were lost – a casualty list greater than that sustained by the British fleet at Trafalgar.

Until then confidence was such that nobody seriously imagined that one of HM cruisers could be sunk. However, in the ensuing enquiry not only were the commanding officers concerned held to blame but the Admiralty were criticized for failing to appreciate the submarine threat. When the news of the tragedy reached Scapa Flow there was a rush to regain the boats that had been landed and to act on a recommendation in the enquiry report that everyone be issued with a cork lifebelt. An MP took Churchill and the Admiralty to task for needlessly exposing untrained youngsters of fifteen to such dangers. But the last word in the public controversy that followed went to the 'Mother of a Dartmouth Cadet' who summed up the patriotic fervour of the day by declaring to the *Morning Post* that 'If my son can best serve England at this juncture by giving his life for her I would not lift a finger to bring him home'.

❖❖❖

There was little difficulty in assimilating large numbers of trained Royal Naval Reserve officers in the fleet, those from passenger liners going to major warships, others appointed to contraband control and to minesweepers. It was in these small ships that the rugged individualism of the 'Rockies', as the RNRs were first called, challenged the rigid traditionalism of the Royal Navy. Fishing trawler men 'possessed that truculent independence, robustness of speech and disrespect of dignity which is the hallmark of those who handle fish'.[13] There were inevitable clashes between retired senior officers appointed to command minesweeper flotillas and fishermen who had no time for naval discipline or polishing brass.

There was also a touch of jealousy between the RNRs and the RNVRs, drawn from the same classes as the Army Territorials and who had answered the call in such numbers that the Navy could not find use for them. At the same time the British Expeditionary Force in France and Belgium, struggling to hold back powerful German forces intent on reaching the Channel ports, was desperately short of trained men. At Kitchener's instigation Churchill had the Reserves organized in battalions to form a Royal Naval Division to defend Antwerp. Not surprisingly the bluejackets were embittered to learn they were to become soldiers and, worse still, be parted from their friends. But they accepted their fate and with the minimum of training and without proper equipment the division was rushed to Belgium. In the event casualties were light but some 1,500 were captured or interned in Holland, the remainder returning to England.

At home public opinion was becoming disenchanted with the lack-lustre way things were going at sea, demanding a more forceful attitude and criticizing Churchill and Battenberg. The latter was subjected to virulent and unfair attacks in the press because of his German birth and there were those who accused him of not keeping a proper check on Churchill. Eventually Battenberg stepped down and Fisher was appointed First Sea Lord on 30 October 1914 at the age of seventy-four. Three days later came the disastrous news of the Battle of Coronel off the west coast of South America in which the cruisers *Good Hope* and *Monmouth* were sunk by a superior German squadron.

Fisher's swift and decisive reaction to Admiral Craddock's defeat makes a striking parallel with the South Atlantic operations of 1982. *Inflexible* and *Invincible* were hurriedly prepared at Devonport to proceed with all dispatch to the Falklands. Arriving at Port Stanley they joined the cruisers *Caernarvon*, *Cornwall*, *Kent*, *Bristol* and *Glasgow*, a survivor from Coronel. Within twenty-four hours Admiral Count Von Spee appeared with two heavy cruisers *Scharnhorst* and *Gneisenau*, together with *Leipzig*, *Nürnberg* and *Dresden*. As the German squadron made off Admiral Sturdee's ships gave chase, battle-cruisers engaging the heavy cruisers and light cruisers their opposite numbers. Then followed the systematic annihilation of the German squadron, the last old-style purely gun action between surface warships; the losers fought valiantly against impossible odds.

Aboard *Inflexible* Stoker Bullock was off watch and asleep as the German ships approached: he woke up to the bugle of 'Action Stations' accompanied by the pipe 'Hands shift into clean underclothing', as a precaution against possible contamination of wounds by dirty clothes. When firing started at 2 p.m. 'clouds of coal dust were everywhere and at each salvo the ship shook and rattled. I was fire party amidships but abandoned it now and again to have a look at what was going on'.[14] Up in the foretop Rudolf Verner, the Gunnery Lieutenant, opened fire at 7 miles; *Scharnhorst* retaliated causing one of the crew to ejaculate 'They are *firing* at us', to which Verner replied: 'What did you think we came all this way for?' The two battle-cruisers took two hours to overwhelm *Scharnhorst* before concentrating on *Gneisenau* which went on firing until the last moment.

The engagement was shared by *Caernarvon* where the newly joined Midshipman Royer Dick had his first taste of battle: 'I don't mind admitting freely that I was in the deuce of a funk when we sallied out, I hope I did not show it. But I got so excited that I soon forgot about the purely personal view before we were an hour out of harbour . . . these remarks apply to most people . . . and once we got firing we had no time to think.'

As *Gneisenau* vanished Dick was sent away in a cutter to rescue survivors:

> When we got to the spot there was a huge quantity of wreckage, stools, hammocks, timber and all sorts of things, all bearing a freight of men. Most of them could not climb into the boat and we had the most awful job to get them in. They fought and bit and held on to one's legs. . . . The horror of that two hours' rescue work will live with me for many a long day. . . . It brought the ghastliness of war very, very close.[15]

Coronel had been avenged and Britain rejoiced in what turned out to be the only total naval victory of the war. For the moment Fisher had injected new life into the Admiralty's direction of naval affairs.

❖❖❖

To relieve pressure on the Russian front, occupy Constantinople and create an offensive when the Allied armies were bogged down in France the Dardanelles venture was Churchillian in concept and very nearly succeeded. It failed because there was no organization to plan and execute such a complex operation involving an armada of surface ships, submarines and aircraft, weapons of every description, amphibious landings of troops and, above all, inter service co-ordination. It was also too late.

In the face of strong currents, minefields, shore batteries and surface patrols early success was achieved by submarines. On Friday 13 December 1914 Commander Norman Holbrook in the eight-year-old submarine B11 with a crew of twelve penetrated the Narrows and sank a Turkish battleship off Chanak:

> I fired one torpedo because lights were getting low . . . and batteries failing. We found ourselves aground astern. . . . By using full revs we got off but I couldn't see the way out of the bay. The coxswain said the spirit compass lenses had packed up and all he could see were black spots. . . . I told him to follow them and at full submerged speed in twenty minutes a sea horizon appeared. We made for it and were more or less swept out of the Straits. We had been under water nine hours. What a wonderful crew – each a first class man – but we had been very lucky.[16]

For this exploit Holbrook was awarded the first naval VC of the war; every member of his crew received a decoration or mention in dispatches. In 1915 British submarines continued to intercept Turkish communications, bringing the total bag to two battleships, one destroyer, five gunboats, nine transports, seven auxiliaries and 188 sailing vessels.

In February 1915 *Agamemnon* was among the battleships bombarding the Dardanelles and Narrow forts from a position at anchor at a range of 3 miles. The forts responded with gunfire, and an account is provided by Midshipman Henry Denham who noted:

> one shell had already hit us amidships killing three men . . . while I was strolling round the upper deck recording the enemy shots falling. The commander was trying to get the disengaged side painted, *but the men were not very willing* [author's italics] and I really cannot blame them. Seeing shells falling all around us the flagship ordered us to weigh. [This meant getting the cable party up from below and] I thought I would go up and see the anchor weighed. No sooner had I got to the screen door than a large shell landed in the oilskin locker and burst right over me. . . . I saw red for two seconds and got a bit of a blast which knocked down most of the men behind me, wounding many.

Agamemnon was hit several times before withdrawing clear but not seriously. It transpired that: 'When Yeoman Bishop was hit by a large splinter from the first shell he was reading a signal and continued to shout it out although his leg had almost been shot off. When taken below he was most cheery all the time and even smoked a cigarette just after his leg was amputated.' Next day the ship's company cleared up the wreckage and during divisions Denham noticed 'what an impression yesterday's show had made on the men; for instead of the usual skylarking at prayers they all looked very solemn and quite melancholy, which I have never seen them look before'. In the afternoon *Agamemnon* went to sea:

> to bury our three dead; a very appropriate place – beautiful, clear, blue water. At 2.20 we started the burial service. The three bodies were borne on stretchers sewn up in their own hammocks and covered with ensigns. They were committed to the deep in turn by sliding down a gangplank into the sea, whereupon they sank immediately. . . . The rifle party fired three rounds, after which there was the 'Last Post'. It was very, very, impressive. . . . One cannot realise disasters or people getting killed, even though they aren't one's closest friends.[17]

❖❖❖

Early in 1915 the Eastchurch wing of the RNAS – No. 4 Aeroplane Squadron – under Wing Commander Samson was sent to the Dardanelles, the advance party travelling with baggage and equipment across France by lorry and motor car. Eventually twenty-two aircraft arrived at their hastily constructed aerodrome in Tenedos, to be supported by the converted carrier *Ark Royal* with its 130-ft flight deck and six seaplanes. Their job was reconnaissance, gunfire spotting and photography of beaches. But Samson had more belligerent ideas: 'I started bombing the Turks. I didn't hit anything, but it was good practice and I felt it was time the Turks realized that Eastchurch had arrived on the scene. From then on all aircraft, whatever their mission, flew armed. . . . By degrees the Fleet's respect for our usefulness grew; but some ships were always better to work with than others.'[18]

Meanwhile the assembly of ships in Mudros harbour had grown in size and variety even before landings were contemplated. Here the fleet could off-load the wounded, provision, ammunition and gain a little respite. As well as swimming and water polo there were football grounds ashore; perhaps the best feature was the regular arrival of mails from England dispatched over land to Taranto, thence by mail steamer, a journey of eight to ten days.

After the tranports arrived barely a month was allowed for practice landings. Although it was known that the enemy was well forewarned two aspects stood out in subsequent events. Firstly, the gallantry of midshipmen and their crews in towing boats laden with troops to the beaches. The second was the incredible bravery of the soldiers in getting ashore in the face of strong opposition, which led to the bond struck up with sailors as they worked and fought together for more than six months under formidable conditions.

On 24 April the invasion force sailed for Gallipoli. One squadron was led by the battleship *Queen*, her band playing *Fall in and follow me* and which included *Bacchante*, where Midshipman Eric Bush, aged fifteen, was detailed to command a 45-ft steam picket boat. As soon as the squadron anchored boats were lowered, filled with troops and taken in tow to join a flotilla of twelve picket boats in line abreast steering for a beach 2 miles distant barely visible in the darkness. After slipping the tow:

> a bugle call ashore gives the alarm. Verey lights . . . starshell. The enemy opens fire and down comes a rain of bullets. The time is 4.30 a.m. and dawn is breaking. There is no cover for our soldiers . . . several are wounded. After they leap out I see them lying flat behind packs and firing. We pick up the launch full of casualties. Fresh troops (from the destroyers) clamber in and the wounded have to make several trips inshore before anyone can attend to them.[19]

Throughout the day and into the night under shell and small arms fire picket boats from the fleet brought troops in and wounded out. An Australian soldier told a story of a midshipman (Denham) whose picket boat got a rope round his propeller while under heavy fire. 'All the same he dived under the water to clear his propeller despite our rather heated objections to him bathing in a danger zone. All midshipmen were wonderful. Bullets left them completely unmoved.' At the landing of the famous *River Clyde* at V Beach a midshipman was among those awarded a Victoria Cross; several gained DSCs during the campaign.

Finally came the evacuation in December and something of the understanding established between sailors and soldiers was expressed by Commander Longden Griffiths in the monitor *Roberts* on meeting the Australians back in Mudros. 'It is a sad sight to see them all, with just what kit they could save strapped to their backs . . . marching wearily to a camp prepared for them . . . having fought against overwhelming odds. And to what purpose? Having lost thousands . . . and suffered privations and hardships untold they have come back having accomplished nothing, won nothing but the admiration of us all.'[20] As a consequence of the Dardanelles failure both Churchill and Fisher resigned their appointments.

❖❖❖

The real trouble about the war at sea was the continued absence of the enemy in any degree of strength. Ever since 1914 the Grand Fleet had been waiting patiently for the big day and for more than a year ships and their companies were sustained by tactical exercises and sweeps into the North Sea. Interesting, perhaps, for senior officers and gunnery lieutenants but deadly dull for most. Starting before dawn the long hours at actions stations; endless procedure and drill at guns and torpedo mountings; hypothetical damage reports for fire and repair parties to tackle. The great Atlantic swell surging by as escorting destroyers took it green over the foc's'le; the cold penetrating wind; the fug and smell below decks; the monotony of meals; the eager anticipation of the noonday tot of rum; the slowly rolling battleships as they headed into the grey mists, eyes straining in search of an enemy that was never seen. And on return to harbour the inevitable coal ship. 'Coaling, coaling, coaling,' sang the sailors. 'Always ....ing well coaling' to the tune of a well-known hymn. A routine that seldom varied.

'Cooks to the galley' to collect the dinner dishes

Ships were commanded and fought from open bridge structures and gun platforms that afforded little weather protection. To keep warm and dry, those exposed to the elements (in particular signalmen and lookouts) wore layers of underclothing, jerseys and woollen socks under oilskins and leather seaboots. Lifebelts were at hand, but because the cork type was bulky and uncomfortable and its successor dangerous if not properly put on, it was left to Messrs Gieves to design and produce a life-saving device. Worn as an ordinary garment before inflation and supplied with a small brandy flask for 'additional support' the Gieves waistcoat was deservedly popular and saved numerous lives. One officer, however, complained that 'a garment that could save a Wardroom Messman was bad enough but when that messman was able to save the wardroom account book as well, it became a menace to the Navy'.[21] Throughout the war it is true to say that Gieves never raised their prices – despite escalating costs of material – and showed great compassion to the next of kin of those killed in action and leaving accounts to settle.

Keeping 70,000 officers and men healthy and happy was no easy task and it says much for the leadership and enterprise of officers and petty officers that they managed to do so in the bleak surrounds of Scapa Flow, the Grand Fleet's base for four and a half years. For example, men from the fleet were landed on Flotta Island to select rectangular areas of heather, as level and free from bog as possible, put up goal posts and label the patches 'football grounds'. Sailing regattas flourished in the summer months but ships mostly relied on their own built-in facilities to stage boxing, deck hockey, tug o' war, band concerts, cinema shows and amateur theatricals. Battleships and cruisers made a point of taking destroyers and submarines under their wing. Leading Signalman H.J. Smith of the new fleet submarine K6 alongside the battleship *Ajax* wrote in his diary: 'I was invited to supper in the signalmen's mess and afterwards went to a Singing Concert which was very good.' Sponsored by the Junior Army and Navy Stores the steamer *Borodino* was brought up to the Flow as a mobile shopping centre, stocking food, books, games and clothing. SS *Ghourko* was the theatre ship that could seat about six hundred in her main hold where ships gave performances of home-made revues and well-known plays.

Some officers shot grouse on the north shore of the Flow, others took up gardening in allotments; perhaps the most popular pastime was on the eighteen hole golf course laid out on Flotta, each big ship undertaking to design and construct one hole:

> One battleship brought sufficient turf from St Andrews to provide an immaculate green and very soon crowds of officers, from Sir John Jellicoe to the most junior snotty, lined up on the first tee – 200 yards down hill. There was no mercy if one lost a ball and the usual procedure was one couple hastily putting and scurrying off the green, another approaching, a third running downhill after their drive and a fourth impatiently swinging their clubs on the tee.[22]

The 'Gieve' waistcoat saved lives in two World Wars

Periodically ships were sent to Invergordon in Cromarty Firth to give each watch of the ship's company a spell of leave: there were also playing fields, a wet canteen, shops and the sight of civilization. Based at Rosyth the battle-cruiser force fared even better, ships being either at short notice for sea or long notice (up to four hours) allowing local leave in a neighbourhood renowned for hospitality.

War-time routine may have been tedious but it brought about a better sense of discipline and relationship between officers and men than pre-war conditions ever achieved. Much advancement and educational training was undertaken, and officers were further encouraged to organize inter-divisional sports and games. Social life in the wardroom and messdeck was aptly and vividly recorded for posterity by authors with pseudonyms like Bartimeus and Taffrail.

Then came Jutland. Acting on information received on 30 May 1916 that the German High Seas Fleet was leaving harbour Jellicoe was ordered to concentrate his numerically superior forces in the North Sea. At 2.30 p.m. on the following day Beatty's battle-cruisers were about 200 miles north of the German coast and 60 miles south of Jellicoe's main fleet, also steering south. Unexpectedly one of Beatty's light cruisers spotted enemy ships and the six battle-cruisers turned to intercept, opening fire at Hipper's battle-cruisers at 3.45 p.m. from a range of 8 miles. General engagement followed and according to Chatfield, Flag Captain in *Lion*: 'Both our own fire and that of the enemy seemed good. . . . We were hit several times and were going joyfully when at 4.00 p.m. the yeoman of signals reported seeing the rear ship, *Indefatigable*, blow up. A vast column of smoke rose to the sky. This seemed at the moment just a disappointment . . . and was not a really serious tactical loss.' Following up astern the 5th Battle Squadron of new fast battleships opened fire at very long range; at that moment Chatfield 'heard a resounding clank behind me . . . I saw a large flame spring from Q turret. My order to flood Q magazine . . . had been forestalled by Major Harvey RMLI, the turret commander. It was lucky he had done so . . . he gave the order with his last words. . . . What an example of the wonderful training of that great corps'. At 4.25 the third ship in the line, *Queen Mary*, blew up: 'Beatty turned to me and said "There seems to be something wrong with our bloody ships today", a remark that needed neither comment nor answer.'[23]

All orders to ship's company were passed by pipe

Petty Officer Francis was gunner's mate in charge of the gunhouse crew in X turret of *Queen Mary* when:

> there came what I term the big smash and I was dangling in the air on a bowline, which saved me from being thrown down on the floor of the turret. These bowlines were an idea of mine . . . men who had them were not injured. Everything in the ship went quiet as a church . . . the guns were absolutely useless . . . there was not a sign of excitement. . . . After speaking to the officer of the turret I ordered 'Clear the turret' and out they all went. PO Stares was the last coming out from the working chamber and reported water coming up the trunk from the shell room. Then I said 'Why didn't you come up before?' He replied 'I heard no order to leave the turret'.[24]

Although temporarily blinded by oil Francis was one of only twelve survivors out of 1,260 officers and men.

At 4.45 p.m. Beatty turned his battle-cruisers 180 degrees to the north; the German battle-cruisers made a similar turn. This brought the 5th Battle Squadron under heavy fire in an area known as 'Windy Corner'. *Warspite* was badly hit and from 5 p.m. till about 6.30 the executive officer, Commander Walwyn, and her fire and repair parties, never had a dull moment. There were fires to tackle, holes in the ship's side to plug, damaged bulkheads to be strengthened and shored up and – most important of all – the ship's fighting efficiency to be maintained. Yet Walwyn found time to note and remember many examples of the sailors' imperturbability and humour in moments of stress. First thing was to stop two stokers enthusiastically trying to chip the fuse out of an unexploded German shell. When a 12-in shell entered the galley and blew down through the deck a rating remarked: 'There goes my ....ing dinner'; and he found the marines (whose guns were not in action) cheerfully playing cards on the deck in the middle of the battle. There were remarkably few casualties.[25]

Less fortunate was the 1st Cruiser Squadron steaming gallantly between the opposing battlefleets and taking the brunt of heavy fire at close range. *Black Prince* and the flagship *Defence* were sunk and *Warrior* so badly hit she could no longer move nor fight. In the starboard engine room Engineer Commander Kitching (later awarded the DSO) was present when 'there was a tremendous explosion in the after end . . . and most of the lights went out. Several men came running forward, including one streaming with blood and I realised fully what cold drawn funk is like'. The engine room was flooded, steam was escaping at full blast, the exit hatches were jammed and the only way out was through the shell hole on top.

For the next two hours Kitching tackled the fires, initially having 'the greatest difficulty in getting my brain to work at all . . . on such occasions evolutions rehearsed at drill work automatically, and I found my subordinates readier than myself in carrying out measures I had myself devised'. The port engine room crew was trapped for nearly three hours with no lights, but thanks to Morgan, the senior engineer, they got out just before the water rose to the top. After being towed by the seaplane carrier *Engadine*, the battered *Warrior* was abandoned in a sinking condition and everyone transferred to *Engadine*. Kitching concluded: 'As we steamed past the old ship the men gave three cheers and then started our old pantomime song "It's a long, long way to the *Warrior*". That was too much for me. I was thankful that I was inside a cabin where no one could see me; for then I quite broke down.'[26]

Officer's Chief Steward Ernest Fox was captain's valet in *Marlborough*, flagship of 4th battle squadron and part of Jellicoe's battle line that extended for more than 7 miles:

> She was a magnificent ship and I was as proud of her as the captain was. At 6 p.m. we sighted the German fleet and opened fire – the *Marlborough* had a very good record of gunnery. We lost touch and . . . at 7 p.m. there was a terrific explosion. Torpedoes struck us on the starboard side and lifted the ship like a rubber ball. My action station was first aid in one of the flats and I felt the ship going over and over. We had a Surgeon Lieutenant Commander in charge. All our faces went white and we looked for the ladder when he said 'There will be no VCs at this station. You'll remain where you are' and sat on the companion way. Then we all steadied up.

On passage to Immingham for repairs, with two stokers killed and several wounded, Fox joined other stewards in the boiler rooms to keep steaming watch and help out.[27]

In another battleship, *Benbow*, Assistant Paymaster Noel Wright had a grandstand view of the battle from the foretop as torpedo lookout and found:

> It was quite a sensation being under fire. . . . Most of the stuff fell about 800 short or 1,000 over. . . . Only one salvo came really close and made a horrid noise – cross between a wail and a whistle. Our men were perfect, as happy and cheery as if at a picnic. Stokers came up on deck, parties of twenty at a time, to have a look at the fight. The commander was the worst offender. He and his 'doggie' – a snotty of sixteen – were walking about the deck the whole time.[28]

Control Top battleship *Neptune*, 70 ft above the upper deck

In the battle-cruiser *Princess Royal* the senior medical officer was in the fore dressing station when 'there was a terrific crash, lights were extinguished and several members of our party made violent acquaintance with the deck'. A combination of fighting candle lamps and heavy whitish fumes caused them to move to the deck above where 'we dressed several cases of burns and . . . I amputated a leg in semi-darkness – but the patient survived'. Another casualty was a Blue Marine (artilleryman), a great personality who 'I always remember saying "Lor, bless you, sir, they fires a lot, but they never 'urts each other!" – this somewhat contemptuous opinion of the gunnery world based on his experience at the Bombardment of Alexandria in 1882'. The fleet surgeon's only complaint was the complete absence of 'authentic news reaching us between decks, combined with enforced idleness at commencement of action, which was very trying'. He concluded with the sentiment that 'officers and men were brought much closer together and had a better understanding of each other after being in action than they did before'.[29]

There were eighty British destroyers in the battle, of which eight failed to return and several more were badly damaged. Steaming at 30 knots just ahead of Beatty's battle-cruisers, Sub-Lieutenant David Wainwright described his experience of the approaching battle in a letter to his parents from a prisoner-of-war camp after his ship was sunk:

> Think of the worst peal of thunder you have ever heard, try to imagine it going on continuously and that you are standing in the corridor of the *Royal Scot* with windows open passing another express train going in the opposite direction. You will then have a faint conception of what it felt like on the bridge of the destroyer in the van of the battle-cruisers.

'A lull in the action', battleship *Conqueror*, Jutland, 1916

> The state of tension while waiting was the worst period that I passed through, because it gave imagination a chance to work. My tongue was dry and I smoked a cigarette hard, hoping that with its aid an illusion of *sang froid* and devil-may-carishness was accepted by my neighbours at its spurious value. I busied myself with testing voice pipes and other accessories to my official function, that of fire control.[30]

One of the more dramatic moments of the battle occurred in the evening of 31 May when Jellicoe was steaming south at speed with his twenty-four battleships, each displacing 25,000 tons, in a six-column line abreast formation. On receipt of the signal from Beatty reporting the sighting of the enemy battlefleet bearing SSW Jellicoe stepped quickly on to the bridge compass platform and – in the words of his flag captain, Frederic Dreyer: 'Looked in silence at the magnetic compass card for about 20 seconds. I watched his keen, weather beaten face with tremendous interest, wondering what he would do. . . . Then he looked up and broke the silence. . . . "Hoist equal speed pendant SE by E".'[31]

Deploying the fleet into the line of battle on the port wing column was a master stroke because it gave the Grand Fleet every tactical advantage, as well as cutting off the retreat of the German High Seas fleet. The stage was set for a substantial British naval victory. During the night, through failure of the Admiralty to communicate an intercepted message of German intentions and the inability of British light forces engaged in the rear to inform him that the enemy was crossing his stern, Jellicoe remained unaware that Scheer was making his escape. When day broke on what should have been a Glorious First of June the Grand Fleet was patrolling an empty sea. It was all over.

After Jutland arguments raged for many years as to what Jellicoe or Beatty should or should not have done, the controversy eclipsing the finer points of the Navy's first full-scale fleet action for more than a century. Throughout the two-day battle visibility was obscured by fog as well as funnel and gun smoke, discrepancies in the estimated geographical positions of British and German main units exceeded 10 miles, wireless communications were inconsistent and magnetic compass accuracy affected every time the guns fired. Yet such was the standard of ship handling and engine room performance that sixty-five heavy warships and seventy destroyers were manoeuvred successfully at high speed by flag and light signals only, not more than a few hundred yards between ships and often under enemy gun or torpedo fire. The need for rigid tactical control under the conditions of Jutland may have been arguable but the fighting efficiency and morale of the Grand Fleet was never in question.

CHAPTER SEVEN

Years of Crisis

There is no danger seamen have not run
Tempests have drowned them since the world began
They have dared shipwreck, frostbite and the sun
But they have dared a greater danger, Man.
John Masefield

Chief Engine Room Artificer Leggatt, serving in the light cruiser *Galatea* at Jutland, never forgot the moment when:

> I saw the *Queen Mary* blow up, the *Agincourt* fire her broadside over us and the Chief Buffer I was talking to exclaimed 'I hope to God there are no shorts, Chief!' . . . But it was a lamentable business because it wasn't a victory. We lost as many ships and more men than the Germans did. It's true the German High Seas Fleet never came out again as such; but it wasn't a victory in the sense that Trafalgar was a victory or Matapan was a victory in the latter days. Moreover it was badly handled by the Admiralty. When we got ashore and went into Dunfermline they were under the clear impression that we had had a good walloping because we had lost this, that and the other.[1]

First news of the battle was a German wireless broadcast stating that the High Seas Fleet had encountered the Grand Fleet off the Skagerrak and had sunk one battleship, two battle-cruisers, two armoured cruisers, a light cruiser and a large number of destroyers before returning to base. German losses were only partially revealed. Since the next of kin of 6,000 British casualties had to be informed the Admiralty had no option but to issue a communiqué based on Jellicoe's report. This admitted the losses of *Queen Mary*, *Indefatigable* and *Invincible*, three armoured cruisers and at least five destroyers while claiming a battleship, two light cruisers and many destroyers. Not surprisingly the impression of defeat, even of disaster, was initially reflected in the Press; within a week further statements indicating heavier German losses and that Jellicoe had 'driven the enemy into port' helped restore public opinion. But damage had been done; the aftermath of the battle proved a moral shock to the nation and a heartbreaking disappointment to the Navy. Months would pass before realization that the Grand Fleet still held the ring and that the High Seas Fleet had suffered a technical knock-out from which it never recovered. The problem of getting the message across to the public was not made easier by the ban imposed in 1914 on the pre-war practice of embarking correspondents in the fleet, despite efforts by Admiral Brownrigg, the Chief Censor, to make some exceptions. Senior naval officers continued to regard the press with suspicion – and all publicity as undesirable.

On publishing the Jutland honours and awards the Admiralty came in for further criticism, this time more justified. After an encounter with the enemy it was the practice for commanding officers to include in their reports citations for exceptional gallantry or skill on the part of officers and ratings. Subsequent decoration with medals or mentions in dispatches were distinct from occasional awards recommended by the commander-in-chief for exemplary duties over a period. After Jutland, Commander James of the battleship *Benbow*, whose squadron had barely engaged the enemy, remarked that instead of keeping the awards separate:

> The Admiralty directed Jellicoe to merge meritorious service honours with those for the battle. The result was ludicrous. A surgeon commander in our squadron was awarded a DSO for good arrangements for the wounded, of which there were none; while a surgeon commander of a ship that had been heavily engaged, who had been at the operating table lit by candles throughout the night, received nothing. Some of the notations against the names of officers of ships that had not been engaged were quite fantastic.[2]

Similar sentiments were echoed by Lieutenant Stephen King-Hall of *Southampton*, flagship of the 2nd Light Cruiser Squadron, that had fired nearly an outfit of ammunition, torpedoed and sunk a German cruiser and sustained more than eighty casualties. Indicating that his admiral (Goodenough) was one of those who 'did not choose to say much about what happened' he complained that 'the Flag Lieutenant [Peters] was the only one mentioned and fully deserved his DSC, but the Navigator and "Torps" did equally good work. . . . The great silent Navy is a beautiful idea, a very fine tradition but can be overdone'.[3] The high regard felt within the service for personal decorations made their award a sensitive and controversial task, with inevitable repercussions in the wardroom and messdeck. As a morale booster for the wounded a silver war badge was introduced, followed in 1918 by the entitlement of chevrons that could be worn on the sleeve to indicate years of service, The introduction of the Most Excellent Order of the British Empire in 1917 (Civil Division) and 1918 (Military Division) did much to restore the balance between gallantry and meritorious service awards.

Certainly after Jutland life in the Grand Fleet was never quite the same. At Scapa and Rosyth there was noticeably less tension in the air and the prospect of an operational incursion by heavy ships became less likely, particularly after two light cruisers had been torpedoed by U-boats. It was left to the experts to decide what lessons could be learned from the battle as thoughts focused on the next leave period and the gratuitous issue of a railway travel warrant. The younger, unmarried libertymen headed for the bright lights of the cities, pubs and clubs, the company of women and up to fourteen days of glorious unrestrained freedom, aptly expressed by a ship's concert party that sang:

> Goodbye – I've got to go
> From dear old Scapa Flow
> I'm heading for Soho.[4]

Cheap beds and food were to be found at Aggie Weston's, the YMCA and service clubs; and because sailors in uniform were deservedly popular the British public made sure they had a good time and turned a blind eye to lapses in behaviour. Older officers and men spent all or part of their leave with their families in surroundings where few households were unaffected by service casualties. After long months of separation there was no substitute for homecoming and reunion with relatives and friends, the journey south from Thurso to Euston via the Midlands being made by a 'naval train' that took just under twenty-four hours. All too soon the time came to return by the dreary trek north. Of course there were absentees but the majority of men came back from their leave, if a little late, since it was unwise to be on the run as a deserter in wartime Britain.

In the Grand Fleet everything was done to keep spirits high to offset the resumption of drills, exercises and forays into the North Sea. As well as regattas and sports there was a drive to help out the Ministry of Munitions in which officers and men devoted themselves to making equipment for the Army. Artificers constructed spare parts for guns and carriages while the wardroom and mess decks turned out tens of thousands of rope grommets for the protection of artillery shell driving bands. Everything was done, too, on a competitive basis.

Another consequence of Jutland was changes at the top in the Grand Fleet. German naval strategy switched to a submarine offensive, and to put new life into the U-boat countermeasures – hitherto ineffective – Jellicoe was appointed First Sea Lord, taking with him members of his staff. On 28 November, after bearing the greatest single responsibility on any man in the war for over two years, Jellicoe went on with scarcely a day's break to undertake an equally daunting task at the Admiralty. On leaving his flagship the ship's company gave him three tremendous cheers, the band played 'Auld Lang Syne' and a staff officer wrote in his diary: 'The confidence that the fleet had in him was unbounded; and every single officer and man in *Iron Duke* loved him, of that I am certain.' His successor was Admiral Sir David Beatty who shifted his flag to *Queen Elizabeth* early in 1917.

One aspect of warfare that Jellicoe wholeheartedly approved was the performance of the Royal Naval Division. After taking a battering in the Dardanelles campaign and resisting pressure to disband it altogether the Division reached France in May 1916. Its battalions named after famous admirals and strengthened by Royal Marine contingents, the Division fought at Beaucourt in one of the last battles of the Somme, at Arras, through the swamps of Passchendaele, with the tanks at Cambrai and right on to the Armistice. Throughout their existence the Division clung tenaciously to the naval way of life and:

> Over their camps flew the white ensign; their company flags showed anchors. Their gun limbers and equipment bore a stencilled naval anchor, not the Army broad arrow. Their language was of the wardroom and messdeck. The nicknames given were shipboard. Men going on leave were mustered for the 'liberty boat' and 'went ashore'. Men were 'rated' and 'disrated' to leading seaman and petty officer. They attended 'sick bay' when ill and in the 'wardroom' the King's health was drunk sitting, not standing as in the Army. Men requested 'permission to grow' a beard.[5]

The Army did not like this. Orders were given to replace the Division's more senior officers with regimental martinets, eager to purge the seemingly casual naval conduct. However, the new officers either succumbed to the ways of the Navy or else moved on to deal with less determined characters. As time passed the original RFR, RNR and pre-war vintage RNVR contingents

Members of the Royal Naval Division going over the top at Gallipoli, 1915

returned to sea. The huge casualty list accounted for others more tragically and by 1918 the great majority of the Division were enrolled straight from civilian life as sub-lieutenants RNVR or, if ratings, Z class reservists. Leadership at company and battalion level was outstanding and, as in the Army, the proportion of officer casualties noticeably high.

Such was the surge of patriotism in the first two years of the war that the Navy never lacked officer volunteers. Veterans on the retired list answered the call in droves, many over sixty; the oldest officer afloat and in command of an armed yacht, Lieutenant Commander Gartside Tipping, was seventy-two when he was killed in action off Zeebrugge. After basic training at the Crystal Palace, the vast glass-house near London that accommodated the Great Exhibition of 1851, many RNVRs took over weapon control duties in smaller warships and a greater number became captains and first lieutenants of motor launches, coastal motor boats and armed yachts patrolling home waters. Volunteer Reserve officers in large ships were less happily employed, facing the old prejudices against 'weekend sailors' and rarely given responsible jobs. In contrast surgeon probationers RNVR were in urgent demand and one young Scot in his final year as a medical student portrays a vivid impression of the small ship navy:

> I went to London without delay and presented myself with perturbation. The Fleet Surgeon who examined me was not worrying about varicose veins and when I told him that I hoped to join the Royal Navy in the regular way, he said it did not matter as I should soon be dead in

> any case. My Lords Commissioners accepted my application and I was told to return to Edinburgh, get my outfit and to hold myself in readiness. An over worked and specially expensive tailor was entrusted with my first appearance in King's uniform.

Appointed to a 960-ton oil-burning destroyer with a complement of five officers and seventy-five men the surgeon probationer arrived at Cromarty to find:

> There was no spare cabin but the settee in the wardroom was converted into a bunk, with a drawer underneath for my meagre wardrobe. The drawer used to come loose in heavy weather and I retrieved my belongings from the deck where they were swimming in an inch or two of water. One lived in that atmosphere known as 'fug' both at sea and in harbour. I used to turn into my bunk in a haze of tobacco smoke after midnight – when the last officer had retired to his cabin – and at sea there was the indescribable smell of sea water in closed spaces which is more nauseating than anything I know. I was dreadfully ill to start with.
>
> My professional duties were performed in the round house, which is the service term for officer's water closet. Surgical operation in such circumstances is cramped, and the bland dignity of the bedside manner laid aside. In peacetime the duties of medical officer are performed by the coxswain who is in charge of a chest containing first aid gear and medicines. Our coxswain was an old petty officer who regarded me with a fatherly air. He thought I was an unnecessary luxury but judged I was to be treated kindly and saw that no young sailor took advantage of my ignorance.
>
> In the first winter of war we were overwhelmed by comforts knitted by kind and anxious ladics. Great packages of socks, Balaclava helmets and mufflers arrived by almost every mail. No matter how many mufflers were handed to the older sailor he would wear them all at once; and when they were dirty he would throw them away.[6]

❖❖❖

The exodus of Dartmouth cadets on mobilization was more than balanced by an increased entry, necessitating additional accommodation at Osborne and Dartmouth colleges. To serve the fleet the intake was doubled, training reduced and Churchill's 1913 Special Entry scheme from public schools sent direct to Keyham (engineering college), the training cruiser having been withdrawn. And because Dartmouth accommodation was not yet ready the 'Pubs' at Keyham were joined by the 'Darts', as the first term of a hundred cadets were called. This introduced an interesting comparison between the two forms of entry which continued in the gunrooms of the fleet.

At sea a battleship's gunroom could accommodate some twenty subordinate officers, including an assistant paymaster or clerk and two sub-lieutenants, the senior being mess president. When not on watch midshipmen were under instruction or in the gunroom where they ate their meals, wrote letters and played the gramophone until it was time to climb into their hammocks. Until aged eighteen they were forbidden to drink spirits but could spend 10*s* per month on duty-free wine and beer. Aboard ship there was plenty of sporting activity, not that much was needed by young gentlemen who ran messages, climbed to their action station in the foretop and accompanied officers on their rounds below decks the length and beam of the ship. The atmosphere in most gunrooms was happy and wholesome but there were exceptions. In the battleship *Superb* Midshipman Simpson served with a senior sub-lieutenant who made life hell for the junior 'warts' by subjecting them to 'evolutions' that were little more than organized sadism. If wardroom officers were aware of what was going on then a blind eye was turned, probably because they themselves had been through the mill. The lower deck knew and were sympathetic, a petty officer remarking to Simpson: 'I would not have come up through the gunroom for all the beer in Pompey.'[7] Special Entry midshipmen, being two years older and having experienced fagging and prefects' beatings at public school, had little time for these childish practices and said so.

When war started the old entry engineer officers were in senior positions, belonged to the civilian branch and wore purple between their stripes that had no curl. Their subordinates, the lieutenants (E), were of military branch, ranked with executive officers and featured above the old entry in the *Navy List*, the well-thumbed publication found in every wardroom. On re-appointment as First Sea Lord Fisher quickly rectified this anomaly by granting the executive curl to all engineer officers, many of whom marked the occasion like the chief of a destroyer, an engineer lieutenant commander of some seniority, who gave a champagne dinner ashore for the wardroom to celebrate his elevation.

The first course of Selborne Scheme lieutenants to opt for engineering joined Keyham in 1913, after two terms' study at Greenwich. In August 1914 they went to sea and it was not until January 1918 that (E) training re-started, when a shortfall in Osborne/Dartmouth volunteers had to be made up from Special Entry officers, a practice continued during the inter-war years.

There were no Portsmouth courses for sub-lieutenants during hostilities. Navigation, torpedo, gunnery and signals specialists continued to be trained in the schools, their courses reduced to six months and including a spell in the Grand Fleet.

'The work was fairly strenuous but very interesting,' wrote Lieutenant King-Hall in *Vernon* torpedo school, aboard four wooden hulks moored in Portsmouth harbour. 'Nearly every Friday afternoon I went up to London for the weekend and was there when the great German spring offensive started in 1918 and continued its irresistible advance. It was a wonderful experience to be in the heart of the Empire during those days of tremendous peril.'[8]

The outbreak of war did wonders for the Mate Scheme. In 1914 some thirty-five mates were at sea and a further twenty-six finishing courses, including the first Mate (E). Early in 1915 the original mates were promoted lieutenant; from then onwards the demand for officers resulted in over a hundred per year being qualified, with a healthy reduction in age so essential to the scheme. By 1918 many lieutenants (ex mate) occupied responsible jobs in small craft or, if suitably qualified, were appointed 'in lieu of a specialist officer'. In fact, three subsequently became flag officers. Warrant officers did equally well, fifty being promoted lieutenant in 1918 under the age of forty-two, half for long and zealous service and half for younger officers by examination. Buttons on their sleeves were replaced with a thin stripe of gold lace, which became a thick stripe when promoted from warrant to commissioned officer. While the great majority were a credit to their branch the decision to stop their daily issue of neat rum was not entirely unconnected with cases of alcoholism and the court martial returns.

By 1916 over a hundred executive branch lieutenant commanders were promoted annually to commander in two six-monthly batches; similarly forty commanders were promoted to captain. As might be expected leadership and personality carried more weight than the powers of intellect and

administration, qualities associated with peacetime promotion. A new breed of senior office
was emerging that contrasted with the highly conformist and rather taciturn battleshi
admirals and captains who had fought at Jutland. Midshipman Layard in the battle-cruise
Indomitable remembers the latter as 'remote and mysterious people who did not consider
necessary to establish personal contact with those under their commands. In two years, as fa
as I can recall, there was never an occasion when our captain ever addressed the men with
pep talk. . . . Not once did our squadron admiral come on board, neither did Admiral Beatt
even after Jutland'.[9]

Although the demand for lower deck personnel in 1914–15 was much greater than anticipatec
the Admiralty Manning Department seldom failed to find ratings to commission new ships o
'stone frigates', as shore establishments were called. More boys were recruited to be trained in les
time than pre-war; short-service ordinary seamen were put through an intensive six-week course i
Devonport barracks before going to sea. The bulk of extra ratings was provided throug
temporary additions to the reserves and men entered for 'Hostilities Only'. More crucial was th
problem of training; to man new vessels petty officers and leading rates had to be drafted fror
seagoing ships and replaced by boys and untrained men. Very soon the Grand Fleet became on
vast advancement school – all the while still keeping an eye on the High Seas Fleet.

In 1889 an unwise decision to remove qualified seaman schoolmasters from the fleet ha
committed the academic education of ships' companies to a 'competent person' appointed by th
captain. Even with help from officers the system could not cope with the flood of young sailor
anxious to better themselves scholastically with higher rate in mind. So Jellicoe arranged fo
certificated civilian schoolmasters to be enlisted and appointed to the fleet; results were highl
encouraging, leading to the inception of Higher Education Test for warrant and commissione
ranks.

Specialized gunnery, torpedo, wireless and signals training stopped in August 1914 when rating
were mobilized but started again as soon as sufficient instructors could be found. From the
onwards the schools in and around home ports turned out thousands of men for the fleet an
armed auxiliaries. The prospect of a month or two ashore ensured that there were plenty c
volunteers to take whatever course was on offer.

Men volunteering to serve for the period of 'Hostilities Only' featured increasingly in ship
complements after 1914. What was their relationship with regular servicemen? Able Seama
Trystan Edwards joined as an HO and reckoned that his colleagues were mostly:

> manual labourers or clerks with an occasional sprinkling of commercial travellers . . . that could be divided up into two main classes. The first consisted of youngsters who joined at an age when they were sufficiently malleable to receive the Navy Stamp. After two years many of these, in their manners and outlook, became almost indistinguishable from regular ratings, so compelling are the social standards established on the lower deck. The others, a much smaller class, were too old to become exactly like bluejackets, but each made an individual adjustment to his new environment. But whether educated or uneducated, modest or immodest, capable or incapable, rich or poor, they one and all were submitted by the bluejackets to certain test of character, by which their status in this strange world of natural men – where money values do not count – was determined with extraordinary precision.[10]

Others took less tolerant views, finding fault with the HOs' clumsy and inconsiderate manners which they called 'ignorant', implying failure to measure up to the social standards of the lower deck. Occasionally they were segregated, as happened in one battleship where two steel crowfoots suspending the mess tables were fitted half-way down the mess table and marked the barrier:

> Between the 'haves' and 'have nots'. Towards the ship's side sat the senior hands, leading seamen and a few three badge ABs recalled from pension. These people argued for ever about the Channel Fleet, Charlie Beresford and training brigs in which they first went to sea. Up the other end sat the HO able seamen who discussed Leeds United, Newcastle and life in the coal pits.[11]

Despite the introduction of Military Service Acts in 1916, culminating eventually in general conscription, the manpower shortage in 1917 became sufficiently acute for the Admiralty to decide on recruiting 'an organization of women', their purpose to relieve men from shore duties. Walker, the Assistant Secretary revealed that:

> We were fortunate in obtaining the services of Dame Katherine Furse GBE as head of the new service, who had up till then been Commandant-in-Chief of the Women's VAD. She attracted several former helpers and at the first meeting at the Admiralty the Second Sea Lord explained what was needed. After inviting questions he turned to Dame Katherine saying 'Now you know what is wanted, go away and produce a scheme. If you want any help ask the Assistant Secretary.' The women were astonished . . . and could hardly believe they were being given a free hand and not tied down by a multitude of regulations.[12]

Choice of an appropriate name was important as some women's corps had acquired less than attractive soubriquets. Women's Auxiliary Naval Corps (WANKS) and Women's Auxiliary Naval Service (WANS) were discarded in favour of Women's Royal Naval Service, a title quickly approved by the Sovereign. From that moment the Wrens never looked back.[13]

Terms of service, pay, allowances, regulations and design of uniform were announced in Admiralty Weekly Orders and a *Times* advertisement asked for 'Women for the Navy – New Shore Service to be formed.' This took care of the officers, ratings being recruited from single girls over eighteen at employment exchanges. Right from the start the selection boards demanded high standards from applicants, a policy that soon paid off. Wren officers were given broadly martial training with parade ground drill, gymnastic exercises and how to fire a

Dame Katherine Furse, Commandant WRNS

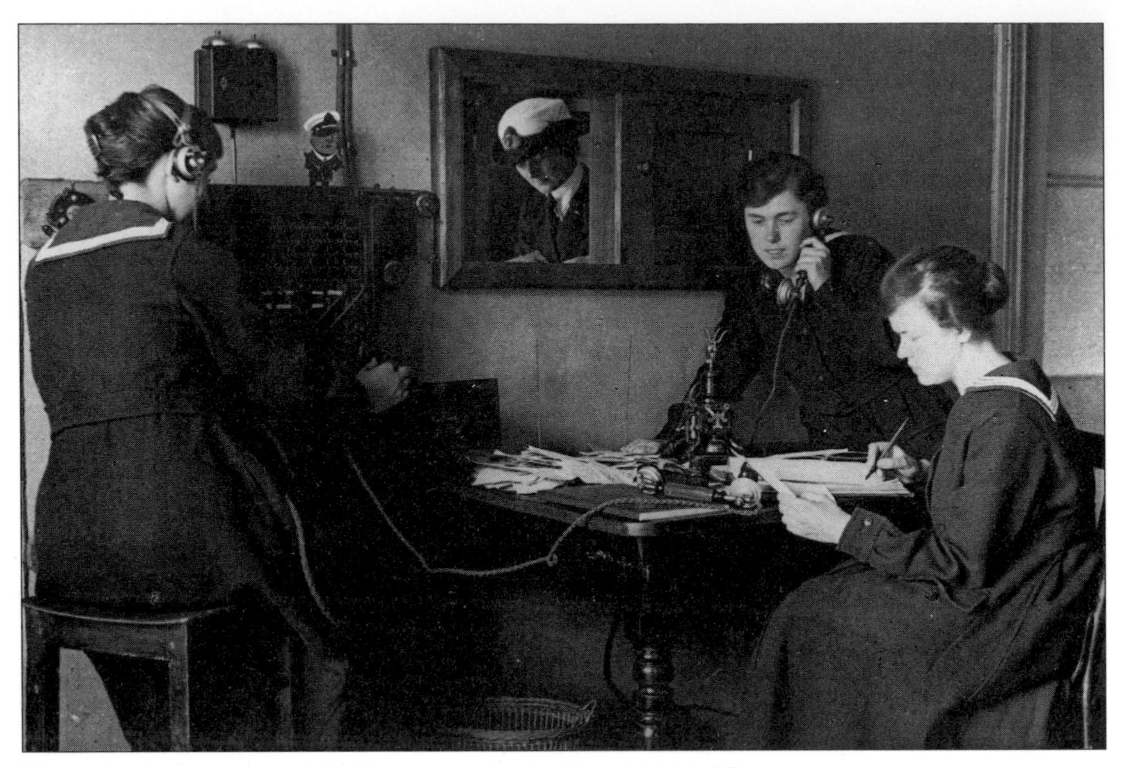

Wren telephone operators, 1917. Note the miniature effigy of Admiral Beatty

revolver. They attended lectures on naval history and the naval way of life, while ratings received similar basic training at the Crystal Palace. From there Wrens were sent all over the country for more specialist instruction as cooks, stewards, writers, telephonists, telegraphists, coders, drivers, dispatch riders, porters in victualling stores, sailmakers, turners, fitters and storekeepers. By the end of 1918 their strength exceeded 7,000, and many were employed overseas in Malta and Gibraltar; all had released officers and men for the fleet. In time they were acknowledged as the best among the women's services.

It came as no surprise that the more conservatively minded officers and senior ratings regarded girls in uniform with scepticism and disapproval; women had only just emerged from the crinoline stage figuratively speaking and had yet to receive the Parliamentary vote. There were cynics, too, among the younger officers if one accepts the opinion of an RNAS pilot who wrote from his air station: 'Wrens only waste time and retard work. Women are no use whatsoever as outside workers and these dear souls are in the WRNS because of its novelty rather than its utility.[14]

In HMS *Excellent* Wrens served as waitresses and cooks in the wardroom. Even so the strait-laced commander took a pessimistic view, remembering the activities of sailors in foreign ports and the evening amusements of young officers. In fact he saw sex rearing its ugly head – on Whale Island of all places. But as is so often the case when the worst is expected the Wrens turned out to be a great success and everybody was sorry when they were demobilized after the war. There was one untoward incident, recalled by Captain Crooke when:

> About a week after the Wrens arrived the commander came to my office with a very glum face, to report that on the previous evening he had come across one of our men embracing a Wren in the Rock Garden. I directed the Wren officer to deal with the female delinquent – in public before the rest of the detachment – and said I would see the man.
>
> Him I found to be a 3rd class Officer's Steward and very ill looking to boot. I sentenced him to 14 days' No. 10A and told him to tell everyone else that the next offender would get a fortnight in cells and that the east end of the bridge was the limit for osculation.[15]

Wren writer, *c.* 1919

1917 found the Allies in low spirits. At sea the Germans had started unrestricted submarine warfare and commerce sinkings rose to an alarming scale before convoys could be properly organized. On the Western Front there was little to show for the great push on the Somme, except for another half a million to add to the long list of British casualties sustained on land and sea. Prices were mounting in the shops as losses of merchant shipping caused food shortages and the inevitable queuing. Air raids precipitated black-outs in towns and cities; road and rail transport had deteriorated. No one doubted ultimate victory but it was taking much longer than expected and the British people were weary. On the lower decks of the fleet the mood was changing. In ships with large and varied complements ratings worried about the inadequacy and irregularities of pay. Not only had inflation all but overtaken Churchill's pre-war pay improvements but feelings of injustice became more pronounced as men in the fleet saw one increase after another being granted to civilian workers while they, the fighting men, were ignored. Again, Royal Fleet Reservists received pension as well as pay, but men reaching pensionable age had to forego their pensions until finally released. The pay of HO ratings also caused resentment. Some were paid more than their active service opposite numbers while others received bonus reimbursements from former employers. To the average bluejacket trying to make ends meet it didn't seem fair.

Yexley published some of the grievances in *The Fleet* early in 1917 and in July senior ratings on leave in London at the Union Jack Club drafted an appeal containing five requests for better pay and conditions. This was taken up by newspapers and discussed in Parliament but elicited no reaction from Whitehall. However, when the General Federation of Trades Unions – many of whose members were serving – applied pressure on the government for increases in service pay the alarm bells started to ring. A Committee on Soldiers and Sailors Pay was set up under a former First Lord and early in September the Admiralty, with Cabinet approval, agreed to some concessions. These included paying the progressive increase of 3*d* per day to able seamen after three years instead of six, a slightly increased messing allowance, abolishing the stoppage of pay after men had been thirty days in hospital, raising the basic pension by 1*d* per day and paying pensions on reaching the required date. Since clothing prices had risen by 30 per cent a kit upkeep allowance was also granted, thus conceding the principle of a free uniform issue. These concessions came into force on 1 October.

Meanwhile from mid-July the Grand Fleet spent two months in Rosyth where the canteen was patronized by ratings to congregate and discuss the situation. Soon after return to Scapa men exchanged ship visits to put finishing touches to a further 'petition and statement of demands presented to the Admiralty by the Chief Petty Officers, Petty Officers and Non Commissioned Officers of His Majesty's Grand Fleet'. There were six 'demands' on the same lines as the London appeal, except that a 50 per cent pay rise was sought, together with a substantial increase in messing allowance. The text of the preamble claimed that an appeal of this nature was the only method of airing complaints, inferring that the previous petition had been ignored. Phraseology included 'deepest resentment' and 'intensified discontent' among ratings and that concessions were 'indispensably necessary'.[16]

The Board and most senior officers believed that outside agitators, aided by serving trade unionists and home port lower deck societies, were stirring up trouble. Commander-in-Chief Portsmouth stated: 'the spirit of Trades Unionism seems to be slowly permeating the different branches of the service in RN Barracks, but at present with very little effect'. And he cited Yexley as someone whose activities 'might be suppressed with advantage'. Commanding the 2nd Battle Squadron Vice-Admiral de Robeck went further by stating: 'the lower deck has lost confidence in the powers of the Board of Admiralty and . . . have gravitated towards trades unionism . . . it does exist and to such an extent that the fact should not be neglected, as if allowed to grow it will be impossible to eradicate'.[17]

In the 1st Battle Squadron Admiral Madden attributed much of the unrest to deterioration in standards of HO ratings, which infected ships' companies with 'socialistic ideas'. Beatty wrote to the Admiralty emphasizing 'the urgent necessity for an immediate increase in pay' but did not consider that serious discontent existed on the lower deck. What upset the Commander-in-Chief and his commanding officers about the Grand Fleet petition was not the nature of its contents but that a committee of responsible senior ratings had submitted a list of 'demands' contrary to King's Regulations and, more seriously, subversive to discipline. That the authorities were uneasy was underlined when the master-at-arms and gunner's mate of the battleship *Resolution* were arrested and tried by court martial in Scapa Flow for fomenting sedition. Significantly they only received nominal sentences.

When announced in October the Admiralty concessions were coolly received by the lower deck. What they wanted was a fair increase in pay and messing allowance; it was not until a deputation from Trades Unions and Parliament complained to the Prime Minister that the Admiralty took a second look. At the end of November the Cabinet agreed to increase service pay. Within a week the Admiralty announced to the fleet a 2*d* per day increase for able seamen rates with 5*d* for chief petty officers. For the time being the heat had been taken out of the situation.

Moving the fleet base from Scapa to Rosyth in April 1917 was a wise and popular decision. It coincided with the arrival of the vanguard of the United States Naval Forces in Queenstown (Cobh) then commanded by Vice-Admiral Lewis Bayly. Between Vice-Admiral Sims, United States Navy and Bayly developed strong mutual respect and affection; harmony between the two navies followed and the first milestone in Anglo-American naval relations had been reached. When the US battleships joined the Grand Fleet later in the year the same occurred. 'Nothing would have been easier than a clash of ideas', remarked Chatfield, Beatty's chief of staff, 'between two Services which had never been to sea together before.' The Americans adopted RN signals, administrative orders, codes and in all manner acted as a unit of the fleet. Occasional friction ashore between bluejackets and enlisted men was of little consequence. 'They (US Navy) are really heart and soul in the business,' wrote Jellicoe to Beatty, 'and they are not influenced by the national jealousies which apparently must always exist between European nations.'[18] The first sign of a special relationship?

On going to sea the fleet was now better armed and better protected against shell fire; everyone was required to wear anti-flash hoods and gloves at action stations to prevent the terrible burns experienced at Jutland. Heavy ships carried an anti-Zeppelin fighter plane on one turret and a two-seater reconnaissance on another, both ready for launching; the aircraft either landed ashore or flopped down in the sea near a destroyer for crew rescue. In the new battle-cruiser *Furious*, partially converted to aircraft carrier, Squadron Commander Dunning became the world's first aviator to make a flight deck landing – the Naval Air Service clearly possessed talent. All too late because the day bombing of London by German aircraft in 1917 led to the creation of a unified Royal Air Force. On 1 April 1918 the RNAS ceased to exist, handing over some 2,500 aircraft and 55,000 officers and men. The Admiralty had to accept, albeit grudgingly, and for the rest of the war the change made little difference. Unfortunately the Establishment still treated aeroplanes with scepticism, disparaging their potential and the performance of pilots and observers – those 'unconventional and outspoken young men with little or no knowledge of the sea and ships'. In July 1918 seven Sopwith Camels took off from *Furious* to bomb and destroy the Zeppelin sheds at Tondern – the first positive proof of naval air power.

With spirits restored in the Grand Fleet it was unfortunate that its former distinguished commander proved less successful as First Sea Lord. In 1917 the war entered a crucial stage as monthly merchant ship losses reached the million ton mark and the possibility of national defeat was contemplated by Lloyd George and his Cabinet. Jellicoe found the going hard. His obsession for centralized control frustrated delegation of business; his cautiously pessimistic attitude did not suit the Prime Minister. Only just in time was the convoy system adopted. In a July Cabinet reshuffle Sir Eric Geddes, a man of ability and driving power, was appointed First Lord when public opinion was losing confidence in the Admiralty and the Young Turks in the fleet were openly recommending that changes be made in the Navy's direction of the war. The slow decline in U-boat attacks was offset by more than one disappointing minor action in the North Sea; the Navy's stock was low. Just before Christmas Jellicoe was curtly, if not brutally, dismissed by Geddes who appointed Admiral Sir Rosslyn Wemyss to succeed him. Two days later Vice-Admiral Roger Keyes replaced Bacon in command at Dover.

In March 1918 German armies launched a massive offensive on the Western Front in a final desperate attempt to overwhelm Allied forces. Field Marshal Haig issued his famous 'backs to the wall' Order of the Day and the War Cabinet in Whitehall virtually demanded that every marine in the Grand Fleet should be sent immediately to the Front, a proposition that Wemyss successfully resisted.

All, however, was not gloom. The idea of blocking the Zeebrugge and Ostend exits to the canal from Bruges to prevent the passage of U-boats and light craft had been broached for some time. Various schemes had been suggested but not until February was Keyes's audacious plan approved; there was no lack of volunteers. After two postponements the raiding force sailed from Dover on the eve of St George's Day, 23 April, with three blockships in company with the old cruiser *Vindictive* and a number of RNVR-manned motor launches. At midnight under cover of smoke *Vindictive* secured alongside the Zeebrugge mole, landing 700 marines and 200 seamen to divert attention and destroy the enemy batteries; meanwhile the blockships approached the canal entrance escorted by Keyes in a destroyer. In the face of heavy shell and machine-gun fire the blockships were sunk as intended and their crews rescued. The viaduct in the mole was blown up by an old submarine filled with explosive and the landing parties recalled after effecting some damage. As *Vindictive* withdrew under cover of smoke Private Feeney RMLI recorded that on going below: 'we saw the result of our landing; one thing was certain – it cost a great deal of blood. I shall never forget the sight . . . dead and dying lying on the decks where, but a few hours before, they ate, drank and played cards. In the light of day it was a shambles.'[19]

Personal bravery was exceptional – eight VCs were gained – and casualties heavy, the marines sustaining the bulk of the 635 killed and wounded. But although the canal was only blocked for a week or so the psychological effect was staggering. Congratulations poured in as the exploit caught the popular imagination of the whole country. It boosted the Army's spirits reeling from the German onslaught and above all restored faith in the Navy. 'We can put our heads up again' wrote an admiral to Keyes, while Churchill reckoned that Zeebrugge had given the Navy back 'the panache it had lost at Jutland'. Captain Carpenter of *Vindictive* wrote: 'The crux of all fighting lies with the personnel, a fact borne out again and again on this particular night just as throughout past history.'

❖❖❖

In shore lower-deck circles the unusual means by which the December 1917 pay increases had been achieved led the agitators to seek a more fruitful method of redressing grievances. The existing rules whereby a complainant submitted his case through his commanding officer was, in their view, long winded and biased towards higher authority. Instead they wanted direct access to the Admiralty, either through a spokesman appointed by the Commodores of Barracks or through approved benefit societies or through a permanent lower deck staff at Whitehall. Another idea was the election of a lower deck MP. If Charlie Beresford was able to address the House why not an active service or pensioner rating? On the grounds that any form of grievance petitioning would inevitably tend to alienate men from their officers the Admiralty flatly refused to consider any of these ideas. Officers were reminded of their responsibilities for ratings' welfare and warned to be on the alert.

Yexley was careful to distance himself from these approaches; instead he published a proposal early in 1918 for an Admiralty Welfare Department, an idea that must have appealed to the Second Sea Lord because he set up in August a Naval Personnel Committee, responsible for lower deck service conditions.

On 29 August the entire London police force went on strike in support of a pay rise and union recognition; both demands were appreciably and immediately met by the government. To forestall the possibility of the lower deck following suit, Yexley sent a confidential memorandum to Geddes advising action because of 'present grave discontent' and describing the lower deck as 'one great combustible mass . . . should an explosive point be touched – the whole Navy would burst into flame'. He specified sixteen separate complaints 'many of them trivial in themselves but in aggregate forming a very dangerous combination of pin pricks'. Pay was highlighted as top

Damage to cruiser *Vindictive* after Zeebrugge Raid, April 1918

priority and in a Navy with 38 per cent married ratings he stressed the 'great irritation' caused by petty leave restrictions in home ports. Copies of the memorandum were sent to the King, the Cabinet and members of the Board of Admiralty.

During the ensuing investigation Yexley was invited to the Admiralty by Geddes to discuss the grievances. At the end of September Geddes informed Lloyd George that 'although there is a certain amount of dissatisfaction on the lower deck there is no probability of this assuming proportions that would impair discipline or lead to any serious incident'. He added that some concessions had been announced, more would follow but the root cause was pay. This he had already addressed to the Treasury but it still had to be settled. If a crisis existed it had been averted for the present.[20]

Throughout the summer the Grand Fleet suffered a serious blow in the shape of a Spanish 'flu epidemic. 'Almost every ship was heavily affected,' wrote a midshipman, 'in *Revenge* we had over 600 cases. The lucky ones who avoided the infection were sent ashore in watches for a route march each day as it was thought that plenty of fresh air might keep the bug away.' There were many deaths in ships and shore training establishments and in home waters the operational strength of naval forces fell to a perilous level of efficiency. Fortunately the outbreak coincided with the collapse of the German armies which also marked the end of the war for the High Seas Fleet. An intended sortie to raid the mouth of the Thames and Dover as a last ditch effort, triggered off mutinies; by 4 November the red flag was hoisted in their naval ports.

When the armistice was declared on 11 November London went mad; a crowd surged up Whitehall calling for the Board of Admiralty to appear, which they did, to great acclamation. In the Grand Fleet assembled in the Forth was the destroyer *Tobago*, where Leading Seaman Henry Hill:

> received the good news at 10.15. But only when the signal came through from the flagship 'Splice the mainbrace' was there any sign of excitement. . . . Tonight we are engaged in making as much noise and commotion as possible. . . . Every ship is ablaze with lights, the large ships playing their searchlights and the small ones firing Verys and rockets. Every ship . . . trying to outdo the others. Drums and bands in full swing. Bells are ringing. Sirens and foghorns. . . . Everyone is shouting himself hoarse. A motor boat has just passed decorated with flags and lights . . . the band is playing all the ragtime music.[21]

Such exhilaration was not unreservedly shared by Beatty and his officers, nor by the Admiralty. Their mood was caught by Wemyss who recorded: 'There can be no naval officer who does not see the end of war without a feeling of incompleteness that . . . does not arise from any sense of failure. . . . The Navy has won a victory greater than Trafalgar, though less spectacular.'[22] And the sentiment expressed by more than one senior rating was 'Why stop fighting when we have got them on the run?' Ten days later an augmented Grand Fleet sailed to escort the German fleet to its anchorage in the Forth. 370 warships manned by 90,000 officers and men in two long columns met the German fleet in single line ahead. Turning sixteen points (180 degrees) in succession to form up on either beam, the British fleet brought their former adversaries into the Forth, thence to their anchorage at Inchkeith. Finally, as each ship of the Grand Fleet passed *Queen Elizabeth*, they cheered the man whose leadership had inspired such confidence in the last two critical years. The flagship's company were assembled on the quarterdeck so that Beatty could say a few words. He preferred to say nothing, but as he went down to his cabin he turned and faced them: 'Didn't I tell you they would have to come out?'

CHAPTER EIGHT

The Navy in Trouble

In ships where the complaints are not strictly attended to, duly investigated and endeavoured to be removed, they are only smothered for a time: and if they do not break out in some acts of insubordination, deep seated discontent is produced.

Captain Francis Liardet, Recollections, *1849*

In 1919 the country faced a world that was not yet at peace, an economy plagued by colossal war debt and the spectre of mass unemployment. On demobilization the fighting man received a suit of civilian clothes, a pair of medals, a small cash gratuity and – if he was lucky – the thanks of his commanding officer. In 'civvy street' he found bitterness and disillusion at the way Government was being mismanaged by a privileged class, a factor that turned the electorate towards socialism and in some cases communism. When the Labour Party came into power in 1924 and 1929 neither Government lasted long but the writing was on the wall; in 1926 a revolutionary situation was created by the General Strike. During the first twelve post-war years the social structure of the Navy took some hard knocks.

In the opinion of the seagoers, experience of war had not improved the reputation of the Admiralty in which few officers had served or were aware of its functions. The younger element believed the Lords Commissioners to be an amorphous body of elderly gentlemen, while the more senior blamed wartime disasters on inefficient staff work. The answerability for personnel, split between the Second Sea Lord and Fourth Sea Lord (pay and pensions), was not always sensitively handled and the lower deck imagined Admiralty officials as a tight-fisted bunch with no thought for their welfare. The Board would argue that wartime conditions and increase of personnel from a pre-war peak of 150,000 to over 38,000 officers and 410,000 ratings in 1918 had presented unforeseen and near insuperable problems. By far the most crucial was pay.

During hostilities, prices in the UK had risen two and a half times. Furthermore, officers and men were quick to notice the substantially higher pay enjoyed by US and Australian personnel; only a few HO entries wanted to sign on for further service because of inadequate reimbursement. When granted twenty-eight days' post-Armistice leave some ratings had to return to duty early simply because they could not afford to live at home. Much of what they found ashore was unpalatable, according to *Queen Elizabeth*'s chief yeoman of signals who told Captain Chatfield: 'My wife, sir, lives in a small house in Portsmouth. I send her all I can, but she can hardly exist and pay the rent. Next door there are wealthy munition workers, their wives and daughters wearing fur coats and playing new pianos. It is hard to bear.'[1]

Officers were also feeling the pinch, hardly unexpected as their basic pay had not been reviewed for fifty years; only engineer, medical and marine officers had benefited after their rates were slightly increased in 1903. Pension scales had not changed since 1870.

At the end of 1918 the Admiralty's Financial Secretary warned the Board of the 'need for prompt and sympathetic consideration'[2] and the First Lord approached the Cabinet 'for an immediate and liberal increase in pay'. The Treasury agreed, inferring that recommendations of an investigatory committee would be more or less accepted.

Chaired by Admiral Sir Martyn Jerram, a Naval Pay Committee was set up in 1919, their instructions to review ratings' pay and allowances. A similar committee under Rear Admiral Sir Lionel Halsey was convened to do likewise for officers. Twelve advisory representatives from the lower deck were officially attached to the Jerram Committee, who visited home ports to obtain evidence from elected witnesses; unofficially a hundred lower deck delegates met in London, with reporters present, to discuss pay claims. This event may have influenced the Government to announce at the end of January the grant of large interim pay increases pending final recommendations. Jerram reported on 27 March, coinciding with a similar committee set up by Beatty in the Grand Fleet. Six weeks later the Cabinet accepted forty-two out of sixty recommendations, ten were stood over and eight overruled. This time there were no half measures, an AB's pay increased from 1*s* 8*d* to 4*s* per day, a petty officer from 3*s* to 7*s* and a Weekly Order referred to 'the great permanent improvements in pay, allowances and pensions'.[3]

News of pay increases were widely acclaimed in the Navy and indeed throughout the country, the *Daily Telegraph* (10 May) remarking: 'An old scandal, which lay heavily on the nation, has at last been removed.' Rather less favourable reactions followed Halsey's recommendations; officers gained substantial pay and allowance increases, a lieutenant receiving 70 per cent more, a commander's pay doubled and a captain's pay rather more than doubled. The new rates were linked to variations in the cost of living; those for the lower deck were not, an oversight that caused serious misgivings later. Although ratings over twenty-five were granted marriage allowance in 1920 the Board turned down a recommendation for officers' marriage allowance, which would have brought the Navy in line with the Army and RAF, on the grounds that it would be a detrimental step. Presumably the pre-war sentiment that an officer should be wedded to the service still prevailed. When the Admiralty moved in 1924 to change their decision the Treasury argued that the 1919 rates incorporated an element of marriage allowance and would not budge unless all officers accepted a cut.[4] Lack of an allowance certainly put a strain on early married life in the wardroom, while the continuation of half pay for unemployed officers was another tribulation.

On promotion to Admiral of the Fleet Beatty hauled down his flag in *Queen Elizabeth* on 7 April 1919; from this date that incomparable force, the Grand Fleet, ceased to exist. Admiral Sir Charles Madden was appointed to command the newly formed Atlantic Fleet, supported by the smaller Home Fleet. In May it was the turn of the 1st Battle Squadron led by Admiral Fremantle in *Revenge* to guard the German fleet in Scapa Flow where they had been anchored since November 1918. Supplied with indifferent food from Germany and forbidden to go ashore the crews of the German ships were demoralized and mutinous. Officers lacked authority, orders were countersigned by the men's committee and in the words of an officer in *Malaya* 'the sight of discipline and efficiency gone to pot. The messdecks were in an appalling condition of dirt and the officers dumb with shame when our men came on board'.[5] The possibility of the Germans scuttling their fleet was not overlooked and plans had been made to seize their ships after the Armistice period expired on 23 June. All appeared normal when Fremantle took his squadron to

German battle-cruiser *Hindenberg* sunk at Scapa Flow

sea for exercises early on 21 June; shortly after noon he received a signal from Scapa Flow: 'German battleships sinking.' Returning at full speed there was little that could be done; by 5 p.m. the great majority of the German ships were sunk or beached.

Next day Midshipman Kenneth Harkness in *Revenge* saw the big German battle cruiser *Hindenberg* sunk upright in shallow water with upper deck awash. Obtaining permission to sail over in a whaler with four other midshipmen to have a look, the party arrived alongside, and took off their boots and trousers, which they hid in the superstructure:

> [We] wandered about seeing what loot we could find. I tried to get hold of the enormous copper steaming light but that was too heavy so I found a smaller trifle. My fellow midshipmen also managed to gather up something and we were just about to shove off and return to *Revenge* when we saw an Admiral's barge approaching. Feeling a bit worried we dashed under cover in the superstructure. It was Rear Admiral Commanding Orkneys and Shetlands. So when he had gone round and had both arms full of equipment we came out and said 'Please, sir, can we take away what we have got?' He was in no position to refuse. Returning later to *Revenge* we saw a general signal 'Nobody is to go aboard German ships.'[6]

In contrast to the prompt settlement of the pay dispute the order to commence demobilization was not given until January 1919, when pamphlets and notices were distributed throughout the fleet to explain the procedure. The Government insisted on priority being given to those needed to revitalize industry, releasing men who had been among the last to be called up, and contradicting the popular 'first in first out' principle, that became the main cause of Army mutinies in France and England. With smaller numbers involved the Navy was more successful, although it took time to find sufficient long-service men to relieve reservists and HO personnel that comprised 80 per cent of most ships' companies. By April there were still 40,000 men awaiting release.

As expected the Navy played a significant role in making good the after-effects of war. First task was to clear the North Sea of German and Allied minefields; in HM Patrol Boat P47 the commanding officer addressed the ship's company:

> The Mine Clearance Service has been inaugurated by Lloyd's to clear the seas of the menace of mines. It is a purely voluntary service. . . . The money is good. We get a bounty of five pounds for every German mine and one pound for every Allied mine we sweep up. On top of our service pay we receive two guineas per week danger money. Think it over, men, before making your decision. You have the choice of taking long leave with your families or postponing your leave and engaging on further war service. . . . All men who don't wish to volunteer, fall out.[7]

Silver badge of Mine Clearance Service, worn on cuff

The only two who moved were ex-coalminers awaiting discharge after six months' service. For most ratings, 'danger' money more than doubled the new rates of pay.

Service in the Baltic, for which many officers volunteered in hopes of a scrap, did not meet everyone's expectations. In 1919 the Baltic Squadron, under the command of the intrepid Rear Admiral Sir Walter Cowan, comprised cruisers, destroyers, submarines, coastal motor boats, auxiliaries and the new cruiser *Vindictive*, converted to seaplane carrier. In protecting the newly declared independence of Esthonia, Latvia, Lithuania and Finland against aggression by Bolshevik and other forces they faced a highly complex international situation. Rising to the occasion the Navy achieved its purpose, if success can be measured in terms of gratitude received from Baltic states. Coastal motor boats gallantly torpedoed Bolshevik battleships in Kronsdadt harbour, *Vindictive*'s aircraft performed useful reconnaissance and destroyers bombarded; hardly a day passed without action of some kind. At Libau no leave was given as hundreds of ravenous refugees thronged the jetty, but at Reval and Riga officers and ratings received a tremendous welcome from the people.

Nevertheless, much went wrong. The service was hard, winter weather severe, there was no proper base, and distribution of provisions, canteen supplies and cigarettes was faulty. Even the pay was sometimes in arrears. Men would have put up with these things cheerfully if they felt that they were unavoidable. Since Britain was not at war they did not understand why they were there; a few were influenced by wireless broadcasts of Bolshevik propaganda. The First Flotilla of Destroyers that left the Baltic in August to give leave was considered by Cowan to be 'a model of discipline and cheerful high war spirits'. Yet on learning they had to return to the Baltic in October, 150 seamen broke out of their ships in Port Edgar leaving half the flotilla to be made up from the Atlantic Fleet. Most deserters gave themselves up in Edinburgh but forty-four made their way to London to present a petition to Whitehall. Arrested by the police at King's Cross they were escorted to Chatham. Grievances added up to a thorough dislike of Baltic service and a desire for extra pay as given to the Army in North Russia and the mine clearance ships. Officers and petty officers must have known that disaffection existed yet did nothing to report it.

In November an outbreak of mutiny in *Vindictive* at Copenhagen was dealt with firmly and successfully by the commanding officer, with the loyal support of most of the ship's company; there was also trouble on board the minesweepers. In December a large number of ratings refused duty in Cowan's flagship, the cruiser *Delhi*, after hearing of a change in the ship's Christmas programme, an incident not well handled by the captain. And although Cowan considered Baltic service sufficiently arduous to justify extra pay and additional leave, he failed to move the Government, through the Admiralty, to make any concessions.

❖❖❖

As the Navy rejoiced over the generosity of the pay code the Admiralty heaved a sigh of relief and turned their attention towards a better system of handling lower deck requests and complaints of unfair treatment. The task was not made easier by the various Benefit Societies, which included pensioners and civilians, assuming a political role and exposing their members to subversive influence. Before Jerram submitted his pay recommendations Admiral Heath, Second Sea Lord, told the Board:

> an organized attempt is being made by socialist and syndicalist circles to introduce into the Navy a Lower Deck Union on Trade Union lines. . . . The position with which we are now faced is this: if we do nothing there is the possibility that the Lower Deck Union will become an accomplished fact. On the other hand, if we are prepared to allow the men a recognized means of presenting their grievances (real or imaginary) and aspirations collectively, then I believe that the danger of an unauthorized union will be averted.[8]

The Admiralty's method of defusing the situation was to set up a Welfare Committee comprised of senior officers but with elected lower deck representatives attached to it in an advisory capacity. Admiral Jerram chaired its first meeting early in 1920, declaring the agenda to be pay, pensions, promotion, messing, canteens and uniform but not naval policy, discipline or grievances. Some of the 300 submissions were quite impracticable and it was not until July that the Admiralty approved only a quarter of them. Exasperated by this news and encouraged by rising membership a deputation from the Benefit Societies led by two chief writers stormed up to Whitehall for an interview with Beatty, now First Sea Lord, to discover Admiralty intentions. After heated discussion they left unappeased; the Welfare Committee had failed and was suspended. Meanwhile a wave of political and industrial militancy swept the country nourished by Labour activists. A revolutionary rally of ex-Servicemen in Trafalgar Square was followed by a TUC conference at Portsmouth where naval ratings were harangued to refuse service in the Baltic. At this stage the Admiralty had had enough. Special Branch officers moved in, civilian agitators were arrested, tried and sentenced and two ratings discharged from the service. In December an Admiralty order recognized the proper functions of the Benefit Societies but ordered them to confine activities to benevolent matters and not engage in the 'aspirations, grievances and disabilities' of the lower deck. Naval newspapers, e.g. *The Fleet* and *The Bluejacket*, were scrutinized for disruptive articles, while attempts by ratings to state grievances to MPs were frowned upon. Although Yexley continued to edit *The Fleet* his health was deteriorating and he was unable to keep up with developments. Between 1919 and 1927 he lectured at RN Staff College on lower deck welfare. He died in 1933.

A year later the Welfare Committee was replaced by a Welfare Conference, the first being held in May 1922. It was not a success, mainly because the Treasury blocked all proposals involving extra expenditure, a point never grasped by the lower deck. At any rate, to give more time for requests to be handled it was decided to hold future conferences every two years at each home port in turn. Although little was achieved they did act as a useful safety valve, especially as the Admiralty Personnel Committee had been downgraded in status and, at Beatty's suggestion, was in 1928 made the responsibility of the Director of Physical Training and Sports. Admittedly the Admiralty went to some length to discover the true feelings of the Navy and to distinguish between genuine and fictitious grievances; perhaps their philosophy of remedial action lacked human understanding. By insisting that King's Regulations be upheld in channelling lower deck complaints through officers to higher authority both the Admiralty and Fleet failed to remove the old fear that men would be penalized for stating a grievance. Worse still, commanding officers felt that any complaint forwarded to the Admiralty cast a slur on their ship's reputation. On the brighter side came the conversion of the Grand Fleet Fund into the Royal Naval Benevolent Trust, its purpose to provide relief in distress for serving and ex-service ratings, as well as assisting those seeking employment after leaving the Navy. Administered largely by elected ratings the RNBT has continued its admirable work until the present day. Another substantial benefit occurred in 1922 when the Navy, Army and Air Force Institutes took over the canteen business for all three services as a non-profit-making concern. Various discounts became allowable to messes and individuals, while those for purchases by the ship's company and general mess – known as rebate – were paid into the ship's fund, less a small deduction for the RNBT. Every ship and shore establishment had its Canteen Committee (renamed Welfare Committee in the Second World War). The executive officer sat in the chair with elected representatives from all branches of the ship's company to administer the Ship's Fund to finance sporting activities, hire films, make grants to charities and assist dependents of men who had lost their lives. It was also a useful sounding board.

Between 1914 and 1919 the absence of shore courses for junior officers led to an imaginative decision by the Admiralty to send all wartime-promoted sub-lieutenants to Cambridge University for two terms to study 'naval and scholastic subjects with appropriate naval instructors and professors'. It was, of course, much more than that. During hostilities over 1,000 'young gentlemen' between fifteen and eighteen had served in the fleet, fought in every major action, gained many decorations and lost one third of their number. Not for nothing Army officers at Gallipoli asked the question: 'How do you train your cadets at Dartmouth?' A spell ashore in a different environment was now justified, public opinion called it 'an interesting experiment' and Rudyard Kipling summed it up in his poem 'The Scholars' with:

> They have piped the children of all the seas from the Falklands to the Bight
> And quartered them in the Colleges to learn to read and write
>
> Their eyes are sunk by endless watch their faces roughed by the spray
> Their feet are drawn by the wet sea boots they changed not night and day

Tenderly, Proctor, let them down if they do not walk as they should;
For, by God, if they owe you half a crown, you owe them four years food!

Hallowed River, most gracious Trees, Chapel beyond compare
Here be gentlemen sick of the sea – take them into your care

'I don't know we were worthy of such sentiments,' remarked one sub-lieutenant at Trinity. 'At first I found it frightfully difficult to settle down in class. So did many others. We wore plain clothes and came under the jurisdiction of our senior officers who were rather thin on the ground. . . . When picked up by a proctor for committing some breach of University discipline, all we had to say was "Naval Officer" whereupon the proctor would raise his hat and walk magisterially on.'[9] Another sub reckoned: 'It was a very good eight months, meeting not only friends in my own term but the two strata of undergraduates – those from the Army who . . . had to work hard to get their degrees and then those from the public schools. The opportunity for games was, of course, unrivalled.' Sub-Lieutenant Harkness at St John's confessed that 'we behaved rather badly. We had a branch of the University Roof Climbing Club . . . over the roofs to our next door neighbour, Trinity College, and came back with eight lavatory seats'. Examinations were held at the end of each second term accompanied by the announcement: 'No naval officer is to leave the classroom until five minutes have expired from the commencement of the examination.' Happy days. For four years Cambridge gave the subs the break they needed until a similar course could be started at the Royal Naval College at Greenwich.

Probably the Navy's most regrettable error of judgement in manning a wartime fleet was to create far too many permanent commission officers. The business of paying off warships was elementary compared with 'the most painful task that had to be carried out . . . the removal of officers who, owing to the shrinkage of the Navy, became redundant'.[10] Although similar but proportionately fewer cuts were imposed on long-service ratings they endured less hardship since many reductions were obtained by voluntary discharges under special terms. Officers of all ranks who had made the Navy their life-long vocation were a different matter.

Late in 1919 the Accountant General's committee estimated fleet peacetime requirements and with Treasury approval for compensation the Admiralty made the first attempt to persuade officers to retire. This failed and so six months later a revised scheme was launched with more generous terms for lieutenant commanders and below; only 407 out of the 650 target accepted. More difficulty was experienced with captains and commanders; as for flag officers the Board hedged a decision. At Dartmouth more vigorous measures were taken when the captain announced that there would be a 'forty per cent reduction in the four junior terms and in the big terms at Osborne. . . . Parents who gave notice before the end of the summer term . . . of withdrawing sons would be given £300'. If there were insufficient voluntary withdrawals then reductions would be made on merit. A Dartmouth master wrote:

> During that leave there were anxious discussions in many families. Very few cadets came from rich homes. In many instances the parents of a cadet had pinched and scraped to send him to Dartmouth and to keep him there until 17 after which he would cost them little. . . . There was much disappointment. . . . To continue to enter terms of a hundred or more at Osborne until January 1919 was inconsistent . . . and showed little foresight.[11]

In 1921 the Prime Minister invited former First Lord, Sir Eric Geddes, to chair a committee to review the whole field of national expenditure, which was at that time running excessively high. Among recommendations was a drastic reduction in naval expenditure. Many years later an officer wrote: 'In due course the Geddes Axe, surely the most cruel and unjust instrument ever used on a splendidly loyal service, descended with brutal force. None of us who saw those days can ever forget the stunning effect of that monstrous measure.'

A third of the captains' list were retired, also 350 lieutenants over and above the 200 who left voluntarily. All officers axed were given retired pay and gratuities commensurate with length of service; opportunities for civilian employment were slim. 'Every time a list of retirements was published', wrote the Second Sea Lord, 'I got a number of indignant and often abusive letters.'[12] Further cuts were necessary in 1926, 1929 and even later as the run down of the Navy continued, leaving the Admiralty in a no win situation. They did not want to be seen as a bad employer, but neither did they want the lists to be congested with officers they could not employ. It is interesting that the Treasury were supportive in giving retired officers reasonable terms but objected when the Admiralty tried to get preferential treatment for flag officers. In retrospect, Geddes did what had to be done and ostensibly took the blame, his name abominated by a whole generation of naval officers. The Navy's standing with public suffered appreciably but at least the same mistake was not repeated in the Second World War.

In 1922 the post-war boom in the UK started to collapse and the economy moved into recession. Early in March 1923 the Chancellor of the Exchequer announced the setting up of a committee under Sir Alan Anderson to 'enquire into the present standards of remuneration and other conditions of employment . . . in the Civil Services and in the three Fighting Services, and to make recommendations'. There was no service representation on the committee, referred to by the Secretary to the Admiralty as one of 'three business men having no prior acquaintances with the subject'. When Anderson reported in October that the pay of junior officers and ratings was too high in relation to the salaries and wages of other members of the community the Admiralty objected strongly, refuting the assumption that naval pay was adequate in 1914, arguing that the committee was ignorant of naval conditions 'and that men presently serving would undoubtedly consider it a breach of faith if any reduction were made in rates of pay'.

Rumours about pay cuts caused widespread indignation in the fleet; similar feelings were expressed by lower deck societies and the press. But when the Army Council cut the ground from under the Navy's feet by accepting Anderson's recommendations the Admiralty had to follow suit; at least they obtained the Chancellor's assurance that men now serving would not be affected. In 1925 an Admiralty Fleet Order stated that men who entered the Navy after 5 October would receive a reduced scale of pay, a cut of 1*s* per day or 25 per cent of an AB's basic salary. Junior officers were treated less harshly, a lieutenant's pay reduced from 17 to 15*s* per day. The order also stated: 'It must be clearly understood that men are not entitled to claim a right to any rate of pay or other emolument under existing scales in the event of reduced scales being introduced [but that] subject to the above – men who are serving . . . on 4 October 1925 will continue to be paid under existing scales until discharged.'[13]

Men clung to this last sentence ignoring the caution that went with it, later to be embodied in King's Regulations. Already the cost of living decrease had been applied to ratings' allowances – victualling, leave, marriage and kit upkeep – as it was to officers' pay in 1924, 1927 and 1930. On the lower deck the majority were on the 1919 scales but would sustain a further reduction in allowances in 1931, while a much smaller proportion of younger ratings were on the lower 1925 scales. It seems astonishing that the service could be run with two different rates of pay for the same work and with officers periodically losing 6 per cent of their pay.

A post-war casualty was the Royal Naval College at Osborne. As Fisher's brainchild it had served its purpose and almost every naval officer under the age of thirty had absorbed its education. Life was rigorous, discipline strict and the health of cadets unusually affected by epidemics allegedly emanating from the old stables. Three royal princes started their naval career in the college, of whom the eldest was destined to be King Edward VIII, his brothers to become King George VI and the Duke of Kent. In 1909 Osborne received unwelcome publicity when Cadet Archer-Shee was charged with stealing a 5*s* postal order from a messmate's locker and cashing it at the post office. Although the boy pleaded not guilty his parents were required to withdraw him from the service; subsequent appeals to the captain and the Admiralty were turned down. Eventually the case was taken to court, when thanks to an eminent QC the cadet was vindicated and his innocence publicly declared amid scenes of great furore. The verdict was not lost on the lower deck, conscious that in similar circumstances a rating stood little chance of challenging Admiralty ruling over miscarriage of justice. In fact the family was broken financially by the protracted legal battle.

Economy cuts put an end to any chance of the college's survival; it was formally paid off on 20 May 1919 after several instructors and teaching staff had transferred to Dartmouth, where additional accommodation had been constructed. College buildings were demolished and playing fields returned to grassland as Osborne passed into history.

Almost the last term to join were the Grenvilles, that included Hugh Gairdner who rose to captain after specializing in engineering. Writing about his experiences of the Interview Board conducted by Admiral Tupper in Whitehall, he wondered:

> What was the Board looking for? Poise? What they saw might have been sedulously laid over a shaky interior. Brains? Certainly not. Many of the boys they passed were astonishingly stupid. Manners, breeding or smartness? Perhaps those were sought but how difficult to detect smartness in a boy when he is palpitating with anxiety and has just endured hours of waiting in a billiard room. . . . Yet there is no doubt the system had merits. Guided . . . by confidential reports from headmasters . . . influenced by their knowledge of gunroom officers, the Board had unquestionably an eye for the country. They aimed to pick not so much the ready made article as those of malleable qualities. . . . From my year have come a VC, triple and double DSOs, submarine commanders whose names will go down in history, airmen, destroyer captains of renown, musicians and scholars. A few have fallen by the wayside but the greater number remained and did not let old Tupper down.

Commenting on the training his term received Gairdner judged:

> The college did little to inculcate the good behaviour expected of the NO ashore and afloat. That came later. Nor did it try to inject intelligence which is after all something one is born with and which doubtless the Interview Board tried to spot. But education on a broad front

A dormitory at Osborne – identical to those in the early days at Dartmouth

was very much Osborne's business. Term officers were there to turn us into embryo seamen and the civilian staff to give us good education, no easy task under the peculiar Selborne–Fisher set up.

One-third of instruction was spent in engineering and as much again in seamanship, navigation and signals, leaving little time for history, English, languages and the 'humanities':

Nevertheless work at Osborne was tremendously enjoyable. . . . From ships' models we let go miniature anchors and got inextricably tied up with mooring swivels, as later we were to do in the *Thunderer*. Upon the sluggish waters of the Medina we sailed in cutters or, taking the helm of steam pinnaces, steered exultantly past Samuel White's yard and into Cowes Roads. . . . When it came to engineering few held this to be a waste of time, however much we may have seen ourselves to be future captains of ships. It was borne upon us that everyone had to know at least something of the other man's job and the upper deck officer needed to know the problems of the engineer and the conditions under which the stoker worked. . . . Under the Selborne–Fisher common entry scheme executive officers could turn themselves into engineers – as 13 of our term did – and, at least on paper, engineers could return to the upper deck. . . . We accepted engineering training as part of the scene and either exulted in it or hated it according to taste.[14]

After the war, only the engineer branch remained convinced that common training and appointing was feasible and would lead to engineers achieving command. From a committee convened in 1918 to review engineer officer careers it emerged that the branch was sceptical of promotion prospects, resentful at having to wear a purple distinguishing stripe and indignant that the engineer-in-chief of the Fleet and ten engineer rear admirals were not included in the executive flag list. In addition there were grumbles that the new (E) officer was not up to his job while young executive officers complained that too much time as cadets was spent on engineering training.

Concluding that they must show their hand on the method of selection for higher posts and clarify the position of lieutenants' specialization, the Admiralty announced in July 1920:

> There is a definite distinction both as regards knowledge and capabilities between those who are to be trained in the science of naval war . . . and those who are to deal with the upkeep and maintenance of engineering and mechanical appliances . . . necessitated by complex machinery and weapons. Each side requires a special study and for this reason final separation of the branches is essential.[15]

To sugar the pill the engineer-in-chief was given extra responsibilities *vis-à-vis* the naval staff on policy matters and that although 'comparatively few higher posts' remained open to the branch it was insinuated that engineers might become Admirals Superintendent of Dockyards. But the order hastened to add that they would 'not be eligible to command the port' since that is 'the province of the Deck Officer'. Further down, the option of reverting to upper deck duties was withdrawn from lieutenants (E). A spark of hope emerged with the announcement that the engineering branch might take over the responsibility for the rapidly increasing electrical equipment in warships; in fact the Board was evenly divided on this issue. In 1929 it was agreed that engineers should take over high power installation leaving the torpedo department to maintain their hold on low power equipment, a compromise that defeated any chance to form an Electrical Branch in the foreseeable future. In comparison US naval officers continued to serve afloat in engineering or deck appointments, possessing equal status without social or professional prejudices. Free state education and open competition to Annapolis Naval Academy enabled the US Navy to be years ahead of the Royal Navy in many aspects of officer training.

Embryo engineers had not shown much interest in acquiring a knowledge of their executive duties and as further indication that the Selborne Scheme was doomed it was decided that they would start their career with four years as midshipmen at Keyham College. Apart from the older engineers no great surprise was exhibited in 1925 when the Admiralty abolished the five branches of officers established in 1915 – military, medical, accountant, naval instructor and artisan. These were replaced by twelve categories, composed of executive, engineer, medical, dental, accountant and instructor officers, chaplains, shipwright, ordnance, and electrical officers, schoolmasters and wardmasters, the last five being warrant officers.[16] By abolishing the military branch and returning the engineer to his original status with no expectancy of sea command, the decision was known among 'plumbers' as the Great Betrayal and the schism re-opened. In future (E) would merge with 'Engineer' ranks and wear the same uniform with a 'more distinct shade of purple' between the stripes, a detail that might have been more tactfully worded. The announcement was not popular in some quarters and in the technical press, although the *Morning Post* took the view that the order would 'establish the engineering officers as the highly skilled specialists they are'. Arguably the decision may not have been the best for the Navy but at least everyone now knew where they stood; a few (E) officers reverted to executive duties but the vast majority remained engineers. At Keyham the long course was firmly established with most entrants coming from public or grammar schools as Special Entries and a minority from Dartmouth.

Because mates promoted from the lower deck were generally too old to go far in the service, the Director of Naval Training proposed early in 1918 that promising young ratings should be considered for cadetships. Admiral Heath, the Second Sea Lord, disagreed, insisting that 'to be a good officer it is necessary to be a gentleman'; what he meant was that, in his opinion, a junior rating could not possess the attributes of background, education and upbringing associated with an officer. This attitude and the forbidding cost of Dartmouth training did not impress MPs, or for that matter middle ranking officers; when a committee recommended the eligibility of young rating candidates for Special Entry cadetships the Board gave way. In 1920 it was announced that provided 'a man takes a first class certificate in further special courses . . . he can become a lieutenant at 23 . . . [and] would be on a precisely similar footing to other lieutenants with regard to promotion'. The Treasury agreed to rescind fees of impecunious parents with Dartmouth cadetship in mind and arrangements were cleared for talented boy artificers to be trained as midshipmen (E). By 1926 the Revised Mate Scheme had made little headway in the seaman branch – mates (E) had done better – and in April the Admiralty exhorted the fleet 'to give every encouragement' to suitable candidates, complaining that all too few had chosen to specialize. In 1927 the first pre-war mate was promoted commander, followed by three mates (E) to engineer commander. For the next four years, however, the scheme failed to reach expectations.

After the upheaval of war the fleet took time to settle down and adjust to peacetime complements. By 1921 the Atlantic and Mediterranean fleets became major commands while lesser flag officers led cruiser squadrons in the North America and West Indies, China, East Indies and Africa stations, as well as heading Australian, Canadian and New Zealand embryo naval forces. At home there were local defence and training flotillas, a sizeable Reserve Fleet and traditional naval bases at the Nore, Portsmouth, Plymouth and Rosyth. Despite the Government's Ten Year rule which 'assumed that the British Empire would not be engaged in any great war during the next ten years' there were still world-wide interests to protect. By 1923 the Navy had reduced to 100,000 officers and men.

Naval policy in the 1920s was further influenced by the need for strict economy, especially in the consumption of oil fuel, the popular appeal of disarmament, Washington Treaty limitations on what was now a One Power Standard Navy and the Anglo-American insistence that the battleship with the big gun was still the battle winner. Thus new construction included two 35,000-ton 16-in gun battleships (*Nelson* and *Rodney*) and eight 10,000-ton 8-in gun County class cruisers whose long endurance suited protection of trade routes. Ships' company accommodation was better, including new kit lockers, and the general messing system was built in with bakeries, oil-fired galleys, steam chests and catering machinery. In 1917 Paymasters had adopted new titles to bring them in line with the executive branch and to acquire the executive curl on their stripes of rank; an extensive overhaul of the branch took place after the war. In 1922 the Supply Branch was formed and a Central Storekeeping System introduced to cut irregularities and save money, each department in a ship being allocated a monthly cash allowance.

While the Admiralty was locked in a struggle to wrest control of the Fleet Air Arm from the Air Ministry lengthy conversions produced the aircraft carriers *Hermes*, *Furious*, *Courageous* and *Glorious*. Admiralty policy on submarines was inconsistent; first they tried to get them abolished internationally then experiments were made with monster submarines carrying big guns and aircraft before resuming conventional classes. After small beginnings the Navy's Anti-Submarine School and Experimental Establishment was established in 1924 at Portland as HMS *Osprey*; top secret ASDIC (submarine detection) equipment was fitted for trial in all classes of warship. Ignoring the views expressed by Jackie Fisher and Percy Scott that submarines and aircraft had rendered the battleship obsolete, the preponderance of serious naval thought led by Beatty concentrated on battle fleet action and the lessons of Jutland. Fleet exercises of the 1920s reflected those trends, the air and underwater threat posed by naval aircraft and submarines of that era taking second place. Everywhere the Navy returned to punctilious ceremonial, brightwork stations and competition to be the smartest looking ship, the first to hoist 'Evolution completed' in general drill, the winner of the Arbuthnot Trophy marathon race, 'cock' ship in the regatta and producer of the best concert party. The fallibility of senior officers was seldom questioned;,the report of an inspecting admiral could make or mar the promotion prospects of more officers than just the captain.

One lesson of war in an increasingly technical navy was the value of specialist officers and ratings, a trend supported by Chatfield who believed specialization created 'a sphere of personal interest according to the inclination of each officer; tuned up the intellect by giving it something to feed on'. The 1920s saw the build up of seaman specialist schools, emphasis on longer courses of instruction, influence on weapon design and the emergence of 'tribal' authorities that appointed their officers and drafted their senior rates to the fleet. HMS *Vernon* moved ashore in 1923 from the hulks to occupy the whole of HM Gunwharf, superbly sited at the entrance to Portsmouth Harbour. The Signal School commanded the cream of boy entries, its officers designing their own diagonal striped tie associating 'blue blood' with 'grey matter'; the *Excellent* celebrated its centenary in 1930 with an evening tattoo on Whale Island attended by royalty. Keyham continued to train engineer officers, while instruction for engine room, electrical and ordnance artificers was now combined in four hulks comprising *Fisgard*, which in 1932 moved from Portsmouth to Chatham.

The merger of the Royal Marine Artillery and the Royal Marines Light Infantry was considered in 1919, but there was much opposition within the Corps and it was not until 1923 that amalgamation of Blue and Red Marines actually took place. For many years afterwards the story goes that the bridge fours in the officers' mess at Eastney were always one colour. As well as continuing to man part of the fleet's gun armament the Corps were earmarked to provide a striking force of infantrymen wherever needed and in 1927 a thousand Royal Marines guarded the international settlements in Shanghai against the Chinese Nationalist armies. Royal Marine Bands continued to flourish as an integral part of daily routine ashore and afloat.

Abandonment of the RM Barracks at Gosport enabled its conversion to the Boys' Training Establishment – HMS *St Vincent* – in 1927. *Impregnable* at Devonport was closed down, leaving *Ganges* and *St Vincent* to train long-service recruits. As an economy measure short-service seamen entry was re-introduced in 1928, this time seven years in the fleet and five in the reserve. Early in 1929 all recruiting was stopped temporarily as the manpower ceiling had been reached and could not be exceeded.

In 1921 the Admiralty Fleet Orders replaced Weekly and Monthly Orders. Signed 'O. Murray' – an outstanding holder of the office of Permanent Secretary – fleet orders under his guidance embodied every aspect of administrative and technical information. The section titled 'Personnel' helped to bridge the gap between the Admiralty and the fleet by producing newsworthy items written in the language of Whitehall about pay, welfare, training, health, sports and personal awards; its emphasis and coverage revealed a portrait of service life. For instance, nobody could be in any doubt that the new Asdic branch was having difficulty in recruiting volunteers. One 'order' described the musical salute appropriate for the Pope while another rather whimsically mentioned 'the discovery of a gold ring found on the golf course at Ascension Island. Claimants are to write to the Secretary of the Admiralty'. Was it ever claimed? A confidential order of 1929 expressed concern at the large number of unnatural offences in the fleet, stressed the supportive value of steadier, more reliable men to overcome the age-old problem caused by small homosexual minorities in ships' companies.

Measured in terms of crime and punishment the quality of lower deck life was in better shape. Recruitment of ratings with good character, the accent on progressive training to meet ever increasing technical requirements, the liberalization of leave arrangements and the ruthless weeding out of undesirables all tended to make for more relaxed discipline and happier ships. Although the dole queue may have influenced some men there were fewer desertions and fewer cases of buying a discharge from the service, as well as fewer summary punishments and courts martial; the latter's procedure was changed to benefit the defendant by allowing a 'prisoner's friend' to be more supportive. One important step towards better discipline was an Admiralty decision in 1919 to give recently promoted chief and petty officers a course of disciplinary training and character building at the RN Barracks; it was some years before the benefits of this scheme were felt in the fleet.

With an abundance of sport, good plain food, proper dental facilities and accent on personal hygiene the Navy of the 1920s was also becoming a healthier service; since 1914 there was far less venereal disease. Grog was still popular on the mess decks and cocktails were the fashion in the wardroom. With cheap 'pusser's' tobacco and habits acquired in wartime there were few not addicted to pipes or cigarettes; in those days nobody thought of smoking as a danger to health, which it certainly was. Until 1920 petty officers were dressed in 'square rig' and men wore sennet hats with No. 1 uniform. The daily working clothes were a white duck suit with silk and lanyard (no blue collar) while officers donned serge or superfine cloth monkey jackets. On Sunday officers wore frock coats, swords and white kid gloves for divisions, inspections and church. Every night except Sundays the dress for formal dinner was mess undress with butterfly collar and stiff shirt, Thursday being usually guest night. On hot weather stations officers and senior ratings wore throat-constricting white tunics and trousers, with pith helmets when ashore or in boats.

Stepping back into the 1920s what would be the impression of the naval officer of today? In the opinion of Commander Layard, who served in the battleship *Benbow*:

> He would find a far lower standard of education on the lower deck, many coming from a poverty background or from orphanages and Barnardo Homes. . . . Officers were less highly educated and, except for the padre or 'schoolie', he would never meet a university degree. In a foreign commission lasting two or three years he would be in a wardroom where very few

General mess dinner ready in the galley, *c.* 1922

> lieutenants were married, hence an essentially male society where the mess was . . . an officer's home and life was always fun . . . nicknames like Pilot or surnames, but throughout a commission never Christian names. . . . Without family ties and less work on board there was plenty of time for leave and recreation . . . the most rewarding feature of all was the making of deep and lasting friendships.[17]

After thirty years in the Royal Navy, over half of them on the lower deck, Lieutenant Commander Harvey remembered his first battleship, HMS *Marlborough*, sister ship to *Benbow*; as a young ordinary seaman he sat at the end of No. 4 Mess table, next to the shelf that held cutlery, condiments, tea, sugar, mess plates and bowls from which were drunk tea, cocoa or rum. He always reckoned that the dog watches (4 p.m. to 8 p.m.) were:

> the pleasantest and most interesting period on the messdecks. At one end of the table a game of solo, euchre, brag or any other of the innumerable card games was in progress, usually with slightly resented 'advisers' hovering in the background; Spoff Hammond who ran the 'gopher' shop would be mixing a concoction in a bucket to sell as lemonade; 'Brigham' Young would be writing to one of his many girls, sorting out their photos in his ditty box; 'Nobby' Hall, prospective Med Fleet light heavyweight champion, doing his shadow boxing; cooks of the mess peeling spuds and over all a buzz of conversation, jokes, taunts and cat calls making a noisy, happy background, repeated in all sixteen broadside messes.

Then came sunset and the sounding of the 'Last Post' by the bugler, its notes reaching the messdeck where: 'To hear the haunting, lovely phrases of this splendid call, echoing from the quarterdecks of half a dozen ships of war in harbour, is a most moving experience. It has for me a strange, sad beauty like a "Requiem". The Fleet is saying an evening prayer which many a sailor, though afraid to kneel, echoes in his heart.'[18]

Battleship *Rodney*'s invincible tug o' war team, trained by Royal Marine Commissioned Gunner A.F. Vickery

In 1928, when Admiral Sir Roger Keyes's command of the Mediterranean was drawing to a close, there occurred a minor dispute on board the battleship *Royal Oak* which made the Navy look extremely foolish and probably cost Keyes the post of First Sea Lord. The case revolved around Rear Admiral Collard who flew his flag in *Royal Oak* and was barely on speaking terms with his Flag Captain, Dewar or the ship's executive officer, Commander Daniel. The latter was present at a ship's dance when Collard lost his temper with the performance of the band led by Bandmaster Barnacle, shouting: 'I won't have a bugger like that in my ship.' After another occasion when the admiral publicly accused the captain and commander of incompetence, Dewar officially complained about Collard's behaviour to the Commander-in-Chief, with a letter that temporarily postponed the sailing of the Mediterranean Fleet for Gibraltar until a court of enquiry could be held. Keyes ordered Collard to strike his flag and when the press realized it was Collard of 1906 Portsmouth Barracks fame the case hit world headlines. Unaware of the facts the Admiralty had nothing to say; neither could any comment be released before the court martial of Dewar and Daniel at Gibraltar in the full glare of publicity. Daniel was charged with writing and making public subversive letters and Dewar was charged with accepting and forwarding them. Both were found guilty, dismissed their ships and severely reprimanded. Summing up the unfortunate affair *The Times* expressed 'a sense of relief and thankfulness' it was all over; in the fleet's wardrooms the word went round: 'Why shouldn't the admiral call the bandmaster a bugger. I want to know who called the bugger a bandmaster!'

By the 1930s lower deck advancement had become sluggish. The average age for promotion to leading seaman had risen from twenty-four to over twenty-seven and to petty officer from twenty-eight to thirty-two. It was rare to see a leading seaman with fewer than two badges and a petty officer with fewer than three. 25 per cent of seamen had more than twelve years' service and in most ships there were 'stripeys', old hands with no thought of promotion who posed a discipline problem since many were older than petty officers. Some would be hit by the announcement of pensions being reduced for those starting their second period of engagement after 31 March 1930. Anxiety about pay began to make itself felt.

Soon after Ramsay MacDonald's Labour government was elected in 1929, Mr A.V. Alexander, the new First Lord, proposed that officer entry to the Navy should be widened by accepting more candidates from the lower deck at a time when the Admiralty was concerned about how to reduce the excess numbers of lieutenants and lieutenant commanders. Alexander had in mind the need to 'democratize' the Navy by attracting sixteen-year-old boys with School Leaving Certificates from secondary schools to join Dartmouth, an idea flatly opposed by the Board – with the exception of the Parliamentary Secretary. An investigatory committee set up in 1931 did establish that the Dartmouth and the smaller public school intakes were 'widely democratic' but also admitted that boys owed their origins to a predominantly middle-class background and that a degree of wealth was necessary to pay Dartmouth fees. Alexander persisted with his proposal to increase the Direct (lower deck) Entry to about half the total intake, with Government and sponsored grants; a fleet order later announced the abolition of the rank of mate in favour of acting sub-lieutenant. To overcome the high age and disparity in qualifications there would be 'a system of intense tuition' for officer candidates in all subjects. Alexander was also concerned that fifteen to eighteen-year-old boys at Training Establishments were being caned too severely; but a committee that looked into the matter judged that 'caning was the most suitable punishment for boys'. Since regular caning had been inflicted on cadets and midshipmen for over a century one wonders why Alexander did not take exception to this practice too; it did not feature, of course, in punishment returns rendered to the Admiralty.

Meanwhile Admiral Sir Frederick Field became First Sea Lord and the year started badly for the Navy. In the submarine depot ship *Lucia* at Devonport there occurred mass indiscipline amounting to mutiny. *Lucia* was an unhappy ship, its crew ineptly handled through excessive working hours and restriction of Sunday leave to paint the ship before sailing for fleet exercises. Ring-leaders were punished, officers censured and the ship paid off.

But worse was to come. After the Wall Street Crash in 1929 came the failure of credit and the start of the Great Depression; early in 1931 Britain approached a grave financial crisis as unemployment nudged the three million mark. A committee on National Expenditure was formed under Sir George May to assess the nation's position and recommend how public expenditure could be cut to defend the pound and retain the Gold Standard.

At the end of July the May Committee reported that there would have to be extensive cuts in the wages of civil servants, teachers, police and armed forces, pointing out that as far as the forces were concerned 'No officer or man . . . has any legal claim to a particular rate of pay.' Despite vigorous protests from the Fourth Sea Lord about the undertaking given to men on the 1919 rates of pay Alexander informed the Cabinet on 19 August that the Navy would accept cuts in pay provided equivalent reductions were applied to other public servants. Four days later the Government resigned, to be replaced by a National Government with MacDonald as Prime Minister; his Cabinet accepted the May Committee proposals and on 1 September publicly announced its decision to enforce them.

Meanwhile summer leave was taken by each watch of ships' companies in the Atlantic Fleet from 21 July to the end of August when men had time to reflect uneasily on the impact of probable pay cuts. On 3 September the Board telegraphed confidentially to all commanders-in-chief – the

Atlantic Fleet was then assembled in home ports – to the effect that: 'For the Navy the sacrifice involves . . . placing all officers and men at present in receipt of pay on 1919 scales on the revised scale introduced in October 1925. . . . The new regulations are to come into force from 1 October next.' The Board also decided to issue an explanatory Fleet Order, in co-ordination with the Army and RAF; but the Treasury objected to anything being promulgated until the Chancellor's Budget speech on 10 September. When Admiral Hodges commanding the Atlantic Fleet returned from leave on 7 September he went sick to Haslar hospital, command automatically devolving on Rear Admiral Wilfred Tomkinson, flying his flag in *Hood* and in charge of the battle-cruisers. Before the Atlantic Fleet sailed for exercises en route for Cromarty Firth on 7 and 8 September it is unlikely that all captains of ships were aware of the contents of the Admiralty telegram. But because the September issue of *The Fleet* contained a letter signed NEUTRALIS hinting at reductions of pay to the 1925 rates it can be assumed that the lower deck knew what was in the wind.

Since 94 per cent of chief and petty officers and 72 per cent of other rates were on the 1919 higher scale of pay ships were swarming with 'buzzes' (rumours); officers were just as much in the dark as the men. Confident that the pay they received was inviolable the older married ratings with children were living up to the limit of their incomes, the margin between making both ends meet and getting into debt being pitifully small. By self denial the vast majority had entered into commitments spread out over years to pay accommodation rents, hire purchase of furniture and insurance, all of which demanded fixed weekly payments. A reduction in pay might mean eviction or forfeiture of furniture and the problem of what to do with the family. Marriage allowance was not payable until the age of twenty-five, a factor that affected many young ratings on the 1925 scale of pay. A feeling of insecurity persisted and certain men, who were later to become mutiny ring leaders, discussed action to be taken if the situation deteriorated.

On Friday 11 September Tomkinson arrived off Invergordon with the battle-cruisers *Hood* and *Repulse*, the battleships *Rodney*, *Warspite*, *Valiant* and *Malaya*, the cruisers *Dorsetshire*, *Norfolk* and *York* and the minelayer *Adventure*. Sailing late from Portsmouth with the commander-in-chief's staff on board, *Nelson* did not arrive until the evening of the 13th to join the ships anchored in two lines with a total of 8,000 officers and men on board. Official news of the actual reductions did not reach all ships until late on Saturday the 12th; in some cases newspapers forestalled a clumsily edited Fleet Order on the notice-board that aroused resentment and suspicion. Confirmation of their worst fears came as a bitter blow to men who had hoped for an all round 10 per cent cut. Instead 1*s* was deducted from all rates, which meant 25 per cent for an able seaman but only 11 per cent for an officer, hardly an example of equal sacrifice. There was also an unexpected reduction in pensions and, worst of all, the new scales would take effect in three weeks, leaving little opportunity for men to communicate with their families. The lower deck felt they had been badly let down and were angry. Captains did their best to explain matters to their ships' companies without success. The mood was ripe for agitators to move in, hold meetings aboard ships and in the beer canteen ashore with a view to organizing mutiny, although the actual word was never used. The sailing of heavy ships for exercises on Tuesday the 15th was to be the signal; ships would refuse to go to sea.

Most of the leaders at Invergordon were able seamen, staid hands with an average age of twenty-eight – they had joined as boy seamen in 1919 – together with a few leading seamen and marines. There is no proof that any petty officer was involved: whatever their sympathies they were deliberately excluded from a positive share in the mutiny, although they must have had some inkling of unrest. There was also no evidence of subversive influence from outside the Navy; later information implied that the Communist Party in England and Russia were taken by surprise by the turn of events. It is probable that Able Seaman Len Wincott, aged twenty-four, of *Norfolk* was the chief ringleader and Able Seaman Bond of *Rodney* the most effective speaker. Meetings in the canteen were monitored by officers of the shore patrol, notably Lieutenant Elkins of *Valiant* who noticed that most speakers were long-service men wearing good conduct badges. Neither ashore nor afloat was any violence offered to officers; all were treated with respect.

Despite unmistakable signs of discontent on the nights of Sunday the 13th and Monday the 14th Tomkinson did not pre-empt it by cancelling the exercises, preferring to leave initiative with the Admiralty. He did, however, inform the Admiralty by signal of disturbances in the canteen. On Tuesday morning the crews of *Nelson*, *Hood*, *Rodney*, and *Valiant* either refused to raise steam or physically prevented anchors being weighed. *Warspite*, *Malaya* and *Repulse* sailed but had to be recalled; the Admiralty were informed that some ships of the Atlantic Fleet had mutinied. By Wednesday morning the situation was deteriorating, with no action by the Admiralty and a refusal to work by men in *Adventure*, *Norfolk* and *Valiant*. More cheering and shouting took place between ships. At 3 p.m. on Wednesday the Admiralty ordered all ships to return to home ports and late that day they sailed. The mutiny may have been over but the repercussions were staggering. Enormous damage was done to Britain's national image throughout the world. In less than a week the government abandoned the Gold Standard and the pound fell in value from $4.86 to $3.49.[19]

CHAPTER NINE

Recovery and Re-armament

Remember then, that your life's vocation, deliberately chosen, is WAR – WAR, as I have said, as a means of peace. But still WAR: and with singleness of purpose, for England's fame, prepare for the time when the welfare and honour of the Service may come to be in your keeping.

Introduction to Seamanship *by Captain Alston, December 1859*

As ships from Invergordon steamed towards their home ports on Thursday 17 September 1931 to give weekend leave the First Lord was addressing the House of Commons. Austen Chamberlain stated that no one should be penalized for what had happened: 'The past is past. It is in the interest of everyone in the Navy or out of it to forget it. I am not going to look back.' Public opinion, on the other hand, felt that the Atlantic Fleet and the Navy had let the country down badly at a time of financial crisis.

On the credit side the destroyers and submarines berthed at Rosyth had been unaffected, partly because of closer relationships between officers and men and partly due to prompt action of Leading Seaman Diavle of the destroyer *Vivien* who reported the activities of an agitator sent from Invergordon to incite refusal of duty. Commodore (D) was thus able to instruct officers to collect a dossier of problems for immediate dispatch to the Admiralty, thus heading off unrest. On foreign stations news of the pay cuts were received calmly on the whole; in most cases ships were widely dispersed, senior officers had time to study the Admiralty signal and ships' companies accepted them dispassionately. The situation at the Cape was aggravated by South Africa remaining on the Gold Standard after Great Britain left it, causing an additional cut of 20 per cent on pay, particularly serious because there were several families on the station. Eventually the Government paid full compensation for the rate of exchange. Only in *Delhi*, light cruiser flagship of the North America and West Indies station, was there a refusal of duty by principally younger ratings wishing to show solidarity with the Atlantic Fleet. Again, the Commander-in-Chief and captain of *Delhi* acted soundly and there was no further trouble. Neither were there side effects in the Navy's schools and barracks, nor in the Army and RAF, who were less seriously affected.

Over the weekend of 19/20 September Special Branch and MI5 officers were active in home ports trying to identify ringleaders and flush out communist agents. Seamen and stokers were in a restless frame of mind, a few militants tried to stir up further grievances, officers were apprehensive, the atmosphere tense. On the afternoon of the 21st the Prime Minister told the Commons that pay cuts for teachers, police and the three Defence Services would be limited to 10 per cent; in the Navy, ratings on the current 1919 rates would lose 10 per cent pay but those on the 1925 rates would be unaffected. Fleet orders announcing the original pay cuts were cancelled and a special fund was set up to relieve financial distress among married ratings under twenty-five who had been badly hit. At Portsmouth, the Nore and Plymouth commanders-in-chief personally headed enquiries into immediate measures to relieve hardship and to make longer term recommendations. On 3 October captains of ships explained the new system of pay and allowances; five days later the Atlantic Fleet resumed its interrupted autumn cruise with a new commander-in-chief, Admiral Sir John Kelly.

Joe Kelly may not have been one of the Navy's intellectuals but he possessed the priceless asset of a personality that could reach into a man's heart with warmth and humour. A born leader of men he was a classic choice at a critical time to take over command since Hodges was still on the sick list. To ensure a free hand Kelly insisted on men known to be mutiny ringleaders being discharged from the fleet before sailing. As a first step to restore morale he went aboard each ship in turn, lower decks being cleared so he could address officers and men on these lines: 'When this trouble blew up the Admiralty looked around for an Admiral with a good record. They hadn't one. So they said they'd have one with a bloody awful record and that's why I'm here. Now take a look at me – I'm no oil painting – but take a good look so that when we see each other ashore you won't say "Who's that funny old bugger over there?".'[1]

Gradually the Atlantic Fleet – later renamed the Home Fleet – settled down under their charismatic leader.

The aftermath was prolonged, with 124 known mutineers, including twenty leading rates and Royal Marine corporals, being drafted from ships to various barracks where the First Lord's amnesty pre-empted disciplinary action. But twenty-four ratings, all from Devonport, were discharged from the service on the grounds that they had been engaged in subversive activities after return from Invergordon. The remainder were put under surveillance and treated reasonably well; some were victimized, others were allowed to re-engage for pension. Seven captains were relieved of their commands, a draconian measure but not unexpected when it was known that in addressing their ship's companies at Invergordon one had said: 'The country is in serious trouble . . . we must all tighten our belts . . . I have written to my wife to sack one of the maids.'[2] Another is alleged to have told the men that they would have to put up with the cuts, that his pay was cut too and that if they could not manage 'they would have to send their wives out to work'. Certain commanders were never promoted; in wardroom messes Invergordon was not a topic of conversation. Tomkinson was censured by the Admiralty, mainly for 'omitting to take decided action on 13 and 14 September' and was later retired.

At all levels of naval society the part played by the Admiralty was criticized; Admiral Tyrwhitt at the Nore stated: 'the men do not regret Invergordon, nor are they ashamed of themselves . . . their chief grievance being against the Board of Admiralty'. In his report Kelly was even more outspoken, pointing out: 'one thing stands out beyond everything else; that officers and men alike, from the highest to the lowest, appear to attribute the mutiny . . . directly to the action of the Admiralty in accepting the "Cuts" as at first promulgated'. He inferred that 'complete confidence in the Administrative authority will not be restored so long as the present Board remain in office'. In his defence the First Sea Lord, Field, protested that the Government had announced the cuts without warning. Even so the Board were caught unawares by the turn of political events, too many were unavailable on leave at a crucial time and when re-assembled they failed to appreciate the effect of the pay cuts on the 1919 men – in other words they had lost touch. After the mutiny evidence pointed to discord at the top, as efforts were directed to put the blame on Tomkinson. While nobody resigned no admiral was re-employed except Dreyer, the Deputy Chief of Naval

Staff, who missed his chance of commanding one of the main fleets. After taking over the battle-cruisers from Tomkinson Admiral James remarked: 'There is no parallel in the Navy's history for such an upheaval in the senior ranks and for so many ruined careers. Perhaps it is because mutinies so seldom occur that we handle them so badly.'[3]

During the enquiries officers and senior ratings complained that the Atlantic Fleet's three leave periods each year and frequent changes in complements – as much as half the seamen within twelve months – made it difficult if not impossible to get to know their men. Disappointment was expressed over the failure of the Welfare Conference system on which many had set high hopes. Requests submitted took far too long to be dealt with, and men were dissuaded from forwarding requests through the chain of command. Indeed there was much in what Tomkinson felt when he reported: 'The more the officers urged upon the men the futility of their action and encouraged them to resort to proper service methods, the more did it appear to many, who had hitherto been opposed to the outbreak, that these methods would have no effect and the only way to secure a real consideration of the complaint was that which had been adopted.'[4]

Since strikes to right grievances were commonplace among industrial communities a 'strike' or 'passive resistance' presented itself as the only weapon of redress. The thought that the Navy considered it mutiny hardly occurred to most of the men refusing duty.

The Board remained obsessed with the possible recurrence of 'mass indiscipline', instructing commanding officers to 'put down any further disturbances . . . with a strong hand' and then issuing 'Notes on dealing with insubordination', all of which appeared typical of the unimaginative administration of Admiral Field, who had been a sick man for much of 1932. More positive was the appointment of a Director of Personal Services – to advise the Board on welfare and service conditions – and setting up committees to handle the candid recommendations of the Kelly Report and other enquiries. The Welfare Conference was replaced by a Review of Service Conditions, the first being held in 1935 by which time 5,000 requests had been received on every imaginable subject. The Review may have allowed men to let off steam but it did not achieve much in the opinion of the lower deck. A poster with printed instructions for dealing with 'Complaints of Unfair Treatment' was displayed in every ship and a Confidential Admiralty Fleet Order issued that emphasized the importance of leadership and developing the personal qualities of individuals in the fleet.

Not until Sir Bolton Eyres Monsell, a former naval officer, was appointed First Lord in November 1932 did matters take a turn for the better. In appointing Admiral Chatfield recently commanding the Mediterranean to be the new First Sea Lord he chose a man of distinction and one who could bridge the gap between the Admiralty and the fleet; with a clean sweep of naval members on the Board the Navy started to pick itself up. First indication that the Lords Commissioners were making an effort to gain the confidence of the lower deck was when they wore uniform instead of top hats and frock coats on their visits to ships, civilian members wearing double-breasted dark blue suits with yachting caps.[5]

For some years the events of Invergordon, politely called 'unrest', gave officers much to think about; they felt deeply ashamed over the harm done to the country and that the Navy no longer occupied that high position in the hearts of the British people that it had held for centuries. What went wrong? What had destroyed the mutual trust between officers, petty officers and men? Writing in 1932 an officer concluded:

> We always thought we were in 'close touch' with our men. If we really had been – would not every officer have realized immediately that a general cut to the post-1925 scale of pay would make things difficult for certain of his men? Conversely would not the man in 'close touch' have gone to his officers with his complaint, sure in the knowledge that they would fight hard to get him a fair deal?
>
> How then have we lost this touch? Since the war ended officers and men have had no real purpose common to both. An excess of officers has led to many appointments in which an officer sees little of those under him; it has also caused the average officer to think too much about his chance of promotion – in which ratings are totally disinterested. Furthermore it has led to officers being employed on work which is more suitable for petty officers; thus the petty officer is short-circuited with corresponding loss of prestige.[6]

Through well-meaning efforts to invigorate the divisional system the officers in some larger ships had started to usurp the position of senior ratings, a chief boatswain's mate arguing that it introduced bad feeling rather than healthy competition between divisions, as well as a lack of uniformity in such matters as discipline and dress. Because their organization was different, in that officers and senior ratings were in closer contact with their men, destroyers and submarines found less difficulty in sustaining morale.

The desire to shoulder some of the blame prompted soul searching among younger officers over their private lives and personal habits. Marriage was a favourite topic of wardroom argument between the bachelors and those married, the latter represented by, say, 25 per cent of all lieutenants and about 50 per cent of lieutenant commanders. There were those who stated that marriage and navy life were incompatible while others insisted that married officers always put the Service first. Comparison was made with the attitude of the lower deck who tended to look on the Navy as employment rather than a profession, felt deeply about family life and dreaded the separation that foreign service entailed.

In harbour the amount of drinking in officers' messes and leave habits came in for introspective criticism. In ships where leadership and example were lacking there was often over-indulgence in both; for instance, in more than one destroyer the hands were detailed off for work at 1.15 p.m. by officers who had been drinking gin in the wardroom since noon and seldom finished lunch before 2 p.m. And it was a standing joke in big ships that senior married officers regularly caught the 3.30 p.m. boat ashore before the end of working hours.

❖❖❖

During the aftermath of Invergordon the fleet continued with the many tasks that fell to a widely deployed peacetime Navy. A typical assignment was to foster trade relations, show the flag and keep in touch with isolated pockets of British community in various parts of the world. Ships' companies had plenty of work on hand and officers were expected to show the diplomatic touch that has characterized their upbringing over the ages. One such ship was the 6-in. gun light cruiser *Durban* of the South American division of the America and West Indies squadron based at Bermuda. In the early 1930s she steamed over 47,000 miles in two years visiting fifty different ports, with barely any change in complement throughout the commission.

Visiting Santiago a party of officers and men led by the first lieutenant were invited to ride out to Cartagena with the colonel and best part of a regiment of Carabineros for a picnic. On arrival they were given light refreshment and a tour of inspection finishing up at the town hall where to their horror, waiting on the steps in full regalia, were the Mayor, Town Clerk, Medical Officer of Health and several dignitaries. Formal greetings were exchanged and the party conducted into the council chamber where the Mayor rose to his feet and started his speech of welcome in Spanish. Ten minutes later he was well in his stride, his audience applauding at discreet intervals, until in his final burst of impassioned oratory the names of Ramsay MacDonald, Admiral Cochrane, Nelson, El Roy Jorge V and General O'Higgins were coupled together. The Mayor resumed his seat amid tumultuous handclapping. On rising to reply the first lieutenant cautiously opened in English and although unable to counter with the names of Chile's more famous men, brought his speech to a triumphant end with 'Viva Chile' in fluent Castilian. Fortunately the proceedings were interrupted by the timely arrival of trays containing a wonderful cocktail of the Mayor's invention and the party soon began to go with a swing. Leaving the Town Hall the assembly moved to an 'Asado' roasting in the backyard of a house, with a small string orchestra to play the national songs of both countries in strict alternation. As their knowledge of English music was confined to *Tipperary* and *God Save the King* the feast was frequently interrupted by the company having to get to its feet while all three verses of the latter were played *lentissimo*, which added considerably to the duration of the meal.[7]

❖❖❖

As early as 1921 the Navy started its fight with HM Government to regain control of its air service, then known as the Fleet Air Arm of the Royal Air Force. Because the FAA was an integral part of the fleet the Admiralty argued that it must be operated, administered and controlled by the Navy; that under the existing system the Navy would never get senior officers with air experience so vital to sea warfare; that divided control was entirely dependent on goodwill and that naval officers were deterred by a feeling of insecurity and lack of promotion prospects from becoming aviators. As a first step the agreement between Air Chief Marshal Sir Hugh Trenchard and Admiral Sir Roger Keyes in 1924 went some way to remove friction between the two services, in particular to make flying specialization a more attractive proposition. However, the Air Ministry resisted the Navy's proposal to train petty officer pilots on the grounds that they were technically inferior to sergeant pilots RAF.

In aircraft carriers the two services operated together in complete harmony and as a symbol of unity air crew in the wardroom of *Glorious* wore one RN button linked to an RAF button in their mess jackets. Flying Officer Cracroft RAF remembers joining *Furious* in 1928 after deck landing training and watching his friend, Lieutenant John Martin, Royal Marines, making his first approach in a Fairy Flycatcher to:

> hit the deck amidships and go smartly over the side . . . to be rescued by the attendant destroyer and returned to *Furious*, bruised and smelling strongly of rum. . . . Then I heard the stentorian voice of the Wing Commander, 'Come on, Cracroft, your turn next.' I emerged from the nets . . . and was sitting in the cockpit of my Flycatcher feeling lonely and apprehensive when a signalman . . . thrust a signal pad under my nose and said 'Name and address of next of kin, sir, please.' Subsequently I did four successful deck landings.[8]

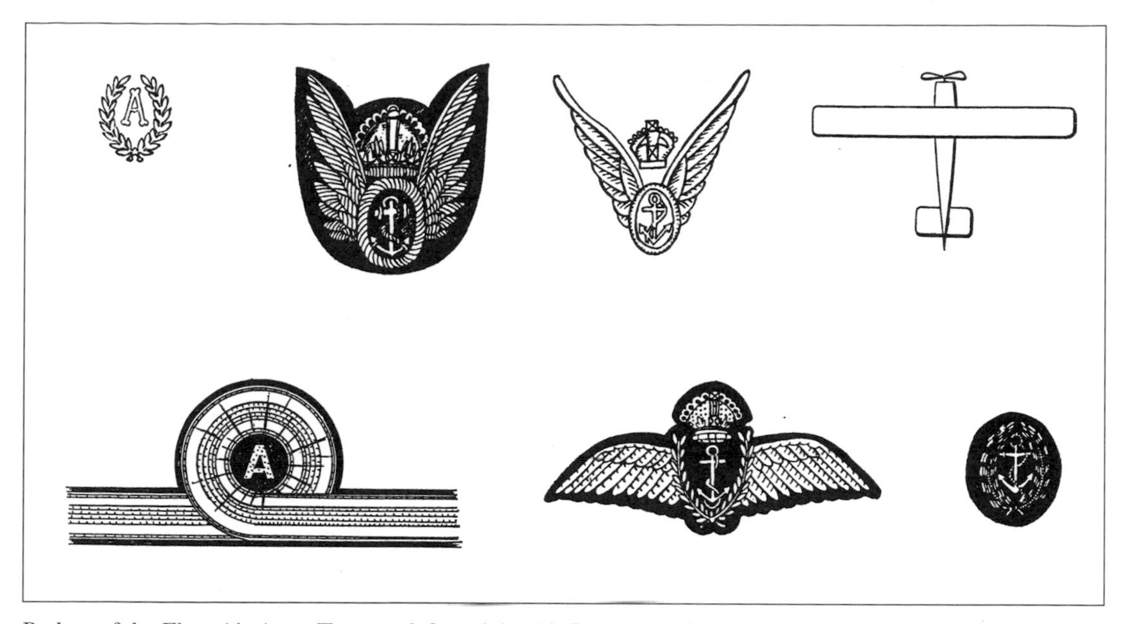

Badges of the Fleet Air Arm. Top row, left to right: Air Branch, observer, aircrewman, telegraphist air gunner. Bottom row: Fleet Air Arm Branch, pilot, RAF officer serving with the Fleet Air Arm

In 1931 the first flag officer to be appointed Rear Admiral Aircraft Carriers was Reggie Henderson, a brilliant officer who did much to promote flying in the Navy. He encouraged officers to go aboard carriers and get airborne, instituted short air courses for midshipmen, re-organized FAA squadrons and improved the tactical handling of carriers. Nonetheless, when Chatfield became First Sea Lord in 1933 prospects were bleak. The Air Ministry was determined to keep control, naval aviation developments were stunted through subordination to the RAF and the Cabinet was in no mood to make any change. 'Of all the battles with which I was faced', wrote Chatfield, 'this was the only one that gave me real anxiety – namely control of the Fleet Air Arm.' Bit by bit and despite two changes in Prime Minister and First Lord, he built up his case, arguing that interchangeability of flying personnel between RAF and FAA was no longer practicable and that air operations at sea were now so highly specialized that training, equipment and technique had to be handled by the Navy. After Chatfield threatened to resign a decision was reached, and on 30 July 1937 the Government agreed that shipborne aircraft should be placed under the administrative control of the Navy, but that Coastal Command should remain with the RAF. Although a great triumph for the Navy there was a tremendous amount of ground to be made up and time was running short. Admiral J.H.D. Cunningham was appointed Fifth Sea Lord and Chief of Naval Air Services, with captains to direct Air Material and Air Personnel; at that time the Navy was desperately short of commanders (O) and (P) to fill Admiralty posts. From the RAF came 1,500 volunteers to join the Fleet Air Arm, as well as aerodromes that became Royal Naval Air Stations at Lee-on-Solent, Gosport, Ford, Worthy Down and Donibristle. In June 1939 an admiral was appointed to administer shore stations from HMS *Daedalus*, as Lee-on-Solent was called. With notable exceptions such as Caspar John, later to become First Sea Lord, naval aviators

Sunday Divisions on the flight deck of HMS *Courageous*, 1928. Note RAF Division in the foreground

of the 1930s were gifted amateurs who had opted for the 'freedom of the air' as opposed to pacing the teak as officers of the watch. Being fiercely independent and devoted to making the best use of indifferent material their flying was of high quality, though somewhat idiosyncratic as each pilot tended to develop his own style. It was fascinating to watch a well-trained squadron break formation and hover around while waiting to catch the affirmative to land on. There was one pilot, for example, whose ploy was to side slip from 200 ft to the end of the 'round down' and then straight into the arrester wires. Nobody minded such eccentricities and provided the squadron was got on board quickly and safely, that was it. The observer was the link between the seamen and aviators and when the latter disembarked to Lee or Gosport the observers remained on board to augment the watchkeeping rota. To meet a shortage of (O)s the Admiralty conscripted two or three courses of lieutenants in the late '30s; most but not all became enthusiastic supporters of the branch.

To meet rapid expansion the Naval Air Branch was formed in 1938 to recruit aviators for seven years, their uniform identified with the Air Branch badge – a capital A in silver surrounded by a gold laurel wreath. Later that year the RNVR Air Branch was introduced to provide pilots and observers on similar lines but only for a war emergency. Lower deck pilots from seaman and communication branches were recruited for twelve months' shore training and final qualification in a carrier. A large number of technical officers were needed from naval engineers and the newly formed Air Branch for aeronautical training with the RAF; several new rates were recruited as apprentices for training as air artificers, air fitters and air riggers while the semi-skilled, drawn from volunteer seamen and stokers, were designated air mechanics.

The worst bargain the Fleet Air Arm inherited was obsolete aircraft. The Torpedo Spotter Reconnaissance Swordfish – top speed 100 knots – embodied the functions of reconnaissance and shadowing, torpedo and dive bombing attack, gunfire spotting and convoy protection as well as an amazing heavy load capability. It was alleged that an officer remarked 'No housewife on a shopping spree could cram a wider variety of articles into her string bag.' From that moment pilots referred affectionately to their Swordfish as a 'string bag' – and a very robust aircraft it was too.

It is to the credit of the Admiralty and Admiral Commanding Reserves that soon after the First World War they found time to overhaul the Royal Naval Volunteer Reserve. In 1921 new regulations were published that not only confirmed the value of the RNVR as an effective fighting force but encouraged ratings to specialize and, in the case of lieutenants, stipulated that they must qualify in a specific direction. As soon as they had done so RNVR officers would then assume equal status and responsibility to RN and RNR officers of similar rank and seniority. This was an enormous step forward for the volunteer. Sea and shore training became obligatory at full naval rates of pay; the Navy took over the ownership and maintenance of all headquarters and training ships and a permanent paid RNVR commander was appointed to ACR's staff to liaise with divisions all over the country.

In 1931 2,000 RNVRs trained with the fleet; as the prospect of war loomed larger so recruitment rose until in 1938 there were over 9,000 officers and men. In 1937 a chance remark by the First Lord in his Estimates speech about inviting yachtsmen and experienced amateur seamen to join a Supplementary Reserve caught the attention of the press; the result was staggering. So many applied to join from all parts of the UK that the list had to be closed. The RNV(S)R were given every opportunity to train at sea, were nominally attached to divisions and in conjunction with the RNVR were mobilized in 1938 and 1939. To enhance fleet AA defence eight old 'C'-class cruisers were converted to anti-aircraft cruisers, their 4-in. high angle armament totally operated by an RNVR unit of three officers and fifty men who had been trained as a team in one of the drill ships ashore.

Royal Naval Reserve officers were paid a £25 annual retainer but what really counted was the prestige of holding an Admiralty commission; by the 1930s there was a waiting list, so keen were they to reach their quota of 1,500 and take training billets in cruisers and destroyers. But with RNR ratings it was a perpetual struggle to keep established numbers up to strength. RNR seamen were enrolled from the Merchant Service for periods of five years up to a maximum of twenty-five, serving in the RN at sea and in the barracks for training periods. There is evidence that the RN were often casual in supervising RNRs and that their jobs were at risk while away under training.

In May 1929 the author was among forty-four cadets aged thirteen and a half that joined Dartmouth from preparatory schools to start a naval career. Our social background was fairly typical of cadets during inter-war years – predominantly middle class, of moderate means and with one third from naval or army families. Having passed an Interview Board we took medical and written examinations in London, at which stage Messrs Gieves stepped in to supply an outfit of uniform and a booklet – *How to become a Naval Officer.* At Dartmouth rules of personal conduct based on hierarchal custom were rigidly enforced throughout the college, principally by cadet captains selected from senior cadets. Each 'term' was named after a famous admiral – ours was Blake – and the first year was the most rigorous, our feet barely touching the ground as we doubled from gunroom to classroom to messroom, conforming with age-old naval routine. Etched in the memory was waking to the bugle 'Reveille' and the raucous tones of our Term Chief PO, grabbing a towel to rush to the bathroom, splashing through a salt water plunge, receiving verbal orders to 'brush your teeth' and later 'say your prayers', putting on clothes in double quick time. There was a brief respite four times a day as we sat on backless benches in front of bare tables to eat our meals – the food was consistently good; or in the classroom where masters, who included survivors from RNC Osborne in 1905, patiently taught us maths, chemistry, geography and naval history. In charge of the Seamanship Room was a pensioner chief who could recite every order for 'making plain sail' while demonstrating knots, splices and fancy ropework in an atmosphere of tarred hemp and canvas aprons. In the afternoons physical exercise was mandatory; if you did not play in an organized game then you were 'on your honour' to swim, play squash or run for twenty minutes.

After 'Evening Quarters' on the quarterdeck and an hour's 'prep' came the orderly process of turning in. Clothes were folded and laid out on each chest, a practice that led to cultivating habits of a lifetime; dormitory windows were lowered exactly to the same extent. As the duty officer did his rounds each cadet lay motionless in bed stiffly at attention, below his chin four inches of sheet, then four inches of counterpane and across his feet a dark blue rug carefully folded, with his initials in red letters correctly centred. Climax to the day came after lights out when those who had stepped out of line and received an excess of 'ticks' (warnings) were summoned by the cadet captain, told to 'Buck yourself up', then 'bend down' for three cuts over pyjama trousers. It was all part of life which became progressively less demanding as we climbed the ladder through Junior to Senior College. Since the cadets who passed through Dartmouth from 1919 to 1939 formed a large proportion of the career officers who fought the Second World War it is appropriate to ask if the Dartmouth system was successful.

The Board of Education inspection report of 1932 evidently thought so – 'a highly efficient educational institution' and 'no visitor could fail to notice that naval discipline is the essence of the place'.[9] Certainly Dartmouth taught us to show initiative, go 'flat out', be punctual, obey orders and revere authority – qualities that almost amounted to a religion. But there were rebels who did not conform to these ideals and were none the worse for it. At the end of nearly four years' training one or two decided the Navy was not for them and resigned – a weakness of the early age entry. Among less than perfect features was the 'term' system that segregated cadets and forbade them to communicate with senior or junior terms until the 'house' system changed all that in 1938. Compared with a public school there was little contact with the outside world and a curiously detached attitude towards the opposite sex. Married term officers were not allowed to reside closer than 30 miles, Saturday night dancing on the quarterdeck was 'men only' – except for the hospital Nursing Sisters who had the whale of a time – and apart from neighbouring farms for cream teas on Sundays everything else was strictly out of bounds. Personally I found little wrong with Dartmouth but would not argue with Charles Owen of our term who wrote:

> For the most part what emerged was a definite breed of fit, tough, highly trained but sketchily educated professionals, ready for instant duty, for parades or tea parties, for catastrophes, for peace or war; confident leaders, alert seamen, fair administrators, poor delegators; officers of wide interests and narrow vision, strong on tactics, weak on strategy; an able, active, cheerful, monosyllabic élite. But while most thrived on Dartmouth diet, not every cadet was satisfied.[10]

Arising from Invergordon and taking a cue from foreign navies the idea of sail training to bring young officers and ratings together was discussed at high level; it was in fact declared by an enthusiastic First Lord in presenting the 1932 estimates. Brought up in sail Chatfield held strong reservations on the value of such training in a technological age and the scheme was dropped in favour of converting the heavy cruiser *Frobisher* to cadet training ship. However, for some years the idea of forming a naval sailing club had been talked about and with the support of submariners with notable sailing experience the Royal Naval Sailing Association was formed in 1935. Its principal objective was to 'encourage sailing throughout the service'; by 1939 RNSA yachts achieved distinction in ocean racing circles and were responsible for the Royal Navy winning the International Naval Races at Kiel.

Early in January 1933 the Blakes and a large batch of Special Entry cadets straight from six months in *Erebus* joined the *Frobisher* in Chatham. The ship had a reduced seamen complement so that cadets could work the ship under supervision and alongside seamen counterparts. We slept in hammocks, fed at messdeck tables, kept watch, ran boats and provided guards for morning colours. Going ashore in the West Indies during the first cruise we tasted our first rum cocktail, danced with the girls and swam off coral beaches. The second cruise took *Frobisher* to Scotland and Scapa Flow thence to Scandinavia and the Baltic, finishing up at Kiel where the German Navy arranged an impressive five-day programme. The Nazi party provided much of the hospitality in a hearty sort of way, expressing admiration for Britain while eulogizing about a man called Adolf Hitler.

It was later apparent that six months in *Frobisher* was rather better value for cadets than a similar period spent in the gunrooms of the fleet. Perhaps the best part was getting to know the lower deck, sharing their jobs and listening to a caustic view of the Navy from an unambitious three badge AB sitting in an upper deck 'caboose'. It was also a good introduction to the Special Entry 'pubs' who impressed us with their wider educational background.

❖❖❖

In April 1933 Kenneth Avery joined the Sick Berth Branch of the Navy. After kitting up at RN Barracks Devonport, he was sent for three months to HMS *Impregnable*, the new entry training establishment just outside Plymouth. As an introduction to service life, routine and discipline were strictly enforced with instruction spread between seamanship, parade ground, rifle shooting, swimming and naval history; above all he learnt how to live in a warship. An unexpected feature was when: 'a representative from Agnes Weston's came round on the first week, pointed out the evils of alcohol and persuaded as many as possible to sign the pledge. I signed one and have it to this day, but I must confess I have since broken it'.

For the next year Avery was a probationary sick berth attendant at Plymouth's RN Hospital at Stonehouse – often referred to as the 'boneyard' – where each class was given periods in the laboratory, medical and surgical wards, operating theatre, administration, dispensary, zymotic or fever wards and in the physiotherapy, X-ray and venereal departments. On the first occasion of attending a major operation:

> I passed out. The operation was the amputation of a leg and involved cutting and sawing with all the blood vessels being arrested to prevent bleeding, in a hot atmosphere and with the

smell of anaesthetic. I did exactly what I was told many others had done before me; but after some water and fresh air was able to return. . . . The other significant occasion in those days was the first cut at the post-mortem and the use of the spinal two edged saw to remove the spinal column.

Crossing the line: King Neptune and Queen Amphritrite arrive on board to open the proceedings, HMS *Sussex*, 1935

As a leading sick berth attendant Avery was sent to the Middle East via Port Said where he disembarked and travelled by rail across Egypt to join the minelayer *Adventure* at Haifa during the Jew–Arab confrontation. Returning to Plymouth he married late in 1936 before being sent to Singapore where he served in several ships on the China Station, travelled all round the Far East, survived a typhoon and was still serving in the depot ship *Medway* at the outbreak of war.[11]

For sheer size, variety and independence of command the China station was hard to beat. Under a full admiral the China fleet included five 8-in gun cruisers, an aircraft carrier, the minelayer *Adventure*, a 6-in cruiser at Hankow 600 miles up the river, nine destroyers, a submarine depot ship with twelve submarines, thirteen gunboats in the Yangtse under a rear admiral and five gunboats in the West River (Canton) under a captain. In 1935 the 15-in monitor *Terror* was brought out to strengthen the naval base and dockyard at Singapore that was to become the great British bastion of the Far East. As flagship the cruiser *Kent* was a particularly happy and successful ship serving the typical two-and-a-half years on the station. Leave was liberal, cost of living cheap and opportunities for sightseeing at the Navy's expense superior to any modern package deal costing thousands of pounds.

In Hong Kong large numbers of Chinese 'boys' lived on board, one being allocated to each mess to scrub out and wash the dishes, their only reward unwanted food. In the days before ships' laundries all washing of clothes was undertaken by 'dhobey' girls, mending and darning by an old 'sew-sew' woman, a suit of uniform or plain clothes tailored by 'Jelly Belly' while 'Tomato Face' could produce a pair of handsewn shoes or boots in twenty-four hours. Tradesmen worked to a high standard, accepting payment over several pay days. In Hong Kong with its swirling life of business, banks and commerce, officers were granted honorary membership of most clubs; and a run ashore for libertymen was all the better for the building of the magnificent China Fleet Club overlooking the harbour. For training periods the fleet went to Wei-Hai-Wei, a delightful little island off the Shantung Peninsula with a pleasant summer climate (unlike Hong Kong), playing fields, tennis courts, skittle alleys, canteen, library and officers' bungalows.

Shanghai's international character held a special appeal for the lower deck; the First Lieutenant of the destroyer *Wishart* remembers looking inside a honky-tonk dance joint to find:

> sailors and soldiers of every sort all mixed up and in various stages of intoxication. Here would be a British AB, there an American marine, an Italian petty officer, a French signalman, a Tommy of the Lincolns, a kilted sergeant of the Argylls, a Philippino officers' steward from an American destroyer, an Annamite [Indo-Chinese] sailor from a French merchantman, a Libyan stoker from an Italian cruiser, two corporals from the 'Thoirty Foist', one of the US regiments from Manila; all dancing away as happy as larks or perhaps lying in a rather comatose condition, embraced by their partners who were probably trying to pick their pockets.[12]

In another part of the world Malta had been the principal base of the Mediterranean fleet for well over a century. In the basin and creeks of Grand Harbour were deep-water berths for battleships, aircraft carriers and cruisers, while in adjacent Marsamusciett Harbour three flotillas, each of eight destroyers, could be tightly packed in Sliema creek, leaving room for submarines off Manoel Island. In fact the whole Mediterranean fleet could be safely moored in weather-protected harbours within easy reach of a well-equipped dockyard, a range of sports grounds and the attractions of Valletta and Sliema:

> The first night in I went ashore with three of my mates [wrote a destroyer's able seaman]. I was to show them the sights as the expert, having been there before. After a couple of Farson's beers at one of the seafront dives we caught the bus to Valletta and made our way to the Gut,

Crossing the line: another victim for the 'bears'

> the sailor's name for a notorious street called Strada Stretta. This narrow alleyway was about a couple of hundred yards long with bars, restaurants, dance halls, cabarets and anything else one could think of to provide entertainment for sailors a long way from home! Some of these were low dives indeed and it didn't pay to stop too long or be alone, but the majority were well run and very cheap. In fact we could have a rip-roaring evening with lots of beer, food, dancing and female company, at little expense. What more could anyone ask for?[13]

There were two large ratings' clubs called the White Ensign and the Vernon close to the jetty in Grand Harbour where beds, drinks and meals were to hand and where a tombola was run every evening for hundreds of eager sailors. The big 'house' at double stakes paid £100 to £150; winners were advised to return on board immediately or put the money in the club safe. Each ship would have its favourite bar on the waterfront and although vast numbers were landed nightly there was little trouble among libertymen. In the afternoons and weekends football, cricket and hockey were played on hard sandstone pitches, rugger at the Marsa and every ship fielded two or more water polo teams. With such a life-style men were fit and spirits high.

During inter-war years Malta was also the heyday for officers. Those married usually managed to get their wives to join them, paying as little as £10 for a sea passage from England. Accommodation, food and servants were inexpensive and life was highly social, revolving around a programme that emptied the harbour of ships three times a year for exercises and cruises to other parts of the Mediterranean. Membership of the Union Club in Valletta, with its famous lower bar and dining room for men only, was *de rigueur*; on the ground floor was a door to the ladies section unflatteringly called the Snake Pit. There was tennis, golf, polo and a race course at the Marsa – the only green patch in the island – dining and dancing at the Sliema Club and swimming from flat rocks into deep water off Tigné Point.

The most notable social events occurred when the fleet was in harbour during the winter months and unattached girls, known as the Fishing Fleet, flocked to Malta to find a husband. Social etiquette expected officers arriving on the station to write their names in the commander-in-chief's visitors' book at Admiralty House in Strada Mezzodi, while young bachelors could be counted on to pay a social call on the houses of married officers that were known to them; if nobody was at home then visiting cards would be left. Tea parties, drinks parties, dinner parties and picnics flourished. At carnival time in the New Year Malta erupted with processions and bands all over the island. After dark there were noisy firework displays and in the Opera House a dance floor was placed over the stalls and a fancy dress ball held on three successive nights, attended mainly by the British community.

The fact that life in the fleet was happy and rewarding makes it all the more difficult to understand why the Maltese were treated in such a derogatory manner. The masses were desperately poor after the First World War and yet we paid little attention to their plight, giving them our 'gash' (unwanted food) and tossing an odd coin to the dghaisaman, not realizing it might be his sole earnings of the day. The Navy's attitude, which included the lower deck, was to regard Maltese as inferior citizens who made cheerful and willing servants and were always good for a laugh. The middle or upper classes were not invited to parties on board ships, neither were they admitted to British clubs until Chatfield as commander-in-chief persuaded the Union Club to accept them as members.

Final of the 'Ukkas' championship on board the cruiser *Sussex*, 1936

Late in 1932 Admiral Sir William Wordsworth Fisher succeeded Chatfield in command of the Mediterranean. A man of striking personality and physical presence he was the archetypal British naval commander-in-chief, known as 'WW' by contemporaries and 'The Great Agrippa' by everyone else. He came to national notice as a potential war leader during the 1934 combined fleet exercises held in the Atlantic. The Home Fleet's objective was to escort a mythical convoy from the Azores to an unknown destination on the Spanish–Portuguese coast, which Fisher rightly sensed would be Arosa Bay. In a full gale with heavy seas running that precluded air operations he effectively shadowed 'enemy' battle-cruisers while his heavy ships, screened by Rear Admiral Andrew Cunningham's destroyers, pressed on at high speed into the night to surprise the main force and convoy with starshell and overwhelming 'gunfire'. 'These bold and masterly tactics not only put an end to the exercise,' wrote Cunningham, 'but settled once and for all the much debated question as to whether or not British heavy ships could and should engage in night action.' In those pre-radar days 'First to sight, first to light, first to fight' was the criterion of night fighting; Fisher was hailed by the press as the great naval genius of modern times.

The following little-known story illustrates why he was regarded with affection by the lower deck. When the combined fleets assembled at Gibraltar for the customary post-exercise discussion and get together the battle-cruiser *Hood* was berthed at one of the moles. Marine Bugler McCarthy, aged fifteen and 5ft 2in tall, was on watch on the quarterdeck at about 7 p.m. He remembers:

It was a beautiful evening and everything seemed so peaceful. Suddenly it dawned on me that I was quite alone . . . walking forward on the starboard side I saw an officer in uniform on the jetty approaching the gangway. When close enough I noticed he had one thick gold band and four normal bands. 'Bloody wars' I thought. Being sure he was coming aboard I manned the side. Just me. Better than nothing at all, I thought.

'Good evening' said our visitor. I saluted smartly and replied 'Good evening, sir'. He was smiling, a nice smile but cautious.

'Do you know who I am?' No room for lies, I thought. This lad is an admiral. Watch it.

'No, sir,' I answered.

'I am,' he said, 'commander-in-chief of the Mediterranean fleet.' He asked me my name which put me more at ease and spoke of other things that made me calm and normal. He was a true specimen of his kind.

'Where is the officer-of-the-watch?' he asked.

'None of my responsibility, sir,' I replied.

'Good boy,' he said. He enquired about everyone else, the whole of the watch staff, before he disappeared down the half deck hatch. Then all hell was let loose. The officer of the watch appeared like magic and asked me why I didn't tell him about the admiral. I told him straight what had happened.

An hour later the admiral re-appeared with our admiral and the captain; the side was fully manned, as it should be. Our visitor was piped over the side and all seemed to end nicely. But no; on reaching the jetty he stopped, turned and faced us all. Then he said 'Thank you, bugler, for welcoming me aboard and doing your job properly. I salute you!' And he did just that.[14]

As the storm clouds gathered over the Middle East, Fisher's battleships and cruisers joined King George V's Jubilee Review of 160 warships at Spithead in July 1935. On return to the Mediterranean Italy showed aggressive intentions towards Abyssinia and because Malta was highly vulnerable to air attack the fleet base was shifted to Alexandria. In October Mussolini invaded Abyssinia, the League of Nations imposed sanctions on the aggressor and prospect of war with Italy became real.

Alexandria harbour was well able to accommodate a fleet reinforced with cruisers, destroyers, store and repair ships; the remaining facilities were limited and shore activities confined to a few sports grounds and an exciting though expensive run ashore. When Tubby Clayton, founder padré of the First World War Toc H, arrived to reinforce naval chaplains he and the Revd Charles Paton, chaplain to the destroyers, set about establishing a fleet club. With Fisher's blessing a disused hotel was taken over and Claridges Fleet Club opened for business to become an instant success. In Claridges sailors could eat, drink, sleep, dance, get a haircut, meet friends and lead a more sophisticated life more cheaply than anywhere else in Alexandria; the turnover was so large that the Club could hardly avoid making a healthy profit.

In March 1936 Admiral Sir Dudley Pound hoisted his flag in *Queen Elizabeth*, Fisher taking up his appointment as Commander-in-Chief, Portsmouth.

No sooner was the Abyssinian crisis over than another emergency arose in the shape of the Spanish Civil War fought by the Nationalist forces of General Franco backed by Germany and

Twenty-first birthday party in Claridge's Fleet Club

Italy against the Republican government supported by Russia. The Navy's main job was to rescue refugees of many nationalities fleeing from combat zones all over Spain; Home Fleet units looked after the Spanish Atlantic coast while Mediterranean ships covered the coastline eastwards from Gibraltar. First on the scene at Barcelona in July 1936 was HMS *London*, cruiser flagship of Rear Admiral Max Horton, the first rescue warship to arrive and the only one to berth inside the harbour. To organize a reception centre for over 1,000 distressed people half the messdecks and officers' cabins were cleared and every available space prepared to meet contingencies ranging from childbirth to death. British nationals were the first to come aboard, including a party of British Communists of both sexes wearing red ties and riding bicycles; in the first three days 900 people were given sleeping and eating quarters according to age, sex and state of health. Young children were fed during the day and tucked up at night by domestic minded sailors who pooled their scanty pay to buy them sweets and gifts from the canteen.

One night the officer of the watch saw an old lady wandering about the deck and so enquired: 'Have you not been given anywhere to sleep, Madam?' 'Yes,' she replied, 'I have a cabin but I am not going there – oh, no. I have remained a virgin for over seventy years and I take no chances on board *this* ship.'[15]

Evacuation continued through a system of ferry trips by destroyer to Marseilles; during her two months' stay over 3,000 persons of fifty-six different nationalities passed through the ship. Just

Children's party: in the hands of the 'pirates'

before *London* was relieved by *Shropshire* a letter was published in the *Daily Telegraph* calling attention to 'the wonderful work being carried out by the British Navy . . . on the coasts of Spain'. The daughter of the writer was in a party of sixty-two, including a twelve-day-old baby, that spent two nights aboard *London*:

> You never knew such kindness and hospitality as we received. I don't think anyone belonging to the ship had anywhere to sleep, eat or sit. We had everything . . . from the Admiral down to the sailors who carried our bags on board and the stewards who made coffee and sandwiches all night, everybody slaved for us – and we must have made an infinity of work and trouble for them all. . . . I would so very much like them to get a little public appreciation from at least one unspeakably grateful recipient of everything they gave.

Destroyers worked harder than most during two and a half years of refugee evacuation; red, white and blue vertical identification bands were painted on 'B' gun shields, 'darken ship' every night and semi-war routine adopted at sea. *Hunter* was mined off Almeria, *Havock* was narrowly missed by an Italian submarine torpedo and destroyers anchored periodically off the port of Gandia reported near misses from bombs.

Shortly after German bombers destroyed the Spanish town of Guernica at the end of April 1937 a naval review to celebrate the Coronation of King George VI took place in Spithead. The Reserve Fleet was commissioned and amongst the 140 British warships present were cruisers and destroyers from the Dominions and those that could be spared from the Mediterranean. Altogether fourteen squadrons of the Fleet Air Arm from four aircraft carriers flew past but the review was best remembered for the immortal words of Lieutenant Commander Tom Woodroffe, the BBC commentator on the fleet illuminations after dark: '. . . The Fleet's lit up. We're all lit up . . .' before the programme was taken off the air. The public loved it but the BBC was not amused.

The Munich crisis of September 1938, which precipitated mobilization of naval reserves and brought the country to the brink of war, could not have occurred at a worse time for warship modernization and new construction. International treaty obligations, largely ignored by Britain's potential enemies, had delayed re-armament until a serious start could be made in 1936. Thus the breathing space afforded by Chamberlain's 'Peace in our time' was providential; but it was plain that the country's financial resources were inadequate to provide the Navy with sufficient strength to meet the combined threat from Germany, Italy and Japan, even with support from Dominion navies.

Yet Chatfield's building programme, which embraced every type of warship and introduced motor torpedo boats, was certainly a morale booster as the Navy grew in numerical strength. This did not obscure an uncomfortable feeling that fleet weapons were not all that could be desired, particularly in long and close range anti-aircraft gunnery and anti-submarine measures. When Lieutenant Howard Johnston qualified as a 'ping man' in 1931:

> A/S was looked on rather poorly in those days and many friends raised eyebrows that I should head for such a backwater full of lazy, hard drinkers. As Staff A/S officer of a destroyer flotilla in the Spanish Civil War I found that among the four Asdic operators in each of the nine destroyers half only managed to get in FOUR HOURS operating their sets in a YEAR![16]

Radio direction finding (radar) had barely arrived on the scene and the fleet's steaming radius was limited, as was the operation of carrier aircraft at night or in bad visibility. In view of these and other shortcomings what was the social state of officers and men in the run up to 1939?

The Navy's active service strength in 1936 was 119,000 – nearly 10,000 officers and over 109,000 ratings. Lower deck recruiting was buoyant and re-engagement for a second period to complete time for pension averaged 64 per cent, including a large proportion of married men. Although fleet expansion helped clear the blockage in leading rate and petty officer advancement rosters it also caused an upsurge in foreign service, due to more ships being sent to troublespots in the Mediterranean and Far East. Ashore and in large ships general messing was, with reservation, reasonably popular, its quality dependent on the ability of the paymaster commander and the ships' cooks to please everybody all the time; canteen (standard ration) messing was the norm in smaller warships. Arrangements at sea for sleeping, eating and washing had hardly changed since 1919; even in new construction ships fitted with recreation spaces habitability was not impressive.

In matters of pay half the 10 per cent cut had been restored in 1934 and there was a generous increase in marriage allowance for ratings in 1938. In this year the announcement of marriage allowance for officers over thirty proved one in the eye for bachelors. To achieve a grant of 5*s* 6*d* per day for captains, 4*s* 6*d* for commanders and below and 3*s* for warrant officers the Treasury insisted that *all* officers' pay should be docked by 2*s* per day. 1938 also saw the end of the seemingly iniquitous regulation whereby older officers were placed on half pay between appointments.

For ratings, but not officers, a basic form of family welfare was started in 1935. Welfare and Marriage Allowance Sections were established in all three naval barracks to investigate cases of matrimonial difference, neglect of children and requests to stop allotments to dependants. This hardly affected the fleet and years later an ex-naval rating remarked: 'The pre-war service was largely devoid of welfare provision and the attitude of many commanding officers to social problems was one of irritation if not intolerance. A man's marriage took second place and little consideration was given to the needs of his family.'[17]

'Arrangements for . . . washing had hardly changed since 1919'

As always naval attitudes reflected those in society generally; state support for welfare was negligible and when girls married sailors they were 'expected to know what they were letting themselves in for'. Coming from home port areas most of them did. Similarly the wide disparity that typified Britain's class structure still existed between wardroom and messdeck in terms of pay, food, conditions and prospects. Although relationships were healthy ratings remained wary of representing grievances through divisional officers, a situation not helped by the platitudes expressed in an Admiralty confidential letter sent to commanders-in-chief in September 1937 following a case of indiscipline in the battleship *Warspite*. Old prejudices die hard, pay was still a sensitive issue – a point that had not escaped the Admiralty. Even so, to be referred to unknowingly by ratings as 'a gentleman' was still the greatest compliment an officer could wish for.

Throughout the 1930s weapon, signal and engineering schools trained men at all levels to meet the needs of new ships joining the fleet. Less encouraging was the shortage of candidates applying for Direct Promotion to sub-lieutenant, applicants being disheartened by firstly having to overcome the 'suspicious attitude barrier' of their messmates. An element of snobbery amongst selection committees was another drawback, a senior officer complaining that candidates had 'so pronounced an accent that they cannot be said to be capable of speaking "the King's English"'.[18] Nevertheless some forty-five seamen were promoted to acting sub-lieutenant in 1938/9 and many went on to reach commander and captain. The engineering branch had an even better record. In these circumstances it was unfortunate that nothing was done to improve the lot of the older warrant officers 'who were stuck there for ten years before receiving a commission (thick stripe),' wrote a commissioned gunner, 'whilst the midshipman you had taught, in part, was wearing two-and-a-half stripes. Then you lingered on for another ten years before reaching your zone for promotion to lieutenant; this step needed a little bit of luck since only 5 per cent of those qualified got their second stripe'. A feeling of frustration among a loyal and capable hard core of officers was not confined to executive branch but included 'engineers, electricians and schoolmasters, many of whom were far better qualified than their seniors but were condemned to the long wait'.[19] After war broke out many warrant officers were promoted lieutenant and gave splendid service.

During the last years of peace mortality and illness robbed the Navy of some prominent flag officers with consequent effect further down the lists. In March 1936 Admiral Sir Roger Backhouse succeeded Chatfield as First Sea Lord, but due to overwork and ill health he resigned in June 1939 to die a month later. Worse still, in June 1937 W.W. Fisher died suddenly at the age of sixty-two, a great shock since he was destined to go to the top. And so Dudley Pound became First Sea Lord, although he himself was not fully fit. After four exacting years as Controller, Reggie Henderson gave up early in 1939 medically unfit, to be relieved by Admiral Bruce Fraser. Two up-and-coming admirals, Geoffrey Blake and James Somerville, were both invalided from the service, although the latter subsequently returned to active duty. By far the most popular sea appointment was Pound's successor in command of the Mediterranean fleet, Admiral Sir Andrew Cunningham. Known as ABC, his leadership in the early years of war was in a class by itself.

Compared with their 1914 predecessors the flag officers of 1939, all with last war medal ribbons, were men of higher calibre, particularly in their attitude to staff work, which had improved enormously both ashore and afloat. Though he used his staff to the full Cunningham professed to despise staff training, thrived on controversy and a typical remark to a newly joined member was: 'I hate staff officers who agree with me.'[20] Among captains and commanders was a wealth of professional talent in all branches, many having served in Admiralty staff divisions or with the engineer-in-chief, and who knew how the Admiralty functioned, unique among fighting services because it combined operational and administrative control in its Whitehall headquarters. Through encouragement to seize the initiative seagoing commanding officers had regained much of that confidence of independent judgement so lacking earlier in the century. When serving in the Mediterranean, especially under ABC, it was accepted that praise had to be earned, even if indicated by cessation of criticism for brief periods. Captains were traditionally referred to by the names of the ships they commanded, and in the run up to war life for everyone at sea became increasingly exacting.

In the mid-'30s the prospect of war caused many young officers of the executive branch to ponder. Should they remain as 'salt horses' or should they specialize? As officers of the watch they had learned the rudiments of ship handling, that most absorbing of seamanlike activities which attracted officers like Tony Pugsley to have one ambition: 'to command destroyers. Those slim quivering thoroughbreds of the sea which, once you have lost your heart to them, never lose their fascination. In the slow maturing days of peace it required a long and patient apprenticeship, a steady scaling of the mountain side with one's eyes firmly on the peak, to achieve the desired summit of command.'[21]

Re-armament, on the other hand, brought the need for more specialists and in 1938 the Admiralty required each sub-lieutenant to state his preference in order of choice. With added responsibility specialization carried extra pay, the highest being submarines and aviation and, moreover, featured markedly in half-yearly promotion lists to commander and captain. In general most lieutenants got what they wanted, despite the shortage of officers due to reductions in Dartmouth entries in the early thirties. Between 1936 and 1939 about 1,500 junior officers joined the Navy; of these 60 per cent were Special Entry, 25 per cent Dartmouth and 15 per cent ex-RNR.

In retrospect it was a memorable experience to be serving in 1939. Officers and men were convinced of the righteousness of the cause for which they were being called upon to fight and supremely confident that they would be on the winning side. People were quietly proud of being members of the Senior Service, regarding it as one big bureaucratic family. As a lieutenant one could go aboard almost any ship and find friendly, familiar faces in the wardroom; the same could be said of ratings in ship's company messes of the same port division. Deep down we were all rather excited at the prospect of war – after all that is what we had been trained for. We were certainly not conscious that for the country – or for the Navy – 1939 would be the end of an era. Nor did we realize that the forthcoming struggle would be so long and hard and completely different from the course so confidently predicted by the experts.

❖❖❖

On 3 September the Admiralty dispatched a MOST IMMEDIATE signal to all ships and shore establishments signed by the Head of the Military Branch. It was timed 1117/3 and read: 'Special telegram TOTAL GERMANY repetition TOTAL GERMANY.'

CHAPTER TEN

The Navy in Adversity

The foundation of success in battle is a good team well led. . . . Whatever advances are made in the scientific development of weapons, the man who wields the weapon is still the most important single factor in war.

The Fighting Instructions, *1939*

The Navy took the outbreak of war in its stride. On weekend leave in Rainham, Kent, Stoker Wigby heard 'Mr Chamberlain announce that we were at war with Germany. It shook us throughout. . . . I left home with a heavy heart. . . . Next day the drafting office informed me that I would be going to a new corvette. . . . I just had time to say goodbye to my wife and son.'[1]

In Alexandria harbour Admiral Cunningham was watching the fleet regatta: 'standing on the foremost turret of *Malaya* when I was given the signal stating that Great Britain had declared war on Germany. There was little to be done. So far as possible all our preparations had been made. As I wrote to an aunt, I never expected to have nothing to do but go ashore and have tea with my wife.'[2] The destroyer *Firedrake* was oiling ship in Scapa Flow when the announcement was made. Asked how the lower deck took it the coxswain replied: 'They were all crowded round the loudspeaker listening to the old boy's speech; when he finished somebody said "About bloody time too!". That was all.'[3] On patrol off the coast of Norway was HM Submarine *Spearfish* commanded by Lieutenant J.H. Eaden. Four minutes after receiving the signal *Spearfish* was attacked by a German submarine; the torpedo missed.[4] In the destroyer *Walpole* engaged in convoy duty off Milford Haven Lieutenant Commander Burnell-Nugent received the Admiralty signal and within ten minutes had attacked a possible submarine contact with a pattern of depth charges. The sudden realization that there was a war on came as something of a shock to all on board.[5]

Quite the best stimulant was the signal that followed – 'Winston is back'. Here at last was a First Lord who knew the Navy, a man of character and drive to bring fresh air into the corridors of Whitehall and get things done. Churchill wasted little time; arriving at the Admiralty he 'spent a good part of the night of the 3rd meeting the Sea Lords and heads of departments and from the morning of the 4th I laid my hands on the naval affair . . . in spite of certain serious deficiencies, notably in cruisers and anti-submarine vessels, the challenge, as in 1914, found the fleet equal to the immense tasks before it'. He insisted on vetting the appointments of flag officers as well as resuming his personal interest in lower deck matters. In 1940 one of his notable 'prayers' was to overturn an Interview Board decision on Dartmouth entry that failed three candidates on the grounds that one had a slight Cockney accent and the other two were sons of a chief petty officer and a merchant navy engineer. 'The whole intention of competitive examination', he wrote, 'is to open the career to ability, irrespective of class or fortune.'[6] He also abolished the precept that automatically court martialled commanding officers of ships that had been lost by enemy action, on the grounds that it was bad for morale. That did not prevent holding Boards of Enquiry if ships were lost or badly damaged under unusual circumstances.

With so much warning the fleet effortlessly shifted into war routine, issued identity discs, started letter censoring, unpacked lifebelts and checked first aid kits. Many people made out their wills, settled home affairs and prepared for long spells at sea. Wise planning by the staff of the Second Sea Lord and Admiral Commanding Reserves, updated by 1938 experience, ensured the smooth running of mobilization; in fact most ships and shore establishments were topped up to war complement by August 1939. The organization at each of the naval barracks was ready to accept and deal with a continuous stream of Emergency and Fleet Reserves in answer to their call up telegram; among them were ex-instructors, which enabled shore training to continue as before, releasing key men for the fleet.

All instructional courses were halved in length but this did not stop training staffs being fully stretched as hordes of miscellaneous officers and ratings swamped the schools. Additional establishments had to be set up and for the next five years a greatly expanded training machine ran at top speed, indoctrinating the individual with sufficient grounding and proficiency to make a useful contribution to his next job at sea. Time was always short; new entry officers and ratings had to be introduced abruptly to naval discipline through the medium of drills and routine that seemed, at the time, to bear little relation to life in the fleet. None of it was made easier by the observance of air raid precautions entailing frequent interruptions for real or false alarms; or the carrying of anti-gas respirators as a permanent article of everyday uniform. The latter was possibly the greatest personal inconvenience imposed by war; not only did these cumbersome burdens prove embarrassingly awkward when proceeding at the double, which many were required to do, but the shoulder strap revealed the name of the owner on occasions when he or she may have wished to remain incognito.

To train large numbers of Royal Naval (Supplementary) Reserve officers HMS *King Alfred* was set up, partly in Lancing College and partly in a sports arena on the sea front in Hove, to become a principal officers' training establishment. Volunteers had arrived during August 1939: 'in taxis, on foot and some even in limousines driven by liveried chauffeurs. They sported top hats, bowlers, trilbies and cloth caps and they wore morning suits, tweeds, grey flannels and shorts . . . there was scarcely a naval uniform among them'.[7]

The majority were experienced seamen holding Board of Trade Certificates; all they needed was an introduction to the Navy from the 'permanent' RNVR staff, some of whom were given a rough ride. As soon as the volunteers got their uniform they were away to sea to man anti-submarine trawlers, corvettes and minesweepers.

To fill dormant appointments many retired officers were back in harness before September 1939 and the response from thousands more of all ages and backgrounds was little short of miraculous; in 1940 the average age of the captain and three sub-lieutenant watch keepers of the armed patrol motor yacht *Campeador* operating from Portsmouth in all weathers was over sixty. Some retired officers found sea service too arduous and had to quit, but by then the Navy had gained valuable breathing space. Very soon educationally qualified Hostilities Only ratings with six months' sea experience as CW (Commissions and Warrants) candidates – they wore white cap bands – were found acceptable for training at *King Alfred* to emerge as officers.

In 1936 a Special Sub-Committee of Imperial Defence reported: 'Women's Reserve deemed not desirable'. A year later Dame Katherine Furse wrote to the Admiralty offering the services of the Association of Wrens, its purpose to keep former members in touch with each other; in 1938 the

Admiralty decided to re-introduce a Women's Royal Naval Service. Mrs Vera Laughton-Matthews was appointed its director and soon set about organizing a nucleus of officers, which by the outbreak of war was ready for expansion. By December 1939 there were over 3,000 WRNS, numbers steadily increasing, until in 1944 their strength exceeded 74,000.

As before their function was to replace active service personnel in such duties as plotters, coders, writers, cooks, stewards, supply ratings, telephone operators, drivers, dispatch riders and messengers. Not only did they perform their duties admirably – in many cases better than the men they replaced – but for the hitherto monastic regimes of many naval establishments they were definitely good news. In the rush to join the women's services the WRNS set its sights high and usually got the best from all levels of society, to the envy of the Army and RAF. A Major RA from Larkhill on a bombardment course at Whale Island was ecstatic about service in the wardroom and went so far as to sit in his cabin every evening, ostensibly for private study but in reality so he could hear the discreet tap on the door followed by 'Permission to darken ship, sir, please?'[8]

To meet the urgent demand for pilots, batches of fifty Naval Airmen 2nd class were given two months' initial training in *St Vincent* at Gosport before learning to fly as Air Branch officers:

> At *St Vincent* [recollects NA Godley] we learnt things we hoped we would never do again. Square bashing under Chiefy Wilmott. Seamanship. How to tie knots, the reef, bowline, clove hitch, sheepshank. Flags and pendants, the Morse code, even semaphore. And traditions . . . Never whistle. Say 'Aye, aye, sir', never 'Yes, sir'. Salute with the palm turned downward. Wear your cap straight across your eyes, never tilted or flat aback. Tie a tiddley bow.

Out of fifty trainees about half would get their wings after nine months' training and become officers, the rest falling by the wayside or in naval parlance: 'dipped. Very few indeed would yet be killed. Perhaps they were found to be LMF [lacking in moral fibre] or deficient in OLQ [officer-like qualities]. But mostly it became clear they'd never make pilots. They found themselves still in the Navy but as plain ordinary seamen hauling on a rope somewhere.'

Elementary flying training with the RAF at Luton was hampered by the proximity of London, which was experiencing nightly air raids. These did not detract from entertainment value because:

> We could always hitch anywhere in bell bottoms. Almost everyone, not only the nice girls, really did seem to like a sailor . . . especially if he were standing at the roadside. Elsewhere we were bought drinks, people called us Jack and dear old ladies came smiling up to us – 'Touch a sailor's collar'. We wore HMS cap ribbons as everyone did in war time. . . . As far as anyone knew we were on shore leave after months of reckless daring at sea. It was only other sailors who could tell at once we hadn't been in the Navy a dog watch from such giveaways as the colour of our collars (not yet faded), the swing of our bell bottoms, the way we wore our caps. But there was a shop in London where you could buy ready-faded collars, just like jeans today. They also sold cap ribbons with the legend FLEET AIR ARM . . . completely unauthorized but some thought them a better line than plain HMS, switching ribbons as we left the airfield.[9]

Godley got his wings the day he left RAF Netheravon as a twenty-year-old temporary acting sub-lieutenant RNVR Air Branch, better known as an 'A boy'; he opted for Swordfish and after seven weeks at Crail joined Arbroath for deck landing training. He saw action in Russian convoys and in 1945 commanded a squadron of twenty aircraft.

In the First World War it was the British Army rather than the Royal Navy that bore the brunt of fighting, suffering more casualties than at any other period in its history. In the second conflict circumstances changed. The RAF came into its own to play a key role; but once the British Expeditionary Force had been safely escorted across the Channel the first seven months were known as the 'phoney war', because nothing much happened on land or in the air. In sharp contrast the Navy, from the moment war was declared, never stopped fighting for all of six years; and by reason of the conditions under which they fought it could be argued that sailors as a whole were in relatively greater danger than airmen or soldiers. An HO rating maintained that:

> In the Navy *everyone* went into action – cooks, stewards, writers, stokers, bandsmen, supply assistants, canteen staff, the whole lot shared the dangers equally. Nor was it only in battle. At *any* moment throughout all the hours and days and nights that ships spent at sea there could be that torpedo on its way towards you, that mine ahead of you, those bombers suddenly appearing. Almost non-stop from the beginning to the end of the war the sailor, from boy to admiral, was in danger.[10]

In his book *The Anatomy of Courage* Lord Moran referred to the Navy, admiring the efficiency and self confidence of its people, derived, in his view, from its traditions, loyalties and professional pride. He detected other sources of strength such as the high standards set in personnel selection and recruitment.

> That a boy has set his heart on this tough service goes for something. He has initiative; he is a cut above the ordinary. Then the ship herself helps; when the time comes the sailor must fight it out whatever the odds, there is no alternative. But more than anything else it is the influence of the machine which kept the Navy from going to seed in peace as soldiers were apt to do.

Whatever his rank or rating a sailor's potential is put to test in war, which invariably brings out the best – and worst – in people. I have therefore chosen, once again, a cross section of personal recollections to describe the outlook and reactions of officers and men as they encountered war, almost all for the first time in their lives.

On the afternoon of Sunday 17 September 1939 the aircraft carrier *Courageous* was operating in the Western Approaches on a U-Boat offensive, screened by four destroyer escorts. In the opinion of Lieutenant (A) Charles Lamb, a Swordfish pilot:

> the attitude of everyone was carefree and casual. We flew on various types of search in answer to distress calls that came flooding in from all directions but only affected aircraft and aircrew, not the ship where the atmosphere was beguilingly peaceful. The ship's company remained at cruising stations by day and scuttles remained open until darken ship at sundown. Officers dressed for dinner each evening and at times it was difficult to realize the country was at war.[11]

Suddenly disaster struck. Two escorts were detached to assist a merchant ship in distress; *Courageous* was turning into the wind at 7 p.m. as Lamb landed on the last Swordfish when U–29 fired three torpedoes, of which two hit the carrier amidships, causing her to list heavily to port. It was then a case of every man for himself, the majority jumping into the sea from right aft with or without life belts. The destroyer *Impulsive* lowered boats and rescued the majority of the 682 survivors out of a complement of 1,200. Able Seaman Marsh was among those helping: 'to pull up survivors with lines – we had no nets at that time – and we did what we could for them. Many were badly burnt and covered in oil fuel. As the ship sank bow first men were still jumping in the water and I saw one man falling on the propellor that was still turning as she went down . . . a sight I shall never forget. It was all over in less than twenty minutes.'[12]

A few days previously the carrier *Ark Royal* had a narrow escape from torpedoes, and a month later *Royal Oak* was sunk in Scapa Flow by U–47 finding a gap in the defences. As in 1914 there were many set-backs. The submarine threat had again been gravely underestimated, Carley floats could not be quickly released, and neither were they suitable for wintry conditions; inflatable lifebelts were either incorrectly used or not to hand. Picking up survivors from the water became a frequent task for which little preparation had been made.

❖❖❖

In 1939 the torpedo school HMS *Vernon* anticipated that the enemy would resort to magnetic or acoustic influence mines to block British ports. Already the German moored mine campaign had met with success and there was evidence of an 'influence' mine immune to normal sweeping methods. Serving in *Vernon* was a seasoned mining specialist, Lieutenant Commander J.G.D. Ouvry, well passed over for promotion but who combined cool courage with quiet efficiency. Cast in similar mould was Lieutenant Commander Roger Lewis; together with Chief Petty Officer Baldwin and Able Seaman Vearncombe they formed a team that was alerted to a report that a parachute mine had been dropped on the tidal reaches of Shoeburyness on the night of 22 November. At low water in darkness and rain the party trudged across the flats to find:

> a cylindrical shape embedded in the mud. Meticulous about detail Ouvry insisted that all metal objects such as money, cigarette cases and buttons be discarded. While the rest kept clear Ouvry and Lewis advanced to investigate the mine . . . seven feet in length, two feet in diameter . . . constructed of a light aluminium type of alloy . . . there was no indication whether it was magnetic or acoustic. Speaking in subdued tones they continued the examination . . . with a sheet of signal pad an impression was taken of the screwed ring so that a spanner could be made in a local workshop. . . . On the way back to the shoreline they discovered the parachute.

While the party was resting a second mine was discovered; at low tide next morning it was decided that Ouvry and Baldwin would tackle mine number one while Lewis and Vearncombe stood by in close touch making notes of progress. According to plan Ouvry and Baldwin started on:

> the screwed ring which secured the aluminium fitting close to the nose. On discovering that one of the holes intended for the spanner was masked by a copper strip Ouvry instructed Baldwin to bend it back. In his enthusiasm Baldwin began to tear it off but was stopped just in time. Had Ouvry not done so both would have been 'blown to kingdom come'. Ouvry then said a little prayer . . . unscrewed the ring . . . and prised out a primer and detonator. Lewis and Vearncombe were signalled to help . . . with the aid of a rope the mine was turned.

Confident that all was now safe the mine was loaded on to a tractor lorry for despatch to *Vernon*. At 10.30 pm that night Lewis reported to the Admiralty, where he found himself describing the operation to Winston Churchill and some sixty admirals and captains.

At 2 a.m. on 25 November *Vernon* reported that it was a magnetic mine. Immediate steps were then take to initiate countermeasures with magnetic sweeps and the 'degaussing' of warships and merchantmen. Ouvry and Lewis were each awarded the DSO, Baldwin and Vearncombe the DSM, the first naval honours of the war.[13]

❖❖❖

To intercept and destroy the German pocket battleships *Deutschland* and *Graf Spee* eight hunting groups were organized to cover the Atlantic trade routes. Composed of the 8-in gun cruiser *Exeter* and the 6-in gun cruisers *Ajax* and *Achilles* Group G was commanded by Commodore Harwood, who correctly anticipated that *Graf Spee* would head for rich pickings off the River Plate. Shortly after the British ships had dispersed from dawn 'action stations' on 13 December to resume patrol off the Plate *Graf Spee* was sighted. Employing tactics already rehearsed Harwood closed to attack from either bow of his adversary. Able Seaman Eric Smith in *Ajax*:

> could see the outline of a large warship. At first I had a feeling of numbness, this was the real thing. I . . . shot down two ladders leading from the bridge, crashed into Commodore Harwood clad in his pyjamas as he left his sea cabin. Shouting a quick 'Sorry, sir' I dashed to B turret just as *Exeter* opened fire. Next into the cabinet was Les Dennis, the turret layer, soon followed by the trainer clad only in a towel; he had been on his way to the bathroom when action stations sounded and entered complaining about all officers who wanted to play war games twice in one day. It was a few seconds before I breathlessly convinced him that this was 'the real McCoy'.[14]

In *Achilles,* manned by the Royal New Zealand Navy, the gunnery officer, Lieutenant Richard Washbourn, by instinct turned to his captain on the bridge; simultaneously they exclaimed: 'My God, it's a pocket battleship.' Scrambling up to the director control tower Washbourn remembered: 'realizing that all one's life's training was about to be put to test and I confessed to a certain thrill of excitement. *Spee* came on in . . . at about 25,000 yards she opened fire, one 11-inch turret on *Exeter*, the other on *Achilles* and *Ajax*. *Spee* only fired a few salvos in our direction before deciding that *Exeter* was her first trouble and put both turrets on her.'

Exeter was soon heavily hit by accurately controlled gunfire assisted by radar ranging – British ships had no radar – losing one turret, then another before listing heavily to starboard. By 7.30 *Exeter* could keep up no longer and so turned to the south-east to effect repairs. Meanwhile *Ajax* and *Achilles* had concentrated their 6-in fire on *Graf Spee*, apparently undamaged, drawing her fire away from *Exeter* and on to themselves. After 20 minutes' firing *Achilles* was straddled by an 11-in salvo:

'Bloody but unbowed': Lieutenant (later Rear Admiral) Richard Washbourn immediately after the Battle of the River Plate, for which he was awarded the DSO

> and the splinters peppered us from truck to waterline. On the bridge one splinter took a chunk out of each of the Captain's legs before shattering the knee of the Chief Yeoman. Up top in my DCT we got more than our fair share. There was a hideous clang, fairly heavy concussion and I remember crouching down in my seat nursing a head that was streaming blood. I gave a bellow 'ACP [after control] take over' and took stock of the situation. The DCT resembled a busy day in the slaughter house. Six bits had come inside. Both my telegraphists were inert bloodstained bundles of blue serge; one operator had tumbled back on top of the spotting observer with nauseating wounds . . . the spotting observer himself had lost large portions of both buttocks but said nothing at the time and stuck it out. Another operator had been in the way of splinters . . . unnoticed and we continued to fire with a dead man resting in a natural position against his instrument.
>
> 'One cannot speak too highly . . .' is a formula that I have always despised and disregarded but it is difficult to put it by after an experience like this. Five out of the ten of us were out, three for keeps and the others took over quietly and did their stuff like absolute veterans. My young communication number, a pretty effeminate looking boy sixteen and a half years old and with little to do except look around him . . . was well spattered with blood, and yet remained as cool as a cucumber.
>
> One never knows how one will react to the violent death of one's friends until it has been experienced. I rather dreaded the showdown . . . and concluded that one must be either a good philosopher or a callous brute. Secondly, there was no suffering. The shock, mercifully provided by nature, overcomes physical pain; that may come later when anodynes are available. Also there was no fatigue. One is too much on the crest of a wave to worry about physical tiredness.[15]

The range was now 8,000 yards. *Graf Spee* broke off the engagement to enter the River Plate with *Achilles* shadowing until she was called off. British reinforcements arrived and in the evening of 17 December *Graf Spee* scuttled herself.

❖❖❖

On 8 April 1940 German troops supported by naval and air forces invaded Norway and Denmark – the initial stage of a major offensive that would lead to German control of the coast of Europe from the Arctic to the Bay of Biscay. Captain Warburton-Lee commanding the 2nd Destroyer Flotilla was ordered to Narvik to prevent enemy troops from landing; he was then informed by the Admiralty that Narvik was in German hands. On hearing from Norwegian lighthouse keepers at the entrance of the fjord that enemy destroyers were there in superior strength he reported to the Admiralty, adding: 'Intend attacking at dawn high water.' A bold and experienced destroyer officer 'Wash' Warburton-Lee signalled a straightforward plan of attack before leading his ships 30 miles up the fjord to Narvik in a heavy snowstorm. Arriving at 5 a.m. *Hardy* first went in alone, the hearts of all on board beating a little faster as they sighted German destroyers among the shipping anchored off the port. Achieving total surprise the leader fired torpedoes and engaged with gunfire, supported by *Hunter* and *Havock*. In the second attack *Hotspur* and *Hostile* joined in with considerable success.

At that stage luck deserted them. Five heavily armed German destroyers arrived on the scene and in the mêlée that followed *Hardy* was hit, *Hunter* sunk and *Hotspur* badly damaged. The shell that struck *Hardy*'s bridge killed the signal and gunnery officers, seriously wounding Warburton-Lee and the navigator. Only Paymaster Lieutenant Geoffrey Stanning, Captain's Secretary, was left amid the wreckage, with dead and dying around him. His left foot useless through a wound, Stanning went below to the shambles of a wheelhouse, found an able seaman to take the wheel and on return to the bridge conned the ship – still under fire – to beach in shallow water. Warburton-Lee's last order was 'Abandon Ship.' The gunner, Mr McCracken, managed to lower Warburton-Lee into a Carley float but he was dead when they got ashore; subsequently for his action on this day he was posthumously awarded the first VC of the war; Stanning was awarded a DSO.

Three days later some of the survivors heard the sound of gunfire in the fjord and saw a British battleship and destroyers driving German destroyers towards Narvik.

Wearing the flag of Admiral Whitworth and preceded by nine destroyers, *Warspite* entered the fjord for the second battle of Narvik. Petty Officer Reardon, Gunner's Mate of 'A' 15-in twin turret recalled that there was:

> An early dinner today before going to General Quarters. My own crew are on the fo'c'sle for a smoke, some wag rolls a snow ball and one of the 'B' turret's crew gets it in the neck. This was a general signal for a snow fight between the two turrets when 'Action Stations' sounds. Gun house, shell room and magazine crews are correct . . . the turret officer tells me I can load. We hear the orders repeated to the men below, the cages come up with a thud and out go the rammers. We can feel that we have increased speed as the ship has begun to vibrate. Then 'Enemy in sight' and the sight setters chant the ranges. It is just like a practice shoot.

Then the 'ding-ding' of the fire gong, the right gun moves a little, comes steady and there is a 'woof' which rocks the turret. 'B' turret firing away overhead, blows away our blast bags and the turret fills with smoke – like London on a November night. The turret officer calls out 'Tell the crew we have hit a destroyer and she is burning nicely.' Good work, boys, keep it going.[16]

Up in the air defence position Lieutenant Commander Fitzroy had a grand stand view of the proceedings and:

as we passed the narrows at the end of the long fjord I remember thinking it was like a forward rush in rugger. We belted along at high speed with destroyers doing magnificent work ahead of us. The roar of our 15-inch guns reverberated from the steep, snow covered sides of the fjord but the explosions of the enemy torpedoes when they hit the rocks were even greater. . . . Tall columns of smoke soon marked the spots where the big German destroyers met their end.[17]

❖❖❖

Throughout the war there were many occasions when warship crews were adrift in boats or rafts, in all sorts of weather and without food or water, for days after their ship had sunk:

The behaviour of men in this ordeal [observed Surgeon Captain McDonald Critchley] depends on how they are led and on their moral fibre. If an officer or senior rating is in the boat, then provided he knows his job . . . and looks after the comfort of his men, boldly assuming responsibility for everything, he will prove the salvation of that boat. He does things and spreads a feeling of purpose. There is a general desire to be like him, for in such a plight men revert to the instincts of a herd and crave leadership. The British sailor in adversity is himself; he is given to a kind of facetious humour, witticisms pass from one boat to another, interspersed with singing which may go on for hours.[18]

Conditions in the water were abnormally bleak when the aircraft carrier *Glorious* was sunk on 8 June 1940 off the north coast of Norway by the German battle cruisers *Scharnhorst* and *Gneisenau*. Men swam to the Carley floats and at first the overcrowded rafts were very low in the water. Some sat with one leg in the sea and the other inside the float. Soon their legs became numb; they were without power or sensation:

Men did not feel hunger after the first day, but they were tormented by thirst. . . . Those who fell asleep did not wake again. The will to keep awake seemed to run parallel with the will to keep alive and sleep was the first sign that a man had abandoned the struggle . . . men became quiet. . . . As men died they were tipped overboard to make more room. . . . Like men lost in the desert who see mirages so the sailors suffered from hallucinations. One man saw warships in action, there were flashes and clouds of smoke; some said 'Don't be daft' but others thought they also saw them. . . . A petty officer had a vivid impression of a distant outline of a dockyard . . . ships seemed to be entering. This vision lasted 15 minutes and then kept coming and going. . . . Men copied one another. If one man stood up the others did the same; if one man waved his hand so did his mates. Suggestion had been given new powers by their distress. It seemed they had been on their raft for years . . . no more aware of thirst and cold; they did not think, they were in a maze helpless to do anything. One sailor who had been silent for nearly two days announced 'I'm just going to get a packet of fags' and stepping in the water was immediately drowned.[19]

On 11 June three officers and thirty-five men out of a complement of 1,200 were picked up by a Norwegian trawler; five more became prisoners of war. Lord Moran asks: 'What is it in the spirit of the Navy that stopped these poor tormented sailors from quarrelling after sixty-five hours adrift in the Arctic circle?'

❖❖❖

During the winter of 1939/40 weather in the North Sea and Atlantic was particularly severe: gale followed gale, snow storms were frequent and the sea froze in many east coast ports. While the newer classes of destroyer worked with the fleet the brunt of convoy work was borne by some sixty 1916–18 Emergency War Programme destroyers; with names beginning with V or W they were amongst the best ever built for the Navy. Although complements increased by 50 per cent to man new weapons or equipment, improvements to habitability were shelved and conditions below decks during the first six months of war were 'almost intolerable', according to Petty Officer 'Bob' Burns. In *Wild Swan* he reckoned that:

fresh provisions became exhausted after three days at sea, the interminable diet of tinned food, no fresh bread and no fresh vegetables caused more distress to the troops than any U-boat or air attack . . . living conditions were primitive beyond measure; never enough billets for hammocks to be slung, so a place on deck sufficed for many. In the cold inhospitable Atlantic salt water was often awash in living spaces and there were no facilities to dry wet clothes. For HO ratings pitched in after minimal shore training it must have been heart breaking. Many suffered permanent sea sickness and their vomiting did not always take place on the upper deck. Smells from inadequate heads facilities permeated everywhere.[20]

Convoy escort duty was probably more exhausting for officers and men in the smaller corvettes where the galley was right aft and the crew slept in bunks in the forecastle. In fact a sub-lieutenant considered it:

sheer, unmitigated hell . . . even getting hot food from galley to fo'c'sle was a tremendous job. The mess decks were usually a shambles and the wear and tear on our bodies . . . something I shall never forget. But we were young and tough and, in a sense, we gloried in our misery and made light of it all. What possible connection it had with defeating Hitler none of us bothered to ask. It was enough to find ourselves more or less afloat the next day and the hope of duff for pudding and a boiler clean when we reached port.[21]

Afternoon watch in destroyer *Douglas*, December 1939

There was indeed a feeling in the Navy that sailors were tough and thrived on discomfort, a view shared by the captain of the destroyer *Whitshed*. Although Commander Conder was a hard character the ship's company had implicit faith in his ability to pull them through any crisis. Morale was high and the first lieutenant remembers that:

> There was no illness on board, except between convoy trips when men might be able to go home for 24 hours or so. They would return with all the complaints brought on by over exposure to too much comfort ashore; hot baths, heated rooms and crowded cinemas . . . which would all disappear as soon as we put to sea. The 'blue water' cure is often a better remedy for minor ills than any physic the doctor can prescribe; a short, sharp dose of sea sickness is the finest treatment for a hangover! The skipper revelled in these harsh methods. After a couple of nights in port he would drive the ship specially hard into a head sea, using more helm and greater speed than was operationally necessary – 'to get the canker out of the system, planted there by over-caring mothers and too-demanding wives' he would say.[22]

Fortunately North Atlantic weather was not always unfriendly and as long as the spirit of understanding and community between officers and men prospered the majority of ships had contented companies. There were exceptions and in the 1918 construction *Curlew*, converted to anti-aircraft cruiser, Ordinary Seaman H.V. Messer was one of several well-educated RNVR ratings to be critical of the 'humourless attitude' of the wardroom – but to a man worshipped the skipper. They criticized the inflexibility whereby 'all routines and disciplines were carried out in the time honoured manner from which no deviation was permitted' and disliked living on the mess decks where:

> everything was reduced to its lowest common denominator, there was no subtlety of any kind. Privacy was non-existent, ablutions, evacuations, reading, letter writing, sleeping and eating were all conducted in a bedlam of half-naked, singing, 'dripping' [grumbling], swearing and seldom silent messmates. One early problem was getting used to the various dialects which, in many sailors, had become so mixed as to be all but incomprehensible. . . . Naval routine left one little time for one's own avocations. The gulf between the messdeck and the wardroom was enormous; it was seldom that an officer spoke to a sailor other than to give him an order.

'Home was one's mess', where Messer learnt to make tea by putting two or more spoonfuls per head into a kettle, adding condensed milk and finally boiling water. The brew was allowed to stand until the colour, even with milk, was dark brown before being poured into cups heaped with sugar: 'when used to it – a most satisfying drink'. Similarly 'pusser's Kye [cocoa] was almost a meal'. Slabs of cocoa were sliced into cups, occasionally sugar and condensed milk added, then boiling water and the result a 'thick, cockle warming drink'.

One aspect that struck Messer loud and clear was:

> the comradeship, sense of humour and eternal optimism of the regular sailor. Although the majority had no ambition, hardly thought for themselves but relied . . . upon leading seamen, POs and officers to run their lives, their support for each other was quite touching. . . . Tomorrow was always going to be better, their last ship was their best ship, their present one the worst; there was always the possibility of finding a willing 'party' on the next run ashore; Chiefs, POs and leading hands were tolerated and respected if they warranted it; a grudging respect, also, was granted to those officers who deserved it.
>
> The opposite side of their character could be equally exasperating; their 'cut off my nose to spite my face' attitude, their foolish disregard for regulations which resulted in penalties far in excess of the misdemeanour, their susceptibility to the extra pint and the soft calls of the shore maidens. However, what can never be denied them were their fighting qualities, their composure in difficult situations whether in war or peace and their wonderful sense of humour. One thing which RNVR sailors learned from their time on the lower deck was respect for their active service messmates.[23]

❖❖❖

Withdrawal from Dunkirk gave many ships their initial taste of air attack. Lieutenant Commander R.L. ('Boggy') Fisher, commanding the destroyer *Wakeful* was in Dover harbour when ordered to 'Proceed to the beach east of Dunkirk with utmost dispatch to embark troops. This is the last chance of saving the BEF'. Arriving at Dunkirk Fisher took aboard his first load of troops and returned to Dover. After re-fuelling *Wakeful* returned to Braye Dunes in daylight, being attacked en route by nine twin engined aircraft:

'Aircraft – Red 60'. Dunkirk was the Navy's first experience of dive bombing

> Thanks to weaving at full speed as soon as we saw the bombs leave the aircraft we managed to dodge all except one near miss which made a hole above the water line in the engine room. Forty to fifty bombs altogether were dropped, some quite close, and I remember vividly the shock of realizing as they exploded with a crack on hitting the water that this, my first experience of somebody trying to kill me, was real war.

Anchored off Braye Dunes beach where long queues of soldiers were waiting *Wakeful* embarked several boatloads until they had 640 on board. Because of top-weight risk they were 'stuffed into engine room, boiler room and store rooms' as low down as possible to preserve stability if required to manoeuvre at high speed. Embarkation took time and it was dark when *Wakeful* headed for Dover, passing close to the flashing light of Kwinte buoy, when Fisher: 'saw two tracks like white swords coming towards us. . . . We avoided one but the other torpedo hit us in the forward boiler room with . . . a brilliant white flash. *Wakeful* was cut in two and the halves sank immediately until their broken ends grounded on the bottom . . . within 15 seconds I found myself swimming off the bridge.'

About fifty survivors, but very few soldiers, were in the water to be picked up by two Scottish drifters en route for Dunkirk. Fisher persuaded the skipper of *Comfort* to return to the wreck where he had last seen men on the stern. On arrival they went alongside the destroyer *Grafton* which was almost immediately torpedoed, putting Fisher again in the water and leaving *Comfort* steaming around in a wide circle with everyone on deck blown overboard. As *Comfort* approached she was engaged by another drifter *Lydd*, which took *Comfort* for an enemy vessel, and rammed her just as Fisher was trying to get aboard. After that Fisher swam around till morning in his Gieves waistcoat, to be picked up by a Norwegian coaster full of Senegalese soldiers en route for Cherbourg. Persuading a minesweeper to take him to Dover he reported to Admiral Ramsay, thence to Chatham to compile a list of casualties. After an Admiralty enquiry it was decided to fit one scuttle in every lower deck compartment big enough to allow a man to escape.[24]

Another warship to be involved was the destroyer leader *Keith*; the captain had been killed and the ship badly damaged while engaging German troops in Boulogne harbour. After two days' rest, repairs and replenishment at Chatham *Keith* was ready again, Able Seaman Iain Nethercott meeting:

> my first HOs on the messdeck. They were ODs [Ordinary seamen] who had been sent as replacements and the poor little chaps hadn't got a clue, they really thought they were on a pleasure cruise. They didn't live the week out. Our new skipper [Captain Berthon] cleared lower deck and gave us a Noel Coward-type speech. Thus fortified we sailed for Dunkirk. [For the next three days *Keith* lifted troops from Dunkirk harbour.] I must admit that it looked very fearsome . . . we were closed up at Action Stations all the time . . . existing on corned beef sandwiches and cups of tea. We catnapped on the guns but were getting more and more tired, especially at night. . . . Most modern destroyers had been withdrawn and soldiers taken off the beaches to older ships and sweepers.

On 1 June Admiral Wake-Walker, in charge of beach operations, hoisted his flag in *Keith* and the next day they were attacked by Stuka divebombers, one bomb going down the funnel to explode in the boiler room causing: 'clouds of smoke and steam to pour out . . . the ship slowed to a stop and started to list to port. An MTB took off the admiral . . . the captain ordered "Abandon Ship" . . . Carley rafts were launched . . . boats lowered . . . and everyone made for [the minesweepers] *Skipjack* and *Salamander*. . . . I could see [the destroyer] *Basilisk* going down to starboard.' The tug *St Abbs* was among those coming alongside to take off survivors, last to board being Nethercott, who looked round and: 'thought my *Keith* would sink any second . . . suddenly more Stukas appeared . . . bombs landed . . . and she just rolled over and sank. . . . I went up forward where someone had a jar of rum. I managed a tot . . . minutes later a bomb hit us and I was blown clean overboard, bobbing up in my whaler's lifejacket looking for *St Abbs*. She had gone.'

Nethercott swam around to climb aboard an abandoned merchant ship, joining other 'Keiths' including the captain. They decided to row back to England in one of the lifeboats, Nethercott laboriously stocking it up with food and water. They had hardly started before being picked up by a motor lighter proceeding to Dunkirk. Finally they transferred to a Sheerness cement carrier which brought them home. Nethercott's concluding remarks: 'I was bloody annoyed, after all that work.'[25]

During the nine days of Operation Dynamo the Navy lost six destroyers and 7,000 lives; Fisher and Nethercott were among the lucky ones. Supported by the Merchant Navy and abundant volunteers the Navy threw everything they had into the evacuation, turning apparent defeat, if not into victory, at least into one of the most brilliant combined operations in history. Once again it showed the unbreakable spirit of the British sailor who is at his best when on the losing side. He certainly earned the undying gratitude and admiration of every one of 338,226 soldiers brought across the Channel.

As soon as the troops reached Dover there were many willing hands eager to help, not least among the WRNS at naval headquarters. In charge was First Officer Nancy Currie whose girls:

> did their own jobs and anything else there was to do, and then came back for their next one. . . . We grudged the time we had to eat and hardly slept for more than an hour or two at a stretch. We helped to deal with men coming ashore. We undid the boots of those lying along the seafront. We improvised pillows for some who were too weak to tell us their next-of-kin. We drove any car anywhere – to and from the hospitals and back to the pier heads to fill them up again with men too exhausted to walk. We cut sandwiches and poured cocoa; we rolled bandages. Meanwhile work at the Castle and the base went on . . . and I never once heard a Wren say that she was tired. History was being made and we were in the front line and the envy of every Wren in the Service. Some of us were in the wardroom when Churchill's great rallying speech came through and we laid down our knives and forks and wiped our eyes: 'We shall fight them on the beaches'. We, we were there. God help us all.[26]

❖❖❖

As a prelude to total war the Luftwaffe started sporadic bombing of Britain from the middle of 1940, which included raids on south coast naval bases; in September the London blitz started. Apart from the damage caused the exaggerated reports of air raids spread to the fleet causing widespread anxiety among those whose homes were in danger. Concern about families continued for most of the war, adding another dimension to the responsibilities of divisional officers and welfare services.

Inevitably the dispersal of naval establishments clear of target areas became top priority, particularly in Portsmouth where training was concentrated; the raid on 10 March 1941 was the last straw. *Vernon* was reduced to a shambles; already many of its activities were conducted elsewhere but major training was transferred to the girls' school at Roedean. The destruction of two Sailors' Homes was a serious loss; although the authorities were quick to make other arrangements, thanks to voluntary efforts and the enterprise of a naval chaplain. The move of *Dryad*, the Navigation School, to Southwick House, near Wickham, was also precipitated by this raid. An unexploded bomb passed through the cupola on the roof, through several floors to reach the basement where Wrens and ratings sitting on chairs were under instruction. As it rolled across the floor to rest against a wall they lifted their legs – without turning a hair! The sub-lieutenant fire watcher in the cupola fell through the hole and escaped unscathed. Haslar hospital was hit and many patients were moved to county hospitals; and when Admiralty House became uninhabitable the commander-in-chief moved his office to the Great Cabin in HMS *Victory*.

Due to its central location the overcrowded naval barracks suffered severely. An urgent investigation into a new site for the Signal School led its commanding officer, Captain Cunningham Graham, accompanied by his commander, to Leydene House, near Petersfield, the property of

Lady Peel. Arriving in uniform in the pouring rain they were led inside by the butler who threw open the door to announce: 'The men have come, your ladyship.' In due course the signalmen moved to their country home, which became HMS *Mercury*. Near Fareham was built a large and highly successful training establishment for ordinary seamen, HMS *Collingwood*; another, HMS *Royal Arthur*, was set up in a holiday camp in Skegness. Mainly on the coast but all round the country small naval commands sprang up away from centres of population to prepare officers and men for the fleet.

❖❖❖

Participation in an air raid on shore was not an enviable experience, although it made sailors realize the suffering of a civilian population unaccustomed to the sort of ordeal intended for the fighting services. On the night of 21 March 1941 Engine Room Artificer George Finch was in the Palace Theatre in Plymouth when:

> we heard the wailing of sirens, but this was commonplace and few people took notice. The first explosion was uncomfortably close . . . the show continued. At about 11 p.m. there was an enormous detonation . . . dust wafted towards the audience. Panic began to spread. Suddenly the clear note of a trumpet blared out . . . some genius in the projection room switched on a spotlight and there was the maestro Billy Cotton standing imperturbably rendering the *Trumpet Voluntary* as if it were Sunday afternoon on the local bandstand.
>
> Several naval men . . . gathered in a group and decided to offer their services to a warden's command post. We left the theatre and entered Union Street. A wave of hot air hit us like a tidal wave, choking, full of the stench of burning buildings, rubber, oil – indescribable. On both sides of the street looking towards what had been the city centre, every building was burning . . . we decided to run the gauntlet towards the centre keeping to the middle of the street . . . towards Derry's Clock where I knew there were several escape routes to the Hoe. . . . We felt the ground shuddering with sickening thuds – the preliminary showers of incendiaries had set the target alight and now it was the turn of high explosives.

Finch and his party reached the Hoe to find a scene of devastation, stopping to assist civilians digging in the debris for survivors from what had been the Nurses' Home and the YMCA. Next day he got permission to render assistance during a raid when he met: 'a small party of naval men wandering aimlessly and persuaded them to join me. They were in a carefree mood . . . ready for anything. . . . The roof of Charles church was well alight . . . a cleric stood at the entrance staring down the nave at the altar. . . . There seemed to be plenty of time.' Within minutes they had rescued the ornamental hangings before the roof collapsed.

During the weeks that followed volunteers from the Army, Navy and RAF joined civilians in a massive clearing up operation; just when it was thought that raids were over Devonport barracks and hospital were hit. Finch was again involved, his shoregoing uniform irreparably stained. But as he remarked: 'Fortunately the Service had by then approved the introduction of blue battle-dress, which we wore as standard dress most of the war.'[27]

❖❖❖

Ted Whitley was one of the 200 or so RAF Halton apprentices who transferred to the RN in 1939:

> and became even more pro-Navy than many who joined directly. . . . Our first contact with the RN were Chief Gunnery Instructors and Leading Seamen who seemed to have been carved from solid pillars of blue serge and who tried in the short time available to ready us for our first ship. [At a holiday camp in Ryde, Whitley was] introduced to 'Blue Liner' service-made cigarettes and excellent food until the camp staff were replaced by naval cooks. From ex-seamen and stokers trained as Air Mechanics we learned tricks like asking a girl to hold your collar from the front whilst donning overcoats. The girl's arms were then trapped and one saw the advantage of sailor's rig.

Joining 819 squadron (Swordfish) at RN Air Station, at Ford, Air Fitter (A) Whitley embarked in *Illustrious*, first of the new aircraft carriers to complete early in 1940. After a work-up based on Bermuda, Captain Dennis Boyd took his ship to join Admiral Cunningham in the Mediterranean, her aircraft a valuable addition to his striking power. Aboard *Illustrious* Whitley found:

> work at sea in a carrier in those days was hard graft, the aircraft flew all day on anti-submarine patrols and were serviced – or the role changed – at night. . . . We hardly had time to wash our overalls and had a lot of stick from the other wearers who were watchkeeping while we were watch on – stop on. The ship's chapel was the only place where one could enjoy a little peace. At sea we slept on camp beds in the hangar as our mess was on the water line.[28]

Engine Room Artificers' Mess, aircraft carrier *Ark Royal*, 1940

As soon as Italy declared war on 10 June 1940 Cunningham seized the offensive, inflicting damage on forces off Calabria before turning his attention to Taranto. To attack the Italian fleet in Taranto harbour had been seriously contemplated in times of crisis pre-war but it was not until November that Rear Admiral Aircraft Carriers, with aircraft from *Illustrious* and *Eagle* at his disposal, could formulate a strike plan. In the event *Illustrious* had to undertake the operation alone with Swordfish from *Eagle* on board. After a stint of night flying training and last minute reconnaissance of the target, weather conditions were favourable on the 11th. 'My first intimation of the Taranto attack', wrote Whitley, 'was a cryptic notice on the blackboard in the starboard forward corner of No. 1 Hangar, "Blitz on Taranto", with a list of aircraft and loads. By the morning of the attack all was prepared.'[28]

At 8.30 p.m. Lieutenant M.R. Maund of 824 squadron was aware that:

> the Klaxon had gone and all starters are whirring as, stubbing out our cigarettes, we bundled outside into the chill evening air. It is not so dark now, with the moon well up in the sky, so one can see rather than feel one's way past the aircraft which, with their wings folded for close packing, look more like four poster beds than front-line aeroplanes . . . the fitter bends over me, shouts 'Good Luck, Sir' into my speaking tube, and is gone. . . . 4F rocks in the slip-stream of aircraft ahead of her as other engines run up, and a feeling of desolation is upon me, unrelieved by the company of ten other aircraft crews, who doubtless entertained similar thoughts. . . . A green light waves away our chocks, orders us to taxi forward, the wings are spread with a slam and as I test the aileron controls; green waves again. We are off . . .[29]

Taranto Harbour was heavily defended by anti-aircraft guns of every calibre, augmented by anti-torpedo nets and barrage balloons. Operating as a flare dropper to illuminate the target, Charles Lamb of 815 squadron noted that:

> Before the first Swordfish dived to attack the full throated roar from the guns of six battleships . . . cruisers and destroyers made the harbour defences seem like a sideshow. . . . Into that inferno, one hour apart, two waves of six and then five Swordfish . . . danced a weaving arabesque of death and destruction with their torpedoes, flying into harbour only a few feet above sea level – so low that one or two of them actually touched the water with their wheels as they sped through the harbour entrance. . . . It seems incredible that only two were brought down.[30]

Turning to look back as his aircraft got away at sea level, torpedo and bombs expended, Maund spoke to his observer: 'Just look at that bloody awful mess – look at it,' as a huge weeping willow of coloured fire showers over the harbour area. Finding his way home by radio direction beacon, Maund:

> circles once before the raised deck-lights go on. The three bright lights ahead are the deck landing-control tell us 'steady approach' – the flight deck is suddenly underneath us. Back throttle stick – a pause – the gentle brush of wheels on deck and the wires have got us. . . . A crowd of people in the glaring Ops Room . . . I am giving evidence. A *Littorio* battleship, I

> think. Yes, a clear run of 1,000 yards. A good drop? Oh – about thirty feet. . . . The wardroom warm and sane. Three rapid whiskies and soda, followed by bacon and eggs I can scarcely taste. A camp bed on the quarterdeck in the grey light of dawn. A jumble of scattered pictures chases through my mind. Unconsciousness.[31]

In 819 squadron Whitley remembers 'an almost carnival atmosphere of relief and the sweet smell of success in particular as all four of our aircraft returned unscathed'.

It was, indeed, a brilliant victory for the Fleet Air Arm, to be celebrated annually after the end of the Second World War. In six-and-a-half hours' flying time twenty aircraft had inflicted more damage on the Italian fleet than was inflicted on the German High Seas fleet at Jutland. On rejoining the fleet they were greeted with the flag signal '*Illustrious* manoeuvre well executed', seemingly faint praise but Cunningham was never one to waste words, even when he really meant it.

Early in 1941 *Illustrious* left Alexandria to escort a convoy to Malta and Greece, when an élite force of Junkers 87 struck with perfect timing and devastating accuracy shortly after noon. Peeling off at 12,000 ft to start their aiming dive, their engine notes rose to a scream as they aimed unnervingly at the carrier to release 500-kg bombs at barely 1,000 ft before pulling out. The first bomb went down the after lift to explode in the hangar starting innumerable fires and heavy casualties. Those surviving threw themselves on the deck as bullets from burning aircraft whizzed around. The heat was unsupportable and people were lucky to get out alive. Amid the perpetual noise of gunfire could be heard the cheerful voice of the chaplain, the Revd Henry Lloyd, giving a running commentary on the action and between bomb explosions 'keeping insanity at bay'. When he went below to tend the casualties he found a young seaman mortally wounded who asked 'Is the captain alright?' When assured that he was the youngster replied: 'Don't worry, padre. As long as the captain is on the bridge he will bring the ship home.' Then he died. There were many examples of great bravery on that fateful day.

Under the indomitable leadership of Dennis Boyd *Illustrious* survived the attack to limp into Grand Harbour and secure alongside Parlatorio Wharf, only to be subjected to further air raids before sailing for Alexandria, and thence for repairs in USA.

❖❖❖

Taranto more than confirmed the moral ascendancy established over the Italian Navy by Cunningham's aggressive policy; in Greece it was evident that the Italian invasion of October 1940 was running into trouble and would soon need German support. Meanwhile convoys with British troops and supplies were being rushed to the aid of Greek forces; it was to attack these convoys late in March 1941 that a considerable force of Italian cruisers and destroyers led by Admiral Iachino in the battleship *Vittorio Veneto* were at sea. Sensing that a decisive fleet action was imminent Cunningham concentrated his light forces to the south of Crete and sailed his battleships and the aircraft carrier *Formidable* from Alexandria to intercept the enemy.

With only a few ships fitted with radar, but with the priceless advantage of aircraft for reconnaissance and strikes, Cunningham's heavy ships gradually overhauled the Italian main body that was headed for home. At 10.20 p.m. on March two large cruisers were spotted from *Warspite*'s bridge, and Cunningham spoke for all present when he wrote:

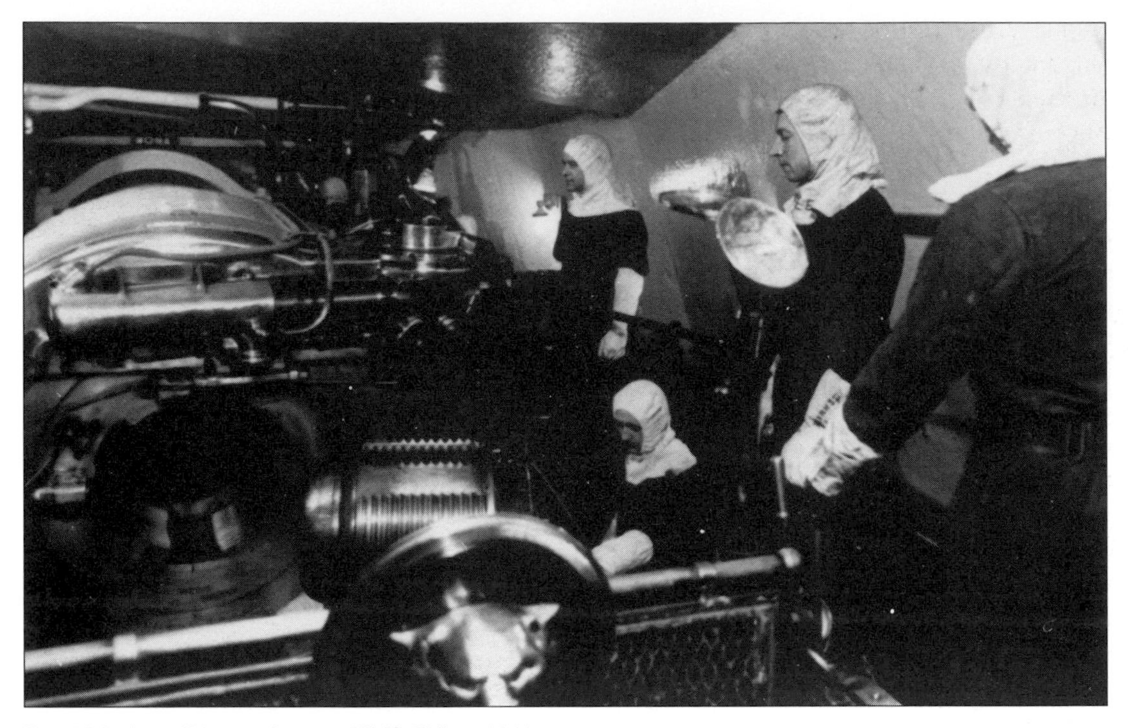

Royal Marines: 'B' turret's crew, HMS *Valiant*, 1941

> I shall never forget the next few minutes. In a silence that could almost bc felt one heard the voices of control personnel putting the guns on to the new target. Never in my whole life have I experienced a more thrilling moment than when I heard a calm voice from the director tower 'Director layer-target'; sure sign that the guns were ready and that his finger was itching on the trigger. The enemy was at a range of no more than 3,800 yards – point blank.'
>
> One heard the 'ting-ting' of the fire gongs. Then came a great orange flash and the violent shudder as the six big guns bearing were fired simultaneously . . . our searchlights shone . . . for what was a ghastly sight. Full in the beam I saw our six great projectiles flying through the air. Five out of six hit . . . and burst with splashes of brilliant flame. The Italians were quite unprepared. Their guns were trained fore and aft.[32]

The action was a massacre. Three heavy cruisers and two destroyers sunk; over 2,000 officers and men lost; British casualties were very light. On the following morning ships returned to the scene of battle to rescue survivors until interrupted by German aircraft attack. On 1 April a special thanksgiving service was held on board all ships.

❖❖❖

After Matapan the situation deteriorated. With overwhelming air power German forces swept through Greece. In mid-April Cunningham ordered his cruisers and destroyers to evacuate some

50,000 British and Commonwealth troops from Greek ports, lifting them to reinforce Crete; without air support fleet losses were providentially small. After the German airborne invasion on 20 May, and with little or no rest, ships were then confronted with the battle for Crete. Based 400 miles away at Alexandria, cruisers and destroyers endured almost continual air attack, firstly when preventing enemy convoys reaching the island and subsequently, when the situation ashore became hopeless, in evacuating the troops. Conscious of the deadly and relentless dive bombing, 'hearts were heavy as news of our casualties kept coming in' wrote Cunningham. 'In my office I came to dread every ring on the telephone, every knock on the door and the arrival of every fresh signal. . . . Most of the ships were woefully short of ammunition and I very well knew the anxiety and physical strain under which their devoted officers and men were working.'

Admiral Sir Andrew Cunningham, 1941

As senior engineer of the anti-aircraft cruiser *Naiad* Admiral Le Bailly later wrote:

> During a prolonged bombing attack such as we endured, engine room and boiler rooms resemble the inside of a giant's kettle against which a sledge hammer is being beaten with uncertain aim. Sometimes there was an almighty clang; sometimes the giant in his frustration, seemed to pick up the kettle and shake and even kick it. The officer detailed to broadcast a running commentary suffered a breakdown during the battle so we heard little below but through the noise and heat of the machinery spaces we came to understand something of what was happening on deck. . . . We could hear our 5.25-in turrets opening fire which told us aircraft were attacking. Next, the bridge telegraphs might signal Emergency Full Speed and we would see the rudder indicator move . . . at the moment of bomb release. This would be followed by the sound of the short range weapons as the bomber pulled out of his dive. . . . We learned to interpret by the ensuing shake or shudder or clang the success or otherwise of our navigator's avoiding action.
>
> From time to time my chief or I would visit the boiler rooms. Here, for hour after frightening hour, with ears popping from air pressure the young stokers knew and heard little of what was going on apart from the obvious near misses and the scream of the boiler room fans. On their alertness, as they watched for orders to open or shut off oil sprayers to the furnaces, depended the precise supply of steam available to meet the sudden changes of speed ordered . . . on which *Naiad*'s survival depended.[33]

Almost worse than reports of sinkings was when the commander-in-chief and his staff watched the battered ships limping into Alexandria harbour only to be told that they would have to re-fuel and re-ammunition overnight and return to Crete. The morale of more than one ship's company was near breaking point and if ever there was an occasion when the leadership qualities mattered, then this was it. Indeed, it was said that some 'ships were held together by string and the personality of their commanding officers'. One such skipper was Commander Aubrey St Clair Ford of the destroyer *Kipling* who, having rescued the survivors from *Kelly* and *Kashmir*, was observed going alongside in Alexandria by an officer in the cruiser *Naiad*:

> at full speed astern with that abandon destroyers seem to display. The quay seems about to be rammed when a sudden race of her propellers pulls the stern down and stops her. She is a very special ship, crammed with men in all sorts of uniform . . . equipment lies scattered all over the deck. She has a heavy list and looks tired and worn. Our commander calls all hands aft to cheer and her captain on the bridge waves a cheery hand in acknowledgement. He is happy, too, because he has achieved the impossible, bringing his crippled ship home with some 300 survivors despite constant air attack. Alongside the quay she shudders and stops. The *Kipling* has come home.[34]

In some incredible way the Navy had done it again, snatching the miracle of yet another evacuation out of certain defeat. As well as preventing a seaborne invasion 18,000 troops had been taken off but at an appalling cost; three cruisers and six destroyers sunk, many more severely damaged, some two thousand lives lost. Was it worth it? Cunningham never faltered in his single minded determination not to let the Army down. In his exhortations to 'stick it out' there was more than one grumble but when it was all over the Navy knew that they could never hold up their heads again if they had shirked the issue. 'It takes three years to build a ship. It would take three hundred years to rebuild a tradition,' was one of Andrew Cunningham's remarks that passed into history.

CHAPTER ELEVEN

Long Haul to Victory

There was no question of enjoying the war, nor of considering it glamorous, nor of hating our opponents. It was all far simpler than that. The war had been entered; it had to be won. Much of what we had to do was unpleasant and frightening; being a destructive task it was never truly satisfying. But we were young and the freshness of youth saw only a challenge to be accepted and took away much of the bitterness of war.

An RNVR officer in Coastal Forces

Outbreak of war saw an immediate increase in the offices of the Admiralty in Whitehall, almost all the 2nd Sea Lord's departments moving to a block in Queen Anne's Mansions off St James's Park where they remained for many years. One of the busiest offices was that of the Director of Personal Services (DPS), whose responsibilities for ratings included welfare, advancement and drafting.

The sheer magnitude of the task can be judged by comparison with the First World War, when in four and a quarter years of war the Navy grew from 150,000 to just over 400,000, an expansion of two and two-thirds. From September 1939 to January 1944 the Navy expanded more than four times, from 161,000 to 750,000 – in the same time the thickness of the Navy List increased from 1 to 6 in. Secondly, because of energetic rating recruitment for three years before war, half the 1939 active service strength were comparatively new entries. The combination of these with the influx of elderly pensioners, many of whom were out of touch with modern developments, accounted for a severe shortage of experienced ratings. Since it took longer to train a key rating than to build a destroyer it was some time before the balance was restored.

Supply of naval man-power was controlled by the Ministry of Labour and National Service, who ordered men of certain ages to register before deciding who should remain in industry and who should be called up for a fighting service. Those registering could state a preference and until the end of 1942 the Navy had little to complain about. However, 1943 witnessed the greatest expansion in man and woman power that the Navy has ever known, 50 per cent higher than in 1942 and thirty times more than in one peacetime year. The physical and mental standards of trainees, as well as training programmes, were reduced to minimum levels, which meant that the Navy had to accept all men offered, except complete illiterates and the almost mentally deficient. Such was the demand for personnel that, provided they were reasonably intelligent, those of Medical Grade II were given remedial exercises at a special establishment before undergoing initial training.

Boy volunteer entry continued to be a promising source of supply, as well as youths of seventeen and eighteen who were trained in one of the many New Entry Training Establishments. Another means of joining the Navy was through the Y scheme, run by Admiral Commanding Reserves and designed to recruit mainly pilots and observers and, to some extent, various types of petty officer.

In each of the three home port naval barracks were seldom fewer than 12,000 men. Of these some two thousand were under New Entry training to become stokers, cooks, stewards and writers; another 2,000 would be learning gunnery or torpedo; those on foreign service leave amounted to 2,000 while a similar number were being kitted up or sent on leave before a foreign draft. The remaining 3,000 included a variety of occupations – CW candidates awaiting interview board, mechanics under specialized training, about seven hundred medically or dentally unfit, men taking course for higher rating, Allied naval personnel under training, a large permanent staff and the inevitable quota of 'barrack stanchions' – men who surreptitiously made themselves so indispensable as to remain in barracks for the whole war. Throughout the whole day and most of the night the tempo of activity in the depots never ceased as men arrived to be documented, accommodated, clothed, fed, paid, medicated, inoculated, sorted out, drafted and dispatched to a ship or station at home or overseas with the minimum of delay.

To DPS the term welfare covered everything that affected a sailor's life – leave, pay and allowances, advancement, victualling, uniform and clothing, accommodation, complaints and representations, discharge and rehabilitation, film shows and live entertainment. Leave became a desperately important factor, not only for the man but also for the family who reaped the joy of a homecoming only to endure the agony of a farewell that might be terminal. To avoid inter-service bickering it was agreed to standardize leave arrangements, although with its different conditions the Navy usually found this impracticable. Pre-war regulations applied in the granting of general leave, plus foreign service leave at a rate of seven days per six months. This did not stop the office of DPS receiving a constant stream of callers asking for extensions of leave on compassionate grounds, varying from illness of close relations, funerals and domestic troubles to the man who asked for an extra few days to supervise the mating of his pigeons. Another sailor called with a baby in arms and a child trailing behind whose wife was in hospital, insisting that as he could not get an extension he would take them back to his ship. The welfare section of his port division handled this and many similar cases.

London was full of ratings on leave and the word got around that Queen Anne's was the place to call if short of cash. Men were often incorrectly paid, had been robbed or were just plain broke, a plight common with Canadian ratings – reputedly big spenders; all were dealt with by a paymaster commander who had the wisdom of Solomon and the patience of Job. Similarly the officer handling requests for discharge or release on compassionate grounds received indignant letters from wives and mothers all of whom needed appeasement. In particular the Directorate had to feed a constant flow of information and advice to port division and naval base welfare authorities, grappling with problems ranging from divorce and bigamy to the provision of fish fryers for sailors' hostels. The measure of its reputation for achieving the difficult at once was illustrated by Captain Caspar Swinley, Deputy DPS, who 'was rung up by someone at Waterloo late one night to say that there was a naval corpse on the platform and what was I going to do about it. Apparently the local undertaker was drunk in a pub and had refused to play. Solving this problem was an interesting middle watch occupation.'[1]

❖❖❖

When Max Horton was appointed Vice-Admiral Submarines in January 1940 he inherited control of fifty-seven submarines in five flotillas, four in the North Sea and one in the Mediterranean.

With one or two notable exceptions the submarine service had not done too well to date and in Max Horton they had just the right man to lead them.

Pre-war submarine ratings were volunteers and picked for exemplary character. By 1941 the demand for trained men made it impossible to continue this system, so Horton decided to accept men with minimal experience and train them at *Dolphin* followed by instruction in the training flotilla. To make up numbers impressment had to be applied, for example, among torpedo gunners' mates who in each submarine would be responsible for some seventeen torpedoes.

To replace officers lost in twenty-six submarines sunk during 1940 and to meet an accelerated building programme, conscription was necessary of junior officers due to insufficient volunteers. Furthermore Horton decided to replace most but not all commanding officers over thirty-five with younger men, on the grounds that it was going to be a long, tough war and submarine operations needed the qualities of youthful captains. How right he was. In any case some older COs felt deep down in their hearts that it was time for a staff job or General Service. Even so the loss of half the 1939 strength of the branch made the crew situation critical.

Early in 1940 the Admiralty started to recruit RNVR officers from *King Alfred* for the submarine service; the first to be selected for six weeks' training at HMS *Dolphin* was Edward Young, a former publisher and weekend yachtsman. On his first war patrol in one of the 1918 construction H class, he remembered:

> It was with a disturbing mixture of apprehension, pride and curiosity that I went into the control-room to take over my watch from Number One for the first time. He took me first to the chart-table, an uncomfortably small space in the passageway leading forward, pointed out our position on the chart and the landmarks on which I must take a fix every half hour, and then showed me those landmarks through a periscope to make sure I could identify them. Finally, with a cheery 'She's all yours, chum' he retired to the wardroom and left me in charge of the ship.

While on patrol off enemy coast H28 was at 'watch diving', the crew divided into three watches, two hours on and four off. The watch consisted of sufficient men to maintain required depth and work the periscope, two planesmen keeping the trim with control wheels as they watched depth gauges, the helmsman steering by gyro compass, an ERA at the vent-and-blow panel and the lever which raised and lowered the periscope, an LTO in the motor room who obeyed the speed telegraphs, a seaman hydrophone operator, and finally a stoker in a compartment under the control room to operate the ballast pump motor and valves to flood or pump the trimming tanks on order. The crew off watch would be sleeping, reading or eating, a routine with which Young became very familiar during the next four years.

As 'Third Hand' and torpedo officer, Young's job when attacking was to work a calculator known as the 'fruit machine' that, among other things, calculated the director angle or aim off for torpedo firing (in degrees relative to the ship's head) and assisted the captain to manoeuvre into the firing position. This occurred towards the end of the patrol when the captain decided to attack a heavily laden barge escorted by two minesweepers. Young continues:

> As each torpedo was fired in the tube-space forward I felt a sudden increase of pressure on my eardrums and a slight backward lurch, as though the boat had bumped into something

large and soft. And then we waited for the bangs in almost unbearable tension . . . the seconds dragged by interminably.

In the event the torpedoes missed causing bitter disappointment. When the captain took H28 down to 100 ft. Young experienced his first depth charge attack, after the hydrophone operator reported propeller noises astern:

> Almost at the same moment a sharp crack, as of a giant hammer, struck the pressure hull, followed by a frightful reverberating row which seemed to echo through all the subterranean ocean caves of the world. To my astonishment the lights stayed on. 'Not very close' said the captain. Not close! As he spoke there was a second almighty crack and again that thundering, rumbling, aftermath. And still we suffered no damage. . . . A little while later the captain, listening intently, said 'I think I can hear his asdic,' and presently I too heard a faint, slow regular knocking, as though someone was tapping gently on the outside of the hull. I thought of Pew's stick tapping along the road in *Treasure Island*. . . . Perhaps the enemy had already detected our echo from his transmissions and was even now closing in for the kill.

There were no more depth charges and Young reckoned he had been let off with an easy baptism.

Young's career then followed the usual wartime pattern, serving in the 7th flotilla at Rothesay, which gave practical sea training to newly qualified submarine officers and ratings, simultaneously acting as submerged targets for destroyers and escorts – a role known as the 'clockwork mouse'. As third hand in *Umpire* Young survived a collision with a trawler on convoy off the east coast – the submarine sank with half her complement – and in 1942 was first lieutenant in *Sealion* briefly and then *Saracen* under Lieutenant Mike Lumby, who had the distinction of sinking a U-boat in his 'working up' patrol in the North Sea. As well as being answerable for the organization, efficiency and welfare of the crew Number One had the life or death responsibility for the submarine's trim.

RNVR Sub under training in a submarine

In July 1943 Young became the first RNVR officer to command a submarine. A year later, in HM Submarine *Storm*, he gained a DSO after conducting a spirited attack on Japanese shipping off the Burma coast when he ran on the surface into confined waters and used his 3-in gun with great effect. One of the best recollections of his naval service was overhearing a junior submarine officer, in the presence of his commanding officer, refer to submarine pay as 'danger money'. 'Danger!' roared the CO, 'Danger! What you get extra pay for, my boy, is skill and responsibility. What the hell do you mean, *danger*?'[2]

In the Mediterranean British submarines had endured bitter loss for small success. And when Horton appointed Commander 'Shrimp' Simpson to command the 10th Flotilla early in 1941 he arrived at Malta to find the island under ferocious air attack. During rest periods between patrols and manned by half crews, submarines had to dive in the harbour at the onset of daylight raids to remain immune from damage. Nevertheless during 1941 and 1942 the flotilla operated with increasing success against Italian warships including submarines, escorted convoys en route for the enemy army in North Africa, individual merchant shipping, shore targets and in clandestine exploits with commando forces. On return to harbour elation was demonstrated by the traditional skull and crossbones flag fluttering above the conning tower, with its insignia depicting the type of action accomplished.

Because so much depended on submarine commanding officers, whose decorations were among the hardest earned in the Navy, Horton directed that 'they were to be treated as Derby winners'. Describing five in his command Simpson reckoned that their contrasting characters set the tone of the flotilla, and that the secret of their success lay in their ability to make instant decisions. All were between twenty-eight and thirty; by the end of 1942 ages had dropped until the youngest – Lieutenant John Roxburgh – was only twenty-three.

Simpson noted that:

> Richard Cayley always appeared light hearted, almost flippant, when in harbour. He carried a mouth organ . . . was a great asset to the mess but behind his cheerful appearance was a shrewd, tough and brave man. . . . At sea he was the only CO who slept at night in the conning tower . . . in a broad, short hammock under the chart table. When submerged by day he would relax in the wardroom either reading or doing gros-point needlework. . . . Experience and skill were nicely balanced with gaiety and resolution.

The next was David Wanklyn who stood over six feet and:

> . . . was an enthusiastic games player but not an exceptional eye for the ball . . . excelled at dry fly fishing, he was a precise person with a good brain. . . . He made such a poor start . . . that I feared he might never make the grade. . . . But wherever Wanklyn was sent the enemy appeared . . . this gave him much practice and confidence . . . turning fleeting opportunities into complete success. His modesty made him loved and respected by all.

E.P. Tomkinson, about 6ft 2in tall, powerfully built and the Royal Navy golf champion, was:

> in a class by himself . . . and the qualities of concentration, a strong will and tenacity demanded by it were plain in his character. With an impressive black beard he looked formidable when serious but he was a gay personality with a gentle nature who hated war. . . . When his great friend and companion Wanklyn was awarded his VC . . . Tomkinson, whose skill was comparable . . . said 'I'm glad Wanks got his VC. He's earned it, it suits him and it

HM Submarine *Trump* returns to harbour after a successful patrol

makes him happy. But, sir, if you want to know what medal would make me most happy, it's the one they haven't struck yet. It's the end of war medal.' . . . Like Wanklyn, his ability, presence and intelligence made him a born leader.

Lieutenant John Wraith appeared to be an:

average, rather shy officer who seemed self-effacing and possibly lacking in self confidence. This was the veneer to a very modest man with a great sense of humour who in action was entirely self confident. . . . On return from a successful patrol . . . his typical explanation was 'They simply committed suicide, sir, just ran into my torpedoes.'

Lieutenant Teddy Woodward possessed exceptional stamina, was a superb swimmer and had a particularly good eye for periscope attack. However:

the pace he set himself in harbour would have put most men in hospital. He would arrive in Lazaretto Creek . . . looking pale and in need of complete rest. He would climb to the conning tower and say 'Let go everything. Slow ahead port.' . . . Once clear of the harbour his First Lieutenant would take over and direct *Unbeaten* to her patrol position. On arrival Teddy was . . . as fresh as a daisy and would apply his fully revived talent to sinking the enemy.[3]

Of these, Woodward alone survived the war.

Having transferred to submarines, Leading Seaman Nethercott DSM joined *Tactician* in the builders' yard, commanded later by Lieutenant Commander Collett of whom he thought highly, and:

During the two years aboard the boat from commissioning to paying off we had no defaulters and no real trouble. We knew that in an operational boat any punishment would send us back to General Service, the worst disgrace the Admiralty could think up. Ashore we were a wild bunch, but naval authorities in all ports abroad kept well clear of stirring up trouble with submarine crews.

During a shake down patrol off Norway in appalling weather Nethercott took turn at conning tower look out, when 'we wore safety belts with steel chains and dog clips to hold on to the rails on the inside of the cab as we were totally submerged in huge waves half the time'.

Soon after arrival in the Mediterranean, *Tactician*:

sank a merchant ship in convoy . . . to be attacked by three escorts. . . . Down at 200 ft with everything shut off for depth charging and at Silent Routine. Some depth charge patterns were so close that you could hear the 'click' of the pistols just before the charge exploded. One string of charges exploded just over the engine room hatch. 'Shiner' Wright, the Chief Tiffy, was standing under the hatch . . . the explosion sheared the hatch clips right off and . . . about a ton of water shot in, most of it on poor old Shiner who wasn't used to sudden baths in his own engine room.[4]

Meanwhile the Battle of the Atlantic was giving cause for concern, Winston Churchill going so far as to confess that 'the only thing that really frightened me during the war was the U-Boat peril'. Added to a lack of escorts for convoys and effective submarine countermeasures was an officer problem. A former convoy escort commander, Vice-Admiral Sir Peter Gretton, commented:

> For the first few years of the war the Home and Mediterranean fleets got all the best officers. It was considered somewhat unfashionable to be in the Western Approaches Command, which . . . received many failures from Scapa Flow, many retired officers and many incompetents. There were a few young lieutenants in their first commands, a very few more senior officers to support the reserves who were such splendid material; but the good regulars were desperately few.[5]

By 1942 the rapid increase of warships had overrun the supply of RN and RNR officers. Thus the RNVR became sufficiently important for the Admiralty to announce that in future the fleet would be manned by reserve officers with a leavening of active service rather than regular officers diluted by reserves. This, and the need for captains and first lieutenants of destroyers with combat experience to remain with the Home and Mediterranean squadrons, explains the shortage mentioned by Gretton. In the early stages of Western Approaches work-up training for convoy escorts was neglected, but by the time Gretton achieved his support group four of his corvettes were commanded by RNVRs, two of whom were Australian; in the wardrooms were Canadians and New Zealanders.

Early in 1941 Western Approaches Command was set up in Derby House, Liverpool by Admiral Sir Percy Noble in close co-operation with RAF Coastal Command and with responsibility for the whole business of protecting trade, routing convoys and destroying U-boats – in other words winning the war. A far-reaching part was played by the Tactical Unit established under the skilful direction of Commander Gilbert Roberts, who had been invalided from the service with TB shortly before the outbreak of war and by sheer determination rejoined the Navy.

Anti-submarine training was transferred from Portland to Tobermory late in 1940 where Commodore Stephenson and his staff gave destroyers, frigates and corvettes a work-up programme to bring them to operational readiness. Many ships came straight from the builders' yard with crews who had never been to sea before; 'Monkey' or 'Puggy' Stephenson, as the retired vice-admiral was called, handled them all with unremitting energy and an old-fashioned sense of humour. A corvette's lieutenant wrote:

> Daily we exercised everything with a wild sense of crisis. We abandoned ship, we repelled boarders, we got out the kedge anchor, we closed up action stations against a stop watch, we fought fires, we prepared to tow . . . we fired guns . . . and demolished the target . . . on the other hand we made a supreme hash of our first depth charge drill, due to a fault in the electric buzzer system. . . . But we learnt quickly during those weeks; almost before we knew it had happened we emerged as a ship's company instead of a crowd of individuals. It was hard work . . . we could see the results from day to day and they were encouraging in every particular.[6]

Retired officers may have had their limitations in commanding small ships but both Roberts and Stephenson possessed the burning enthusiasm and decisive personality that also characterized many convoy commodores. And when Max Horton succeeded Percy Noble as Commander-in-Chief Western Approaches in November 1942 he found a well tuned organization to which he could apply his drive and genius.

Ships' companies of escort vessels were a typical lower deck cross section and, since they rarely saw warships larger than a destroyer, regarded themselves as rather special. Unlike other forces they were able to see with their own eyes the contribution they were making to the Allied cause and regularly derived immense satisfaction in delivering a convoy safely across the Atlantic. Periodical boiler cleans afforded the only chance of a few days' leave; otherwise it was the pubs and clubs of Greenock, Londonderry or Liverpool. At the latter Signalman Dossett of the destroyer *Havelock* remembered:

> the Flotilla Club on the quayside of Gladstone Dock as being very exclusive; crew members could go in overalls and a naval cap so it was a favourite spot for those of us a little short of the ready and those on duty who thought they would not be missed for a moment. From the darkness, with shaded quayway lights of . . . ships alongside the only illumination, you stumble through a door and blackout curtains into a long wooden shed with refreshments one end and a bar at the other. The canteen was manned by women – wives of Liverpool business men who worked voluntarily. Everywhere were sailors (no women except the staff), the noise, the fug, the pilchard sandwiches and, of course, the beer – all made a haven of rest where we could forget our troubles for a little while.[7]

With his background as watchkeeper, first lieutenant and commanding officer of corvettes Nicholas Monsarrat RNVR captured some of the atmosphere and life in small ships. As a convoy approached a U-boat danger zone tension mounted, and 'it is almost a relief when the first explosion is heard and the first flare goes up and you think "Oh well, this is it"'. Admiration by the RN for the Merchant Navy became deep and unbounded because warships could at least take positive action:

> we can crack on a few revs, fling ourselves about a bit, strike back formidably if the opportunity arises. But they have to wallow along as if nothing had happened. . . . Imagine being a stoker, working many feet below the water-line, hearing the crack of explosions, knowing exactly what they mean and staying down there on the job shovelling coal or turning wheels . . . disregarding what you *know* may be only a few yards away and pointing straight at you.
>
> No amount of publicity, no colourful write ups . . . above all no medals, can do honour to men like these. Buy them a drink ashore, if you like; but don't attempt an adequate recompense. You won't get in the target area.[8]

In the escorts it was no joke when circumstances dictated watch on – watch off at night on the bridge because:

> Strain and tiredness at sea induces a sort of hypnosis; you seem to be moving in a bad dream, pursued not by terrors but by an intolerable routine. You come off watch at midnight, soaked,

twitching, your eyes raw with the wind and with staring at shadows . . . you strip off the top layer of sodden clothes . . . thereafter a few hours sleep between wet blankets, with an inflated life-belt between your ribs reminding you all the time that things happen quickly. And then, every night for seventeen nights on end, you're woken up at ten to four by the bosun's mate and you stare at the deckhead and think: 'My God, I *can't* go up there again in the dark and filthy rain and stand another four hours of it.' But you can, of course; it becomes automatic in the end. And besides, there are people watching you.[9]

About his corvette Monsarrat wrote:

If sailors are not the most sentimental of men then I'd like to know who are. More than half the crew . . . are married but all of them seem to have a love of home grafted deep inside them. It is complementary to the ship, as the inner centre of their world. It stands behind everything; when the mail is delivered and distributed to various messes the atmosphere of the ship is quite distinctive, compounded by sentiment and a sort of unassailable concentration. Plans for the future all seem to centre, not round jobs or a steady income but on a house, a family, a private world which, no matter how cramped or how poor it may be, will give them peace against all comers. That is what they are fighting for – the sure welcome, the old woman, the kids. Their day dreams are the least ambitious and the gentlest of any I know.

This is probably as vital a source of strength and endurance as can be found anywhere. Men who fight with the heart, *for* the heart, are unbeatable.[10]

❖❖❖

By 1943 sea routine in most ships settled down to a steady rhythm verging on boredom and tiredness. There was a sameness about so many features. The same dawn action stations, the same meals served up with monotonous regularity in the wardroom and messdeck, the same German surface warship silhouettes staring at you in the heads and the same thirst for news that sent 'buzzes' circulating through the ship. Dinner time was the main social occasion of the day, preceded by the tot enjoyed among 75 per cent of the ship's company; wardroom drinking, on the other hand, was by choice quite restrained. Communications with the outside world became vitally important and the arrival of mail lifted morale sky high. Censorship of letters was already an unwelcome chore for officers who thought it an intrusion into a sailor's private life, occasionally enlivened by cryptic messages like HOLLAND, ITALY or BURMA as the writer signed himself off.[11]

❖❖❖

For three years the Royal Naval College at Dartmouth continued as every four months forty-five Dartmouth and forty Special Entry cadets went to sea. The college also trained cadets from the Dominions and those from the Free French, Norway, Belgium, Holland, Poland and Greece. As a coastal force base and a convoy staging port Dartmouth was a vulnerable target; it was effectively bombed in September 1942. Being empty of cadets there were few casualties but the college was badly damaged; early in 1943 all naval cadet training moved to Eaton Hall, the Duke of Westminster's seat near Chester.

Towards the end of 1942 it was apparent that *King Alfred* was unable to grant sufficient temporary commissions to RNVR officers to meet further expansion; other sources would have to be tapped as a matter of urgency. One method was to attract university graduates and a scheme was set up to interview and train potential officers by means of University Naval Divisions. A more promising solution was to overhaul the whole system of selecting and training officer candidates from the lower deck with a programme evolved from a pilot scheme carried out at HMS *Glendower*, a seaman new entry training establishment at Pwllheli, North Wales. This included assessments designed by the Admiralty Senior Psychologist, specialized training and Army Selection Board tests to assist in measuring leadership. After *Glendower* the new approach was introduced successfully in the seaman training establishments of *Collingwood*, *Raleigh*, *Ganges* and *Royal Arthur*; also *Duke*, *Excalibur* and *Gosling* to cover stokers, communications and fleet air arm personnel.

❖❖❖

When Germany occupied Norway, Holland, Belgium and France the Navy's Coastal Forces – three assorted flotillas of torpedo boats – received top priority. As well as defending our own inshore convoys there was enemy shipping to be attacked, protected by well armed German E-boats and trawlers. Nothing less than a rapid expansion of Coastal Forces Command could match the situation; many more MTBs and motor gunboats had to be built and large numbers of RNVR officers and HO ratings trained to fight alongside a nucleus of regular naval personnel.

Coastal Forces operated predominantly in darkness and for every action there were many nights of fruitless patrol. Although boats could not be fought under bad weather conditions crews were exposed to continuously disagreeable conditions of motion, wetness, vibration and noise. Operational conditions contained all the ingredients of exhaustion and in the confusion of night actions mistakes were unavoidable; the actions they fought were usually bloody affairs. As soon as Portland was operating as a work-up base efficiency improved, and a number of able and successful leaders emerged.

These men became senior officers of flotillas based in the UK and later in the Mediterranean, around which the organization ashore and afloat largely revolved. One such officer was Lieutenant Commander Robert Hitchens RNVR, whose peacetime interests, apart from his solicitor's practice in Falmouth, were motor racing and dinghy sailing. Peter Scott, another distinguished Coastal Force CO, records that:

> He was known throughout Coastal Forces as 'Hitch' and most of the tactical theory of motor gun boats was first developed and practised by him. But the chief thing about him was the way he could lead and the confidence he instilled into the officers and men of his flotilla. I remember one of them telling me that his only fear on going into action was that he wouldn't satisfy 'Hitch'. And it wasn't limited to his flotilla, this inspiration. It spread around and developed the spirit which put our Coastal Forces on top whenever they met the enemy, by virtue not of their guns but of their determination . . .

MGB returns to harbour after night patrol

In the summer of 1942 Hitchens's flotilla moved from the North Sea to the Western Channel and on 14 July his MGB was one of three lying in wait for E-boats 12 miles north of Alderney. They decided to enter the Alderney Race when suddenly a light was sighted; Hitchens realized that he was overtaking an escorted convoy and wrote later: 'I made the signal "Enemy in sight" and silently, signlessly, the unit fell into line ahead – the fighting formation.' With a strong head wind and in darkness they could not be heard or seen, and after challenging the rearmost enemy vessel, a trawler, Hitchens ordered: 'Open fire':

> The next few minutes provided a welter of impressions for me, beginning with a crescendo of noise and light, passing through tense anxiety and ending with such stark fear as I have never known before. All our guns burst into life. With the gun muzzles a few feet from one's ear the noise was terrific, the light from the muzzle flashes, the tracer and the bursting shells dazzling and bewildering, the effect most gratifying. That trawler hard hit and surprised, scarcely returned the fire at all.

As soon as they sighted the escorted tanker Hitchens decided to carry out the highly dangerous attack of releasing a depth charge under her bow. Having practised the manoeuvre on one of our trawlers off Harwich his coxswain knew exactly how to steer; increasing speed and firing all guns at the target the 'seventy one foot six' MGB leaped forward 'quivering with unleashed power'.

Clearing the enemy's bows by 10 ft and under heavy fire Hitchens ordered the depth charge to be let go. A few seconds later came a shattering underwater explosion – 'just one of those rare occasions when everything goes right'. But the MGB was in trouble and 'it seemed that we must be irretrievably afire. It was obvious that the entire upper deck crew had been knocked out by that infernal blast'. Hitchens and his first lieutenant battled with the flames in the wheelhouse and, having subdued the worst, turned to the blazing oil aft. Meanwhile Petty Officer Curtis, the coxswain, with the throttle hard up and superb steering had swept the boat away to the north. With one killed and another mortally wounded in his boat Hitchens and his MGBs returned to base, the tanker stopped and burning in a cloud of smoke.[12]

After 148 operations, which included fourteen actions for which he was awarded the DSO and bar, DSC and two bars and was three times mentioned in dispatches, Hitchens was killed by a stray cannon shell during a minor action in July 1943. He left a rich legacy in the development of boats and ideas on the way they should be fought.

❖❖❖

As a doctor in general practice R. Ransome Wallis joined the Navy as a surgeon lieutenant RNVR, to be appointed to the cruiser *London*, based on Scapa Flow. After the German invasion of Russia *London* participated in a number of PQ convoys to North Russia and in May 1942 Wallis was lent to the destroyer *Martin* – her medical officer had gone sick. As the escorts and convoy were being assembled at Hvalfiord, Iceland, for Convoy PQ16: 'I found that all the other officers were younger than I was except the gunner . . . some seemed to be boys. Destroyers are not for the aged and although I was only 32 I did find the wardroom a bit juvenile sometimes. But they were a splendid and most likeable lot and had a first class ship's company.'

Wallis's staff consisted of one sick berth attendant, a schoolmaster in private life, immensely popular with the ship's company but had the habit of vanishing in action to help in a magazine or where he could be useful, leaving Wallis to cope single handed. However, there was a valuable bonus in the shape of a quartermaster who had turned over from being a fully trained LSBA and was available when needed. The convoy sailed on 25 May.

With twenty-four hours of daylight and the sun shining through the night, unless obscured by cloud, the force was attacked almost continually by JU88s, Heinkel torpedo bombers and, to a lesser extent, by U-boats. On the third day out the Russian ship *Starii Bolshevik*, with part cargo explosives, was hit by a bomb and sustained severe casualties. *Martin* closed and Wallis was sent over in a boat with the SBA to take off the wounded as quickly as possible:

> What with gunfire, bombs and the screaming engines of dive bombers the row was terrific, but the effect on our rowing was electrical and the whaler surged along as if it were at Henley. A rope ladder was hanging over the port side of the Russian ship and with a last despairing effort we got close enough for our bowman to grab it and hang on as *Starii Bolshevik* gathered speed, burning fiercely and with black smoke pouring out of the fore hold.

With the help of three Russian women crew the worst cases were lowered into the boat in Neil Robertson stretchers, the walking wounded climbing down the ladder. Back on board *Martin* Wallis and the QM/LSBA continued work in the sick bay. Meanwhile attacks on the convoy continued relentlessly, Wallis's next job being to go aboard an armed trawler to collect wounded, bringing them back to a ship already full of casualties. At this stage 'the strain was telling. Two or three of *Martin*'s ship's company were cracking up . . . the worst case was an Engine Room Artificer. He simply could not stop shaking and this alternated with periods of weeping'.

Earlier the Chief had asked Wallis to show himself occasionally in the engine and boiler rooms 'to encourage the people down below' so he made a point of going to talk to them. 'I was glad to go up to the Sick Bay again. The ERAs and stokers certainly had the worst of it and I found the sledge hammer blows of explosions on the side of the ship particularly frightening in this world of machinery and boilers.'

Like other medical officers faced with a few severely injured men in an intense state of shock among less serious cases Wallis wondered where his duty lay: 'By nature of his profession a doctor has to be a perfectionist. The best is just good enough. The thing that worried me was to know exactly what was the best for the wounded in the prevailing conditions.'[13]

In the almost continuous action of PQ16 he had to decide whether to conduct an elaborate operation that might take hours or devote his skill to others; either way there was no rest for the medical staff, and on reaching Kola Islet Wallis collapsed with fatigue. He was later awarded the DSC for his services in *Martin*.

Removing ice from a corvette's gun mounting after Russian convoy, 1943

Weather conditions and enemy action made Arctic operations an unpopular turn of duty for the ships' companies of small ships and as Senior Officer Destroyers Commander 'Boggy' Fisher in *Musketeer* was confronted with:

> a recurring dilemma dealing with men who deliberately missed the ship when we knew that we were about to go on a Russian convoy that we all hated. To treat them as deserters meant imprisonment ashore (which was what the men probably wanted). There were no cells on board. . . . In some cases these men were more in need of hospital treatment than prison. . . . Additionally there were some very brave men. . . . Once, when I went down below from the bridge to see an injured man I saw in the Petty Officer's mess a figure crouched, trembling, in a corner. I asked Number One what was the matter and he said 'That's the PO Cook. He's always like that after depth charges have been dropped.' *That* man never missed the ship.[14]

It was hard enough to find personnel for the fleet without having to compete with a growing number of men being found medically unfit for sea service, including those whose real ailment was an unwillingness to serve in ships. The problem was unknowingly compounded by medical officers with little or no naval experience, whose natural inclination was the well being of their patients. Experience showed that a man bent on avoiding draft or complaining of symptoms that prevented him keeping watch, or who was a regular attendant at Sick Bay, almost invariably succeeded in getting discharged to hospital. On being found fit he would be redrafted to sea to another ship and the whole cycle would start again. Undoubtedly there were genuine cases of mental breakdown but there were also malingerers, creating an awkward problem for ships' officers trying to discriminate between the two.

It was clearly a job for the psychiatrist to investigate and recommend whether those affected should be graded permanent shore service or sent back to sea or stood over for special treatment. One such case, who was subjected to examination at a naval hospital, later wrote:

> The psychiatrist knows. I hope to Christ he does know. But he hasn't been to sea, he hasn't seen a boy with head on messtable sobbing quietly after prolonged action and no sleep. He hasn't experienced the rough incomprehensible sympathy of men who would laugh at the answer five to the question 'What is twice times two?' When the interview was over the psychiatrist says 'Yes, yes, I understand. Come back next week. Report to Sick Bay three times a day. They'll give you something to quieten you down.'[15]

Eventually the man was discharged from the service.

❖❖❖

On the day that Peter Bull opted for the Navy in 1940 he remarked that 'the sea was not in my blood and I took jolly good care that my blood was not in the sea'. Public school education and the acting profession stood him in good stead in preliminary training at *Raleigh*; by the time he joined the destroyer *Hesperus* he was a CW candidate and on his way to *King Alfred* as a cadet rating. There he maintained that the successful production of Anson Division's concert carried him through his examinations, and in 1942 he was appointed first lieutenant of HM Tank Landing Craft 168 berthed at Middlesborough.

Construction of vessels and training in combined operations, as well as inter-service co-operation, were largely ignored between the wars, partly through lack of interest and disregard of history and partly because the RAF insisted that air power had rendered seaborne landings virtually inoperable. Churchill was quick to alter this thinking; in 1940 he set up a Combined Operations Directorate to develop weapons, craft and training. Moreover, it gave the Royal Marines the opportunity to establish themselves in a role for which they were well suited, in particular the manning and operation of amphibious craft.

After the Dieppe raid in August 1942 and for the next two-and-a-half years Bull commanded Landing Craft Flak 16 with seventy officers and men in the Mediterranean to take part in the Sicily invasion and then to Salerno where: 'I stationed the ship a hundred yards from the shore; it was an unattractive position, but the courage of the LCTs, who were unloading rapidly under heavy fire, inspired us to try to give them moral support. . . . There was something superb about the LCT matelot with a cigarette hanging out of his mouth, a tin hat practically flat aback, joking with the soldiers.'

Life in landing craft was full of anomalies; food had to be cadged, communications were highly unorthodox and when Bull lost an anchor he went aboard a US Salvage ship, bespoke another and sent the bill to the Admiralty. But he had a good ship's company, who walked ten feet tall when Bull, alone among hundreds of landing craft, manoeuvred his ship to survive a fierce storm that left the beach littered with wrecks. On promotion to Lieutenant Commander, Bull handed over to his successor at Naples in May 1944. To say farewell he went below where, at variance with King's Regulations and Admiralty Instructions:

> I was presented with a magnificent inscribed watch and a large signed photograph of the ship's company. I had to leave hurriedly without saying the things which I had intended and retire to my cabin to recover.
>
> There had been few changes in personnel and we knew each other pretty intimately. It is very easy . . . to have unofficial chats with the men, and these, combined with their letters home, were sufficient to keep me in touch with their feelings. If there were grousing comments and veiled complaints I would go down to the mess decks and try to get to the root of the trouble. Some of them were justifiable . . . like absence of mails or lack of promotion among the marines. When I left after two and a half years I still had the same corporals. . . . Not unnaturally enthusiasm and ambition flagged. . . . But general behaviour was at a high level . . . when VD was at its height our ship remained unscathed with an all-time record of immunity. [Among the key ratings was] Sergeant Donald Best, my senior NCO, and impossible to praise enough. From the moment he stepped up from being second sergeant the routine and discipline of the ship went like clockwork. An admirable companion on the bridge with whom to share watches. . . . My coxswain, Luther Hunter, quietly efficient and diplomatic in his relations with the marine element. . . . The Engine room deserves a chapter to itself. It is no joke being in the bowels of the ship at dangerous moments, particularly if as prone to sea sickness as Sandy Horne. Yet I never heard him complain or slacken . . . he and the stokers worked like a team of acrobats. . . . There was Bardsley the wireman who was so

> inefficient that he had only to put one wire a few inches from another to cause a major explosion – but goodness what a footballer! Between the marine corporals there was little to choose. One had a penchant for pinching bicycles and another for finding me several pounds out in my victualling accounts. . . . There was Telegraphist Canavan who used to go into a dewy eyed trance a few miles out of Messina, thinking of his signorina . . . [16]

In command of a flotilla in the Adriatic Bull was awarded the DSC – but the news did not reach him until he read his school magazine after he was demobilized.

❖❖❖

After her battering off the River Plate the cruiser *Exeter* was refitted in Devonport dockyard; the day before commissioning early in 1941 the captain died. 'If sailors are superstitious here it was on a plate,' thought Lieutenant Commander Frank Twiss. 'But so busy was everyone on commissioning day that there wasn't time to brood.'

By the time *Exeter* reached Singapore Japanese aircraft had bombed Pearl Harbor, *Prince of Wales* and *Repulse* had been sunk, convoys of troops were pouring into Singapore and the situation in Malaya was deteriorating rapidly. In February 1942 *Exeter* joined Australian, Dutch and American cruisers and destroyers to form an Allied task force, total strangers to each other and without common communications or methods. In the ensuing battle of the Java Sea the allies lost two cruisers and three destroyers against superior Japanese forces; *Exeter* acquitted herself bravely but a hit in the boiler room necessitated repairs in Sourabaya. In the evening of 28 February *Exeter* sailed with destroyers *Encounter* and (USS) *Pope* in an attempt to fight their way out to the open sea, barely two years after helping to drive *Graf Spee* into Montevideo. Tables were now turned.

In perfect weather and maximum visibility the enemy were sighted – five cruisers and several destroyers. *Exeter* was repeatedly hit, all power failed and the order given to abandon ship. Twiss came down to the boat deck where he met the Chief Ordnance Artificer, who had been his right-hand man for eighteen months and had fought at the River Plate:

> 'Come on' I said, 'We'd better go off together.' 'I can't do it,' he replied, 'I can't leave this ship. I am going forward and will go down with her.' At this moment a shell exploded on board and we were covered with dust and peppered with fragments. . . . So this is what it is like to be wounded, I thought. I looked down at my white tunic, expecting to see it full of holes and bleeding. . . . Surprisingly there were no holes and no blood. I was unhurt. 'Come on,' I said, 'you mustn't be foolish. What good will it do if you go down with the ship? No – you and I must leave together.' We blew up our lifejackets, shook hands and more or less stepped into the sea which was not far below the upper deck.

Twiss and the Chief OA swam away, shells landing around them. The ship was then torpedoed and sunk.

Survivors managed to stay afloat for twenty hours before a Japanese destroyer picked them up. Transferred to a captured Dutch hospital ship they were put ashore in Macassar to become prisoners of the Japanese army:

> We were a pretty bedraggled looking lot. I still had a shirt, a pair of white duck trousers and my lieutenant commander's shoulder straps. Nothing else. . . . No hat, no socks, no shoes. I was in great pain with my eyes which were sore beyond bearing and it was agony to open them. . . . Others were in similar state. . . . Bundled ashore, formed up in column by blows, shouts and kicks we moved off to march . . . a matter of hopping from one place to the next.

The camp was full of Dutch and Indonesian forces as well as civilians. Some were cruelly beaten up as attempts were made to sort out the captives:

> It was a tricky time because *Exeter*'s ratings were separated from officers, though living in the same camp under the same conditions. Officers were concerned to help the men; but the men, seeing the officers so roughly handled, rather naturally felt it was time to look after themselves and let the devil take the hindmost. It was a moment when morale and naval discipline might go for six. Yet to keep up . . . our cohesion and be able to meet the Japanese authorities with a sense of proper leadership . . . it was tremendously important to maintain standards.
>
> The day was largely saved by the Navigator . . . because he was able to establish communication with the sailors sufficiently to gain their respect and admiration . . . and because officers were getting no privileges at all. The anxious wobble in *Exeter*'s ship's company morale was smoothed out. We were as one again.

Without warning the captain, commander, specialist officers and two senior communication ratings were given civilian clothes and sent by tramp steamer to Yokohama to be imprisoned in a purpose-built naval interrogation camp at Ofuna.

Each prisoner was confined to a tiny wooden cell at night, fed on just enough boiled rice and what passed for soup or tea to keep alive, forbidden to speak to anyone else and required to do physical drill two or three times a day as well as gardening work. The general idea of Ofuna was to break the spirit; that done, interrogation would be easier. In fact few if any British were questioned, until the arrival of the dreaded Kempetai, by which time interest was lost on naval matters. All the same:

> it was a very testing time. There we were, thousands of miles from home, in the hands of fanatical and very cruel people, not accepted as prisoners of war and not reported as such. . . . Happily the human mind does find hope where none seems likely. The very antics of the Japanese, the shame of being captives of such silly little men, the desire to do something to get our own back soon led to finding small but important ways of hitting back. The dawn bowing to the Emperor became a competition to think out ruder, coarser and more horrible imprecations to heap upon his head. As we bowed these remarks would be whispered in the ranks. It is some wonder the Emperor survived to surrender.

The highlight, however, was Japanese Army Day when Twiss was ordered to drill the British squad, where:

> the right-hand man of the front rank was my captain and that of the rear rank was my commander. I must say they did it splendidly, marching, countermarching, wheeling, changing step and so on. . . . I think even the Japanese were mildly impressed. Alas, the Americans did not make out so well. They are not by nature able to keep in step, they did not seem to have any fixed procedure and frankly their performance was a shambles. Much to the delight of the guards who spent twenty minutes marching around, singing and shouting Bushido-like noises.

After some months, weak from low diet, one prisoner came out with dysentery; the disease spread and Twiss was among those sent to Yokosuki hospital. On return he was utterly miserable: 'Life at this time was very low. . . . I remember sitting in my cell and hearing the songs of birds outside. One song in particular . . . always made me feel how lovely it must be to be a bird, free to fly away, free to sing, free to go back to its own home. From time to time even now I hear a bird song which instantly and painfully brings back the feeling in that Ofuna cell.'

Meanwhile *Exeter*'s ship's company was split up into groups to work in docks, airfield and in the town of Macassar to dig air-raid shelters. Life was made considerably worse by the arrival of a chief guard called Yoshida, who ruthlessly subjected prisoners to even more painful and degrading punishments. Late in 1942 the 'Exeters' were moved to Japan where hopes were raised as they saw American planes on bombing missions. After meals the routine was to put their tin plates out to dry 'neatly yet not obviously arranged so they spelt EXETER for any Allied plane to see and report'. Despite more and more deaths from malnutrition and disease there remained a grim determination to survive.

In August 1945 the war was over and *Exeter*'s prisoners were rescued by Americans and Australian forces, eventually finishing up in Queen Mary's hospital, Roehampton. When Twiss was interviewed he indicated that any officer trained at Dartmouth was better prepared to stand up to the despair pressures and collective horrors of a Japanese POW camp than those whose previous experience lacked the strict discipline, example and pride-inducing regime of a Royal Naval College.[17]

❖❖❖

Returning from the Quebec Conference in October 1943, the First Sea Lord, Admiral of the Fleet Sir Dudley Pound, was seriously ill. On Trafalgar Day he died; after the funeral service at Westminster Abbey his ashes and those of his devoted wife were scattered in the sea off the Nab Tower.

How will Pound be judged? In condemning his shortcomings some historians, in this writer's view, have overlooked the finer points of an outstanding officer. For four difficult and dangerous years he bore the whole burden of responsibility for war at sea, enduring bitter and often unjust criticism when things went wrong, but always taking the blame and never sparing himself, despite failing health. Having gained the respect of Churchill, restraining some but not all of his wilder schemes, he took, perhaps, too much to heart Nelson's dictum that 'Duty is the great business of a sea officer'. Unwisely he chose not to delegate to his staff and it was said that he often worked nineteen hours a day. Dudley Pound may not have been the greatest First Sea Lord but it is doubtful if anyone else could have done the job better.

Cunningham succeeded Pound and in June 1944 the long-awaited invasion of Europe, codenamed *Overlord*, took place. The naval assault, operation *Neptune*, was planned and commanded by Admiral Sir Bertram Ramsay; Allied naval forces involved 125,000 officers and men, over 6,000 ships, including 6 battleships, 23 cruisers, 104 destroyers and over 4,000 landing craft. It was quite simply the most massive and complicated operation in naval history, its success due to superlative organization backed by intensive training.

Admiral Sir Dudley Pound and Prime Minister Winston Churchill

❖❖❖

From the moment Britain stood alone after Dunkirk the USA proved itself a staunch friend, supplying munitions, handing over fifty destroyers to help fight the U-boats and providing repair facilities for damaged warships in US naval ports on a lend/lease basis. After Pearl Harbor the two countries fought as allies, the Royal Navy making available its war experience and the US Navy contributing training facilities for the Fleet Air Arm, to quote two examples of spontaneous co-operation. As victory in the West became credible the American High Command appeared less enthused over the offer of British naval assistance in the Pacific. The issue was not resolved until the 2nd Quebec Conference in September 1944 when President Roosevelt warmly accepted Churchill's proposal that the British should be employed in the main theatre of operations. Even then Fleet Admiral Ernest J. King, US Navy, Chief of Naval Operations and a declared Anglophobe, did his best to 'keep the Limeys from muscling in' on their endeavours to defeat Japan.

As Controller of the Navy in the early stages of the war, Admiral Bruce Fraser established close relations with the United States Navy and as Commander-in-Chief, Home Fleet, welcomed the arrival of two US Navy battleships and five destroyers as a valuable addition to his force.

At the end of 1943 the German battle-cruiser *Scharnhorst* was successfully engaged and sunk; the formidable *Tirpitz*, severely damaged by midget submarines, was put out of action by the Fleet Air Arm in April 1944 and finally sunk by the RAF, thereby making it possible for British heavy ships to move to the Far East. At the end of 1944 Fraser hoisted his flag as Commander-in-Chief, British Pacific Fleet.

Commanding initially what was a non-existent fleet Fraser faced complex problems. Although serving operationally under Admiral Nimitz, with whom he established cordial relations, he answered to the Admiralty for maintenance of his ships, the support of their crews and the transport of his victuals, stores, ammunition and fuel half-way round the world. With the European war all but over and rumours of demobilization in the wind, even more important was the need to maintain morale among crews manning the auxiliaries and create the will to continue the fight until Japan was defeated. Another problem was communications. Against strong Admiralty opposition the BPF changed over to US Naval signal books but a proposal, as much a courtesy gesture as anything, to adopt khaki uniform as worn by the US Navy was initially turned down. In the end it was widely accepted by RN officers as being more practical than tropical whites.

Since Pearl Harbor the US Navy, supported by a dynamic ship construction industry unimpeded by war, had made enormous strides in building a large, modern fleet. Organized in task forces with a preponderance of aircraft carriers, its logistics furnished by a purpose-built fleet train, the Americans were able to operate on a scale hitherto unimagined by the Royal Navy. When the first British task force arrived on the scene in March 1945, its base at Sydney far from complete and only a small proportion of its fleet train assembled at the advanced base in Manus, the contrast was striking. To those accustomed to European conditions of war the distances involved were staggering, as was the ability of American warships to remain almost indefinitely in the combat area. Thus the British method of fuelling large warships at sea by means of buoyant hoses trailed astern of tankers appeared clumsy and unseamanlike compared with the quicker, more efficient method of fuelling abreast, an evolution that the British fleet was soon to adopt.

During the BPF's first visit to Manus 'in the equatorial heat and humidity for ten miserable and debilitating days, with officers and men erupting in an epidemic of boils and prickly heat' it was evident that RN living conditions were mediocre. That was not all. In a report to the Admiralty before his fleet arrived Fraser pressed home: 'The provision of amenities on board US ships is of great importance; soda water fountains, ice, ice cream, water coolers and movies are all in abundance together with much literature and a mail delivered at sea five days before "S" day [the operation] . . . there seemed to be ample resources.' Cunningham replied: 'I hope our people will not get too blinded by American lavishness. We cannot compete with them in either personnel or material, nor do I think that we should train our men to expect the same waste as is practised in the American Navy.'

Having taken a personal interest in the status, accommodation and living conditions of US Navy officers and enlisted men during long spells at sea, Fraser appreciated the psychological value of making life more bearable and the sailors more effective by attending to their creature comforts. He saw this:

> as perfectly compatible with the long tradition of the Service. . . . In this he was a 'modern', the first British naval Commander-in-Chief to campaign successfully for a modicum of the myriad amenities taken for granted in the Royal Navy of the 1980s. Knowing that he was right Fraser stuck to his guns . . . encouraging his staff to go on finding all they could about what made service in the US Navy more attractive, more endurable and more efficient . . . than in the Royal Navy.[18]

In his dispatch Fraser accepted that the Americans:

> are much quicker than we at learning the lessons of war and of applying them to their ships and tactics . . . the fact that their ships are always up to date helps to engender an essentially modern and experimental habit of thought. . . . We on the other hand are more cautious in our ship construction and in our tactics and, unlike the Americans, we would rather not change anything until the alteration has been thoroughly tested as an improvement. As a result the British Fleet is seldom spectacular, never really modern, but always sound.[19]

Formidable's flight deck after attack by a Kamikaze with a 500-lb bomb

Led by Admirals Rawlings and Vian the BPF acquitted itself well, especially in the performance of its aircraft, its fighter direction and its aircraft carriers after being hit by suicide bombers on the armoured deck, an asset not possessed by US Navy carriers. Early one morning in May 1945 *Formidable* ranged Corsair and Avenger aircraft for the morning strike on targets in Japan. Suddenly an aircraft passed very fast and low overhead, identified as Japanese, which finally approached from astern and then 'an immense crash shook the ship. . . . It was a grim sight. A fire was blazing among wreckage close under the bridge, flames reaching up the side of the island and clouds of black smoke far above the ship'. The ship had been hit by a 500-lb bomb, part of which penetrated the engine room, causing intense fires on the flight deck and accounting for two officers and six men killed. Within six hours *Formidable* reported ready to resume flying operations and the captain gripped the shoulder of the US Navy liaison officer 'What do you think of our bloody British flight decks now?' 'Sir,' came the reply, 'they're a honey.'[20]

War in Europe ceased on 8 May 1945 and after the second atomic bomb was dropped on Japan the Second World War officially ended on 15 August. The Navy could now afford to relax a little, but before covering the long task of clearing up the after-effects it is worth mentioning a few impressions taken away by officers and men as thoughts turned to peace.

Six years of war had been a great leveller, causing the character of the wardroom and messdeck to experience prolonged change. Far from impairing efficiency or ship spirit the introduction of

'In the Royal Air Force, a landing's OK/ If the pilot gets out and can still walk away/ But in the Fleet Air Arm the prospect is grim/ It's bloody hard luck if the pilot can't swim'

people who joined 'for the duration' became a source of strength. Their refreshing outlook, varied background and unconventional approach did a power of good to the regular Navy, endorsing the value of amateurs in a professional service and rejuvenating a good deal of naval thought. And in many wardrooms officers promoted from the lower deck in all branches blended in successfully to indicate the shape of things to come.

There were few unhappy ships in the war. A taste of enemy action early in the commission, even if inconclusive, proved a perfect stimulant for morale, bringing officers and men together in a way that nothing else could. After braving that they felt confident, able to withstand any amount of action and discomfort, acquiring a stamina they never knew they possessed.

The final impression was the respect and admiration felt by the vast majority of ships' companies towards their commanding officers. In the emergencies of war men instinctively looked towards the bridge for inspiration; rarely were they disappointed and many captains, whatever their rank, will be remembered for their calm courage in the face of danger that carried to every corner of the ship. In the destroyer *Laforey*, 'the ship's company idolized Captain Hutton – his quiet, orderly, efficient handling of *Laforey* in countless actions inspired a pride amongst his officers and men', wrote Petty Officer Burns. 'He never forgot to congratulate or thank even the most junior ratings for a job well done. . . . When he left us *Laforey* was for days like a ghost ship; no laughter, just all round depression.'[21]

CHAPTER TWELVE

The Stagnant Years

Set thy house in order.
Isaiah 38: 1

For Britain 1945 was a memorable year. After the Allied armies and air power forced Germany to surrender, it was Churchill's intention to continue the coalition government until the end of the Japanese war. When the Opposition demurred a general election was called, resulting in a sweeping Labour victory; it is probable that the fighting services voted overwhelmingly for the party that promised a better deal for housing, employment and social security. Almost certainly their voting intentions were influenced by the left-wing bias of the Army Bureau of Current Affairs educational pamphlets, officially encouraged for use in discussion groups held in camps, barracks and warships all over the world. By the end of the year a social revolution had started – the British Empire was on the way out and the Welfare State on the way in. Winston Churchill was replaced at the Potsdam Conference by Clement Attlee – an indication to other powers that British people had abandoned interest in world affairs – and American Lend Lease Aid was withdrawn. A virtually bankrupt Britain was consigned to continued austerity with rationing, shortages and an environment visibly changed by the effects of war. By any standards the outlook was bleak.

The abrupt, unforeseen end of fighting in the Far East left the Navy with a range of rehabilitation tasks that kept ships of the British Pacific and East Indies fleets busy for well over a year. Most immediate was the re-occupation of Hong Kong and Singapore and the rescue of thousands of British and Commonwealth prisoners of war and civilian internees. On arrival off the Japanese coast 'scores of wasted POWs struggled out to the fleet, some commandeering boats, the stronger even swimming. It was deeply moving as they came on board in scraps of uniform they'd managed to keep, many weeping, some even kissing the deck'.[1] Medical attention was at hand and aircraft carriers detailed for their repatriation, taking priority over the return of service men for demobilization. But although liaison with American ships and military authorities in Japan prospered and many BPF officers shared Fraser's opinion that the Royal Navy should preserve and develop the close wartime bond with the US Navy, the Admiralty was less enthusiastic. In many departments lurked an in-built resistance to anything American. Paradoxically, the ship that the well-nourished American Fleet Train had not got was the British-designed Fleet Amenities Ship. Comparable to *Ghourko* and *Borodino* of Scapa fame in the First World War, SS *Menestheus* possessed a brewery with a weekly production of 250 barrels of Davy Jones ale, a row of shops including Gieves and the ability to lay on every form of entertainment, ranging from an ENSA stage show or the latest movies to a reception of pre-war lavishness. As the star attraction when Fraser was host to the US Fleet in Shanghai, the ship so impressed the guests 'that they wanted to buy her – offered the Admiralty a million pounds for her. But the Admiralty refused. The Americans were very upset, didn't have anything like her at all . . . and she was just brought home and broken up'.[2]

By 1945 the Navy's strength was greater than at any other time in its history, the composition of the fleet reflecting the characteristics of a long drawn-out, hard-fought war: 15 battleships, 52 aircraft carriers, 63 cruisers, 257 destroyers, 137 submarines, 542 sloops, frigates and corvettes, over 1,000 minesweeping and A/S vessels, 1,389 motor torpedo boats and coastal craft, and 5,000 landing craft. The Fleet Air Arm totalled 1,336 front line aircraft, enough for 70 squadrons and at home and overseas were 300 shore establishments and air stations. In this vast naval and air force were serving over 860,000 officers, men and women. Within two years the Navy's personnel was cut to 195,000.

Economy became the watchword and to strike the correct balance between running the fleet down to peacetime proportions and retaining sufficient ships of the right type to meet a mass of commitments, the business of drafting, retaining and releasing personnel became critically important. Fortunately one of the Navy's most level-headed administrators was Second Sea Lord – Vice-Admiral Sir Algernon Willis. After serving as his Chief of Staff, Algy Willis followed Cunningham to the Admiralty early in 1944 to play a prominent part in demobilization and planning the manpower of the future Navy.

Ranking from midshipman to commodore some fifty thousand Volunteer Reserve temporary officers were serving when war ended, comprising 88 per cent of the Navy's officer strength; over 2,000 had commanded HM ships. Their decorations were a typical cross-section of those gained by the whole Navy; equally significant was their contribution of skills ranging from gifted surgeons and erudite schoolmasters to university-trained marine, electrical and electronic engineers. Thrown in at the deep end with little or no training, 333 Temporary VR chaplains were appointed to minister to ships or squadrons, undertake cipher duties, organize concerts, dispense comforts, run lectures and act as letter writers for inarticulate sailors unable to communicate with their wives and girlfriends.

Widely popular was the announcement that the Navy still needed an RNVR with an establishment of 10,000 officers and men in eleven divisions around the country. This attracted so many applicants for permanent commissions that the Supplementary Reserve had to be enlarged to take the waiting list. And as further reward for their many achievements in ships, aircraft and shore bases, they were allowed to retain the rank and uniform worn on demobilization, a concession extended to petty officers that included many applicants leaving the RN and wishing to keep in touch with former shipmates. In 1951 the RNVR's wavy stripe was straightened out so that VR officers appeared identical to their regular counterparts.

In every shore establishment demobilization became the order of the day, particularly as several regular ratings had exceeded their time for pension. In the words of a chief petty officer:

> Fifty-six days' paid leave was granted from the actual day of release. Those concerned were organized in groups to visit a local warehouse where each individual received a free issue of civilian attire, namely two pin-stripe suits. Resettlement offices were established in most districts to advise and assist servicemen to adapt themselves to a new and, in many cases, unwelcome life. . . . Send offs became a routine spectacular as each demob group reached the final day. Taxis departed well adorned with boots and placards bearing words like 'Paid off' or 'Nozzers for Civvy street'![13]

At least two years were to elapse before the Navy's wartime-only personnel could be fully discharged. Except ratings with prior claim, such as those with special qualifications and pre-war reserves, older men went first while younger ratings moved from ships being laid up to those still active but depleted by demobilization. Many temporary officers were in no hurry to return to civilian life and applied for short-term RN commissions on offer, while others were invited to volunteer for minesweepers to help in the huge task of clearing minefields. Transfers to the RN were especially welcome from the Air Branch officers that comprised 75 per cent of the Fleet Air Arm and from Fighter Direction Officers who were all wartime reservists. Altogether 600 RNVRs took RN commissions in one way or another; the remainder went home to resume their jobs as bank clerks, barristers, bakers, journalists, policemen or to look for employment, confident that the Navy was safely in the hands of its 'caretakers'.

Less easy to resolve were the minds of regular naval people into which feelings of uncertainty had entered after the end of fighting. Victory had been achieved but at what cost? Over 50,000 British naval personnel had lost their lives, 20,000 more than in the First World War. Would the Navy ever be the same again? What had the post-war Navy got to offer? Answers to these questions and more had to be carefully thought through.

There were officers and men whose lives and those of their families had been disrupted by trauma or separation, their homes wrecked and their whole future left in jeopardy. In addition to former POWs were those in need of rest and rehabilitation, time to sort themselves out, resolve matrimonial problems and get to know their children. Was it the right moment to say 'Enough is enough' and look for a new career? Although some bore emotional scars for a long time, the great majority weathered the process of adjustment and quietly got on with whatever they had to do. But as sea and shore commands shrank to a trifle of wartime size and importance, appointing and drafting authorities were hard put to find worthwhile employment for everyone. Former captains of destroyers and submarines had to 'pace the teak' as big ship watchkeepers or become shore based staff officers; senior ratings found themselves committed to responsibilities far inferior to what they had been accustomed. It gradually dawned on everyone that the Navy would have to accept a multitude of changes and that the fleet would become smaller in the years ahead. Also recognized was that a much bigger Admiralty than in 1939 would be needed to deal with unfinished business and to mastermind the post-war years.

First thoughts turned to pay, which had not been a contentious issue during the early years of the war even though minimal increases were awarded; in fact an able seamen in 1943 received the same basic pay as his counterpart in 1919. As would be expected, War Service or Hardship Grants of up to £3 per week tax free for HO personnel who entered the Navy from higher income employment ashore did not pass unnoticed by the regular element of the lower deck; neither did the more lucrative earnings and spending powers of United States and, to some extent, the Dominion armed services. In 1944 an allowance known as Japanese Campaign Pay was granted to those serving in the Far East, but by and large the pay of the average sailor returning home in 1945 compared unfavourably with the rising wages of the average industrial worker.

As the purchasing power of the pound continued to fall, the new Government acted swiftly, rushing through a tri-service pay code without giving the Admiralty much warning or time to study details. For officers a common scale was introduced for all branches with increases averaging 15 per cent; executive officers' specialist pay was abolished, except for submariners, hydrographers and aviators. The age for marriage allowance was reduced from thirty to twenty-five, but in future would be taxable. Ratings fared relatively better, an ordinary seaman's basic pay being almost doubled; there were improvements to allowances including trade pay for artificers, better badge pay adjusted to four, eight and twelve years' service, a flat rate of marriage allowances and a new basic scale for pensions after twenty-two years from the age of eighteen. Senior ratings grumbled over the closing up of junior with senior rates of pay as well as integration with other services; and there were complaints that 'war service increments' were not included as a permanent part of the new rates.

The end of the Second World War was the last occasion of paying prize money. In 1946, there were relatively fewer prize funds at the Admiralty's disposal than in the eighteenth and nineteenth centuries. During the Napoleonic Wars, for example, the amount of money awarded for services rendered in capturing an enemy prize encouraged many sailors to join up and enabled senior officers to retire to a well-endowed country living. In 1919 £40 million was distributed throughout the Navy, an admiral's share being £4,000, a captain £800 and an able seaman £25. Because many enemy ships were scuttled the total prize fund after the Second World War was only £5¼ million and the contributions of the Royal Air Force and the Merchant Navy could not be overlooked. This time government policy ensured a more democratic share out, a flag officer receiving £60 and an ordinary seaman £6.

1946 was a bad year for morale in the Home Fleet. Too many flag and senior officers failed to appreciate the tremendous upheaval in social conditions caused by a long war and were trying to instil pre-war standards too abruptly. Among ships' companies were a high proportion of HO ratings waiting to get out of the service, with no interest or incentive to do anything but stay in harbour. Cases of wilful disobedience escalated and behaviour ashore deteriorated. Matters might have been worse if the Second Sea Lord had not introduced the rate of leading patrolman in 1944 for street policing and set up a Regulating School to improve the standard of provost work. During hostilities many policemen had joined as leading seaman (regulating); on demobilization the leading patrolman came to the fore to become the junior rate in a better structured Regulating Branch. Typical of any new venture the school had its teething troubles, partly in applications from men of dubious background on the pretext that it takes a thief to catch a thief and partly because the school was tossed from one shore establishment to another. In 1950 it became part of HMS *Excellent* on Whale Island where it has remained to this day.[4]

To create a healthy branch emphasis was put on obtaining volunteers from men of sound character, to train for leading patrolman and subsequently for regulating petty officer and master-at-arms. Unlike the other two services who taught their provost corps to be policemen, the leading patrolman was trained to remember that he was a sailor first and to look after the discipline and welfare of servicemen ashore. By the 1960s the branch had acquired a first class reputation within the Navy, with good promotion opportunities to officer rank.

At the top end of the discipline scale a committee was appointed under Mr Justice Pilcher to review the administration of justice in the Navy, following similar enquiries into Army and RAF courts martial procedures. Naval courts martial had risen from 40 in 1938 to a wartime total of 1,134 but declined to 83 in 1950. Pilcher could find little wrong, commenting: 'A naval court martial is attended by considerable ceremonial and enjoys a high degree of prestige amongst officers and ratings. . . . We have heard little evidence of any dissatisfaction with the present administration of justice by court martial.'[5]

It was agreed, for example, that CPOs and POs could opt for court martial if the charge might involve dismissal, detention or disrating. In general the committee tried to bring naval discipline and summary practice into closer conformity with that existing in courts ashore. In the same way a Courts-Martial Appeals Court was set up in 1951 similar to the present Court of Appeal (Criminal Division). Probably because the naval commanding officer has greater summary powers of punishment than his opposite numbers in the Army or RAF such appeals remained comparatively few. And after being in force for ninety years the Naval Discipline Act was revised, mainly to bring the Navy in line with the other two services. In 1966 the Armed Forces Act brought in the power to fine ratings as a punishment, a measure later extended to officers.

Another important change concerned church on Sunday. In October 1946 an Admiralty Fleet Order directed that it was no longer compulsory for officers and men to attend Divine Service '. . . performed every Sunday according to the liturgy of the Church of England'. There is evidence that the Navy had no option but to follow the decision of the Army and the RAF to abolish their compulsory church parades which bore little relation to the Navy's church on Sundays.

The Revd Gordon Taylor, formerly Chaplain RNVR, had this to say:

> The merits and demerits of 'compulsory Church' have long been argued and today they are of merely antiquarian interest. When church attendance on any appreciable scale ceased to be the social custom in civilian life, it was inevitable that the compulsory system which obtained in the armed services could not be maintained and was doomed; but in the Royal Navy, after its unique relationship with the Church for almost a thousand years, the change served the interest of neither.
>
> In the situation which followed the abolition there was much talk of 'moral leadership'; but this proved no substitute for what had been lost. The pious hopes of the idealists for lower deck attendance at voluntary Church were not fulfilled because they did not take sufficiently into account the social pressures which worked against it. Before abolition any sailor who wished to worship could do so without appearing to be setting himself up before and above his messmates; and the majority of those attending could be observed saying the words of the Lord's Prayer and of other prayers in which the service required them to join. There must have been a great number of sailors who after abolition felt like the man who commented to his chaplain 'They have made it impossible for a man like me to go to church.'

The *Church Times* went further, commenting succinctly: 'In a Service routine, where conduct is organized in every detail, where nearly every act is taken corporately, to make church going voluntary is tantamount to making it peculiar.'[6]

New Entries were still required to attend church during the earlier part of their training and to receive religious instruction. Divine Service on a voluntary basis continued to be celebrated on Sundays throughout the Navy and if a chaplain was present it was noticeable how his personality and popularity were reflected in the size of the congregation. A more important task for chaplains was to encourage young sailors, many of whom had never been to church before, into the Christian faith. In the years ahead evangelism and ecumenism became a real challenge for the chaplaincy service.

Another decision to affect the whole Navy was the long overdue question of who should handle the electrical and electronic equipment in ships, hitherto the respective responsibilities of the torpedo branch and RNVR Special Branch officers wearing green stripes. Rather than expand and train members of the Engineering Branch, the Admiralty appointed a committee under Rear Admiral Middleton to consider the formation of an Electrical Branch, taking advice from the industrial and academic field which, among other things, recommended that trainee officers be sent to Cambridge University to read for degree standards. Thus was born the Electrical Branch of the Royal Navy on 1 January 1947, its school to be located in HMS *Collingwood*, a hutted camp built in 1939 to train young seamen on 200 acres of land near Fareham.

Among those who had only known the Navy in war and found it strange to adjust to peacetime conditions was the Fleet Air Arm. In 1940 its hard core had been decimated by the Norwegian campaign, only to be revived by the vast expansion of wartime volunteers that gradually became more experienced and competent than the 'gifted amateurs' of pre-war days. In some indefinable way they also became imbued with the same spirit as their predecessors; they were not just aviators but *naval* aviators and, as such, were an integral part of the Navy.

Because the importance of command of the air over the sea was extensively and consistently demonstrated during the Second World War there was to be no going back. Even although most of its escort carriers and more than half its aircraft had to be returned to the USA and widespread cuts made to personnel and to seventy air stations and repair yards at home and abroad, the mood was one of confidence. To stimulate recruitment the Admiralty announced in 1946 that all junior executive officers, irrespective of specialization, were to be given the chance of obtaining a pilot's 'A' licence as part of their training. But when the idea was floated that the Air Branch should not consider itself a service within a service and an order decreed that 'Naval Aviation' would officially replace 'Fleet Air Arm' reaction was almost hostile. In 1951, the 'Fleet Air Arm' was reinstated by Flag Officer Air Home and a historian wrote: 'With its role at last fully understood, with the Navy behind it, money available and a brilliant team of engineers and designers contributing a flow of novel ideas, the Fleet Air Arm ceased being 'the monkey's orphan' and became one of the most professional flying services in the world.'[7]

Members of 41 (Independent) Commando RM de-ice their equipment during retreat from Chosin, 1951, in bitter conditions

The Korean War broke out when the international outlook was already grim. The Cold War was at its height, Eastern Europe was under Russian control, the Berlin air lift was over, the United Nations was five years old and the North Atlantic Treaty Organization just formed. Response to North Korea's unprovoked attack was the first truly international effort to contain aggression and in June 1950, Britain dispatched troops, ships, naval aircraft and a fleet train. Having minimal enemy ships and aircraft to contend with, the naval role was unspectacular – mainly blockade, air strikes and bombardment. Light fleet carriers, cruisers, destroyers and frigates took their turn off the west coast, while Royal Marines 41 Commando operated successfully with US Marine forces. Needless to add the carriers also acquitted themselves well in prop-driven Sea Furies and Fireflies, carrying out some 23,000 operational sorties over three years and losing thirty-three aircrew.

The idea that the Wrens might be totally disbanded after the war was quickly refuted when the Government announced that Armed Forces Women's Services were to be retained. In 1949 the WRNS became a Permanent Service, separate but integral with the Navy, having their own training establishment at Burghfield, near Reading which in 1953 was commissioned as HMS *Dauntless*.

In searching for suitable acknowledgement for their war services, I came across the following lines from an old copy of *Punch*:

This is in praise of the Wrens –
Boat Wrens, Coder Wrens, Steward Wrens,
Quarters Wrens, General Duties Wrens,
Wrens on shore and afloat
Wren ratings in sailoresque caps
Spry but not musical comedy
Chief Petty Officer Wrens
With sober three buttons on their sleeves
And, as much of the old school of chiefs
The backbone of their service,
Wren officers in their berets
With flaring proud badge of the sea
Wrens in their white shirts or blue blouses
Skirts or bell bottoms
At drill on the square in the forenoon
Eagerly dancing at night
Coming off watch in the morning
Pale with drained faces;
Wrens with purple carbon painted fingers
Rolling off signals – 'Top Secret', 'Important'
Wrens in the Dockyard
Saluting like rather shy children
Wrens on an MTB's deck
With greasy small wrists and a spanner
Plotting Wrens, Messengers, Sparkers
Torpedo Wrens, Ordnance Wrens, Cooks
Trim, bright, staunch, overworked
Good hands and good shipmates
And let it be gladly proclaimed
Utterly indispensable
This is in praise of the WRENS.

WRNS marching in the Victory Parade in London, 1946

From 75,000 in 1945, Wrens fell to 7,000 and by 1950 were serving Naval Air and the three Home Commands, Rosyth, with the Royal Marines and in overseas bases. Overall recruiting figures continued to be the best in the Navy and there were plenty of volunteers from ex-officers and ratings to join the Women's Royal Naval Reserve.

A sailor of Nelson's era would not have found much to surprise him in the broadside messdecks of the Second World War warships that formed the major part of the fleet during the 1950s. Joining a destroyer post-war, Leading Seaman John Cooper recollected:

> The first item of personal gear to be acquired was a bucket – a dhobeying bucket. Not from Pusser's sources but . . . ideally a large galvanized pail from the canteen or ashore.
>
> The destroyer's bathroom would have up to twelve wash hand basins – negative plugs – and mirrors to serve about a hundred men. At peak times, e.g. before breakfast or early evening in harbour, a queue would form in the long narrow passage outside known as the 'Burma Road'. Inside, people would wash, shave or bath standing up or even 'crash out the dhobeying' cheek by jowl in various states of dress or undress from fully clothed to naked except for the inevitable sea boots . . . there was always an inch or two of water sloshing

> around with the motion of the ship. All this could be avoided with the adroit use of one's bucket.

After lashing up and stowing his hammock, Cooper would half fill his bucket with warm water and take it to his favourite spot on the iron deck at the back of the fo'c's'le for morning ablutions. Filling a mug for teeth cleaning and wedging up a pocket mirror, he would shave and if fresh water was short – it often was – he would put his underclothes in to soak and leave the bucket in the mess:

Leading Seaman (later Lieutenant Commander) John Cooper

> Usually in the evening, the daily bath was taken in the bucket, placed on a mess stool or locker top . . . head, shoulders, arms followed by legs were then washed, balancing against lively movement of the ship . . . all this was done whilst one's mess mates were writing letters, playing cards . . . the water could then be used to soak overalls overnight. There being no laundry facilities whatsoever, washing and drying of clothes was a constant task that required planning. Drying lines in No. 1 Boiler Room – with air space in galley flat – reached over grating walkways between a tangle of pipes and valves. It was usual to shout a greeting to the stoker PO on watch far below – which he never heard.

Cooper's description of canteen messing was in the same vein. Breakfast was 'a cup of tea and a quick walk round the table', cooks of the mess 'having no time to linger over such an insubstantial meal' as one would be in the galley fetching the tea while his 'oppo' was drawing the 'daily entitlement of meat from the Able Seaman "Butcher" – a source of much comment – at the upper deck aerated locker or Beef Screen'. Mess members would peel the 'dinner and supper spuds' and if at sea 'the air would be foul and damp. The ship's SRE (Sound Reproduction Equipment) would be full on, distorted and modulating, to flood the crowded messdeck with the daily programme. Sailors would indulge in a favourite pastime of bellowing rough and risqué witticisms back at the loudspeaker'.[8]

After successful trials in the fleet carrier *Implacable* in 1944 centralized messing was introduced in all new aircraft carriers, the latest cruisers and some battleships. This entailed building dining halls and serveries adjacent to galleys so that the whole ship's company could be fed with pre-plated meals during a continuous sitting. For the first time in naval history, food, messtraps and washing-up facilities were removed from messdecks, fulfilling a long-standing request of older ratings. It was of particular advantage to air crews requiring round-the-clock sustenance but due to lack of space it could not be applied to small ships. Nevertheless, it was a promising step forward in modernizing the archaic methods of feeding sailors.[9]

Cafeteria-style dining halls were certainly a popular feature in the new carrier *Eagle* – commissioned in 1951 – and her sister ship *Ark Royal*, where chief and petty officers were waited on by teams of sailors in their dining hall, junior ratings serving themselves in a separate larger space. Galleys were fitted with advanced electric cookers, washing-up machines and waste disposal units. In the wardroom a catering officer was introduced to run the mess on the victualling allowance system; in the ante-room a bar had replaced steward service.

Peeling the dinner and supper spuds

Another overdue change was in uniform. One of the sinecures of war routine was the relaxation of rig (dress), especially when the permitted wearing of non-uniform garments not only added a touch of panache to the individual but made up for deficiencies in service issue clothing. The importance of wearing anti-flash gear to cover the maximum amount of skin surface was, on the other hand, strictly enforced at action stations and undeniably saved lives. Return to peace brought an all round tightening up of dress regulations; it was also appropriate to review the uniform worn by officers and men, some of which had been in abeyance.

In 1939 an officer's wardrobe contained fourteen different 'dresses' – combinations of uniform – which were specified in the appendix to the *Navy List* down to the last button, together with the occasions on which they would be worn. Ten years later, in an era of clothes rationing and stringent economy, the Admiralty abolished ceremonial full dress, ball dress and mess dress, along with frock coats, cocked hats, epaulettes, ceremonial sword belts and white kid gloves that officers had worn for more than a century. That left the former No. 5s – cap, monkey jacket and trousers – as the principal all-purpose dress ashore and afloat. When it came to carrying swords, medals and neck decorations for ceremony older officers deplored the passing of the frock coat that made even well-upholstered figures look elegant. However, captains and above were soon able to adjust their old frock coats to modified ball dress and in 1959 a ceremonial frock/tail coat was instituted for flag officers. White dress, white mess dress and tropical rig (shirts, shorts and stockings introduced in 1937) were retained but the white helmet abandoned. In the 1970s commanders and above appreciated the chance to wear white bush jackets on formal occasions. As a tropical action working dress a light blue shirt and dark blue shorts were introduced, as well as tropical mess undress with open-necked shirt and cummerbund over blue trousers, to be known as Red Sea rig. Meanwhile, blue serge battledress continued as an optional dress, as did a modified mess dress. Ashore in plain clothes it was *de rigueur* until the 1960s for officers to wear hats and for those serving at Whitehall the current fashion was to carry a bowler and rolled umbrella.

For ratings, too, there were changes. Instead of the much cherished overalls, the Director of Victualling produced a new action working dress of light blue shirt and dark blue denim trousers. And at long last, the difficulty of getting into the traditional 'square rig' of collar, jumper and bell-bottomed trousers was made easier by a coat-style, zip-fronted jumper and zip-fronted trousers fitted – officially for the first time – with side and hip pockets. In 1956 the same rig was extended to junior ratings in the Supply, Sick Berth and Coder branches that had hitherto worn 'fore and aft' jackets, straight trousers and peaked caps. PVC fabric impregnated oilskins succeeded the sticky, smelly model that started life in the nineteenth century, and in 1957 the practice of officers wearing white cap covers and ratings wearing white caps in hot or summer weather only was extended to all round the year. White plastic tops could be sponged clean – no need to 'blanco' for Sunday divisions. Introduction of a tropical evening rig of white mess jacket and black bow tie for chief petty officers met with approval and almost all new-look uniform found favour in the fleet. 1974 saw the arrival of dark blue 'woolly-pullies' and windproof jackets for officers and senior ratings, as well as dark blue berets for junior ratings. Following trials in the fleet the traditional square rig was further modernized in 1977, relinquishing the tapes that tied the silk and flaring trousers with a 'fore and aft' crease in lieu of bell bottoms.

Somewhat overdue, Admiralty staff divisions in Whitehall and material departments in Bath gave serious thought to improving fleet living standards. Provision had to be made for men to sleep and stow belongings; the storage, cooking, serving and eating of food; medical and sanitary services; a wide variety of offices and store rooms. Equally important, in producing the right environment, thought had to be given to the choice of materials, supply of air, control of noise, lighting, aesthetics and many other factors.

In reverting to the pre-war practice of giving officers single cabins, it was accepted that increased numbers would lead to smaller cabins, re-design of furniture, adjacent bathrooms and location in the bridge superstructure. Ships' companies would continue to be split up into several small units or messes to give maximum privacy and 'togetherness'. By the early 1950s, space per man had dropped from pre-war standards of 20 to as little as 15 sq. ft for junior ratings and from 25 to 17 sq. ft for senior rates. Besides endeavouring to increase these limitations, it was decided after much heart-searching, to introduce bunks instead of hammocks. A trial in the carrier *Perseus* in 1950 with a three-tier bunk, which could be easily unrigged, showed that bunks would use less space than a corresponding number of slinging billets and that bunk settees could be fitted to ensure everyone could find a seat. Predictably most of these improvements took time to materialize, and not until 1970 was it possible to provide multi-berth cabins for chief and petty officers.[10]

Before the war ended it was clear that methods of officer selection used by the former Interview Boards were on the way out. Based on successful tests by the senior psychologist with potential RNVR officers further trials were made with seventeen- to eighteen-year-old Special Entry officers. As expected post-war Admiralty Interview Boards included a psychologist and they also adopted War Office Selection Board tests enabling selectors to see candidates as individuals and as potential leaders of a group.

For different reasons attention was directed to the recruitment and training of cadets at Dartmouth where, apart from the House System, the regime had not altered since the demise of Osborne in 1921. During the wartime years at Eaton Hall the only innovation was a scheme to award twenty scholarships each year, to preparatory school candidates as well as those from grant-aided schools. When cadet training resumed at Dartmouth there were changes in the wind, largely inspired by the First Lord, A.V. Alexander. Arguing that thirteen and a half was too early for a boy to make up his mind about a career, the Labour government in 1947 decided to increase the age entry to sixteen and a quarter and provide free tuition, board and lodging. The abolition of fees and discrimination over social status and education made good sense – fulfilling, incidentally, one of Fisher's original aims. Raising the age to sixteen stirred up a lot of controversy. Not only did boys from state grammar schools have to hang around until old enough to take the entrance examination, but headmasters of public schools were not prepared to lose promising boys just before entering the sixth form. Moreover, by leaving at sixteen many boys missed leadership experience and responsibility that come from seniority. Adverse Navy career propaganda followed, a prominent educationalist asking openly if the Government's primary consideration had been social equality or service efficiency; and public school entries started to decline.

At the College the two forms of entry worked satisfactorily side by side, together with seventeen- and eighteen-year-old Special Entry cadets from independent and state-aided schools. Pangbourne Nautical College, HMS *Conway* and HMS *Worcester*, ostensibly feeders for the Merchant Navy, also produced a promising and plentiful stream of young officers for the Navy. Initially the old cruiser *Frobisher*, then the big County class *Devonshire* and finally the light aircraft carrier *Triumph* served as training ships for a programme similar to the 1930s. To encourage aviation *Triumph* carried three Sea Balliol aircraft.

From 1950 introductory training was given at Dartmouth to lower deck entries, in keeping with Admiralty policy that 25 per cent of the Navy's officers should come from that source. Most were products of the Upper Yardmen scheme in which outstanding ratings were selected and promoted to acting sub-lieutenants up to the age of twenty-three. The remainder were selected Boy Artificers under training for one term before specializing in the Electrical and Engineer Branches.

Between 1939 and 1945 the spate of promotions from leading rate or petty officer to warrant rank and from warrant to commissioned rank had been the source of much satisfaction. But no sooner had war ended than representations were made through commanders-in-chief that the status and pay of warrant officers was out of line with their responsibilities and that they resented the impression given of being comparable to warrant officers in the Army and RAF. In small ships manned largely by reservists, their background and experience had proved invaluable; in short, they had fought a good war and now wanted something better. After the recommendations of a committee chaired by Admiral Sir Percy Noble, it was decided that on 1 January 1948 warrant officers would become branch officers, their rank prefixed by the title 'commissioned' and that warrant officers' messes ashore and afloat would be closed down so that they could join the wardroom.[11]

Not everyone welcomed this decision. For generations the WOs' mess in big ships and ashore had been a highly respected institution, comparable in spirit with the wardroom and a fruitful link with the lower deck. Even gunroom officers were sad to lose their special relationship. But few at that time realized how fast social change was accelerating within officer ranks and how much remained to be done.

Late in 1944 the title of the Accountant Branch was changed to Supply and Secretariat Branch. After nearly a hundred years the prefix 'paymaster' was exchanged for the less dignified suffix '(S)';

for all that, they continued to thrive as 'pussers'. Early in the war a Royal Naval Supply School had been set up first in London and then in Wetherby, Yorkshire to be commissioned initially as HMS *Demetrius* and then as HMS *Ceres* in October 1946 by a Captain (S). Its purpose was to train writers, stores ratings, stewards, cooks, both continuous and special service, as well as National Servicemen and Wrens. After common training at Dartmouth and in the training cruiser, midshipmen (S) joined the fleet and as sub-lieutenants did an educational and war course at Greenwich, followed by three months in *Ceres*.

In the run down of fighting services, it was predictable that volunteer long-service recruitment would fall off unless inducements were offered. In addition to pay increases, the Admiralty announced a new four year engagement culminating in a £125 bounty, while a bounty and gratuity for each additional year of service would be granted to men who stayed on. To maintain the strength of all services an eighteen month period of National Service conscription was continued but their employment by the Navy was limited, since few could be given worthwhile technical training. Nevertheless, National Servicemen were a useful asset to the service, some being accepted for officer training with successful long-term results. When in 1947 financial cuts lowered conscription to twelve months and the Navy was ordered to reduce to a total of 145,000, manpower planning was thrown completely off balance. Added to a fuel crisis the Home Fleet almost ceased to exist, reductions were made on foreign stations, recruiting plummeted and a US admiral claimed: 'The United States now has more absolute control of the sea than was possessed by Britain.'

During war years regular recruiting stopped, except for young seamen boys, artificers and marines. This made the lower deck seriously top heavy, half being junior rates with less than three years' service, the other half a major overbearing of chief and petty officers. In contrast to a pre-war policy of a continuous service Navy with a sprinkling of special (short) service men, the Admiralty decided on a 50/50 recruiting policy. But this was never realized and during the 1950s was more like 30 per cent CS and 70 per cent SS; at the same time re-engagements dropped from 65 per cent pre-war to 30 per cent and over a thousand purchased their discharge. Reasons were not hard to find – family separation, lack of housing, competition with industry and rising wages ashore. Some relief was launched in September 1950 in the shape of a new pay code, much more generous than the 1946 scales and more in line with the private sector. Pay for an ordinary seaman again doubled with rather fewer increases for more senior ratings; seamen specialist qualifications, technical and artificer branches all received additional pay; kit upkeep and marriage allowances went up. Officers also did well, particularly in the junior ranks; flying pay was almost doubled. In addition, there were better pensions and retired pay with officers given tax-free terminal grants. Other beneficial changes were the establishment of a free gangway (right to go ashore at any time when off duty), permission for senior ratings to wear plain clothes when ashore and legal aid from public funds for officers and ratings facing trial by court martial. To add to a 'Fifth Five' years' re-engagement, senior rates were encouraged to sign on for a 'Sixth Five' with a bigger pension.

After the euphoria of victory parades and farewell parties in 1946, the shore training machine shifted into a lower gear. Through the conscientious service of many former retired officer and rating instructors and the injection of courses on instructional technique, coupled with innovations like multiple answer tests, the standard of wartime instruction was much higher than in 1939. Updated in the latest teaching doctrine, the Instructor Branch of the Navy assumed a more influential role in the running of various schools. It was also evident that due to the proliferation of seaman specialist branches in war the whole structure had to be rationalized.

The first amalgamation took place between the torpedo and anti-submarine branches, logically sensible but not without delivery pains. Feelings varied between sullen indifference on the part of older officers and men, to keen resentment by the up-and-coming anti-submarine branch, accustomed to the small ship officer/man relationships and intensely proud of their role in defeating the U-boats. Their people were essentially user maintainers and senior A/S ratings were upset that, unlike torpedo ratings, they were not allowed to transfer to the new Electrical Branch. HMS *Vernon* at Portsmouth became the principal Torpedo Anti-Submarine School with *Osprey* at Portland for sea training, *Defiance* at Devonport, Chatham Torpedo School, and *Lochinvar* at Port Edgar for advanced minesweeping training. In addition, the TAS branch took over diving training from Whale Island in exchange for anti-gas. When Commander George Blundell joined *Vernon* as executive officer in 1946, he was informed that the Commander-in-Chief, Admiral Sir Geoffrey Layton, had been appointed 'to shake up the Portsmouth Command and bring it up to peacetime standards of discipline and smartness after the relative laxness and dislocation of intensive war'. And well he might. On arrival, Blundell found:

> . . . the general efficiency was abysmal. The standard of dress, the discipline generally and morale was at a low ebb. Hundreds of ancient, passed over for promotion torpedo officers swarmed everywhere offering helpful advice. Chief and petty officers, many long overdue for 'time expired', far outnumbered others in the ship's company. After the battering the place had received, it was all entirely predictable.

At a time when a powerful school of thought advocated moving the school to *Osprey*, the appointment of Captain Jock Hughes-Hallett ensured *Vernon*'s survival. Gradually the school was re-built, torpedo/anti-submarine susceptibilities removed and spirits soared. In the process, Blundell found that:

> One of the essential functions of a commander in the post-war turmoil was to act as a buffer for the moans emanating from officers and men venting their opinions on the new order when a forceful captain was in the driving seat. My job was to listen sympathetically . . . smooth ruffled feelings and enable them to blow off to me. . . . Fortuitously the combination of a brilliant, impetuous, ruthless captain with a tolerant, broad-minded, easy-going commander . . . was a lucky one for HMS *Vernon*.[12]

The other far-reaching event arising from the evolution of ship action information organization, was the merger of the navigation and direction branches. Navigators, fighter direction officers and radar plotting ratings including Wrens, all combined in HMS *Dryad* at Southwick to form the Navigation Direction branch of the Navy. Despite misgivings, there was tremendous activity over five years in conversion training as various categories of (D) learnt about (N) and vice versa. However, by 1951 it was evident that the average officer could not be master of both, so sub-specialists ND(N)s and ND(D)s were introduced; at the same time, buildings to house and train the new branch rose out of the sylvan surroundings of Southwick Park.

RNVR officers comprised 90 per cent of wartime Fighter Direction officers

It was logical that the Signal School, HMS *Mercury*, should remain in its country estate at Leydene. After closing down wartime schools, there remained Signal Training Centres at Devonport, Chatham and overseas; the Naval Air Signal School moved from Arbroath to Lee-on-Solent and a Combined Operations Signal School was set up at Fremington, Devon. The Experimental Department remained at Witley near Haslemere and in 1948 became the Admiralty Signal and Radar Establishment, manned by signals and electrical officers and a complement of civilian scientists. Signal flags were changed to the International Code, and signal books revised to US Navy style and later to meet NATO requirements; similarly, the pre-war phonetic APPLES–BEER changed in 1944 to ABEL–BAKER and subsequently to ALFA–BRAVO – where it stayed.

As with other specializations, long courses reverted to one year, the programme interspaced with foreign and NATO officer courses eager to integrate their navies with the latest techniques. In 1957 the Signal Branch, but not the school, became known as the Communications Branch, Signal officers became Communicators, the century-old title of Yeoman-of-Signals became Communications Yeoman, the PO Tel changed to Radio Supervisor, signalmen became Tactical Communications Operators and telegraphists were called Radio Communications Operators, able to touch type when receiving morse. Electronic warfare was now an important responsibility.

Somewhat belatedly a new and essential school was set up in London in 1942 initially to teach officers how to control ship damage resulting from enemy action. As war progressed the fleet became better organized to cope with the effects of mines, torpedoes, bombs and shells; undoubtedly many lives and even ships were saved as a result. In 1945 the school moved to Tipner in Portsmouth, to be commissioned three years later as HMS *Phoenix*. With the added responsibilities of teaching defence against atomic (nuclear), biological and chemical attack the school rated a captain's command and a sizeable staff of executive, engineering, electrical and shipwright officers with a sprinkling of senior rates. *Phoenix* continued to train as many key personnel as possible in what became known as the ship's ABCD (later NBCD) organization. Virtually everyone was trained in fighting fires, which remained a permanent peacetime hazard. *Phoenix* was also the home of the shipwright branch until the late 1960s, when the beloved 'Chippy' was replaced by a hull engineer artificer.

At the end of 1945, command of *Excellent* assumed imperial proportions with 300 officers and 6,000 ratings borne on the books, mostly under training; Whale Island could even boast to operating the first Sikorski helicopter in the Navy because nobody else knew what to do with it. Rationalization left the pre-war core of *Excellent* with *Fraser* Gunnery Range at Eastney, Devonport gunnery school, with its range at Wembury, and Chatham gunnery school. Among the many peacetime activities revived was the inter-command field gun competition for the first post-war Royal Tournament in 1947. At the time there were those who questioned the publicity value of such an outdated display when the Navy's guided missile was more than a figment of the imagination. But the public loved it because it epitomized all those qualities associated with naval people – courage, team work, skill and the spirit that never gives up when confronted with catastrophe. With crews over-subscribed by volunteers from all branches of the service, the field gun competition continued to be one of the Navy's best selling points and, along with the incomparable Royal Marines Band, the Tournament's top attraction.

Whether marine, aeronautical or ordnance specialists, the engineering branch had come through the war with flying colours, their efforts largely unseen as aircraft took off, torpedoes were launched, turrets fired and captains threw their ships about under maximum helm at maximum revolutions. In most ships there grew up a special relationship between the executive user and the engineering maintainer, each confiding to the other the problems of people and material. After the war the respect felt by the younger executive officers for their technical counterparts had gone up several notches.

The need for more engineer officers in war caused the RN Engineering College at Keyham to look for more beds and classrooms. As long ago as 1939 plans had been approved to build a new college at Manadon just outside Plymouth and every use was made of temporary accommodation erected on its 100-acre site. In 1946 RNEC Manadon was commissioned as HMS *Thunderer* with a Captain (E) in command – a great boost for the branch – with planned accommodation and sports facilities for 500 students and staff. But Manadon was still far from finished and so Keyham, 4 miles distant, was in constant use to share the load for several years. With the need for deeper specialists the whole system of officer training was overhauled to produce the right sort of instruction for officers courses after getting their ER watchkeeping ticket and before specialization. Taking a cue from Dartmouth, *Thunderer* developed its own extensive leisure facilities.

In 1939 artificer apprentice training was transferred from the *Fisgard* block of the Mechanical Training Establishment at Chatham, partly to *Caledonia* at Rosyth and partly to Portsmouth and

Devonport. The former had already started training engine room and electrical apprentices; those at the latter were later accommodated at the new RN Artificers Training Centre at Torpoint in Cornwall, adjacent to HMS *Raleigh.* This was commissioned as HMS *Fisgard* by a Captain (E) in 1946, the name fortuitously handed down from the old hulk that started Boy Artificer Training as part of Fisher's scheme early in the century.

John Lord was among 3,000 candidates from grammar, secondary and a few minor public schools who sat the sixteen-year-old apprenticeship examination in 1939 in which 150 were successful; their four-year course remained unchanged, which explains the consistently high standard of artificer performance during and after the war. 'Training at *Caledonia* was first class,' remarked Lord, 'combining technical subjects in the factory with academic subjects in school – a fairly tightly packed day with time left over for plenty of sport and fun.' Discipline was strict:

> Nobody escaped minor punishments, like stoppage of leave or 'jankers'. A few were caned with great ceremony and fewer still spent time in the Military Prison Wing of Dundee gaol. All rules were meant to be broken, one of the essential skills being that of locksmith. . . . It is said that the man who made the keys at Colditz started life as an artificer.

Lord served his apprenticeship as a coppersmith to qualify as ERA when competition for promotion was fierce. He married in 1946, his wife accepting long absences from home; in fact in his first engagement he had two lengthy foreign commissions interspaced by three months in the Home Fleet and one month in a home port. In his second spell of ten years he spent half at sea and half ashore – 'a more favourable sea/shore ratio'.[13]

Like *Collingwood* at Fareham, HMS *Raleigh* at Torpoint in Cornwall was planned under the Military Training Act of 1938 and commissioned early in the war to train ordinary seamen and National Servicemen. Early in 1948 it became the stokers' new entry training establishment, their title later changing to Marine Engineering Mechanics. In the late 1950s it was decided to integrate the seamen and MEMs Part I (initial) courses and concentrate the new entry training for all branches of the Navy in *Raleigh.* Meanwhile boys' training at *Ganges* (Shotley) and *St Vincent* (Gosport) continued as recruitment concentrated on long-service volunteers, *Impregnable* (Plymouth) and *St George* (Isle of Man) being paid off.

The title of stoker must have appealed to young Leo Sklenar. In 1950 he left school at fourteen for apprenticeship as a metal worker; after three years he found it so boring that he walked into an RN Recruiting Office to join the Navy. Getting parent's consent was no problem but Sklenar's employer objected by refusing to write a reference. The recruiting petty officer soon sorted this out, then persuaded the boy to sign on for twelve rather than seven years on the grounds that it paid a bigger terminal bounty. Sklenar volunteered for stoker because 'it had variety, the petty officer commenting "Smart lad"'.

Sklenar joined *Raleigh* for a six month basic course and to learn the art of stoking. Sea training took place in local destroyers:

> I passed my basic technical tasks with flying colours, though my education left a lot to be desired. . . . I passed out and my first ship was the aircraft carrier *Eagle* as a second class stoker. But there was no stoking for me as I was assigned to the Avfuel and Avgas Party,

> fuelling the planes and manning the catapults. Six months later I was promoted Stoker 1st class and awarded 12 weeks' difference in pay . . . so they must have thought I was good. Then the Suez Canal crisis erupted and it was watch on stop on for me . . . I done a 2½ year stint on the *Eagle* and got stacks of red inkers [accelerated promotion recommends] then I joined the Reserve Fleet at Devonport on the Repair Ship *Dodman Point.*

Two things happened. First his rating title was changed, which he explains: 'When I joined we were called stokers but there were very few recruits as "stoker" does not sound good. So they changed it to Marine Engineering Mechanic; it may have sounded better but I don't think it made much difference.'

The second event was passing Educational Test Part One, thanks to the individual attention of a friendly Coder (Ed) 'whose duty it was to coach solid stokers like me for ETI exam'. Eighteen months later he was rated petty officer and received the Naval General Service medal with the clasp 'Suez 1956'. Petty Officer Sklenar then served in two frigates and four destroyers mainly overseas, where:

> . . . the food was not too bad, not as good as home cooking. They believed in feeding a man up, chips with everything, figgy duff and custard, Windsor soup . . . nothing to write home about. . . . I enjoyed my daily tot of Pusser's neat rum, though I never drunk it before going on watch.
>
> As regards recreation, I was selected for the first XI as goalkeeper. Every port we visited we played the local football talent. At one small island we slaughtered them, the score at half time being 16–nil. Our skipper, who was watching, drew me to one side and whispered in my ear, 'Let in a few goals'. During the second half I was all thumbs and the final score was 18 for us and 16 for them.

As a divisional petty officer Sklenar had his share of welfare work in which he grew to understand the many problems facing young marine engineer officers. A sore point with him was pay which, as a bachelor, was:

> Not bad, but what wound me up was the perks the married man got at the expense of the single man . . . marriage allowance . . . foreign service allowance . . . moving allowance. I got talking to a married M(E)1 called Johnson – not a bad bloke – when on steaming watch. . . . Here was I a petty officer with millions of pounds of sophisticated machinery on my plate yet his take home pay was more than mine, *and* with no responsibilities. . . . Not his fault but I was angry and told him to get out of my sight, then added 'Make yourself useful and brew up the tea'.[14]

In good physical health and with a commendable record, Sklenar was in HMS *Drake* (Devonport) at the end of his engagement in 1966 and resisted personally written overtures from the Commodore to sign on for more. He got a job as a factory engineer and later became director of marine engineering of a West Country dredger company.

Notwithstanding increases in pay and improvements to service conditions the post-war unrest left its mark on many ship's companies. As well as petty crime there was persistent leave-breaking to the point where offenders seemed to think nothing was very wrong in being absent without leave. From 1950 occurred several cases of malicious damage in ships. Steering gear, electric leads and turbines were the principal targets of bloody-minded sailors, some trying to work their tickets. In the aircraft carrier *Indefatigable*, training young seamen at Portland, Captain R.L. Fisher recollected that in 1953:

> the latter months of the commission were made miserable . . . by some wretch committing sabotage by the devilish method of sticking needles into the multi-core cables. There was latent discontent in the Navy at that time and some of the youngsters imitated him by smashing gauge glasses in the engine rooms. . . . The ship became the permanent home of more than one Admiralty detective and we were constantly harried by press reporters. Appeals by me to chief and petty officers to help find the saboteur produced no response . . . we got him in the end – a Scottish Nationalist electrician.[15]

Reports of incidents were taken up by newspapers who published the complaints about poor food and harsh discipline that did the Navy no credit. In two or three small ships mutual trust broke down to the extent that grave indiscipline followed. After one incident, a commander-in-chief reminded the officers of his command that:

> we can none of us feel any complacency about the state of discipline in our ships and establishments unless all of us constantly and consciously take the utmost pains to get to know our men, talk to them off and on duty, study their welfare, respect their pride, commend their well-being and punish their wrong-doing. Perhaps we should use daily King Solomon's prayer for an 'understanding heart to judge our people that we may discern between good and bad'. [I Kings 3: 9.][16]

An inherent problem was the large proportion of men with short-service engagements over whom a minority of long-service ratings had little influence. It was also significant that most cruisers, destroyers and frigates had to manage with scarcely better messing and living conditions than in 1945; what was spartan and tolerated in war was now sub-standard and resented. Shortage of manpower, the indifferent efficiency of weapon systems and machinery, problems of maintenance, excessive commitments and too many abrupt changes in programme that could not for security reasons be explained to ships' companies, all tended to lower spirits. The fleet was over-stretched and something had to give, which explains the reluctance by many men to sign on for further engagement and the number of ratings who bought themselves out of the Navy.

There were, however, signs of better times ahead. Austerity was ending and a pattern of British society was beginning to emerge that was to have a profound effect on the Navy's way of life. Especially in the field of communications – telephones, radio and television – the pace of technological change started to accelerate in the late 1950s, eroding any sense of a steady state in society such as existed in the years before the Second World War. In Britain improvements in living standards, more equal opportunities for men and women and the lowering of class barriers were changes that penetrated the Navy to exert pressure on long established customs and practices hitherto regarded as fundamental or even sacrosanct.

Admiral Sir John Edelsten, C-in-C Mediterranean Fleet, presents regatta prizes aboard his flagship

The most far-reaching factor to transform the lives of officers and ratings was the rapid growth in educational opportunity, arising from the Education Act of 1944, commitment to comprehensive schools and raising of standards throughout the teaching profession. More exciting was the upsurge in higher education after the opening of new universities and polytechnics for students of both sexes eager to gain degrees and diplomas to match job qualifications. It was interesting to note, too, how some educational authorities criticized the examination system as being too meritocratic and the role of the public schools as being too socially divisive, opinions not lost on those concerned with officer entry.

Mainly due to social pressures, naval policies about people simply had to change as better informed officers and men expressed a desire to have a real sense of purpose in their job, a higher quality of life, more consideration for their families and appropriate career management from recruitment to re-settlement in civilian life. How the Navy met these challenges and laid the basis for a more efficient, better contented but leaner service is described in the next chapter.

CHAPTER THIRTEEN

Foundation for the Future

Change is one of those things which we like to encourage others to do but which most people dislike accepting themselves. Skills acquired over a long period are suddenly no longer needed. . . . All these things are profoundly disturbing to the individuals involved. But it is even more painfully true that any organization which refuses to accept change eventually succumbs to extinction or revolution.

HRH Prince Philip, Duke of Edinburgh

On 18 April 1955 Admiral the Earl Mountbatten became First Sea Lord, an office he held for four years. His arrival coincided with an anxious, testing time for the Navy, a predicament persisting well into the 1970s, with endless Defence Reviews, regular cutbacks in personnel, disappointing recruitment and a profusion of Admiralty committees concerned with improving the careers of officers and men. What is more the Royal Navy lacked an established role.

In the first place all was far from well with the officer structure. The dilemma was first brought to light in 1946 when the Second Sea Lord warned the Board of the need for an even flow of officer promotions, avoiding large fluctuations which would only store up trouble for the future.[1] He also cautioned that a diminishing number of ships without a corresponding reduction in executive commanders and captains would curtail their sea time to an unacceptable degree. Regrettably the inauguration of NATO and demands for staff jobs aggravated the situation to the extent that commanders could look forward to only eight months at sea to qualify for promotion to captain. A split list then became a professional and mathematical certainty.

Secondly, there were widespread feelings of exasperation among older Engineer and Supply and Secretariat officers over the unfading predominance of the Executive officer caste in a variety of service appointments involving general administration, warship design and weapon technology. While sharing these views the newly formed Electrical branch had less occasion to complain than the veteran engineers, who recollected the Selborne–Fisher concept of interdependence that never saw the light of day, who felt they were still regarded as second class citizens and who had witnessed the neglect of a proper approach in preparing the Navy's propulsion systems for the late war. Again, Supply officers provided Board members, as well as flag officers ashore and afloat, with their secretariat gaining essential know-how in administration; yet the great majority were denied the chance to exercise it later on in any capacity. Finally, there was little recognition that in wartime, plumbers, pussers and even schoolies had shared the same risks as everyone else and on many occasions had displayed notable examples of leadership and gallantry. To what avail? Career prospects for (E) and (S) branches remained barely encouraging in contrast to their executive brethren.

Not before time these shortcomings were acknowledged by the Board of Admiralty. Under the Chairmanship of Vice-Admiral Sir Aubrey Mansergh, a Committee on Officer Structure and

Training (COST) was set up in January 1954, having representatives from all branches to collect evidence and suggestions. Although a lot of hard work was needed to iron out controversial problems, there was not much disagreement over broadening the responsibilities of (E), (L) and (S) officers. As a forecast of what was to come, the Admiralty abolished in March 1955 the coloured distinction cloth worn between stripes by non-executive officers since 1863. Paradoxically, some (E) and (S) dinosaur-minded individuals insisted on wearing their 'cloth' during the voluntary period until the last possible moment.

Protracted argument surrounded the best way to resolve the executive officer sea time problem. Two solutions emerged; either institute Wet (sea-going) and Dry (shore-going) lists of captains and commanders or else divide them up into first and second eleven groups with only the former going to sea, leaving the latter scant chance of further promotion. In the event the Wet/Dry list scheme prevailed.

On 1 January 1956 an Admiralty Fleet Order was distributed, with an introductory message from the Board. Broadly speaking it was accepted that the executive officer must become more technical and the technical officer must increase in numbers and become more executive; that with more experience in junior ranks outside their technical field, senior (E), (L) and (S) officers would play a more responsible part in higher administration; and it was essential that prospects of promotion to commander be improved for all officers.

The most far-reaching resolution was that from 1 January 1957 all (X), (E) (L) and (S) officers would be formed into a single General List in which '. . . officers must be still more "all of one company"'. Cadets would enter the List with a period of common training before becoming Seaman, Engineer or Supply specialists – initially no decision being made on Electrical officers. After specialization all junior officers would take their turn in day-to-day harbour ship and shore duties, with the carrot that a cadet entering in 1957 would have three chances in four of being promoted commander when the time came. Because of their special professional requirements Instructor, Medical and Dental officers would continue as separate branches.

On the ticklish subject of command it was decided that while sea command would not be the exclusive prerogative of any one list or specialization non-Seaman officers required a specific appointment 'for Seaman duties' or higher direction. For normal working command all officers would be on a similar footing, a principle that was extended to sitting on a court martial or – a nice touch of the old Navy – command of ships' boats. To retain a single standard of justice no change would be made in disciplinary matters by widening the delegation of summary punishments. The whole concept of the General List was that as many jobs as possible would be open to officers of any specialization and that merit rather than branch would be the cardinal factor in promotion.

Great trouble was taken to spell out every detail, including the splitting of Seaman specialist captains and commanders into a Post (Wet) List and a General (Dry) list, the former title harking back to sea service in the eighteenth and nineteenth centuries. In 1960 engineering and electrical specialists were amalgamated into a single Engineering specialization.

To compensate for a smaller cadet entry, more promotions would be made from the lower deck, the Branch List being expanded into a new Special Duties List of sub-lieutenants, lieutenants, lieutenant commanders and a few commanders in order to fill more specialized junior complement billets. Furthermore, a Supplementary List would be introduced to top up the ranks of junior officers with direct entries in any specialization as vacancies occurred. There were many details covering career prospects, junior officers' training, promotion ages, retirements, the reserves and how officers' names would be shown in the Navy List. AFO 1/57 clarified the flag list, promotion procedure and the new centralized appointing organization.

The introduction of the General List was every bit as momentous as the Selborne–Fisher scheme fifty years earlier; but this time reactions were different. After reading AFO 1/56 '. . . it seemed to me', said a lieutenant commander, 'both a revolutionary and a courageous commitment by the Board, and a brilliantly written explanation'. When officers realized that only radical steps could reorganize their structure, comments were almost universally favourable. There were exceptions. Some engineer and electrical officers grumbled over interference to professional training by instruction needed to qualify them for military command while others deplored the disappearance of 'tribal chiefs', former heads of (E), (L) and (S) specializations.

The worst hit were those among the 400 commanders who opened their 'personal' letters to find that they were to be 'dry'. For an ambitious officer with successful sea experience to be told in his late thirties that he will never command a warship, the news was heart-breaking. Most Dry List officers made a go of it and a few achieved flag rank. Others decided to call it a day and retired, the Second Sea Lord receiving angry and bitter letters of recrimination. Reverberations from this divisive upheaval rumbled on for some time.

Gradually former seaman officer appointments at commander and captain's level passed to other specializations and vice-versa; in 1965 a Survey Committee on Officer Structure was able to report that the basic concept of the General List 'is serving the Navy well and should continue, but care is needed to avoid over widening of experience at the expense of specialist professionalism'. They also recommended that 'the Supply Specialization should not merge with the Seaman Specialization', and that 'the term "Post List" be abolished, a seagoing list being retained for administration purposes'. In other words the wet/dry list should be covert, which it soon became.[2]

Equally important in COST deliberations was the cadet entry and training at Dartmouth. After five years of the sixteen-year-old scheme there was, as predicted, a marked fall off in public school applicants; insufficient boys of the right calibre were joining the Navy. An Admiralty working party recommended an entirely new system to cover everything from a common entry to specialization as a lieutenant, terminating midshipmen's time at sea in the fleet and transferring to Dartmouth essential parts of sub-lieutenants' courses at Greenwich and Portsmouth.

Since public and political opinion would never accept a return to thirteen-year-old entry it had to be eighteen for all; in fact age limits were between seventeen and three-quarters and nineteen, allowing boys two bites of the cherry for entry. Cadets either had to have the GCE 'O'-level passes before taking the Civil Service Commissioner's examination or could go for five passes, two at 'A' level. The scheme was better than the Special Entry it replaced because by widening the field some could benefit from being clever and joining early, while others could stay to complete school careers in the normal manner; a reasonably bright boy could still try for a university if not selected for the Navy.

On joining Dartmouth cadets spent two terms mainly on academic levelling, although later the need was felt to add an initial term for basic naval and disciplinary training. Then came a term at sea in frigates and destroyers of the Dartmouth Squadron under a Captain (D). Steaming as far afield as the Baltic, West Indies and the Mediterranean cadets were instructed in professional subjects but more importantly they lived the life of a rating. On return to the college they were rated midshipmen before a further four terms of academic and professional training, including a nine week spell at sea. Rated acting sub-lieutenants they joined the fleet to obtain a Certificate of Competency, in effect the membership card of the General List club denoting that the holder was a capable member of the officer corps and able to take charge. In addition a seaman officer had to gain a Watchkeeping Certificate.

Supply officers and seamen officers – except submariners and aviators who could not be spared for so long – spent three years at sea to be promoted lieutenants with seniority gained from Dartmouth results. Engineer officers broke off after getting the ER Watchkeeping ticket to start training at Manadon, while electrical officers went to a university to gain a degree. Between the ages of twenty-three and twenty-six the plan was for all lieutenants to take the Greenwich War Course; subsequently seamen officers would think about sub-specializing in (TAS), (C), (G) or (ND).

The COST scheme was an improvement in that it dealt with officer entry and training as a whole rather than as a series of parochial problems. But, in spite of the widened field of entry and early scholarships to help boys stay at their schools, barely sufficient acceptable candidates came forward; worse still the wastage rate from the academic failure was alarmingly high.

In 1958 Sir Keith Murray and a high level committee were appointed to go into the whole question once more. Their main recommendations – accepted by the Board and implemented in 1961 – were that educational standards should be raised, sea time in the fleet for midshipmen restored, the attempt to integrate and combine academic and professional training abandoned and that engineering as well as electrical specialists should read for degrees.[3]

Restoring sea time for midshipmen was the result of strongly held opinions by senior officers on the value of such experience being retained. And so once the higher entry standard of five GCE passes, two at 'A' level, was agreed and the need for schooling at Dartmouth eliminated, a period of entirely naval training was a logical sequence. Cadets would spend the first year at the college and in the training squadron; the second at sea as midshipmen, learning management as well as seamanship but accommodated in the wardroom. The third year would see seamen and supply officers back at Dartmouth for an academic course as acting sub-lieutenants, thereafter to do professional courses and return to sea. In their third year and later electrical and engineer officers would read for their degrees, becoming qualified officers rather later than the others. In an open letter to retired officers in 1962 the First Sea Lord stated that the first Murray scheme entry met 75 per cent requirements, candidates were of very good quality and once the school's liaison organization was strengthened the full quota would soon be realized. He did admit, however, that the Navy had a fight on its hands to attract the best candidates.

For various reasons the Murray scheme was changed towards the end of the 1960s, reducing the total length of training at Dartmouth by nearly a year until, in the opinion of a former commanding officer at the college:

> the academic and professional training was only a very thin veneer. The short time spent at Britannia Royal Naval College was not sufficient for what I call the 'rub off effect' – the training by example of staff and the ethos of the place. The young men simply had not the time to develop their officer-like qualities. All this put a strain on the fleet whose training load was enormously increased. . . . I am glad to say that slowly the cyclic wheel was turned, wisdom and common sense prevailed and training time lengthened.[4]

Britannia Royal Naval College, Dartmouth, in the 1970s

In 1965 the first four Seaman and Supply Branch officers were accepted for a degree course at Oxford, and by 1971 so popular were graduate entries that the annual ceiling was raised from twenty to a hundred. To stimulate volunteers naval units were set up at Aberdeen, Liverpool and Southampton and serious consideration given by the Second Sea Lord's office and the Chief of Naval Educational Services towards inaugurating a naval degree course in conjunction with RNC Greenwich and City University, London. It did not come to fruition although a Systems Management degree course featured at a later stage.

Were there too many alterations in officer entry and training after the Second World War? If so, did they deprive the Navy of promising officer potential? The paramount importance of acquiring a fair share of the nation's youth entailed stepping up public relations and improving the Navy's image with schools, in competition with the other services and industry. Equally crucial was the skill of the Admiralty Interview Board, initially located at Dartmouth and later at Gosport. Led by an admiral or senior captain their methods of spotting talent became highly professional and scrupulously impartial. By the middle 1960s, some 70 per cent of successful candidates were accepted from state-aided schools – including Upper Yardmen – and 30 per cent from independent schools, the latter proportion decreasing by 1970. Also subjected to aptitude tests and interview were entrants for short service commissions on the Supplementary List to become aircrew officers.

To compete with ever changing social and educational trends and the need to keep training time short was no simple matter for the Second Sea Lord. With hindsight it was probably right to experiment. By 1970 an impression was gained that standards were satisfactory but there was only just sufficient 'good' or 'very good' potential joining the fleet.

Having remodelled the officer structure from top to bottom the Admiralty turned its attention to ratings. Traditionally their specialist training was in the hands of Admiralty staff divisions and specialist schools. There was a Director of Naval Training, but with so few powers or staff that he was dubbed 'Director of No Training'. All this changed in 1957 when a Director General of Training was appointed with authority to centralize control of training in Whitehall.

The first recommendation of the committee to review the Navy's Rating Structure was to enhance the seamen branch by reducing its numbers to permit seamen to concentrate on seamanship instead of being given jobs of little or no interest.[5] A later development was the establishment of a Seamanship School in Portsmouth, where the few remaining purely seamanship tasks were taught, such as life saving, replenishment at sea and boat work. It was the committee's suggestion that the seaman's former technical duties should be undertaken by 'weapon mechanics' and 'weapon electrical mechanics', combining user and maintainer duties on a semi-skilled basis, an idea taken up by the Electrical Branch when they assumed responsibility for weapons. All this – and the suggestion that communal chores should be shared by all branches – made good sense.

One of the major sociological developments to affect the Navy was the steady increase in marriage among younger people. It was soon clear that the Navy would have to adapt itself to an increasingly married lower deck if there was to be any real chance of attracting and keeping men in the service. Exacerbated by the Korean war the uncertain and irregular lengths of overseas commissions became a source of increasing dissatisfaction in the fleet. To reduce separation, especially for newly married younger ratings, and to keep ships' companies together the General Service Commission was introduced in 1954. Under this system ships would serve an eighteen month commission of which only twelve would be spent abroad. Simultaneously Foreign Service Commissions were reduced to eighteen months; married personnel in shore billets overseas, including those serving in local craft, would be limited to thirty months, besides qualifying for free passages. Home Sea Service, Port Service – home shore posting – and Reserve Fleet made up the other types of commission. A more even-handed sea/shore ratio could be achieved by alternating the different types.

Another trend was the dramatic rise in the employment of single and married women in the country's labour force. Family responsibilities permitting, many naval wives conformed to the national practice of supplementing the family income in this way.

Family sentiments also caused general dislike of the inequitable consequences of drafting and manning ships by separate authorities in the three home ports (by Lee-on-Solent for the Fleet Air Arm). The system had failed to stand the test of war and in 1956 Centralized Drafting was introduced under a commodore based in HMS *Centurion* at Haslemere, its purpose to install a fairer, more efficient method of manning the fleet. Ratings could select a depot or barracks for family welfare and holding purposes, as well as choosing an area in which to serve when their time came for Home Service. Gone were the days of a West Country, Portsmouth or Chatham ship's company whose collective background more than anything else created a ship's character. In fact, by the 1960s the Navy was recruited from much wider sources in the country and away from home ports.

In 1970 *Centurion* transferred to Gosport to swell the concentration of establishments in the south; subsequently the Commodore became responsible for drafting, mobilization, advancement, promotion and next-of-kin records of all naval, marine and Wren ratings. It was logical, too, that the Directorate of Naval Pay and Accounts should also be located in *Centurion* to link up with a fully computerized organization.

Announced as a 'New Deal' for the Navy the substance of the 1956 estimates was to introduce a Regular Engagement of nine years. This superseded the former continuous and special (short) service engagements, except for artificers whose training still required twelve years. As a boost to recruitment and to retain men in service there were obvious attractions in one standard engagement; no obligations to join the RFR and option to re-engage for further five year periods with an enhanced pension. And to keep up with the times the rating of 'Boy' was dropped in favour of 'Junior' to cover seamen and engineering, electrical and naval air mechanics, all of whose basic training was carried out in *Ganges* at Shotley and *St Vincent* at Gosport.

The 1956 Armed Services Pay Code was also well received in the Navy. It was the first review for ten years, with increases in almost every pay scale, allowance and pension. The Second Sea Lord, Admiral Sir Charles Lambe, thought it so important that he flew personally to Gibraltar to address officers and men of the combined fleets. But when added to the cost of new ships, weapons and aircraft the extra expenditure had to be paid for, firstly by reducing naval strength by 5,000 to 128,000, and secondly by drastic economies in the Navy's shore structure. Addressing the Way Ahead Committee Mountbatten stated: 'We must take risks not only in making proposals for the future but in liquidating the legacies of the past. . . . We have been trained to take risks in operating our ships at sea . . . but have been less willing to apply these lessons to our responsibilities ashore. We must do so now.'[6]

Naval bases at Scapa Flow, Invergordon, Harwich and Bermuda were shut down, and that at Simonstown was handed over to South Africa. Gunnery training was concentrated in *Excellent* at Portsmouth and *Cambridge* at Plymouth, communications training was focused on *Mercury* at Petersfield; medical, air, ND, TAS and Royal Marines training was also rationalized. The supply school HMS *Ceres* was absorbed in *Pembroke* at Chatham and *Sultan* was established as the Marine Engineering School for artificers and MEMs at Gosport; in 1958 *Harrier*, teaching air navigation and direction, was closed down. Cutting 7,000 uniformed personnel and 23,000 civilians saved £15 million.

Between 1946 and 1970 the Navy was involved in fifteen or so overseas operations of which Korea and Suez were the most significant. Because the latter stood out as a major national setback and became a turning point in British defence policy it is worth recounting.

Whatever the political reasons behind the abrupt decision of Colonel Nasser, Egypt's Head of State, to nationalize the Suez canal in July 1956 it was in Britain and France's interests to move quickly, secure the canal with military forces and unseat Nasser. Although Commander-in-Chief Mediterranean, Admiral Sir Guy Grantham, was all for immediate naval action Operation

Musketeer took all of three months to mount from the UK. Included in a force under Grantham's command were five aircraft carriers, three cruisers, nineteen destroyers and frigates and every landing craft that could be made serviceable. To find extra personnel for this force precipitated a manning crisis of no small proportions.

After Israeli forces knocked out the Egyptian army east of Suez late in October, British and French forces destroyed most of the Egyptian air force. At dawn on 5 November French paras and British Red Devils floated down to their dropping zones, beach defences were pounded with bombs and shells and the first troops and tanks went ashore. Thereafter 45 Commando Royal Marines was ferried inland by helicopters from carriers anchored offshore, 'the first time this precise operation had been attempted and it had something of a picnic air about it'. Marines piled into the helicopters with ammunition on their laps, and in this haphazard manner five hundred men, stores and equipment were brought ashore and the few casualties evacuated. At the end of the day Allied troops occupied Port Said and were 20 miles down the canal when ordered to stop by Whitehall; a truce was signed and Anglo–French forces withdrew. Afterwards Grantham considered the operation 'a complete success but far too much force was employed . . . it could have been achieved much more effectively with RM Commandos and the Fleet Air Arm'. To be cut short with victory in sight was galling to the fighting services and 'what should have been a feather in the cap of the Navy . . . was relegated to the sub-conscious limbo of defeats'.[7]

Though Suez heralded the end of the British Empire and withdrawal of many overseas commitments at least the campaign underlined the need for a mobile task force ready for deployment at short notice; it also gave the Royal Marines an enhanced role central to Admiralty policy. In future small RM detachments would be included in frigates serving overseas and later *Albion* and *Bulwark* were converted from aircraft to RM Commando carriers. Suez also marked the first step in the decline of the Navy's big fleet carriers.

In April 1957 Mountbatten and his Board were confronted with the first major Defence Review, better known as 'Sandys' White Paper' after Duncan Sandys, the Minister of Defence. Extending over five years its purpose was to reduce and reorganize the nation's armed forces, which had become too expensive to support. National Service was phased out, the fighting services made totally regular and the Navy reduced from 121,000 to between 90,000 and 100,000 by 1962. To keep defence expenditure strictly within limits Sandys was given increased authority with a high-powered Defence Board to assist him. Of the 400 warships in reserve a third were scrapped within a year.

The business of axing some two thousand RN and RM officers from a total of 14,000 was conducted with more compassion than shown by Sir Eric Geddes in 1922. Apart from 25 per cent of the Flag List – retired after one job as rear admiral and thereafter by a reduction in promotions – almost all the officers to go were volunteers to take a 'Golden Bowler' by premature retirement. With a moderately generous tax-free compensation some fifty captains, three hundred commanders, rather more lieutenant commanders and majors RM and a number of Special Duty officers all left the Navy. About a thousand ratings were discharged, the majority volunteers or at the end of their engagements. By and large, a fairly painless operation.

It was one thing to abolish National Service but less easy to decide how best the regular forces could be maintained at full strength by volunteers. Under Sir James Grigg a tri-service committee was set up to examine the factors bearing on the willingness of men and women to serve; these included pay and pensions, training and promotion, discipline, accommodation, food, recruitment, uniform, welfare, re-settlement after leaving the service and public relations. In many of these aspects the Navy had made progress but there was much to accomplish and no room for self-satisfaction.

Investigation revealed that pay was not, at that moment, a major issue. None the less, one of the committee's first recommendations was to institute a biennial review of service pay that took into account civilian wages for comparable occupations in the services. This was completed in time for new rates to be announced in April 1960.

By the time the 1966 pay review was due all three services were facing serious manpower shortages. The Government had set up a National Board for Prices and Incomes, which decided that the entire structure of Armed Forces pay needed re-examination; and in the sweeping reforms that followed the Second Sea Lord, Vice-Admiral Sir Peter Hill-Norton, took an active part. In the first place it was accepted that the complex network of pay, allowances and charges should be replaced by a 'military salary', its prime aim to pay the rate for the job. This would help servicemen and potential recruits better to judge their financial position relative to what it might be in civilian life. Another reason was to abolish the difference in real income between single and married men, a unique feature of service pay. To undertake this survey a detailed job evaluation was carried out in comparing service responsibilities and training with commercial enterprise. The result was to create one basic rate for each rank and trade, subject to tax, out of which servicemen and -women would pay for food, lodging and clothing, but not uniform. In the Navy charges for accommodation and food would not be applicable on board ship.

Finally it was agreed that a provision should be made in the military salary for those aspects of life in the fighting services that have no counterpart in civilian employment. To be called the X factor it would take into account exposure to danger, discipline, total commitment to the service and the frequent uprooting that is inseparable from Service life; any one of these features could be found in some employments but not the combination. Such disadvantages would be set against the benefits of adventure, variety, chance to travel – although this was diminishing – and the greater security enjoyed by service people. Also, those who committed themselves to longer engagements would receive extra pay. It was decided that the X factor should initially be 5 per cent of basic salary, that the resultant increases would also apply to the Reserves and, as a step towards equal pay for women, the rates for servicewomen would be increased to 95 per cent of corresponding scales for men. Kit upkeep allowance and hard lying money were retained, the latter at a single rate; flying pay, submarine pay, diving pay and parachute pay were also retained and increased. With the approval of all three services the military salary came into force on 1 April 1970.[8] To review it biennially an Armed Forces Pay Review Body was set up.

Unlike the Army and Air Force the pre-war Navy was anything but concerned about providing homes for officers' and ratings' families. Traditionally the Admiralty provided official houses for commanders-in-chief and some senior officers, and after Invergordon the Victory Housing Society, supported by the Royal Naval Benevolent Trust, built 130 low rental houses for ratings in Portsmouth. In 1946 a decision was made to build married quarters for ratings and officers but progress was slow; by 1953 only 1,800 houses had been built at home and overseas.

Further projects were launched to accommodate officers and men serving anywhere in a home port area with an expectation of occupation for six months or more; similar arrangements were made for the Fleet Air Arm. Until quarters were ready the hirings scheme was in operation whereby furnished houses and flats could be rented, the Admiralty paying the difference from married quarter charges. By 1970 there was service accommodation for 9,000 families, almost too much for a Navy diminishing year by year; many were located in vast all-naval housing estates, complete with NAAFI shops, community centres, children's playgrounds, tennis courts and bowling alleys. They were economically sound propositions but the absence of husbands overseas generated sociological problems that taxed many a welfare officer.

In keeping with the Welfare State the Navy's Family Welfare Organization continued its good work after the Second World War, establishing major sections in Portsmouth and Devonport and smaller units at Yeovilton for Naval Air Command and at Rosyth. Family Welfare and Liaison officers, all ex-RN and backed up by civilian and WRNS welfare workers, dealt mainly with ratings' domestic and matrimonial problems, most of which arose from family separation due to husbands' absence overseas. They also handled what was called turbulence – changes to ships' movements or an unexpected draft to a new job, known as a 'pier head jump'.

In the fleet the Divisional System of dividing the ship's company into small units led by an officer and petty officers remained the keystone of personnel policy for successive Second Sea Lords. Complementary to the system was the Second Sea Lord's personnel liaison team of two officers and a chief petty officer to provide feedback from the lower deck and the Divisional School at Portsmouth, which did much to remind officers of their responsibilities. But more often the human problems of a young, largely married ship's company were sufficiently deep seated to require lengthy attention by commanding officers and others before the matter could be resolved; the key in many cases being the attitude of the naval wife. In contrast to the old Navy, where most wives stoically accepted their husbands' absence overseas for as much as two years, circumstances had markedly changed. The young wife of a lieutenant spoke for many when she wrote:

> There seems to be a new generation of naval wives. The younger ones will never be the same as their predecessors. They do not fit the traditional role of the naval wife left behind at home, content within the limits of home and children and accepting all the difficulties of Service life. Their husbands have been trained to obey without question, but they have not. Nothing in their school or family background has prepared them for the unquestioning acceptance of domestic and social difficulties. 'Patriotism' and 'the stiff upper lip' are not in their vocabulary. They often want to work, but find it extremely difficult to reconcile with the rigid naval leave periods and sudden disruption. They cannot easily run home to their families when their husbands are away. In short these wives find naval family life more strange and difficult than ever before, and are less able to accept their 'special problems'. It is their husbands who often resign prematurely for family reasons.

Investigating the situation a Naval Welfare Survey Committee recommended that:

> families left behind need considerably greater support than they now receive and the main weight of our recommendation is to remedy this. Most sailors are fully competent to handle their own and their families' problems . . . but there are a significant number where this is not

> the case. In part this is due to the changing nature of the service . . . we were surprised to find that in HMS *Ark Royal* with its complement of 2,600 officers and men, the average age was only 21.[9]

Another benefit to an officer or rating seeking a part- or even full-time naval career was an assurance that the Navy would go out of its way to assist those leaving to find another job. Between the wars the situation had been very different, more being done for discharged ratings than officers. The former possessed a high reputation among employers as reliable and competent workers, and with the help of vocational training classes and the National Association for Employment of Sailors, Soldiers and Airmen it was rare for ex-naval ratings, especially those with technical expertise, not to find work. For officers it was different since most were presumed, quite fallaciously, to have private means and were left to their own initiative to find employment; many became school bursars, secretaries to golf clubs or superintendents of hospitals to supplement a meagre pension.

With the post-war rise in cost of living it was no longer choice but necessity that prompted officers on retirement to find work to supplement their pension, amounting to half their active pay. Two serving officers at the Ministry of Labour advised and assisted job seekers but such efforts were insubstantial, and it was not until the mid-1950s that proper resettlement courses were instituted. Personal assistance was also given by the Second Sea Lord's office, while the Officers Association became one of many sources of job vacancies as employers realized that younger, highly trained officers were on the market. Confidence in ability to handle people at all levels has long been a strong point among RN job seekers, and more recently the possession of civilian technical qualifications has opened the door to even more opportunities. Indeed, few have not made a real success of a second career in another profession or in industry. Much the same could be said of the lower deck, who readily adapted themselves to positions of trust and where integrity was all important. So much so that they often gained preference over other ex-service applicants.

There has always been something about a sailor, as Captain George Blundell found when placed on the retired list at the age of fifty-two. During terminal leave he learnt from the Birmingham Labour Exchange that a well-known manufacturer of vehicle propeller shafts was seeking an electrician's mate. As an ex-torpedoman he knew about amps and volts, applied and got the job. He did not reveal his rank, however, when he reported to the personnel office and was taken by the foreman to meet the man under whom he would work:

> I learnt to respect Len, a brilliant electrician who worked at a tremendous speed with vast enthusiasm. . . . He supplemented his income by adroit use of overtime, by flogging budgerigars or acting as a weekend wedding reception waiter . . . a lovable, difficult, intriguing character who taught me a lot. Our first act was to get my Works Card with a basic wage of £8 16 shillings a week . . . our 'headquarters' was two rickety steel lockers standing against the wall of the Hardening Shop, in which we kept clothing, cleaning gear, tools and tea mugs. . . . The Works Canteen was very class conscious. There was a dismal room for *Labour*, such as me . . . there was a room for *Superiors* and another for *Managers* with a table cloth and waitresses and – glory of glory – a dining room for *Directors* with drinks on the house. During my time in the company I tried them all.

Nobody in the Works knew anything of Blundell's background, and though not openly curious they quickly summed him up as a 'gent' with a history that had to be shielded from 'management'. One day his identity leaked and next morning:

> I placed my bike in the rack as usual. . . . Outside the Time Office stood the Commissionaire, ex-Chief Stoker Arthur Batty, rigidly at the salute as I passed in my overalls to clock-in. 'Good morning, Sir' he hailed. Entering the Hardening Shop I found Len in a great state of excitement, bursting with expletives. I was rather flattered by his pleasure. 'But Len,' I remarked 'I did try to tell you a month ago.' Len looked a bit awkward. 'Well, George,' he said, 'we discussed you in the Shop and decided you must have been in prison and was trying to make good.'[10]

Public relations has never been a strong suit in the Navy's pack and its post-war development under the direction of a Chief of Naval Information revealed an Admiralty department very much out on a limb. It was always a busy office dealing with interminable enquiries, but apart from handling press releases on naval affairs and maintaining liaison with the media Naval Information was not geared to projecting the Navy's image to any great depth. Nevertheless, Navy Days at the three home ports in the summer holidays, Operation 'Shop Window' by aircraft carriers and destroyers during a day at sea for selected visitors and an extensive Admiralty Lecturer programme for schools did much to keep the Navy in the public eye.

Occasionally something happened to appeal to the journalistic mind, such as when a junior rating was lost overboard from the destroyer *Carysfort* in a fleet exercise in November 1957. When his effects were auctioned, for which a ship's company of 180 subscribed £645, *The Times* called it chivalry, because:

> This collective and individual act of generosity was not causeless and fortuitous. Its origin lay in the kind of men these were and are, the life they lead, the outlook which they share, the virtues which are instilled into them which they learn swiftly – and unstintingly put into practice. If men acquire the habit of being disciplined, generous and unselfish . . . and in their every day concerns are capable in a moment of crisis of pulling out that extra effort, whether of heroism or comradely kindness. . . . That is the lesson these men teach us all.

In 1964 the Navy appointed a Director of Public Relations, having a mixed civilian and naval staff with terms of reference that enabled PR to play an increasingly important role. An innovation of the early '70s was the RN Presentation Team led by an articulate and spirited captain, to put the Navy's case before the public up and down the country with a polished performance that included films and slides.

Ships' newspapers were popular in wartime because everyone was hungry for information; the custom was continued later in home ports. In 1954 *Portsmouth Navy News* became the *Navy News*, brainchild of the barracks commander and chaplain, who became the first editor. Its monthly issue of twelve pages, illustrated with photographs to record events and impartially covering all branches of the service, soon filled a long-felt want by serving and retired naval people. Being an independent

Pacific Post was the newspaper of the British Pacific Fleet

newspaper it survived an attempt by the Admiralty to curb its criticism of Government policy and by the 1970s reached a circulation of 100,000, far in excess of the newspapers of other services. *Navy News* continues to remind its readers of the active, colourful and versatile life led by officers, men and women afloat and ashore.

Predictably the combination of better education, better pay and better conditions of service exerted a favourable influence on punishment returns and the impression left by libertymen in foreign ports. In shore establishments periodical visits by specialized units helped to offset addiction to alcohol and drugs, while a leading factor in restoring a higher standard of discipline lay in the work of *Royal Arthur*, the Petty Officers' school. In 1920 the fleet complained that too many young petty officers were lacking in power of command, the remedy being short courses at the three Home Ports, mainly on the parade ground. Experience in the Second World War demanded their re-introduction, and eventually a Petty Officers' school was established at Kingsmoor Camp, Corsham near Bath, in 1946, where within ten years 17,000 petty officers of all branches were given courses of six weeks' duration.

Besides teaching man management the course aimed to improve their understanding of responsibilities and to stimulate pride in their rate; current affairs talks, discussion groups and lectures about the Navy helped to broaden their outlook. With a commander, and later captain, in command there were nine course officers, each assisted by a chief petty officer instructor. One course officer wrote:

> I enjoyed *Royal Arthur* immensely, getting young petty officers away from their trade and instilling the idea of 'All of one company' brought out the best in the students. . . . The chiefs during my time were a chief mechanician, a chief coxswain and an electrical artificer 1st class . . . all superb men and all volunteers. In the Black Mountains where we did our field days during the third and fourth weeks, the officer and chief messed together in the same room. A wonderful experience.[11]

In 1970 the captain reported that the average age of petty officers on the course was twenty-four, that more than half possessed GCEs and that several were educationally qualified for commissioned rank. Their outlook was noticeably conservative and they were rather better informed on world affairs than about the Navy. He continued:

> The petty officer is generally contented with the physical conditions of service – pay, food, accommodation, engagements and amenities. . . . What he wants is a job that is really worthwhile and the opportunity to use his talents to the full. He is liable to have come from the same road . . . the same school and enjoy the same interests as many young commissioned officers. He is not conscious of any social gap between himself and the wardroom . . . but regards his seniors as individuals and does not naturally accept them for their rank.
>
> To give his seniors confidence and respect he is looking for firm command, a real concern for his welfare and something to admire in the shape of superior skill and ability.[12]

Fleet chief petty officer, 1970

For years the Navy had discussed the introduction of a Master Rate for the most senior chief petty officers in order to give them special status, privileges and responsibilities. A survey of chief petty officers indicated that 70 per cent would be prepared to remain in the service if offered a career to within ten years of reaching pensionable age at sixty-five. The difficulty was deciding a fair method of promoting men between the various branches. In 1970 the fleet chief petty officer appeared on the scene, comparable with the highest grade of warrant officer in the Army and Air Force. Although classified as a warrant officer there was no question of a fleet chief equating to the rank abolished in 1949; he would mess with chief petty officers and wear their uniform, except for a more elaborate cap badge and insignia on the cuff. With better pay and pension his work would be principally managerial and a valuable asset in divisional work.

Senior ratings also played a key role in helping to maintain the standard of fleet training when ships were not engaged in contingency roles like the Cod War or anti-terrorist patrols. The sequence of pre-commissioning training, commissioning, equipment trials and shake-down was manifestly improved when Flag Officer Sea Training was established at Portland to work up all RN warships, except aircraft carriers. By introducing down to earth realism into the four week programme, ships emerged with a surge of confidence ready for anything, their officers and men welded together into a team at a time when most needed. Subsequently flag and commanding officers kept up momentum in maritime exercises, mainly with other NATO forces, to counter the Soviet naval and air threat. Again, properly applied imagination was instrumental in creating situations that placed men under stress and taught them to overcome the danger of the unexpected.

Of all the improvements to the quality of life in the lower deck the most appreciated and cost effective was in the standard of feeding. Certainly general messing took a turn for the better when cafeteria-style dining halls were introduced in large ships; but the system still suffered from a 'take it or leave it' attitude, and in small ships the additional drawback of dried-up meals in 'hot' lockers for late arrivals. It was left to the initiative of ship's officers in the cruiser *Sheffield* to experiment with multi-choice menus at the start of their commission in 1957.

With a newly installed self-service dining hall, the latest galley equipment and a team of enthusiastic cooks and supply ratings choices of hot and cold food were instituted from day one. To overcome fears of exceeding General Mess allowance the 'leftovers' at the servery were offered as an extra choice on the following day, instead of being ditched in the 'gash chute' over the side. It was readily apparent that the multi-choice concept was almost by definition cheaper, and after a few teething troubles over queues and meals for senior ratings, became an instant success. There were complaints from the ship's Medical Officer that sailors were getting too fat and, more serious, from the wardroom that the ship's company was getting a better deal.[13]

With increased funds for messing, multi-choice cafeteria-style feeding was installed in new construction warships; in some frigates all cooking was done in a single galley, a system common to ironclads in the 1870s. Coincidentally the culinary expertise of cooks took on a new lease of life after a Central School of Naval Cookery had been set up at Chatham, enabling trainees to absorb City and Guilds qualifications and the more advanced to reach Hotel and Catering Institute standards. With diet in mind caterers planned daily menus for breakfast, dinner and supper, exercised cost control and ordered food ingredients. Identical arrangements were built into shore establishments. In 1968 officers' cooks and ships' cooks branches were amalgamated, reflecting the greater proficiency of the average naval cook and his ascendancy in status within the hierarchy of the lower deck. Having upgraded meals to three star restaurant standards the Navy turned its attention to rum.

That the Admiralty regarded the free issue of rum as a worthwhile social benefit was evident in 1937 when it granted a lower deck request that 'grog would be more acceptable with less water in the mix'. A year later two – instead of three – water rum became the daily tot, a ration that continued until its abolition in 1970. One million gallons of rum per year were supplied to the fleet throughout the Second World War and some 75 per cent of ships' companies drank it; in certain conditions the tot undoubtedly helped to sustain morale. Even so rum was responsible for recurrent crime and punishment and its abuse became far too prevalent, such as in 1945 when a pair of eighteen-year-old twins died from an excess of 'sippers' on their birthday. There were similar fatalities in 1949 and 1960. When the free issue and sale of beer became fashionable in the Far East in 1944 – and to many, more acceptable than rum – the Admiralty were quick to realize that they had a possible substitute. Storage for beer was gradually introduced into all warships.

By the mid-1960s the abolition of rum and its replacement by beer was seriously considered for a Navy that was changing socially and technologically. Although only 30 per cent of personnel now opted for grog and the number was diminishing yearly, the performance of junior and senior ratings in handling complex equipment after a tot of rum washed down with a can of strong beer

Rum issue, 1900

gave rise to anxiety. As Admiral Twiss, Commander Far East Fleet in 1965, pointed out, the tot – equal to three or four pub gins – when added to beer put the sailor over the breathalyser limit. Furthermore, punishment returns showed that nearly all cases of serious indiscipline, such as contempt, striking and skulking occurred after rather than before the rum issue. It was also apparent that the number of cases in Netley (psychiatric hospital) attributed to alcohol was higher in proportion to numbers borne for the Navy than for the other services. Equally serious was that chief and petty officers were bottling much larger amounts of rum than were suspected and keeping it in their lockers.

In 1967 the abolition of rum came to a head and the Second Sea Lord, Vice-Admiral Hill-Norton, proposed a way in which it could be achieved. When Twiss succeeded Hill-Norton later in the year he decided that the rum issue would have to cease in one act for everybody entitled to draw it, and that a worthwhile *quid pro quo* compensation must be found.

As their status improved, chief petty officers and petty officers had been pressing for bar service in their messes, primarily to reciprocate hospitality in foreign ports in much the same way as the wardroom gave official cocktail parties. It seemed reasonable to trust senior ratings to act responsibly and run their bars under no less strict supervision and accountability than the wardroom bar. In accepting rum abolition they would gain considerable prestige – a fair exchange.

To compensate junior rates Twiss discovered that the abolition of rum would save the Navy Vote £300,000 a year in 1968; Sir Michael Carey, the Naval Permanent Secretary, considered this a dangerous step as it would be subject to political pressure and inflation. So why not ask the Treasury to amortize the rum issue over ten years with a down payment of £3 million to put into a trust fund? Unexpectedly the Treasury agreed. In December 1969 the Admiralty was able to announce that as from August 1970 the rum issue would be abolished, bars under supervision would be available to chief and petty officers and the Sailor's (or Tot) Fund of £2.7 million would be set up to provide amenities for the lower deck that could not be funded by Defence votes.

Rum issue, 1970

The First Sea Lord, Admiral Sir Michael Le Fanu, and his Board took full responsibility for this measure, accomplished in a remarkably short but tense period. In January 1970 the abolition of rum was debated in the Commons and taken up by the media. But to little advantage. Admiral Sir Frank Twiss concluded: 'With enormous dignity and plenty of good lower deck fun and poking charley the great issue went through. A naval tradition had been given up. Some said the decision was wrong but most realized it had to be. Splice the main brace was retained but for generations 'Up Spirits' will remain a happy memory of the Old Navy.'[14]

In those seemingly far-off days between the World Wars, when time was found for leisure the normal duties of a rating at sea were sufficiently arduous to keep him fit, while the games enjoyed on the playing fields were relaxation – a break from ship routine and hard living conditions. Emphasis was on team games – soccer, rugby, cricket and hockey – but athletics, water polo and boxing were equally popular. At inter-ship level officers and ratings were evenly represented, although few of the former were either good or keen enough to play for the ship's soccer team. It was socially advantageous for an officer or man to be a good games player, more so if he could represent the Navy whose standards rated highly at national level.

In 1946 sport made a welcome return to naval life, especially in shore establishments, but seldom regained its former widespread popularity in the fleet simply because less time was available for recreation. There were exceptions, of course, where ships' programmes enabled regattas to be held and teams to be landed in foreign ports, but as time went on these opportunities had diminished. The proportional increase in young married officers and ratings added to the intensification of sea and shore training programmes gradually altered the nature of naval leisure activities. Thanks to the Nuffield Trust in providing boats, cruising and ocean racing became much sought after; there was growing enthusiasm, too, for skiing, mountaineering, golf, archery, squash, cycling and all types of outward bounding as interest shifted from team games to more individual sports in which officers and ratings freely mixed.

In 1971 a new Royal Naval School of Physical Training was commissioned as HMS *Temeraire*; physical training instructors were trained to be organizers of sport and propagators of physical fitness rather than star performers. Boosted by grants from the Tot Fund a superb range of recreational facilities was gradually set up ashore. Naval policy remained positive that sporting activity would play its part in building character and leadership as well as keeping men fit.

A new breed of medical officer with wider experience, together with better facilities in sick bays afloat and hospitals ashore, ensured that the Navy's health remained first class. In a report on the Navy's health from 1957 to 1963 the Mediterranean Station came out best and the Far East worst, due to the prevalence of VD and tropical diseases. To make the Medical Branch more attractive to potential recruits the eighty-year-old title of Sick Berth Attendant was changed to either Medical Attendant or Medical Technician.

Serving in the Admiralty with Mountbatten as First Sea Lord was an interesting experience. His strength of character, electric personality and untiring energy left his intentions in no doubt. After success with Way Ahead he set about reshaping the Navy for the future at a critical stage in the development of nuclear propulsion, atomic warheads and computer technology. Yet few realized the size of the fight he had on his hands to preserve the fleet during those difficult days when Duncan Sandys as Minister of Defence was gunning for the Navy, one day to abolish cruisers and the next to chop the Fleet Air Arm. Mountbatten's competitive streak and off-putting manner with people at higher levels may have given him detractors as well as admirers, but his influence won the day and created a role for the Navy, which was what really mattered.

The earl was at his personal best when visiting ships and establishments, meeting sailors face to face as, for example, during an inspection of Portsmouth Barracks in 1958. After addressing officers and men in the drill shed Mountbatten joined Commodore Roy Talbot in his office for a cup of coffee and to peruse a list of sixty 'Old Shipmates'. Talbot continues:

> The commander had all these men mustered in a room below, ranged in order round the walls. The First Sea Lord started off immediately chatting with the men and seemed to know all about them individually, what ship, where, whether married or single, the number of children and so on. It was quite amazing; until half-way round he suddenly said 'But surely your name is McKenzie, not Atkinson, isn't it?' 'Yes, sir,' the man replied. Mountbatten turned to the commander and said 'Look here, Commander, you have got these men in the wrong order, you know.' If I had not witnessed this personally, I would not have believed it. It was certainly the most amazing example of a man with a photographic memory that I have ever experienced.[15]

After stepping down as First Sea Lord in 1959 Mountbatten became Chief of the Defence Staff and aware that Macmillan, now Prime Minister but previously Minister of Defence, had failed in his attempt to unify the three services at top level. With his own experience and the lessons of Suez in mind Mountbatten was determined to succeed; his reorganization of Britain's defence structure was perhaps the crowning achievement of a remarkable career. In 1962 came the proposal to abolish the three Service ministries and combine their functions in a single Ministry of Defence. 'A project to abolish the Roman Curia', remarked Nicholas Rodger, 'would hardly have met with less enthusiasm in Vatican circles than Cmd. 2097 *The Central Organization for Defence* aroused in Whitehall.'[16] A series of monumental rows followed before Mountbatten's plan was finally approved. On 31 March 1964 the Board of Admiralty met for the last time and at sunset the crimson and gold flag of the Lord High Admiral was hauled down in the presence of the Lords Commissioners, a naval guard and the Royal Marines band playing 'Auld Lang Syne'. On 1 April, a date that did not pass unnoticed, HM ships, vessels and establishments came under the direction of the Admiralty Board of the Defence Council, and the Queen assumed the title of Lord High Admiral.

The naval staff with other directorates joined their Army and Air Force counterparts in the Ministry of Defence, a single 'main building' in Whitehall. Apart from a mass of titular changes such as AFOs becoming Defence Council Instructions (Navy) the rest of the Navy was scarcely affected by this high level revolution. The main wrench in leaving the old Admiralty buildings packed with the centuries of history was losing the direct allegiance of the Admiralty Secretariat. However mundane a Whitehall job, most naval officers could usually look forward to something different, such as a spell at sea, an outlook denied to the civil servant. In no way did this alter the latter's fierce loyalty to the Navy or his skilful guidance to generations of desk-bound warriors in the conduct of Admiralty business. Sailors have always rated sea-going rather than bureaucratic experience more important to their professional attainments but in the MOD, with its long working hours in the company of highly staff-trained soldiers and airmen, the future would be different.

❖❖❖

Regardless of innovations to training the Navy upheld a high standard of ceremonial, most of which stemmed from HMS *Excellent.* Early in 1965 the news came that Sir Winston Churchill's health was failing and that it was the Queen's wish that he should be accorded a State funeral. Before his death preparations were under way in Whale Island for the State gun carriage and to select a crew of 156 men. Captain Arthur Power recollected that: 'By the time the very old, very young, very tall, very short, the bearded, the halt and the blind had been weeded out we had just enough for the crew plus spare numbers. By tradition the crew is stiffened by Gunnery Instructors in square rig. The only problem then was who to leave out.'

On 28 January the crew and supporting party arrived in London to be accommodated in Chelsea Barracks, and:

> the dress rehearsal at night through the streets of London to muffled drum beats with a crew who thought that the night life of Chelsea was a suitable prelude . . . was not my most agreeable memory. Perhaps for this reason I was a bit short with the Regimental Sergeant Major of the Grenadier Guards when he started to interfere with the marching of my crew. Certainly he did not do it again.
>
> Saturday morning broke clear, dry but very cold. Contrary to parade orders we decided the gun carriage crew would be in white fronts, negative great coats. . . . Chelsea had been scoured for safety pins so a good deal of non-uniform warm clothing lay cunningly concealed under this façade.

Leaving Wellington Barracks at 8 a.m. the crew marched to Westminster Hall to receive the coffin:

> Like all occasions that have been properly prepared, from then on our worries ceased. We lost rhythm with the band soon after Parliament Square but the rock-like step of the Gunnery Instructor element of the crew never faltered. One remembers others changing arms at intervals but we decided against this. . . . The crowds were large and silent with ex-service men everywhere.

Arriving at St Paul's Cathedral pall bearers carried the coffin inside for the service, while the gun carriage crew waited outside 'in a cold and draughty corner'. It was a relief when the service was over, the coffin returned and the procession was under way for the final phase by the river. Then as the cortège moved off to a brisk pace an officer was heard to remark 'That felt good', an opinion confirmed by television films shown all over the world. For the greatest Englishman who ever lived it was befitting that officers and men of the Royal Navy, for whom he had done so much and in whom he held so much pride, should be accorded the principal honour at his funeral.[17]

❖❖❖

In 1966 the Fleet Air Arm was at the top of its form. With the advent of faster, heavier and vastly more expensive jet aircraft the virtuoso naval aviator was born – no longer the gifted eccentric but a dedicated professional trained for precision flying. Checked out regularly by flying instructors – 'the trappers' – they made precision landings down the 'mirror' glide path on to the angle deck. When a carrier went to sea it operated continuously and after a foreign visit the ship worked up again. The main worry of the command was keeping the aircrew in full flying practice, which required thirty hours' flying a month. With a leavening of General List officers these were mainly short-service officers who joined for a maximum of twelve years; a number transferred to permanent commissions. They were just as dedicated as their predecessors and when flying Phantoms and Buccaneers were among the best equipped and proficient aircrew in the world.

Everything hinged on a carrier replacement programme; existing carriers were wearing out and for two-and-a-half years a new carrier CVA–01 had been firmly in the programme. According to Mr Christopher Mayhew, the Navy Minister: 'It had become, rightly or wrongly, the touchstone of the Government's determination to keep the Fleet Air Arm in being. . . . The choice for the 1970s thus seemed to be between a fleet including CVA–01 or a fleet without carriers at all.' In March 1966 the Secretary of State for Defence, Mr Healey, made the historic decision to withdraw the Navy from certain global commitments to a North Atlantic posture, to operate with NATO under an air umbrella provided by the US Navy or shore-based RAF. The Navy's recommendation to go ahead with CVA–01 was turned down and Mayhew resigned. What then transpired, in the words of Rear Admiral Griffin, just appointed as Naval Secretary, was that:

> The Board had lost a long and hard fought battle over what they considered to be a central policy issue and each of the naval members, the First, Second, Third and Fourth Sea Lords,

the Vice Chief of Naval Staff and the Deputy Chief of Naval Staff sent their resignations to the Naval Secretary.

The Naval Secretary's Secretary, who had been legally trained, pointed out that if these resignations in their present form were to be accepted all concerned would lose their terminal grants and pensions. Revised versions were therefore sent and the Naval Secretary then had the considerable task of restructuring all the top appointments of the Navy.

The resulting picture was a grave one and included the inevitable promotion of the Naval Secretary to First Sea Lord in about 1969. All agreed that this would be an unacceptable blow to the Royal Navy and decided that a more limited but adequate protest might be made if the First Sea Lord alone, Admiral Sir David Luce, retired early and the remainder stuck to their posts. Mr Healey was unmoved. The Naval Secretary therefore put the position to the next most senior officer, Admiral Sir Varyl Begg, then Commander-in-Chief Portsmouth, and conveyed Sir David Luce's invitation to take over from him as First Sea Lord. Before responding, Sir Varyl wanted to know who was leaving and, on being told that the rest of the Board were prepared to continue under his leadership, he accepted. On taking over he quickly established the Future Fleet Working Party to recommend a revised structure for the Fleet. Their report was largely accepted and included provision for 3 *Invincible* class 'through deck cruisers'. These were finally approved by the Conservative Secretary of State, Lord Carrington.[18]

The abandonment of CVA–01 may have sent shock waves through the Navy, but Fleet Air Arm morale remained buoyant as they faced up to transfer from fixed to mainly rotary wing operation.

❖❖❖

Luce's resignation entailed forfeiture of promotion to the admiral of the fleet and considerable personal sacrifice. As he was the first submariner to have held the post of First Sea Lord it is appropriate to note the substantial progress made by the submarine branch since 1945.

Submariners were now less inclined to regard themselves as a private navy, but in contrast to the airmen they were not well represented at higher Admiralty level for some years after the Second World War. All this started to change when the signal was received from USS *Nautilus* as she left her building yard in January 1955: 'Under way under nuclear power.' The first true submarine had arrived, opening up enormous possibilities for sea warfare and a major boost for the branch.

Peacetime training resumed at *Dolphin* with a majority of volunteers. Subsequently ratings served in submarines for five years, but could extend this time before returning to general service; in fact most did. Unlike ratings, who could volunteer up to the age of thirty-three, officers specialized as early as sub-lieutenants for four months at *Dolphin* before working their way through the various duties, eventually reaching first lieutenant. After three years as second-in-command those selected for the 'perisher' course to qualify for command found the ordeal a good deal more technical and rigorous than in pre-war days; about 25 per cent failed. Service in submarines also appealed to engineer officers, many of whom were branch list officers, having been submarine artificers before promotion; the fitting of radar together with complex electric and electronic equipment in new construction submarines also necessitated an electrical officer in the complement.

After Russia exploded the H-bomb in 1954 the US Navy developed Polaris as an intermediate range submarine missile within four years. When the Skybolt air-launched missile with a nuclear warhead was no longer available to the RAF the British government persuaded the USA to supply Polaris missiles. In 1967 *Resolution*, the first of four 7,500-ton nuclear-propelled submarines, was accepted in the fleet, supplied with sixteen Polaris nuclear-headed missiles, with a 2,500-mile range.

Accommodating a crew of about thirteen officers, fifty-four senior and seventy-five junior ratings, the Polaris submarine opened up a new dimension in submarine operation. Commanded by a commander and having a lieutenant commander as executive officer, also with S/M command experience, there were three seaman officers, a supply officer (who could also keep watch), four marine and electrical engineers, two Polaris systems officers and a surgeon lieutenant. A fleet chief petty officer – 'Fleet Chief of the Boat' – assumed the duties of coxswain, and among artificers were those specialized in marine engineering and in control, ordnance and radio electrics.

To enable the submarine to operate for long periods submerged, accommodation and messing were of the highest standard; unlimited fresh water for cooking and laundry, cinema, library, a range of recreational facilities and perhaps best of all a weekly 'family-gram' (radio message) of forty words sent from home. To obtain maximum operational deployment the Royal Navy followed the principle adopted by the US Navy in commissioning each submarine with two crews. By allocating the month's maintenance period to the crew that would take the ship to sea for its eight week patrol a maximum operating efficiency was assured. Equally important the system ensured that crews got their leave and refresher training, as well as being least disrupted by the inevitable changes in complement that amounted to 25 per cent every twelve weeks. This unique arrangement depended for its success on tact and tolerance at each level, especially the attitude of respective commanding officers. Admittedly most pairs of crews were prone to some divergence of opinion at the start of a commission, but the great leveller proved to be patrol experience. When both crews had completed patrols discord, if any, was replaced by mutual respect.

Avoiding offset boredom was easier than anticipated since it was feasible to organize a whole range of indoor games competitions, publish newspapers, take educational courses, run quizzes and discussion groups and encourage individual hobbies. With some crews it paid off to have a rigid weekly routine of training and recreational events, 'big eats' night and tombola, not to mention a different film practically every day. Motivation became important during the 'low' period of mid-patrol; officers and senior ratings had to employ tact and imagination in dealing with welfare problems occasioned by the non-arrival of 'family-grams'.[19] Based with their shore support – HMS *Neptune* – and families in the tight enclave of Faslane, submarine crews developed an aura of élitism within the branch that was to increase as more 'nukes' joined the fleet. It was a pity, all the same, that the rest of the Navy saw so little of their activities. In 1970 it was the majority wish of the branch to seek and gain approval for qualified officers and ratings to wear the dolphin submarine badge in uniform, a similar motif to that worn by other navies.

Consisting of two dolphins supporting a crown over a foul anchor, the submarine badge was worn over the left breast

With the rapid developments in all forms of maritime warfare, the advent of computerized equipment and the direct control of weapons vested in the operations room as opposed to weapon control positions, it was clear that a new philosophy was required to man and fight a ship. In the 1950s the Seaman Officer Sub-Specialization Working Party wrestled with the problem of how to broaden training, without reaching firm conclusions. By the time the County Class missile-firing destroyers and *Leander*-class frigates arrived in the 1960s, in which the whole ship could be regarded as a weapon system, it was apparent that the seamen officers were too narrowly specialized by reason of their background to compete with a modern sea/air battle. The matter was brought to a head by Vice-Admiral Edward Ashmore, second-in-command of the Far East fleet in 1968, who broadly proposed that seamen officers should no longer sub-specialize in weapons, navigation/direction or communications but should be trained as warfare officers with sufficiently versatile capabilities to fulfil every requirement. In the face of undisguised opposition the Principal Warfare Officer was introduced in April 1972 to become the hub of the new Operations Branch.

This decision coincided with a major re-appraisal of responsibilities within specialist branches and the location of schools. In 1967 the Weapons and Radio branch had become the Weapons and Electrical Engineering Branch, sub-divided into ordnance, control and radio departments, each with their own artificers, mechanicians and mechanics. In 1970 the CONSTRAIN plan was launched – to concentrate naval training as far as possible in selected areas of the United Kingdom. There were too many training establishments and there was never going to be enough money to run them properly; for historical reasons many were in the wrong place. In future there would be three main groups; an Operational group of mainly seamen specialists, a Weapon Engineering group and a Marine and Hull engineering group. Additionally there was a fourth group comprising Supply and Secretariat personnel, the Regulating Branch and commitments for Damage Control, Management, Divisional, Leadership and Seamanship duties. While *Collingwood* and *Sultan* were the obvious bases for the engineering groups, *Dryad* at Southwick with *Mercury* as a satellite were chosen as a focus for operational training, and *Excellent* in Whale Island was left with the Regulating and Leadership schools, as well as *Phoenix* under its wing.

It was one thing for the older seaman schools to accept these revolutionary changes as being best for the fleet, which they did with good grace. It was another to swallow the pill and realize that former sub-specialist officers had reached the end of the road. Could one officer possess all the skills necessary to fight the ship? How would the new scheme stand the test of war? Only time would tell.

The two main casualties were *Vernon* and *Excellent*, particularly the latter. Not only was it the demise of Whale Island but the culmination of a dynasty that had lasted for almost a century. Since 1914 there was rarely a year when at least one member of the Board or a commander-in-chief was not a gunnery specialist, a feature shared by nearly half the First Sea Lords. Likewise the gunnery instructor, a versatile leader of men, was the backbone of many a ship's company. In a labour intensive navy armed primarily with guns, it was Whaley's job to teach gunnery and the principles of discipline that went with it; for this the school was often derided, seldom loved but always remembered. In fact Whale Island had given the Navy much more than just the art of gunnery. But all that had changed now and in 1974 *Excellent* became the centre for Naval General Training.

Dryad was quick to realize that one officer could not muster the total expertise of his sub-specialist predecessors and that PWO training must be split between Above Water and Under Water warfare, with courses as long as those of the officers it replaced. More complex was the re-organization of ratings into two main groups – seaman and communications. In each group were three levels of responsibility and skill filled by fleet chief, chief and petty officers; leading ratings; and able rates. On 1 January 1975 the Operations Branch came into being. The fleet liked the concept of a rate-related structure and indications were that it had got off to a good start, to the credit of the School of Maritime Operations.

By the mid-1970s the Admiralty Board could afford to look back on the last thirty years with a sense of achievement, if not satisfaction. Though Defence cuts had bitten deeply and personnel strength had been reduced to 76,000, the Navy had never failed to accomplish the many tasks it had been called upon to undertake. To meet the Soviet threat a new and reasonably well-balanced fleet was at sea with updated weapons, aircraft and machinery, smaller complements in surface ships and immeasurably better conditions afloat. 1976 marked the Diamond Jubilee of the submarine service, which now provided the main striking power. Shore training had been streamlined, work-up training in the fleet realistically invigorated and the WARSHIP series on BBC television was described by a critic as 'making the services disgracefully entertaining'.

Officer structure, training and appointment up to lieutenant commander in all branches had been totally reorganized; similarly rating structure and training was in a continual process of adjustment. Short and full career officer recruitment seemed promising, discipline was sound, allowances to assist house purchase and children's boarding school education had proved popular, rum had vanished and welfare services were just keeping their head above water in an era of rapid social change. Relations between officers, petty officers and ratings were better than they had been for many years. By no means everything was perfect but the Navy had come a long way since the frustrations of the '50s and was now more confident than ever to tackle an emergency. That event was not far off.

CHAPTER FOURTEEN

Challenge at the Falklands

I have always been taught to consider that there is nothing the Navy cannot do.
Captain William Bate of the frigate Actaeon *when confronted with objections to a bold plan of attack by a Naval Brigade on Canton, 28 December 1857*

Despite criticism that the pace was too slow the concept of the truly General List of officers gained ground as promotion prospects improved and more middle management shore appointments were shared by Seamen (X), Marine and Weapons Electrical Engineers (E) and Supply and Secretariat (S). In 1978 there was great rejoicing in the Instructor Branch (I) when they were admitted to the club after twenty years on the touch line during which many 'schoolies' were employed with success outside their specialization. The summit of 'generality' had already been reached by the mid-1970s when first an engineer officer, Attie Turner, and then a supply officer, Peter White, were promoted to full admiral while serving as Chief of Fleet Support on the Admiralty Board. And at a time when the Seaman element represented 40 per cent of GL officers Fisher would have been especially pleased to note the appointment of a former Eng. L, Lindsay Bryson, to be the first non-seaman Controller of the Navy.[1]

In the late '60s and throughout the '70s a number of studies were conducted by the Directorate of Naval Manpower and Training on future career aspects of officers and ratings. Every bit as important as the restyling of the seaman officer and rating structure was the quiet revolution among a large proportion of the Navy's 26,000 engineers. Since 1965 the Weapon Electrical Engineering Branch had become more systems orientated as it absorbed further development in digital computers, satellites and missiles; as a result its rigid three-prong structure of radio, control and ordnance did not match the new generation of weapon systems. Tactically the need for rapid response to missiles and electronic warfare in a multi-threat environment had brought about the Principal Warfare Officer, the Operations Branch and the start of user/maintainer schemes, all aspects of which impinged on the WE Branch. Coincidentally there was a growing overlap with the Marine Engineering Branch as well as a general shortage in most types of artificer. Against this background the Engineering Branch Working Group produced its report in 1975. The first recommendation was to set up an electro-mechanical Marine Engineering sub-branch to look after hull systems, propulsion machinery, 'hotel' services and high-power electrical generation and maintenance. The Weapons Engineering sub-branch would then become responsible for sonar, radar, electronic warfare, action data and communication systems for all weapons, navigational aids and internal communications. Logically they would take over magazines and explosives from the seaman branch.[2] Looking ahead the greater commonality of training and employment of Ops and WE officers suggested further study of their branches with a view to closer relationship.

Reactions to the report among the 'Greenies' (Weapons Engineers) varied between those advocating no change and leave well alone to those who welcomed a new structure. On 1 September

1979 some 10,000 ratings (but no officers) changed their title, of whom 2,600 transferred from WE to ME. Simultaneously new-style weapon artificers, mechanicians and mechanics appeared on the scene as the WE branch concentrated a more rational approach to operation and maintenance.

Whereas most serving officers accepted the sombre implications of successive Defence Reviews with equanimity the recurrent reduction in naval strength, highlighted by the media, hardly reassured those contemplating an officer's career. To attract maximum entrants of good quality candidates were given as many options as possible to fit age, qualifications and ambition; as before a full career had been synonymous with the General List, with short or medium career officers being destined for the Supplementary List. In the latter case a Seaman or Supply officer could now join for eight years but could leave at five; additionally a Seaman officer could join for three-and-a-half years. Those opting for flying duties joined for twelve years with similar opportunities to quit. Although age on entry for the majority remained at about eighteen some applicants could go through a scholarship or reserved place scheme beforehand for a full career commission. In addition two University sponsorship schemes, initially for full and subsequently for short career commissions, showed considerable promise. One was Direct Graduate Entry (DGE) in which graduates joined Dartmouth as a sub-lieutenant for a term, followed by sea training before taking a Fleet Board. The other was University Cadetship Entry (UCE), in which one could enter the RN at any stage before going up to or while at university, with patterns of training to allow considerable flexibility, culminating with a term at BRNC after graduation. Because most youngsters between, say, eighteen and twenty-three are impressionable and apt to change their views, the increase in graduate entries introduced a radically new outlook and attitude among junior elements of the officer corps. By the mid '80s the majority of full career officers were degree trained.

'My job is not to break them down and build them up again. My aim is to show them that they can cope, that if a person gets organized he will – hopefully – manage.' Thus remarked a divisional chief petty officer at Britannia Royal Naval College, Dartmouth where virtually all officers joining the Navy received their initial training.[3] Seaman officers (including aviators), Engineer, Supply and Instructor officers of the General and Supplementary Lists; Special Duties officers; Doctors, Dentists and Nursing Sisters; Royal Marines; WRNS; Chaplains and Reserve Officers, together with a hundred officers per term from Commonwealth and foreign nations all started their naval career at Dartmouth. Questioning and critical, the great majority were far more broad-minded and receptive to new ideas than their predecessors of the 1960s.

By 1980 the general training syllabus for most had been cut to one term in BRNC and one term in the training ship. The first four arduous weeks were devoted to learning the rudiments of leadership, such as living and working together, being in the right place, dressed in the right rig at the right time and becoming physically fit. Practical exercises on College 'cliffs and chasms', the challenging conditions of cold, wet nights on Dartmoor and the use of all types of boat to learn the first principles of seamanship were all part of training. Almost as important was the development of latent officer-like behaviour, which included dress etiquette, wardroom customs and social graces. As one midshipman disarmingly put it to a College wife at a Divisional coffee morning: 'This is the first time I've had to make polite conversation to anyone.' There was emphasis on the Divisional System and the parade ground remained the medium for training in self-discipline and power of command. Even so, when midshipmen joined the fleet there was still much to do in moulding the character, ability and confidence of future officers as the overlap in the qualifications of young officers *vis à vis* young senior technical ratings narrowed or virtually disappeared.

A major success story for the 1970 era was the recruiting of WRNS officers and ratings. With an annual application rate exceeding 6,000 and ten out of a dozen young women being turned away, the resultant high standard augured well for a greater integration of WRNS within the naval service. From 1976 Wren officers regularly attended the RN staff course and both officers and senior rates were appointed to posts ashore previously filled by men. In their Divisional Jubilee year (1977) the WRNS were brought under the Naval Discipline Act to share more evenly with men the opportunities as well as the obligations of naval discipline. WRNS ratings entered on the same engagements as male counterparts and in 1980 their training was transferred from *Dauntless* to *Raleigh.* Inexorably the Royal Navy moved towards the wider acceptance of a feminine role, and it is of interest that the Admiralty Board considered drafting WRNS to survey ships in 1977 – but turned it down on grounds of cost.

Since the end of the 1960s a different story surrounded the recruitment of junior seamen and electrical mechanics; efforts to improve job satisfaction and ease the strain of separation from families made little headway on what became a serious shortfall. Like the Army and RAF, the Navy was also affected by strong competition from industry, and the disenchanted attitude of the British public towards defence; the declining birth-rate of the '50s and the imminent raising of the school leaving age were further drawbacks. In 1969 a tri-service committee chaired by Lord Donaldson was set up to find a solution.[4]

For the Navy a four year engagement was introduced for seamen and electrical mechanics as an alternative to the nine year stint, with further options to change from nine to four years – or the reverse when reaching the four year point. Regulations for discharge by purchase (later called Premature Voluntary Release) were eased and the whole business of enlistment re-examined to simplify and clarify the conditions under which youngsters would join the Navy. The outcome of the Donaldson Report was that ratings received the right to give eighteen months' notice of leaving the service; similarly officers could retire voluntarily having given nine to fifteen months' advance warning. Regardless of the liberal features of the Donaldson report there were critical shortages in officers and men by the late '70s. Press reports of officers queuing up to leave may have been exaggerated, but the increase in applications to retire caused a 6½ per cent deficiency in middle ranking complement billets, despite allowing older officers to retire later or re-enter for further service. It was the same on the lower deck with a 21 per cent shortfall in recruiting and large numbers leaving the service at eighteen months' notice. Main reasons were not hard to find – depressed pay, over-stretched conditions of service and turbulence in drafting. All these resulted in reduced manning standards for the fleet.

Salvation came with the incoming Thatcher government (1979), which implemented the recommendations of the Armed Forces Pay Review Body to increase basic pay by about 32 per cent and a promise to maintain pay at a proper level in future. Although retention remained a crucial factor the manpower situation started to improve at a price that necessitated cutting fleet strength. In 1981 John Nott, as Minister of Defence, produced a White Paper, which stated bluntly: 'we cannot go on as we are. The Government has therefore taken a fresh and radical look at the Defence programme'. Severe reductions, contained in Command 8288, were under way when an unexpected situation developed in the South Atlantic.

On 19 March 1982 the illegal landing of a party of Argentine scrap-metal workers on the island

Falklands planners at Northwood: Vice-Admiral Sir Peter Herbert, Major General Jeremy Moore, Admiral Sir John Fieldhouse, Vice-Admiral Sir David Halifax, Air Marshal Sir John Curtiss, Rear Admiral Peter Hammersley

of South Georgia sparked off a chain of circumstances that culminated in the Falklands operation. The Navy's reactions to events were swift, bold and unerring. In the absence of the Chief of Defence Staff – Admiral of the Fleet Sir Terence Lewin – on a visit to New Zealand, the First Sea Lord, Admiral Sir Henry Leach, became aware of the imminent invasion of the Falklands by Argentine forces. On 31 March Leach personally convinced the Prime Minister that nothing short of a task force would be needed to retrieve the situation and that one could be assembled in a matter of days. When the Argentinians invaded on 2 April orders had already been given by Commander-in-Chief Fleet, Admiral Sir John Fieldhouse to Rear Admiral Sandy Woodward, who would command the naval forces at sea for Operation Corporate. Woodward embarked in the destroyer *Glamorgan* and with some units of the task force fresh from Exercise Spring Train, sailed from Gibraltar; the remainder left UK ports on 5 April for the 8,000-mile passage south via Ascension Island. Eventually 51 warships, 171 naval aircraft, 21 Royal Fleet Auxiliaries and 54 merchant ships taken up from trade were to be involved in the campaign.

The opposition was not inconsiderable. An old 6-in heavy cruiser, *Belgrano*, and an ex-RN light fleet carrier *Veintîcinco de Mayo* were supported by three destroyers and nine frigates, including two Type 42s that had recently scored pass marks at Portland. There were four operational submarines but perhaps more significant was the Argentine Air Force with 200 front line aircraft, including Super Etendards,

Mirages and Skyhawks carrying a range of bombs and Exocet missiles. Up to 12,000 Argentine troops landed on the Islands, supported by fifty light attack aircraft and helicopters.

At Ascension on Easter Sunday the fleet chaplain conducted services in ships and the captains of destroyers, frigates and RFAs present assembled in the destroyer *Glamorgan*. Rear Admiral Woodward remarked:

> We all knew this would most probably be the last chance of such a meeting, for within a few days we would be heading south again, into more dangerous waters where communication could no longer be face to face but only by encrypted voice radio – telephone or computer. Most of us had known each other for years, and I suppose in a sense we each knew something of what the others were feeling. So we maintained a slightly forced air of good humour, one to another, but it was tempered by the chill realization that there could only be one valid reason why we should be in this room in this ship, talking not merely as old friends but as trusted senior commanders preparing to fight a war. Even then, though, one could not suppress the tiny hope, the fantasy, that it might yet all go away.[5]

Since the 1970s Royal Fleet Auxiliary ships – fleet tankers, freighting tankers, store support ships, landing ships logistic and a helicopter support ship – had been an integral part of any task force. In many respects RFA officers were indistinguishable from RN officers, taking naval staff

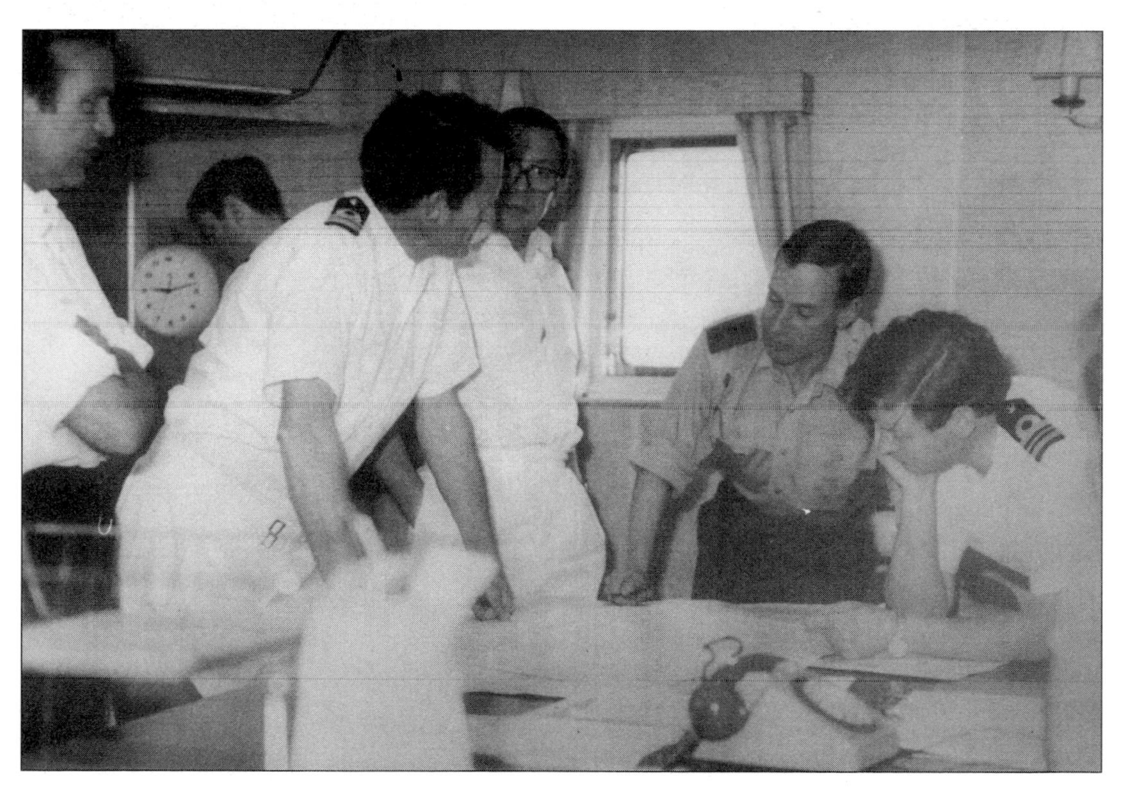

Rear Admiral Sandy Woodward and staff in Flag Operations Room, HMS *Glamorgan*

and specialist courses, such as principal warfare officer. What they may have lacked in background or technical training they more than made up in seagoing and shipboard experience.

Woodward shifted his flag from *Glamorgan* to the aircraft carrier *Hermes* to form the Battle Group and continue towards the 200-mile exclusion zone round the islands. Two other groups were detached, one to re-capture South Georgia and, later, another to operate as anti-aircraft pickets.

On 2 May *Belgrano* was torpedoed and sunk by the submarine *Conqueror*; her commanding officer, Commander Wreford-Brown, remembers his ship's company cheering when they heard the explosion: '. . . Afterwards I had a certain amount of regret about the loss of life. . . We had countered the threat . . . to our Task Group and the loss of life they could have caused us. . . . We had done what we were invited to do and I would do it again.'[6] More important to Woodward, although not realized at the time, the incident kept the Argentine surface fleet out of the operation. But the enemy airforce was quick to retaliate, and within forty-eight hours the frigate *Sheffield* was sunk by an Exocet missile, the first British warship to be so lost since the Second World War. It came as a shock to the task force.

After 3 RM Commando Brigade, together with 2 and 3 Para battalions, had established the San Carlos beachhead on 21 May, the frigates *Ardent* and *Antelope*, as well as the destroyer *Coventry*, were sunk by enemy aircraft in the confined waters in or near Falkland Sound; many other ships were damaged. But 5,000 men and their equipment were landed without a single battle casualty and the Argentine Air Force did not remain unscathed. Some 150 aircraft were destroyed in the whole operation, of which a sizeable proportion was downed by Sea Harriers. Throughout the whole campaign the performance of Harrier and helicopter aircrew was outstanding.

When *Sheffield* was struck by an Exocet a few feet above the waterline just after 2 pm 'there was some doubt that the warhead went off but several men were killed instantly. A large fire was started, releasing great quantities of heat, smoke and fumes which were to cause others to die, many of them in heroic circumstances.'[7] Attended by *Yarmouth* and *Arrow* spraying water each side and with Sea Kings from *Hermes* lowering pumps on deck with fire-fighting and breathing apparatus, every effort was made to save the ship. But it was 'an awful, losing battle as the heat crept inexorably forwards

Men of Recce Troop 40 Commando prepared for San Carlos landing, SS *Canberra*, 21 May 1982

HMS *Ardent* on fire, with *Yarmouth* standing by, 21 May 1982

towards the Sea Dart magazine'.[8] Later Captain Sam Salt gave the order to abandon ship and the remainder of the crew were taken off by helicopter and across to the frigates. *Arrow* took aboard 224 – her own ship's company was about 180 – and some time later Lieutenant Jackman was asked what the survivors were like: 'What would you expect people to be like after their home had been wrecked and they had lost friends and everything they had. . . . They were very quiet. A lot tried to be cheerful . . . but you could see deep down that it was over for them and they realized it.'[9]

Similar graphic accounts surrounded the sinkings and damage inflicted on other ships, in which officers and ratings behaved with the same fortitude and acceptance of fate as their predecessors in two world wars. In Falkland Sound (Bomb Alley) *Antelope* was attacked by low-flying aircraft – one of which was destroyed by a leading seaman's 20-mm Oerlikon – and in a later attack the ship was hit again by a bomb that did not explode. While attempts were made to defuse it the bomb was triggered off, the ship torn apart, set on fire and abandoned just before the missile magazines blew up. Paying tribute to his crew, Commander Nick Tobin commented: 'There is nothing special about them. They are young men who happen to have chosen the Royal Navy as a career and are a product of the English character. A certain amount of pragmatism, good training and pride . . . all combines to make some very good sailors.'[10] In *Coventry* the explosion of three well-aimed 1,000-lb bombs gave the ship no chance and within fifteen minutes she started to capsize. With many officers among those killed or wounded the evacuation was handled by young sailors. 'I sat and watched them in complete amazement,' recorded a badly burnt and shocked Captain Hart-

Flight deck of carrier *Hermes* as a Sea Harrier is launched

Dyke. 'They just went about their tasks sensibly and steadily. Some of them must have been scared out of their wits.'[11].

Resulting from the loss of the container ship SS *Atlantic Conveyor* and embarked helicopters, the troops had to 'yomp' with their heavy personal equipment some 50 miles to the outskirts of Stanley. A brilliant, silent night-attack on Mount Harriet, held by a superior force of Argentinian troops, was then carried out by 42 Commando. 'Once we got into the fighting we switched to auto and got stuck in,' said Sergeant 'Jumper' Collins. 'The guys worked fantastically. We were fighting the enemy at 5 and 10 metres. We were literally knocking the weapons from their hands and going on.'[12] In the face of adverse conditions the stamina and skill of the troops won the day and by 14 June it was all over, men from 40 Commando hoisting the Union Jack once more at Stanley.

J Company 42 Commando (including those repatriated after the Argentine invasion) enter Stanley, 14 June 1982

By any standards it was an epic victory and a

timely demonstration of British sea power that left its mark throughout the world. Royal Marines and naval casualties amounted to 130 killed and 257 injured; the proficiency of medical teams and facilities undoubtedly saved countless lives. Although most ships and units had adequate first aid facilities the knowledge that they were underpinned by a first class rescue and medical organization was a potent morale booster. The latter was partly achieved by the expertise of Reserve doctors and nursing personnel recalled for the emergency to make up numbers.

In the ships of the task force youth was predominant – on first going into action the average age of *Glamorgan*'s ship's company was under twenty. There were ratings who had not been to sea before and almost nobody could claim previous war experience. Yet analysis of Operation Corporate indicated that during the three month campaign the performance of officers and men was more than satisfactory and in many cases exemplary, particularly by those officers in command for the first time. Despite some unfortunate equipment failures in ships and problems associated with control of damage and fires, it was evident that after nearly forty years of peacetime activities the Royal Navy and Royal Marines had lost none of their ingrained professionalism, which says much for training standards and material efficiency. At home the

Welcome Home

reactions of wives and families to the triumphs and disasters were subjected to the full glare of publicity; but judging by media coverage and the amount of mail received by task force ships wishing them well the British public maintained an abiding admiration for their Navy. Certainly the reception on return was overwhelming.

The last word goes to John Fieldhouse, Commander-in-Chief Fleet, in the concluding remarks of his Falklands dispatch: 'Operation CORPORATE became necessary because deterrence failed, but in its execution it represented a triumph of military capability backed by resolute political will. The difficulties of short notice, extreme range and appalling weather under which this operation was mounted were all overcome by a single factor, the quality of our people.'

Epilogue

Still basking in the fame of Trafalgar the Victorian Navy was the supreme symbol of patriotism, self-assurance and tradition that made Britain great and presented Parliament with the freedom of imperial action. In return the people gave the Navy a measure of loyalty and affection bestowed on no other department of State. From the Victorians emerged a hardy, vigorous breed of sailor who regarded seamanship as a religion, whose readiness for war was open to question but who kept the peace of the world through sense of duty and by sheer force of character.

Although segregated in its own private domain the Navy has always echoed the social climate of the day. The traditional divide between wardroom and messdeck mirrored Victorian England's equally distinct gulf between master and servant. When a wave of humanitarianism swept the country in the 1870s the Admiralty responded with uncharacteristic benevolence to initiate reforms on the lower deck of a volunteer regular Navy that attracted recruits with better potential. In no time these men began to question the validity of long established practices such as inadequate leave and unjust punishment, causing personnel administration at Board level and in the fleet to become progressively demanding. The crunch came when those in authority failed in their obligations or lost touch with the aspirations of the men they commanded.

In a labour-intensive fleet life at sea was governed by a discipline imposed by strict regulations, exacting routine and meticulous organization of ship's companies generally larger than found today. For those stepping out of line there was punishment, severe until the turn of the century but seldom inflexible, and diminishing as ratings with education and good character joined the service. Today, willing obedience to orders, as well as conformity to a code of personal conduct that requires little resort to punishment, are symptomatic of the modern Navy.

After 1900 the race for naval supremacy involving huge expenditure on ships and weapons would have ignored the need for social reform, but for Fisher. At a time when trades unions began to exert a strong influence on the working classes he won the confidence of the lower deck and with support from Churchill as First Lord, completed a series of radical reforms in time for the First World War. Though less successful in transforming the officer structure his contribution to social history was momentous. In the aftermath of war the Navy had to fight for itself in a scene of political and industrial strife; even a generous pay increase failed to satisfy a minority of ratings anxious to bargain for better conditions. The Admiralty countered with the 'welfare' committee that temporarily contained the situation while insisting that grievances be handled in the regulation manner.

Recovery from war was also prolonged among the officer corps, shaken by the severity of the Geddes Axe and the feeling of uncertainty at a time of disarmament and disillusion. Unfortunately, the tendency to take the lower deck's intrinsic loyalty for granted recurred and when the national economy suddenly collapsed, leaving the Government with little option but to cut the pay of armed services in line with other public servants, the Admiralty was caught unawares. A chain of ill-starred mishaps led to the tragedy at Invergordon in which the Navy's reputation suffered a serious but not fatal blow. As with other mutinies of the nineteenth and twentieth centuries the cause was absence of mutual trust between officers, petty officers and men. However, at Invergordon it was principally but not entirely the Admiralty who had lost touch with social conditions on the lower deck, transgressing the adage 'You muck about with sailors' pay at your peril.'

Since the days of sail and muzzle loaders the Navy has insisted on excellence in the standard of training. In the 1930s re-armament came too late to modernize an ageing fleet, and at the outbreak of war there may have been flaws in the fleet's defences, failures of weapons to hit the target and equivocal leadership at higher levels, but the irresistible confidence and resource of the British sailor almost invariably saved the day. Life at sea in war has always been a tedious experience; long periods of waiting and watching, repetitious drills, boredom and discomfort. But when the alarm bells sounded it was the swift and instinctive reaction that counted. Another factor contributing to victory was the remarkable facility of RNVR officers and hostilities-only ratings to adapt themselves readily and efficiently to naval duties. In fact, their example was one of the crucial formative influences in later years to make the ruling order more aware of what ordinary people were capable of achieving.

After the Second World War management of the Navy was too pre-occupied with overseas commitments and internal re-organizations to realize that the country had started a social revolution. Though recognizing the need for the General List and overhaul of young officers' training it is hard to understand why overdue improvements were not implemented sooner for ratings. Many saw their work as making very little demand, either on their ability or on their sense of responsibility, while living standards ashore led to demands for a better life afloat. Recruitment and retention suffered and not until the 1960s was a series of fundamental reforms introduced, calculated to attract promising youngsters into the service and keep them there for as long as possible. Nevertheless manning problems affecting officers as well as ratings and amounting at times to serious proportions, continued to cause anxiety for many years.

There was no question of turning the clock back and with a new generation of administrators the Navy adjusted more readily to the increasing pace of change in the community. By the 1980s the better schooling and family background of the adult rating, combined with officers drawn from the whole spectrum of society, contributed to a near classless service. Since birth and upbringing were no longer prerequisites for entry to the wardroom it had to be leadership and kindred qualities that stamped the officer. Events in the Falklands campaign indicated that these were far from lacking in the Fleet.

In reflecting society the old Navy held ultra-conservative views about women; until the First World War they were barely recognized, although two thirds of all petty officers had a wife and family to support. It was, perhaps, typical of Establishment policy in conceding marriage allowance to ratings that officers should wait another twenty years before a similar indulgence. However, war in 1939 changed a lot of attitudes. Wives and mothers kept the family together, tended the children, wrote letters that meant so much and suffered the agony of farewells;

whatever their status women were the unsung heroines. Post-war a noticeable trend was early marriage among younger officers and ratings, whereby the greatest single factor was no longer the man but the man and his family. Able to hold down a good job herself the naval wife became less willing to accept the claims on the family by her husband's career.

The ever increasing part played by women in British society was echoed in the changing attitudes to women in the armed forces; probably the most significant social development in the Navy in recent years has been the gradual but inevitable integration of WRNS officers and ratings. It made good sense when male recruitment was deficient to tap a more fruitful source but it was a courageous act on the part of the Admiralty Board to send WRNS to sea to share combat duties. In due course history will relate this to have been a judicious step, one that is being sustained with customary skill and minimal fuss. Even so the Navy must be careful that recognition of social trends and its duty as an equal opportunity employer does not impair its war-winning capability.

Since 1870 naval people have come a long way. Much has changed and much will continue to change. No longer commanding the passions identified with the world's biggest and most powerful fleet, the Royal Navy has become a social entity, if not in advance of society as a whole, at least far more dynamic than the nation generally supposes. Looking back on service in the late 1930s spirits were high because the Navy was expanding almost daily to fight another war. In this turbulent world of today, decline in national power and accent on 'smaller but better' armed forces – the former so much easier to achieve at the expense of the latter – I am amazed that the Navy consistently displays an aura of total and cheerful confidence in the future. How was it that ten years ago Admiral Leach was able to approach the Prime Minister and state that the fleet would be ready in three days to retake the Falklands? There are many answers to this question, not least the proven ability of the British sailor and marine to react to a crisis. What other profession or career offers the intellectual challenge, variety and comradeship to compare with the Royal Navy? In job satisfaction and in exploiting the full potential of its people the Navy reflects much that is best in our country and is comfortably ahead of the other services. There is, however, another explanation to be considered.

Of all the factors over the years to shape the lives of officers and men the most beneficial has been the ship. Whereas the Army sets great store on the military and moral value of regimental tradition the Navy relies on the ship to mould its crew into a fighting community. It does more than that. Whatever its type or size the ship is a miniature society embracing people with different skills, different backgrounds and different personalities, all of whom unconsciously build the ship's character. To maintain operational efficiency a ship today commissions for a longish period, its crew subject to trickle changes after serving two years. In no way does this weaken the aim to be the best in the squadron, the best in sport or acquire the reputation that years later springs to mind as the ship of happiest memory. Neither does it alter the feeling of security and of being needed, nor that sense of togetherness that sailors feel about a home without being really conscious of it. And when a ship is sunk in war something deep and indefinable in the lives of those surviving is lost as well.

Nearly fifty years ago when asked how the Navy possessed the genius for evoking the best out of people and winning their affection and loyalty a captain replied unhesitatingly: 'a system of manners'. It was, he said, a system based on long experience and the only way in which officers and men could live and work together in the crowded, confined conditions of a ship. Without it, he added, life would be intolerable while discipline and performance would suffer. By manners he meant quite simply, consideration for other people.

That view seems to sum up a large chunk of the Royal Navy's character today.

❖❖❖

And now the old ships and their men are gone; the new ships and the new men, many of them bearing the old auspicious names, have taken up their watch on the stern impartial sea, which offers no opportunities but to those who know how to grasp them with a ready hand and undaunted heart.

Joseph Conrad, Mirror of the Sea

CHRONOLOGY

The Social History of the Royal Navy, 1830–1982

DATE	EVENTS	ACTIVE PERSONNEL [1]/ OFFICE HOLDERS OF SECOND SEA LORD FROM 1872 [2]
1830	HMS *Excellent* commissioned as gunnery training ship (hulk) in Portsmouth. Award and medal introduced for ratings with Long Service and Good Conduct.	30,000
1832	Navy and Victualling Boards absorbed into Admiralty. Direction and administration of RN conducted by First Lord, five Sea or Naval Lords, Civil Lord (dockyards) and Parliamentary Secretary (finance).	
1835	First Chief Engineer and Inspector of Machinery appointed.	
1836	Seaman Schoolmasters established. Examination instituted for First Class (Officer) Volunteers.	
1837	Engineering Branch established by Order-in-Council. Engineers placed in warrant rank with uniform, pay, regulations and training arrangements. Introduction of Good Service Pension for senior officers. RN College, Portsmouth, closed.	
1839	RN College, Portsmouth, reopened for training mates and above	
1840	Leading stoker introduced. Mates commissioned.	35,000
1843	Rank of naval cadet officially recognized.	
1844	First numbered Circular issued by Admiralty to Fleet.	
1846	Cap badge with gold crown introduced for officers.	
1847	Engineers classed in three divisions. Selected Senior Engineers became commissioned officers. Naval General Service medal authorized.	
1849	Good conduct badge introduced with extra pay.	
1850	New ration scale introduced. Rum ration halved to ⅛ pint, evening issue stopped and compensating allowance paid to teetotallers.	39,000
1852	Pursers receive full salaries: title changed to paymaster. Committee on manning the Navy established to consider continuous service.	
1853	Continuous Service introduced by Act of Parliament, together with	46,000

	improved rates of pay. Rate of Chief Petty Officer and Leading Seaman introduced. Act of gallantry by seamen and marines acknowledged by medal and gratuity. Pay increased all round.	
1854	**Britain and France declare war on Russia – Crimean War.** Rating of medical dresser established. Warrant officers appointed to ships in lieu of lieutenants and sub-lieutenants.	61,500
1856	Victoria Cross instituted. **End of Crimean War against Russia.** Executive curl on gold lace instituted for executive officers. Uniform introduced for petty officers, seamen and boys. 'Wardroom mess' and 'gunroom mess' designated. Dirk re-introduced for midshipmen in lieu of sword.	68,000
1857	Journal of Royal United Service Institution first published. Regulations for entry and training of naval cadets issued. Approval given for improved feeding in sick mess.	68,000
1858	Introduction of Bounty system of recruitment. Assistant surgeons commissioned. Captains authorized to grant regular leave.	59,500
1859	*Britannia* commissioned to train cadets (in Haslar Creek, then Portland). Royal Commission on Manning reported. Royal Naval Reserve established. Standard victualling ration improved. Recruiting organization established.	
1860	First Naval Discipline Act passed. First and second classes for conduct instituted. Last man hanged at yardarm. Monthly payment inaugurated for officers and ratings.	79,000
1861	HMS *Warrior* commissioned as Britain's first armoured iron battleship. Combined Queen's Regulations and Admiralty Instructions published as first edition.	
1862	Gratuities for widows of men killed on active service established.	
1863	Coloured bands of cloth introduced to distinguish officers' uniform. *Britannia* moored in River Dart.	
1864	Flag ranks reduced to four and white ensign adopted for all HM warships. Introduction of staff captains and commanders. RNR officers' uniform approved. Commissioned rank of chief gunner, boatswain and carpenter established. Royal School of Naval Architecture and Marine Engineering established in South Kensington.	
1866	Albert Medal instituted for gallantry in saving life at sea. Naval Savings Bank introduced afloat.	67,000
1867	Introduction of Writer rating.	
1868	Engine Room Artificer's rating established as chief petty officer. Cap ribbons officially recognized.	There was no 2nd Sea Lord between 18/12/68 and 5/5/72
1869	Permission given for officers and men to grow beards with moustaches. Circular 5 forbade flag officers to nominate sons as	

flag captain, only as flag lieutenants. Circular 57 drew officers' attention to disapproval of excessive wine bills. Admiralty committee on victualling reported inconclusively.

❖❖❖

1870	**English Elementary Education Act passed.** Circular 26 outlined new ratings of signal boys, 2nd and 3rd class signalmen, yeoman and chief yeoman, etc.	60,000
1871	Circular 61 drew attention of leading rates of need 'to read and write fairly'. Flogging suspended in peacetime. Trade Unions legally recognized by Act of Parliament.	
1872	RN Artificer Engineer and Engine Room Artificers Club and Benevolent Fund founded. Cookery School opened at Portsmouth.	60,000 RAdm J. Walter Tarleton
1873	Admiral Superintendent of Reserves appointed. RN College Greenwich instituted with courses of study for officers. Royal Naval Artillery Volunteers established. Circular 36 introduced colour vision tests in eyesight examination for officers and ratings.	
1874	Uniform for naval bandsmen introduced. Conspicuous Service Medal re-introduced.	
1875	Circular 47 permitted officers to wear plain clothes on leave in UK but not abroad. Subordinate officers permitted to wear plain clothes on leave for sporting occasions only.	59,000 VAdm Geoffrey Phipps-Hornby
1876	First Royal Sailors Rest opened in Devonport. HMS *Vernon* (hulk) commissioned in Portsmouth for torpedo and electrical training and experimental work. Admiral Cooper Key's Committee on Engineering Branch reported.	
1877	Half stripe introduced for lieutenants, navigating lieutenants and civil branch equivalents of over eight years' seniority. HMS *Marlborough* (hulk) established for engineer officer training.	RAdm Alexander Hood
1879	Navigation lieutenants became lieutenants (N). Circular 34 drew attention to importance for all officers and ratings to swim before leaving training ship. Flogging suspended in wartime. Revised uniform regulations issued for officers and ratings.	RAdm The Earl of Clanwilliam
1880	Training school for engineer students opened at Keyham.	58,000 VAdm Lord John Hay
1881	RN Medical School established at Haslar. Circulars 70 and 74 established facilities for Naval Savings Banks ashore and making allotments to families. Gold badges provided for ratings.	
1882		Adm Lord Alcester
1884	Circular 3 instituted places and hours for smoking on board ship. Smoking forbidden if under eighteen. Circular 39 encouraged	

	officers to become interpreters in French, German, Spanish or Italian.	
1885		61,000 VAdm Sir Anthony Hoskins
1886	Distinguished Service Order instituted for officers too junior to receive CB. Ranks of Fleet Paymaster and Staff Paymaster introduced.	
1887	Naval Intelligence Department formed, including Manning Department. First promotions made to lieutenants from warrant officer. Circular 1 limited birching of boys to twenty-four cuts over bare breech.	
1888	*Naval Warrant Officers' Journal* first published.	Adm Sir R. Vesey Hamilton
1889	First Naval Defence Act passed. Navy League established. Monkey jacket (undress coat) introduced for officers. Head Schoolmasters achieved warrant rank.	RAdm Henry Fairfax
1890	Rank of Signal Boatswain introduced. Naval barracks established at Devonport. Naval salute with right and left hand introduced. Approval for junior rates of civil branches to wear long jackets and peaked caps.	67,000
1891	HMS *Excellent* gunnery training school moved to Whale Island. More explicit dress regulations issued for officers and ratings. Naval Exhibition at Chelsea.	70,000
1892	Death of Admiral of the Fleet Sir Provo Wallis aged 100, having served ninety-six years in the Royal Navy.	VAdm Sir Frederick Richards
1893	Official numbers for ratings introduced, together with port divisions. Navy Records Society founded.	76,000 RAdm Lord Walter Kerr
1894	Committee on RN Executive Lists reported. Torpedo Boat Destroyer *Havock* commissioned. Committee on Manning reported.	81,000
1895	Recruitment of 100 RNR officers into the Royal Navy. Navy League founded.	86,000 RAdm Sir Frederick Bedford
1897	Artificer engineer achieved warrant rank.	97,000
1898	*Bluejacket* and *Coastguard Gazette* first published by Yexley.	103,000
1899	**Outbreak of war between Britain and Boers in South Africa.**	RAdm Archibald Douglas
1900	Physical training becomes a specialist branch.	113,000
1901	**Death of Queen Victoria. Accession of King Edward VII.** Committee on training and examination of junior officers reported. Conspicuous (later Distinguished) Service Cross instituted for junior officers.	117,000
1902	Fisher and Selborne launch New Admiralty Scheme for entry and training of officers. **End of Boer War.**	122,000 Adm Sir John Fisher

1903	By Order in Council engineer officers granted military titles of rank. Cigarette tobacco, jam, coffee and condensed milk issued in tins. Goschen committee on executive lists of officers reported. RNVR and RM volunteers established. Lieutenants (N) granted executive command as for (G) and (T) officers. Order in Council instituted rate of Mechanician. Royal Naval School of Music established.	126,000 RAdm Sir Charles Drury
1904	Establishment of rank of lieutenant for 4 per cent commissioned and warrant officers. Band service transferred to Royal Marines. Ratings' messes granted free issue of knives, forks, basins and plates.	130,500
1905	Fort Blockhouse commissioned as submarine depot with hulk *Dolphin*. The *Fleet* monthly newspaper founded by Yexley. Committee on Naval Cookery reported. Stopford Committee reduced costs of ratings' uniform.	127,000
1906	HM Signal School established in RN Barracks, Portsmouth. Start of ration allowance. HMS *Dryad*, Navigation School established in old Naval College (Academy) in Portsmouth.	127,500
1907	Login Committee improved Canteen and Victualling arrangements. Circular drew attention of flag officers to severity of court martial sentences. Battleship *Dreadnought* commissioned. Penny postage authorized for letters from HM ships. Oilskins, watch coats, seaboots, stokehold boots issued on loan. Corporal punishment suspended completely. Interport Field Gun competition started at Royal Naval and Military Tournament at Olympia.	127,000 VAdm Sir William May
1908	Headquarters of RN Physical Training School moved to Pitt Street, Portsmouth. Policy issued on travelling expenses, rail travel warrants, cheap leave tickets, use of own motor cars and subsistence allowance. Battle-cruiser *Invincible* commissioned.	128,000
1909	Detention first awarded as a punishment. Introduction of warrant rank for Writers, Ship's Stewards and Cooks.	VAdm Sir Francis Bridgeman
1910	**Death of King Edward VII. Accession of King George V.** Mobilization Department formed. First specialist course of signal officers qualified in flags and W/T.	131,00
1911	Eastchurch established as first Naval Air Station. First Lord, Winston Churchill, secured pay increases for lower deck.	133,000 VAdm HSH Prince Louis of Battenberg
1912	Naval Staff formed at Admiralty. *Dolphin* commissioned at Fort Blockhouse, Gosport. Brock Committee on punishments reported. Mate scheme launched. RN Staff Course established. Naval Wing of Royal Flying Corps established. Circular 41 emphasized importance of Divisional System.	136,500 VAdm Sir John Jellicoe
1913	*Naval Review* founded. Special Entry scheme for public schools started at Keyham College. Petty Officers 2nd class abolished.	146,000
1914	Naval Wing of Royal Flying Corps becomes Royal Naval Air	250,000

	Service. Rank of lieutenant commander authorized. **British Empire declared war against Germany.** Dartmouth and Keyham colleges stopped training. Separation allowance granted for junior ratings.	VAdm Sir Frederick Hamilton
1915	Engineering branch officers formed part of military branch. Free travelling warrants issued after naval engagements. Junior officers forbidden to keep logs and journals. Distinguished Service Medal introduced.	350,000
1916	Military Service Acts passed in Parliament. Warm clothing issued free to include balaclava, woollen drawers, mitts, jersey and thick socks.	400,000 VAdm Sir Cecil Burney
1917	Women's Royal Naval Service established. Committee on Soldiers' and Sailors' Pay reported: some concessions made. Anti-submarine training started at Portland. New titles introduced for certain non-executive branches.	450,000 VAdm Sir Rosslyn Wemyss
1918	Branch colours instituted for Shipwright, Electrical, Wardmaster and Ordnance Warrant Officers. RN Air Service transferred to Royal Air Force. Paymaster Director General introduced and Paymasters granted military titles of rank and executive curl. Naval Personnel Committee established. Anti-Submarine Detection Investigation Committee instituted. **End of war against Germany.**	450,000 VAdm Sir Herbert Heath
1919	Demobilization went ahead. Jerram and Halsey committees on ratings' and officers' pay recommended general increases. RNC Osborne closed down. Officers' Association formed to assist officers find employment. Naval Welfare Committee held first meeting at Portsmouth. Cambridge University selected for Junior Officers' training.	275,000 VAdm Sir Montagu Browning
1920	AWO 2157 outlined separation between executive and engineering branches. AWO 3657 defined functions of Benefit Societies and naval newspapers. Establishment of formal training of Accountant Officers.	136,000 VAdm Sir Henry Oliver
1921	Geddes Committee on National Expenditure set up. Admiralty Fleet Orders, including Confidential Orders, replaced Admiralty Weekly and Monthly Orders. Technical training of engineer officers started on promotion to midshipman.	124,000
1922	Navy Army and Air Force Institute took over naval canteens. Welfare Committee replaced by Welfare Conference. Royal Naval Benevolent Trust founded. Supply branch formed. Introduction of central storekeeping.	118,500
1923	Royal Marine Artillery and Royal Marine Light Infantry merged as Royal Marines. Canteen committees introduced in HM Ships. *Vernon* moved ashore. Anderson Committee on pay of fighting services reported. Hand salute limited to right hand only.	99,500

1924	RM Barracks, Forton converted to boys training as HMS *St Vincent*. HMS *Osprey* established at Portland for A/S training and experimental work. Examination instituted for command of destroyers.	100,500	VAdm Sir Michael Culme-Seymour
1925	CAFOs 2858/2859 authorized cuts in officers' and ratings' pay. Order in Council 139 replaced five officer branches with twelve categories of 'officer'. Petty officers' course made compulsory for POs of all branches.	102,500	VAdm Sir Hubert Brand
1926	Committee on Executive officers first reported. Welfare Conference reported numerous minor concessions for lower deck. **General Strike in Britain.**	102,500	
1927	Officers' rates of pay adjusted down by 6 per cent to meet cost of living. Association of Retired Naval Officers founded. AFO 74 emphasized the importance of maintaining good relations with the Merchant Navy.	102,500	VAdm Sir Michael Hodges
1928	Short-service seamen entry re-introduced.	102,000	
1929	Navy Weeks instituted at three home ports.	100,000	
1930	Naval Disarmament Conference in London. Naval Treaty between Britain, France, Italy, Japan and USA. Committee established to review mate system of promotion. Distinguishing badge introduced for Submarine Detection Operators.	97,000	Adm Sir Cyril Fuller
1931	Formation of National Government. May Committee on National Expenditure reported. Pay review leading to mutiny of ships of Atlantic Fleet at Invergordon. Rank of Mate abolished in favour of Acting Sub-Lieutenant.	93,000	
1932	Director of Personal Services instituted. Procedure established for making representations of unfair treatment. CAFO 2023 outlined the training policy in the fleet. Larken committee set up to investigate conditions of service in WT and Signal branches.	91,500	VAdm Sir Dudley Pound
1933	Training cruiser *Frobisher* made first cruise with cadets from Dartmouth and Special Entry. **Unemployment in UK reaches almost 3 million.**	91,500	
1934	Failure of Naval Disarmament Conference in London.	92,000	
1935	Welfare Conference replaced by Review of Service Conditions. Welfare and Marriage Allowance offices established for ratings in three home ports.	99,100	VAdm Sir Martin Dunbar-Nasmith
1936	**Death of King George V. Edward VIII succeeds to throne but abdicates in favour of King George VI.** Commissioning of Motor Torpedo Boat flotilla.	119,000	
1937	Royal Navy regained control of Fleet Air Arm and its air stations. Coronation Naval Review at Spithead. CAFO 2648 emphasized importance of giving responsibility to petty officers and leading seamen.	127,500	

1938	Naval Air Branch and RNVR air branch formed. Officers aged over thirty granted marriage allowance. Abolition of half pay for officers. Rum and water ratio in grog adjusted to 1:2. Women's Royal Naval Service re-introduced. Transfer of RNEC Keyham to Manadon planned.	134,00 Adm Sir Charles Little
1939	Gunnery sub-specialist rates reorganized to man new weapons. AFO 2576 outlined procedure for burial at sea after war operations. **British Empire declared war against Germany.** National Service Act (Conscription) introduced in UK.	134,000
1940	Massive expansion and relocation of training and accommodation establishments. Length of training courses ashore reduced by 50 per cent.	276,000
1941	Western Approaches command set up in Liverpool. Working up base for minor warships set up in Tobermory.	405,000 VAdm Sir William Whitworth
1942	Damage Control School formed in St Paul's School, London. Widespread adoption of blue naval serge battledress.	507,000
1943	Unprecedented expansion in naval man and woman power. RN cadet training moved to Eaton Hall, Cheshire. CAFO 1793 highlighted seriousness of the manning situation.	671,000
1944	Accountant Branch renamed Supply and Secretariat Branch. Supply School moved from Highgate to Weatherby as HMS *Demetrius*. **Butler's Education Act passed. Allied invasion of Europe.**	779,000 VAdm Sir Algernon Willis
1945	**Atomic bombs dropped on Hiroshima and Nagasaki. End of war in Europe and Far East.** Demobilization commenced as majority of warships returned to home ports.	865,000
1946	Navigation Direction branch formed. Second Sea Lord warns Board of problems with officer structure. RN Supply School commissioned as HMS *Ceres*. Tri-service pay code introduced with increase of pay all round. Last prize money paid. Attendance at Divine Service made voluntary. Middleton Committee on electrical specialization reported. RNEC Manadon commissioned as HMS *Thunderer*.	503,000 VAdm Sir Arthur Power
1947	Caslon Committee on assessment of complements reported. Electrical Branch formed. Revival of Royal Tournament in London.Five RNVR Air Squadrons formed. Reorganization of RoyalMarine commands. National Service reduced from eighteen to twelve months.	195,000
1948	Manpower Economy Committee reported. Title of Warrant Officers changed to Branch Officers. Introduction of sixteen-year-old entry at Dartmouth. Corporal punishment formally abolished. WRNS became permanent. Training squadron established in Portland. RNEC Manadon opened as HMS *Thunderer*.	152,000 VAdm Sir Cecil Harcourt

1949	Director of Service and Welfare Conditions appointed. HMS *Phoenix* commissioned as Atomic, Biological, Chemical and Damage Control School. North Atlantic Treaty Organization established. Air Branch abolished. George Cross replaced Albert Medal.	148,000
1950	**Outbreak of war in Korea.** Fifth and sixth five year re-engagements introduced. Uniform regulations revised. New pay code improves pay and pensions. Free gangway to go ashore at any time in shore establishments. Stores branch split into victualling and stores specialists.	142,000 VAdm Sir Alec Madden
1951	RN Regulating School established in Whale Island. RNR and RNVR officers adopted straight stripes on uniform. Courts Martial Appeals Court instituted. Introduction of tobacco coupons. Pilcher Committee on administration of naval justice reported.	140,000
1952	**Death of King George VI. Accession of Queen Elizabeth II.** Centralized messing introduced in aircraft carriers. Modernization of shore accommodation started.	148,000
1953	Coronation Naval Review at Spithead. New royal yacht named *Britannia*.	149,000 Adm Sir Guy Russell
1954	General Service Commission introduced. **End of Korean War.** Mansergh Committee on Officer Structure and Training (COST) convened. *Navy News* founded. **All food rationing ends in UK.**	137,500
1955	Special entry of cadets from public schools ceased. Coloured cloth between officers' stripes abandoned. Dartmouth Training Squadron introduced. First batch of married quarters completed. Stokers became Engineering Mechanics. Uniform regulations overhauled.	132,000 Adm Sir Charles Lambe
1956	AFO1/56 described General List of officers. Commissioning of *Sultan* to train Engineering Mechanics and *Temeraire* in Rosyth to train Upper Yardmen. **Anglo-French invasion of Suez.** Nine year engagement and centralized drafting introduced. Select Committee on Naval Discipline Act reported. 'Boy' title changed to 'Junior'. Supply and Secretariat junior ratings adopted square rig as for seamen.	125,500
1957	Reduction in number of officers and senior ratings by normal and voluntary retirement. Signal Branch changed title to Communications Branch. Establishment of Naval Work Study. *Phoenix* paid off to become NBCD School. *Hornet* Coastal Forces Base closed down. RNVR and RNR merged. Branch Officers renamed Special Duties officers. End of midshipmen in gunrooms of fleet.	120,000 VAdm Sir Deric Holland-Martin
1958	Murray Committee on junior officer training appointed. Pay increased for officers and ratings. Committee on Ratings Structure	110,000

	reported. Supply School moves from Wetherby to Chatham. Seamanship school instituted. Flag Officer Sea Training established at Portland.	
1959	New Naval Discipline Act passed. Grigg Committee on Armed Forces established to examine willingness of men and women to serve in Armed Forces. Loyal Toast in future to be drunk sitting when National Anthem played in naval mess. Ceremonial frock coat re-introduced for Flag Officers.	105,000 Adm Sir St John Tyrwhitt
1960	Carlill committee on merging of engineering and electrical specializations reported. C-in-C Home Fleet hoists flag in Northwood, Middlesex. Start made to improve habitability in fleet. Upper Yardmen move to Dartmouth. 73 per cent officers and 60 per cent ratings now serving in shore establishments. Specializations Steering Committee set up.	100,500
1961	Short-service commission scheme introduced for officers. (Supplementary List.) Last National Servicemen left RN. Nore Command formally closed.	97,500 Adm Sir Royston Wright
1962	Multi-choice cafeteria-style feeding established. Guided missile destroyer *Devonshire* commissioned.	96,500
1963	Nuclear submarine *Dreadnought* commissioned. Re-organization of Communications Branch. First engineering specialist (Rear Admiral R.S. Hawkins) appointed Board of Admiralty as 4th Sea Lord. Career offices and staff replace Recruiting Offices throughout UK.	98,000
1964	*Sultan* renamed Royal Naval Marine Engineering School. Service overseas separation reduced to twelve months. Ministry of Defence formally established. Caterer Branch introduced. AFOs replaced by Defence Council Instructions. Director of Public Relations (Navy) appointed.	100,000
1965	Survey Committee on Officer Structure reported. University cadetship scheme started. RN Volunteer (Supplementary) Reserve disbanded.	97,000 Adm Sir Desmond Dreyer
1966	Armed Forces Act passed. Fines introduced as punishment. Introduction of boarding school allowance for officers. Privilege of drinking Queen's health seated extended to Chief and Petty Officers. Manadon granted right to design own BSc course.	100,000
1967	*Neptune* commissioned as Polaris submarine base at Faslane. Appointment of C-in-C South Atlantic and Mediterranean abolished. Introduction of Weapons and Electrical Engineering Branch.	100,000 VAdm Sir Peter Hill-Norton Adm Sir Frank Twiss
1968	Failure of attempt by Transport and General Workers Union to	97,000

	introduce trades union into the RN. Amalgamation of Ship's Cook and Officers' Cook branches.	
1969	Introduction of interest free loans for house purchase. Reforms established in Naval Detention Quarters, Portsmouth. Appointment of C-in-C Naval Home Command at Portsmouth. Commanders-in-Chief Portsmouth and Plymouth abolished. Donaldson Committee set up to review recruitment. RN Polaris assumed responsibility for nuclear deterrent.	92,000
1970	Launch of plan to concentrate training in selected areas of UK. *Centurion* commissioned as Pay, Drafting and Records Establishment. Fleet Chief Petty Officer introduced. Ships first commissioned with trickle drafting schemes. Rum abolished in RN and Sailors' Fund set up. Introduction of Military Salary and Armed Forces Pay Review Body. Donaldson committee reported on conditions for recruitment and retention of ratings leading to shorter engagements.	87,500 Adm Sir Andrew Lewis
1971	**Withdrawal of British forces from east of Suez.** C-in-C Fleet at Northwood assumes command of total seagoing fleet. *Temeraire* commissionedas RN School of Physical Training. Computerization of naval pay started. C-in-C Far East Fleet abolished. Submarine Service badge instituted.	84,000 Adm Sir Derrick Empson
1972	Principal Warfare Officer introduced to replace seaman sub-specialist officers. Nine year engagement instituted for WRNS ratings.	83,500
1973	Seebohm Committee on Naval Welfare reported on closing down *Ganges*; all recruit training transferred to HMS *Raleigh*.	82,000
1974	Naval General Training established on Whale Island. First Supply and Secretariat Officer appointed to Admiralty Board.	79,000 Adm Sir David Williams
1975	Operations Branch introduced into fleet.	
1976	WRNS brought under Naval Discipline Act and WRNS officer candidates arrived at RNC Dartmouth. New voluntary release rules for RN personnel came into force.	77,000
1977	Instructor branch joined General List of officers. Naval Personnel and Family Service inaugurated. C-in-C Naval Home Command took over responsibility for Reserves.	76,500 Adm Sir Gordon Tait
1978	New WRNS officer career structure introduced. Naval Engineering Degree course started at Manadon.	75,500
1979	Armed Forces Pay Review Body increases pay by 32 per cent. Aircraft carrier *Invincible* commissioned. Major reorganization of Engineering Branch implemented. Malta Naval Base closed.	73,000 Adm Sir Desmond Cassidi
1980	RNR Air Branch formed. British Rail permitted servicemen and families same travel privileges as senior citizens.	72,000

1981	WRNS training at *Dauntless* transferred to *Raleigh*. Last general payment of ship's company.	74,500
1982	Closure of *Excellent*, *Vernon*, *Fisgard*, *Pembroke*, *Phoenix* and *Caledonia* as training establishments.	73,000 Adm Sir Simon Cassells
	Britain defeats Argentina in war over Falkland Islands.	

❖❖❖

1987		67,000
1993		59,000

Notes and References

Abbreviations

Adm	Admiralty correspondence in Public Record Office
AFO	Admiralty Fleet Order
AWO	Admiralty Weekly Order
BR	Book of reference issued by Ministry of Defence (Navy)
CAFO	Confidential Admiralty Fleet Order
DCI	Defence Council Instruction
DGNMT	Library of MOD Directorate of Naval Manpower and Training
IWM	Imperial War Museum
JNS	*Journal of Naval Science*
JRUSI	*Journal of the Royal United Services Institution*
MM	*The Mariner's Mirror*
NHL	MOD Whitehall (Naval Historical) Library
NMM	National Maritime Museum
NR	*Naval Review*
RINA	Papers read to the Royal Institution of Naval Architects
USM	*The United Service Magazine*

Chapter one

1. Beresford, *Memoirs*, pp. 11–40.
2. Rodger, *Naval Records for Genealogists*, Chapter 2.
3. Baynham, *Before the Mast*, p. 120.
4. Moresby, *Two Admirals*, p. 43.
5. Bridge, *Some Recollections*, pp. 76–7 and 149.
6. Fitzgerald, *Memories of the Sea*, p. 275.
7. Yexley, *The Inner Life of the Navy*, p. 70.
8. Paget, *Autobiography and Journals*, p. 79.
9. Sloane-Stanley, *Reminiscences of a Midshipman's Life*, p. 283.
10. *Chambers Journal*, vol. 51, pp. 361–2.
11. The *Table of Summary Punishments* was composed by Captain A.P. Ryder of *Hero* and copies on cardboard distributed throughout the fleet. (The author possesses one.)
12. Rasor, *Reform in the Royal Navy*, pp. 42–8.
13. Admiralty Circular No. 283 of 1857 following recommendations of committee chaired by Rear Admiral the Hon. Henry Rous in 1856 (NHL).
14. Fleet, *My Life and a Few Yarns*, p. 59.
15. Riley, *Memories of a Bluejacket*, p. 167.
16. (F.W.) Fisher, *Naval Reminiscences*, p. 42.

Chapter two

1. *Navy and Army Illustrated*, vol. 9, p. 7.
2. Ballard, *The Black Battlefleet*, p. 65.
3. Willis, *The Royal Navy as I saw it*, p. 32.
4. Crowe, *The Commission of HMS* Terrible, p. 338.
5. Baynham, *Before the Mast*, pp. 171–7.
6. Ballard, *The Black Battlefleet*, pp. 45–6.
7. Thompson, *Close to the Wind: Early Memoirs of Admiral Sir William Cresswell*, p. 26.
8. Kerr, *The Navy in My Time*, pp. 14–16.
9. Noble, *Sam Noble AB*, pp. 1–4.
10. Yexley, *The Inner Life of the Navy*, p. 15.
11. *Ibid*, p. 11.
12. Baynham, *Before the Mast*, p. 155.
13. Riley, *Memoirs of a Bluejacket*, p. 74.
14. Noble, *Sam Noble AB*, p. 104.
15. Thompson, *Close to the Wind: Early Memoirs of Admiral Sir William Cresswell*, p. 86.
16. Yexley, *The Inner Life of the Navy*, p. 63.
17. Capper, *Aft from the Hawsehole*, p. 42.
18. Marder, *Fear God and Dread Nought*, p. 64.
19. Scott, *Fifty Years in the Royal Navy*, p. 49.
20. Fleet, *My Life and a Few Yarns*, pp. 122–3.
21. Willis, *The Royal Navy as I saw it*, pp. 32–3.
22. Jarrett, *British Naval Dress*, p. 108.
23. *Active List of Flag Officers and Captains of the Royal Navy* published by Griffin of Portsmouth, 1879. (Copy held by author.)
24. Morris, 'A View of the Royal Navy', *Encounter*, 1973.
25. Noble, *Sam Noble AB*, pp. 113–14.
26. Penrose Fitzgerald, *Memories of the Sea*, pp. 304–5.
27. Chambers, *Salt Junk*, p. 104.
28. Willis, *The Royal Navy as I saw it*, pp. 90–1.
29. Extracts from the private journal of Captain the Hon. Edmund Robert Fremantle Royal Navy, NMM FRE/130 and 131. Courtesy of the Trustees of the National Maritime Museum.

Chapter three

1. Bacon, *Naval Scrapbook 1877–1900*, p. 15.
2. Bowden-Smith, *Naval Recollections*, pp. 149–50.
3. Pack, *Britannia at Dartmouth*, pp. 98–9.
4. Martin, *Adventures of a Naval Paymaster*, p. 5.
5. *Ibid*, p. 46.
6. Report of Committee on the Executive Lists of the Royal Navy, 1894 (NHL).
7. Smith, *A Yellow Admiral Remembers*, p. 54.
8. Lyne, *Something about a Sailor*, p. 88.
9. Capper, *Aft from the Hawsehole*, p. 94.
10. Willis, *The Royal Navy as I saw it*, p. 33.
11. Noble, *Sam Noble AB*, pp. 120–4.
12. Kerr, *The Navy in My Time*, p. 106.
13. *Ibid*, p. 94.
14. Bowles, *Gun Room Ditty Box*, pp. 88–92.
15. An Undistinguished Naval Officer, *The British Navy in the Present Year of Grace*, pp. 54–7.

16. Willis, *The Royal Navy as I saw it*, pp. 197–8.
17. Yexley, *The Inner Life of the Navy*, pp. 119–22.
18. *Ibid*, pp. 132–4.
19. Mr Ashton to author.
20. Padfield, *Aim Straight*, pp. 143–4.
21. Chatfield, *The Navy and Defence*, p. 16.
22. Lyne, *Something about a Sailor*, pp. 106–7.
23. Admiralty Circular 160, May 1903, reported improvements (NHL).
24. Wells, *Whaley*, pp. 54–5.
25. Willis, *The Royal Navy as I saw it*, pp. 337–8.

Chapter four

1. Fletcher, *Some memories of A.L. Fletcher* (unpublished), pp. 6–10.
2. Walker, *Thirty-six years at the Admiralty*, pp. 10–13.
3. Mackay, *Fisher of Kilverstone*, pp. 84, 135 and 172.
4. Bacon, *Lord Fisher*, p. 186.
5. Memorandum dealing with entry, training and employment of officers and men of the Royal Navy and Royal Marines, December 1902 (New Admiralty Scheme), p. 3 (NHL).
6. *Ibid*, p. 4.
7. Mackay, *Fisher of Kilverstone*, p. 284.
8. Marder, *From the Dreadnought to Scapa Flow*, p. 47.
9. Martin, *Adventures of a Naval Paymaster*, pp. 143–4.
10. Walker, *Thirty-six Years at the Admiralty*, pp. 73–4.
11. Marder, *Fear God and Dread Nought*, p. 257.
12. Baynham, *Men from the Dreadnoughts*, p. 79.
    Crime and Punishment in the Royal Navy, August 1920, Admin 1/8941.
13. *Ibid*, p. 151.
14. *Ibid*, pp. 153, 154 and 161.
15. *The Fleet*, May 1905, p. 8.
16. Admiralty Circular Letter No. 7 11498/1907 (NHL).
17. Reynolds, *The Lower Deck*, p. 81.
18. Baynham, *Men from the Dreadnoughts*, p. 88.
19. Tweedie, *Story of my Naval Life*, p. 78.
20. Goodenough, *The Handy Man: Afloat and Ashore*, p. 127.
21. Earl of Cork, *My Naval Life*, p. 48.
22. Baynham, *Men from the Dreadnoughts*, p. 135.
23. *Ibid*, p. 136.
24. Lowis, *Fabulous Admirals*, pp. 237–8.
25. Walker, *Thirty-six Years at the Admiralty*, p. 42.
26. Chatfield, *The Navy and Defence*, p. 34.

Chapter five

1. William Halter – taped extracts – IWM 00721/20.
2. Chalmers, *Max Horton and the Western Approaches*, pp. 5–6.
3. Popham, *Into the Wind*, p. xvi.
4. *Ibid*, p. 2.
5. *Ibid*, p. 3.
6. Bacon, *Lord Fisher*, p. 300.
7. Kerr and Granville, *The RNVR*, pp. 59–60.

8. Bacon, *Lord Fisher*, p. 268.
9. Wright, *Sun of Memory*, p. 14.
10. Baynham, *Men from the Dreadnoughts*, pp. 115–16.
11. *Ibid*, p. 116.
12. Dawson, *Flotillas*, p. 125.
13. Reynolds, *The Lower Deck*, pp. 96–7.
14. Chatfield, *The Navy and Defence*, p. 104.
15. Dawson, *Flotillas*, pp. 1–2.
16. Stephen, *The Dreadnought Hoax*, pp. 29–49.
    Sunday Telegraph, 24 Feb. 1990.
17. Baynham, *Men from the Dreadnoughts*, p. 120.
18. (F.W.) Fisher, *Naval Reminiscences*, p. 282.
19. Brock Committee on Naval Discipline, Admin 397/02 Pamphlet P631 (NHL).
    Gretton, *Former Naval Person*, pp. 104–9.
    Carew, *The Lower Deck of the Royal Navy*, pp. 43–6.
20. James, *The Sky was Always Blue*, pp. 77–81.
21. Marder, *Fear God and Dread Nought*, p. 290.
22. Carew, *The Lower Deck of the Royal Navy*, pp. 47–53.
    Gretton, *Former Naval Person*, pp. 103–4.
23. 'Ex-Royal Navy', *The British Navy from Within*, pp. 81–92.
24. Baynham, *Men from the Dreadnoughts*, pp. 118–19.
25. *Ibid*, p. 119.
26. Walker, *Thirty-six Years at the Admiralty*, p. 70.
27. Young, *With the Battle Cruisers*, p. 10.
28. Churchill, *World Crisis 1911–1914*, p. 93.

Chapter six

1. Bush, *Bless our Ship*, pp. 19–21.
2. Clinker 'Knocker', *Aye Aye, Sir*, pp. 134–5.
3. Dewar, *The Navy from Within*, p. 161.
4. Wells, *Whaley*, p. 75.
5. Liddle, *The Sailors' War 1914–1918*, p. 28.
6. Fairbairn, *Narrative of a Naval Nobody*, pp. 85–6.
7. Dawson, *Flotillas*, p. 130.
8. Liddle, *The Sailors' War 1914–1918*, p. 36.
9. Mrs Beatrice Stokes, widow of Able Seaman Stokes, to author.
10. *The Personality of a Bluejacket*, NR7 (1919), p. 198.
11. Bush, *Bless our Ship*, pp. 31–3.
12. Taylor, *The Sea Chaplains*, p. 337.
13. Turner, *Gallant Gentlemen*, p. 289.
14. Liddle, *The Sailors' War 1914–1918*, p. 49.
15. *Ibid*, p. 51.
16. *Ibid*, p. 62.
17. Denham, *Dardanelles – A Midshipman's Diary*, pp. 34, 37–8.
18. Popham, *Into the Wind*, p. 29.
19. Bush, *Bless our Ship*, pp. 46–7.
20. Liddle, *The Sailors' War 1914–1918*, pp. 83–4.
21. Gieve, *Gieves and Hawkes*, p. 43.
22. 'Etienne', *A Naval Lieutenant 1914–18*, pp. 83–4.
23. Chatfield, *The Navy and Defence*, pp. 142–3.

24. Fawcett and Hooper, *The Fighting at Jutland*, p. 35.
25. *Ibid*, p. 141.
26. *Ibid*, pp. 432–42.
27. Taped interview, Imperial War Museum records 00751/08.
28. Wright, *Sun of Memory*, p. 37.
29. Fawcett and Hooper, *The Fighting at Jutland*, p. 417–22.
30. Liddle, *The Sailors' War 1914–1918*, p. 110.
31. Dreyer, *The Sea Heritage*, p. 146.

Chapter seven

1. Baynham, *Men from the Dreadnoughts*, p. 238.
2. James, *The Sky was Always Blue*, pp. 97–8.
3. King-Hall, *Sea Saga*, pp. 477–8.
4. Liddle, *The Sailors' War 1914–1918*, p. 135.
5. Kerr and Granville, *The RNVR*, pp. 88–9.
6. 'The Idler', *Rolling Home*, pp. 157, 170, 172, 177.
7. Simpson, *Periscope View*, pp. 26–9.
8. King-Hall, *A Naval Lieutenant 1914–1918*, p. 197.
9. Layard, *Junior Midshipman 1915* (unpublished ms), p. 7.
10. Edwards, *British Bluejacket 1915–1940*, p. 61.
11. Bush, *Big Ship Navy* (unpublished ms), p. 20.
12. Walker, *Thirty-six Years at the Admiralty*, p. 132.
13. Fletcher, *The WRNS*, p. 13.
14. Liddle, *The Sailors' War 1914–1918*, p. 170.
15. Wells, *Whaley*, p. 82.
16. Carew, *The Lower Deck of the Royal Navy*, p. 75.
17. Financial Secretary to Admiralty, 27 Sept. 1917, Adm. 1/8498/201.
18. Marder, *From the Dreadnought to Scapa Flow*, vol. 5, p. 121.
19. Holloway, *From Trench to Turret*, p. 75.
20. Carew, *The Lower Deck of the Royal Navy*, pp. 88–92.
21. Baynham, *Men from the Dreadnoughts*, p. 246.
22. Lady Wemyss, *Life and Letters of Lord Wester Wemyss*, p. 398.

Chapter eight

1. Chatfield, *The Navy and Defence*, p. 178.
2. Financial Secretary, minute, 23 Dec. 1918, Adm 116/1728.
3. Admiralty Weekly Order 1809/1919 and 2359/20.
4. Admiral Goodenough's committee of 1924, Adm 167/70.
5. Mid Ian Sanderson to his father 1 Dec. 1918 reporting the impressions of Lieutenant Commander A.B. Downes of *Malaya*. Marder, *From the Dreadnought to Scapa Flow*, vol. 5, p. 271.
6. Captain K.A. Harkness to author.
7. Clinker 'Knocker', *Aye Aye, Sir*, p. 239.
8. Second Sea Lord, minute, 14/12/19 Adm 1/8566/235.
9. Bush, *Bless our Ship*, p. 89.
10. Chatfield, *The Navy and Defence*, p. 198.
11. Hughes, *The Royal Naval College, Dartmouth*, pp. 93–4.
12. Oliver MSS p. 218.
13. AFO 2859/25 – revised rates of pay for new entries.
    See also AFO 2858/25 – revised rates of pay for officers after 5 Oct. 1925.

14. Gardner, *Naval Cradle – Osborne memories* (unpublished).
15. AFO 2157/20, resulting from Board discussions Adm 1 June 1920.
16. Order in Council 139 of 16 Dec. 1925.
17. Layard, *70 years ago*, (unpublished) pp. 10–11.
18. Harvey, *Downstairs in the Royal Navy*, pp. 43–5.
19. Account of the mutiny at Invergordon is based on: Roskill, *Naval Policy between the Wars*, vol. 2, pp. 89–110; Owen, *Mutiny in the Royal Navy*, vol. II BR 1828(1) 1955, pp. 15–34; Pursey, *Invergordon, First Hand – Last Word*, *NR*, vol. 64 April 1976; Divine, *Mutiny at Invergordon*; Coles, *Invergordon Scapegoat.*

Chapter nine

1. Lowis, *Fabulous Admirals*, p. 240.
2. Admiral Sir Guy Grantham to author.
3. James, *The Sky was Always Blue*, p. 162.
4. Report of proceedings, 11–16 September 1931, Senior officer Atlantic Fleet 24 September 1931, Kelly Papers.
5. Account of the aftermath of the Invergordon Mutiny is based on: Roskill, *Naval Policy Between the Wars*, vol. 2, pp. 110–32; Owen, *Mutiny in the Royal Navy*, vol. II BR 1828 (1) 1955, pp. 34–46, CAFO 2023/32 – Training Policy; Pursey, *Invergordon, First Hand – Last Word NR*, vol. 64, April 1976; Coles, *Invergordon Scapegoat;* Divine, *Mutiny at Invergordon.*
6. *NR*, vol. XX – 1932, pp. 46–52.
7. Commission Book, HMS *Durban* 1931 to 1933 – South American Division.
8. *NR*, vol. LVII – 1969, p. 93.
9. Hughes, *The Royal Naval College, Dartmouth*, pp. 100–1.
10. Owen, *No More Heroes*, p. 131.
11. Avery, *A Dose of Salts*, pp. 24–169.
12. Fisher, *Salt Horse*, p. 46.
13. Mack, *HMS* Intrepid, pp. 31, 32.
14. T. McCarthy to author.
15. Wright, *Sun of Memory*, pp. 127–34.
16. Middlebrook, *Convoy*, p. 10.
17. Report of Naval Welfare Committee (Lord Seebohm) 1973, p. 15 (DGNMT).
18. Roskill, *Naval Policy between the Wars*, vol. 2, pp. 342–3.
19. Lieutenant G.A. Bond to author (1990).
20. Marder, *From the Dardanelles to Oran*, p. 37.
21. Pugsley, *Destroyer Man,* p. 10.

Chapter ten

1. Wigby, *Stoker Royal Navy*, p. 95.
2. Cunningham, *A Sailor's Odyssey*, p. 217.
3. Divine, *Destroyers War*, p. 8.
4. Lipscombe, *The British Submarine*, p. 47.
5. Vice-Admiral Sir John Roxburgh to author.
6. Churchill, *Second World War*, vol. 1, pp. 692–3.
7. Kerr and Granville, *The RNVR*, p. 151.
8. Wells, *Whaley*, p. 112.
9. Kilbracken, *Bring back my Stringbag*, pp. 3–16.
10. Poolman, *The British Sailor*, p. 173.
11. Lamb, *War in a String Bag*, p. 11.
12. John Marsh to author.

13. Poland, *The Torpedomen*, pp. 131–7.
14. Connell, *Jack's War*, p. 44.
15. Extract of letter by Richard Washbourn to colleague, 20 January 1940.
16. Roskill, *HMS* Warspite, pp. 206–8.
17. *Ibid*, p. 204.
18. Moran, *Anatomy of Courage*, p. 94.
19. *Ibid*, pp. 97–8.
20. Connell, *Jack's War*, p. 58.
21. Brown and Marshall, *Ships and Men in Rough Seas*, JNS, vol. 5, No. 1.
22. Lombard Hobson, *A Sailor's War*, p. 55–6.
23. Messer, *Able Seaman RNVR*, pp. 26–30.
24. Fisher, *Salt Horse*, p. 120.
25. Poolman, *The British Sailor*, pp. 47–9.
26. Chalmers, *Full Cycle*, p. 96.
27. Finch, *Tiffy*, pp. 107–13.
28. E.W. Whitley to author, 1990.
29. Winton, *The War at Sea*, pp. 86–91.
30. Lamb, *War in a String Bag*, pp. 106–7.
31. Winton, *The War at Sea*, pp. 86–91
32. Cunningham, *A Sailor's Odyssey*, p. 332.
33. Le Bailly, *The Man Around the Engine*, p. 82.
34. Lawrence, *A Naval Schoolmaster Looks Back*, p. 77.

Chapter eleven

1. Minutes of technical Progress Meeting, First Lord's War Room – 28 May 1943 (DGNMT).
2. Young, *One of our Submarines*, pp. 12–241.
3. Simpson, *Periscope View*, pp. 164–7.
4. Poolman, *The British Sailor*, pp. 139–40.
5. Gretton, *Convoy Escort Commander*, p. 104. See also CAFO 137/42 – Shortage of Officers (NHL).
6. Monsarrat, *Three Corvettes*, p. 15. © The Estate of Nicholas Monsarrat 1945, by kind permission of Mrs Ann Monsarrat.
7. Middlebrook, *Convoy*, p. 40.
8. Monsarrat, *Three Corvettes*, pp. 62–3.
9. *Ibid*, p. 27.
10. *Ibid*, p. 157.
11. HOLLAND – Hope our love lasts and never dies.
    ITALY – I trust and love you.
    BURMA – Be undressed and ready my angel.
12. Scott, *Battle of the Narrow Seas*, pp. 35, 77, 79.
13. Ransome Wallis, *Two Red Stripes*, pp. 83–100.
14. Fisher, *Salt Horse*, p. 100. See also CAFO 2156/42.
15. Winton, *War at Sea*, p. 269.
16. Bull, *To Sea in a Sieve*, pp. 111, 162–4.
17. Admiral Sir Frank Twiss to author. See also Johns and Kelly, *No Surrender*.
18. Humble, *Fraser of North Cape*, p. 258–60.
19. Vian, *Action this Day*, p. 196.
20. Wardroom Officers, *A Formidable Commission*, pp. 78–83.
21. Connell, *Jack's War*, p. 167.

Chapter twelve

1. Humble, *Fraser of North Cape*, p. 182.
2. *Ibid*, p. 293.
3. Wells, *Whaley*, p. 138. Boy New Entries at *Ganges* were called 'Nozzers'.
4. AFO 2912/1951.
5. Historical introduction to BR 11.
6. Taylor, *The Sea Chaplains*, pp. 457–8.
7. Popham, *Into the Wind*, p. 223.
8. Lieutenant Commander John Cooper to author.
9. CAFO 147/45.
10. AFO 2701/1952. See also H.D. Ware *Habitability in Surface Warships*, RINA 1986.
11. Noble Committee for Special Entry Officer Candidates, 1945.
12. Blundell, *Naval Anecdotes* (unpublished).
13. John Lord, former Chief Engine Room Artificer, to author.
14. Leo P. Sklenar to author.
15. Fisher, *Salt Horse*, pp. 201–2.
16. BR3226, Ch. 6, p. 17.

Chapter thirteen

1. Memorandum by Admiral Sir Algernon Willis on the necessity for an even flow of promotion for officers, 1946.
2. Report of Officer Structure Survey Committee, 1965.
   Rear Admiral C.C.H. Dunlop to author.
3. Report of Dartmouth Review Committee (Murray), 1958.
4. Vice-Admiral Sir John Forbes to author.
5. Committee on rating structure (CRUST), 1958.
6. Memorandum by First Sea Lord, 1957, circulated to Admiralty staff.
7. Popham, *Into the Wind*, pp. 237–8.
   Admiral Sir Guy Grantham to author.
8. Cmnd 4291 – Standing reference on the pay of the Armed Forces.
9. Report of the Welfare Committee – chairman Lord Seebohm, 1973.
10. Blundell, *Naval Anecdotes* (unpublished).
11. Captain Richard Kirkby to author.
12. Captain C.P.O. Burne to author.
13. Rear Admiral C.C.H. Dunlop to author.
14. Pack, *Nelson's Blood*, pp. 115–20.
15. Vice-Admiral Sir Roy Talbot to author.
16. Rodger, *The Admiralty*, p. 156.
17. Wells, *Whaley*, pp. 178–80.
18. Admiral Sir Anthony Griffin to author.
19. *NR*, vol. 58 (1970) p. 99.

Chapter fourteen

1. Admiral Sir A. Francis Turner KCB, DSC.
   Admiral Sir Peter White GBE, FBIM.
   Admiral Sir Lindsay Bryson KCB.
2. DCI 166/75.
3. Barker, *Ruling the Waves*, p. 342.

4. Report of the Committee on boy entrants and young servicemen, Chairman Lord Donaldson, 1970.
5. Woodward, *One Hundred Days*, p. 85.
6. Underwood, *Our Falklands War*, p. 18.
7. Woodward, *One Hundred Days*, p. 14.
8. *Ibid*, p. 17.
9. Underwood, *Our Falklands War*, p. 33.
10. *Ibid*, p. 66.
11. Woodward, *One Hundred Days*, p. 288.
12. Underwood, *Our Falklands War*, p. 33.

Appendix

1. Active service numbers include Royal Navy and Royal Marines officers, men and women. Personnel strengths based on statistics provided by Accountant General's Department of Admiralty dated 13 October 1913 (which include Coastguards), Naval Historical Branch and AS(M)2, Part of Defence Analytical Services Agency – April 1993.
2. Until 1872 responsibility for naval personnel was often shared by the First Sea Lord and a Junior or Second Sea Lord. From 18 December 1868 to 5 May 1872 there was no Second Sea Lord and by Order in Council of 19 March 1872 the Board were reorganized and responsibility for personnel more specifically assigned to the Second Sea Lord with the appointment of Rear Admiral J. Walter Tarleton. His responsibilities included manning, training, officer appointments and mobilization.

Bibliography

The following books were consulted but this cannot claim to be a comprehensive list. In addition, reference was made to the *Naval Review* (*NR*), *Journal of the Royal United Services Institution* (*JRUSI*), *The United Service Magazine* (*USM*), *The Army and Navy Gazette*, *The Mariner's Mirror* (*MM*), *Navy Lists*, *Sports and Recreation in the Royal Navy*, *Royal Navy Broadsheets* and the *Navy News*. Place of publication is London, unless otherwise stated.

Acland, Sir Reginald, KC, *Crime and Punishments in the Royal Navy during the last fifty years*, *NR* vol. II, (1923).

Admiralty, *Your Ship: Notes and advice to an officer assuming his first command*, 1944.

—, *The Divisional Officer's Handbook*, 1957.

—, *King's Regulations and Admiralty Instructions.*

—, *Queen's Regulations and Admiralty Instructions.*

—, *Naval Staff at the Admiralty: Its work and development*, Sept. 1939.

—, *Circulars.*

—, *Fleet Orders*, including those classified Confidential.

—, *Monthly Orders.*

—, *Weekly Orders.*

Alliston, John, *Destroyer Man*, Greenhouse Publications, 1985.

Ashcroft, William P., *Reminiscences*, *NR* vol. 52 (1964), vol. 53 (1965).

Aspinall-Oglander, Cecil, *Roger Keyes*, Hogarth Press, 1951.

Avery, Lieutenant Commander, K.R. *A Dose of Salts*, Merlin Books, 1988.

Bacon, Admiral Sir Reginald, *The Life of Lord Fisher of Kilverstone*, 2 vols, Hodder and Stoughton, 1929.

—, *A Naval Scrapbook : Pt I, 1877–1900*, Hutchinson, 1932.

Baggett, John, Signalman, *Journal of the Cruises of HMS* Alexandra, *flagship of Admiral John Hay*, NMM, JOD 71.

Ballard, Admiral George, *The Black Battlefleet*, Nautical Publishing Co and Society for Nautical Research, Greenwich, 1980.

—, *The Navy in early Victorian England* (ed. G.M. Young).

—, *Memoirs* Pt 1, *Burneys and HMS* Britannia, *MM* vol. 61 (1975).

—, *Memoirs* Pt 2, *Midshipmen*, *MM* vol. 62 (1976).

Barker, Dennis, *Ruling the Waves: An Unofficial Portrait of the Navy*, Penguin, 1986.

Bartimeus, *The Long Trick*, Cassell, 1917.

—, *A Make and Mend*, Richard Cowan, 1934.

—, *The Navy Eternal*, Richard Cowan.

Bassett, Colonel Sam, *Royal Marine*, Davies, 1962.

Bath, Pay Commander A.G., *The Victualling of the Navy*, *JRUSI*, Feb 1939.
Bayly, Admiral Sir Lewis, *Pull Together*, 1938.
Baynham, Henry, *Before the Mast: Naval Ratings of the 19th Century*, Hutchinson, 1971.
—, *Men from the Dreadnoughts*, Hutchinson, 1976.
Beckett, Captain W.T.N., *A Few Naval Customs, Expressions, Traditions and Superstitions*, Gieves, 1931.
Bennett, Captain Geoffrey, *Charlie B*, Day, 1968.
Benstead, C.R., *HMS* Rodney *at Sea*, Methuen, 1932.
Beresford, Admiral Lord Charles, *Memoirs*, 2 vols, Methuen, 1914.
Blake, John, *How Sailors Fight*, Grant Richards, 1901.
Bowden-Smith, Admiral Sir N., *Naval Recollections 1852–1914*, Army Navy Co-op Society.
Bowes, Arthur, *Diary in HMS* Sultan *1882–1885* NMM, JOD104.
Bowles, G.S., *A Gun Room Ditty Box*, Methuen, 1898.
Boyd, Captain J.M., *A Manual for Naval Cadets*, 1860.
Boys, W.H., *Memoir of Naval Service of Admiral Henry Boys*, unpublished, 1913.
Bradford, Ernlie, *The Mighty Hood*, Hodder and Stoughton, 1959.
Bridge, Admiral Sir Cyprian, *Some Recollections*, John Murray, 1918.
Briggs, Sir John H., *Naval Administrations 1827–1892*, Sampson Low.
Brooke, Geoffrey, *Alarm Starboard*, Stephens, 1982.
Broome, Captain Jack, *Make a Signal*, Putnam, 1955.
Bryant, Sir Arthur, *English Saga 1840–1940*, Collins, 1940.
Bull, Peter RNVR, *To Sea in a Sieve*, Davies, 1956.
Bush, Captain E.W., *Bless our Ship*, Allen and Unwin, 1958.
—, *Flowers of the Sea*, Allen and Unwin, 1962.
—, *How to become a Naval Officer*, Allen and Unwin, 1963.
Campbell, Lieutenant Charles, *The Interior Economy of a Modern Man of War*, *JRUSI* vol. 27, 1884.
Capper, Lieutenant Commander H.D., *Aft from the Hawsehole*, Faber and Gwyer, 1927.
Carew, Anthony, *The Lower Deck of the Royal Navy 1900–1939*, Manchester, 1981.
Chalmers, Rear Admiral W.S., *Max Horton and the Western Approaches*, Hodder and Stoughton, 1954.
—, *Full Cycle: Biography of Admiral Sir Bertram Ramsay*.
Chambers, Admiral B.M., *Salt Junk*, Constable, 1927.
Chatfield, Admiral of the Fleet, Lord, *The Navy and Defence*, W. Heinemann, 1942.
Churchill, Rt Hon. Winston S., *The Second World War*, vols 1 to 6.
Coles, Alan, *Invergordon Scapegoat: The Betrayal of Admiral Tomkinson*, Alan Sutton, 1993.
Connell, G.C., *Jack's War*, Kimber, 1985.
Cork and Orrery, Admiral of the Fleet, the Earl, *My Naval Life 1886–1941*, Hutchinson, 1942.
Craddock, Captain Christopher, *Whispers from the Fleet*, Griffin, 1908.
Cresswell, Admiral Sir William, *Close to the Wind*, Heinemann, 1965.
Crowe, George, MAA, *The Commission of HMS* Terrible, Newnes, 1903.
Cunningham, Admiral of the Fleet, Viscount, *A Sailor's Odyssey*, Hutchinson, 1957.
Cunningham Graham, Admiral Sir Angus, *Random Naval Recollections*, Famedram, 1979.
Davies, John, Lieutenant RNVR, *Lower Deck*, Macmillan, 1945.
Dawson, Captain Lionel, *Flotillas: A Hard Lying Story*, Rich and Cowan, 1933.
—, *Mediterranean Medley*, Rich and Cowan, 1933.

De Chair, Admiral Sir Dudley, *The Sea is Strong*, Harrap, 1961.
Defence Council Instructions (Navy).
Denham, H.M., *Dardanelles: A Midshipman's Diary, 1915–1916*, John Murray, 1981.
Dewar, Vice-Admiral K.G.B., *The Navy from Within*, Gollancz, 1939.
Divine, A.D., *Destroyers War*, John Murray, 1942.
—, *Mutiny at Invergordon*, MacDonald, 1970.
Don, W.G., Deputy Surgeon, *Reminiscences of the Battlefleet of 1855*, Cornmarket Press, 1971.
Douglas-Morris, Captain K., *Naval Long Service Medals, 1830–1990*, privately published, 1991.
Dreyer, Admiral Sir Frederic C., *The Sea Heritage*, Museum Press, 1954.
Dwyer, Lieutenant D.J., *A History of the Royal Naval Barracks, Portsmouth*, Gale and Polden, 1961.
Eardley-Wilmot, Rear Admiral Sir Sydney, *An Admiral's Memories*, Sampson Low Marston, 1927.
Edwards, A. Tristan, *The British Bluejacket: 1915–1940*, Unwin Brothers, 1940.
Elvin, Commander R.H.P., 'The Mechanician 1905–1955', *Journal of Naval Engineering*, October 1935.
'Etienne', *A Naval Lieutenant*, Methuen, 1919.
'Ex-Royal Navy', *The British Navy from Within*, Hodder and Stoughton.
Fabb, J. and McGowan, A.P. *The Victorian and Edwardian Navy from Old Photographs*, Batsford, 1976.
Fairbairn, Lieutenant Commander Douglas, *Narrative of a Naval Nobody*, John Murray, 1929.
Fawcett, H.W. and Hooper, G.W.W., *The Fighting at Jutland*, 1920.
Finch, George E., *Tiffy: Autobiography of a Naval Engineer*, Square One Publications, 1991.
Fisher of Kilverstone, Lord, Admiral of the Fleet, *Memories and Records*, Hodder and Stoughton, 1919.
Fisher, Admiral Sir F. William, *Naval Reminiscences*, F. Muller, 1938.
Fisher, Rear Admiral R.L., *Salt Horse*, Famedram Publishers.
Fitzgerald, Admiral Penrose, *Memories of the Sea*, Arnold, 1913.
Fleet, Vice-Admiral H.L., *My Life and a Few Yarns*, Allen, 1922.
Fletcher, M.H. *The WRNS – A History of the Women's Naval Service*, Batsford, 1989.
Fremantle, Admiral Sir Sydney, *My Naval Career 1880–1928*, Hutchinson, 1949.
Frewen, Oswald, *Sailors Soliloquy*, Hutchinson, 1961.
Gieve, David W., *Gieves and Hawkes 1785–1985*, Gieves and Hawkes, 1985.
'Giraldus' (Gerald O'Driscoll), *Awful Disclosures of a Bluejacket*, Marlborough, 1929.
Glascock, Captain W.N., *The Naval Service or Officers Manual*, Saunders Otley, 1836.
Goodenough, Revd G., *The Handy Man: Afloat and Ashore*, Unwin, 1901.
Grand Fleet Chaplains Notebook, *Grand Fleet Days.*
—, *In the Northern Mists.*
—, *Naval Intelligence*, Hodder and Stoughton, 1918–1919.
Granville, Wilfred, *Sea Slang of the Twentieth Century*, Winchester Publications, 1949.
Grenfell, Captain Russell, *Service Pay*, Eyre and Spottiswood, 1944.
Gretton, Vice-Admiral Sir Peter, *Convoy Escort Commander*, Cassell, 1964.
—, *Former Naval Person*, Cassell, 1968.
Grove, Eric, *Vanguard to Trident – British Naval Policy since World War II*, Bodley Head, 1987.
Hackforth-Jones, Gilbert, *Life in the Navy Today*, Cassell, 1957.
Hamilton, Admiral Sir R. Vesey, *Naval Administration*, George Bell, 1896.

Hampshire, A. Cecil, *The Royal Navy since 1945*, Kimber, 1975.
Harland, John, *Seamanship in the Age of Sail*, Conway Maritime, 1984.
Harris, Admiral Sir Robert, *From Naval Cadet to Admiral*, Cassell, 1913.
Hartford, Commander G.B., *Commander RN*, Arrowsmith, 1927.
Harvey, Lieutenant Commander W.B., *Downstairs in the Royal Navy*, Brown Son and Ferguson, 1979.
Hastings, Max and Jenkins, Simon, *The Battle for the Falklands*, Book Club Associates, 1983.
Hayward, T. and Ashton, K., *The Royal Navy, Rum Rumour and a Pinch of Salt*, Brown Son and Ferguson, 1985.
Her Company, *The Silver Phantom: HMS Aurora*, F. Muller, 1945.
Hewitt, T., *From Dawn to Dark in the King's Navy*, Barrell, 1930.
Hickman, W., RN, *Reports and Opinions of Officers on Regulations for Maintaining Discipline*, 1867.
Hill, Captain Roger, *Destroyer Captain*, Kimber, 1975.
Holloway, S.M., *From Trench to Turret*, Royal Marines Museum.
Holman, Thomas, *Life in the Royal Navy*, Sampson Low Marston, 1892.
Hogg, Anthony, *Just a Hogg's Life: A Royal Navy Saga of the Thirties*, Solo Mio Books, 1993.
Hopwood, Captain Ronald, *The Old Way*, John Murray, 1917.
Hough, Richard, *The Longest Battle*, Weidenfeld and Nicholson, 1986.
Hughes, E.A., *The Royal Naval College, Dartmouth*, Winchester Publications, 1950.
Humble, Richard, *Fraser of North Cape*, Routledge and Kegan Paul, 1983.
'Idler, The', *Rolling Home*, John Bale, 1936.
James, Admiral Sir William, *Admiral Sir William Fisher*, MacMillan, 1943.
—, *Portsmouth Letters*, MacMillan, 1946.
—, *The Sky was Always Blue*, Methuen, 1951.
—, *A Great Seaman – Life of Admiral of the Fleet Sir Henry Oliver*, Witherby, 1956.
Jameson, Rear Admiral William, *The Fleet that Jack Built*, Hart-Davis, 1962.
Jarrett, Dudley, *British Naval Dress*, Dent, 1960.
Jeans, Surgeon Rear Admiral T.T., *Reminiscences of a Naval Surgeon*, Sampson Low Marston, 1927.
John, Rebecca, *Caspar John*, Collins, 1987.
Johns, Chief Ordnance Artificer William, and Kelly, R.A., *No Surrender*, Harrap, 1969.
Jolly, Surgeon Commander Rick, *The Red and Green Life Machine: A Diary of a Falklands Field Hospital*, Century, 1983.
Kemp, Peter K., *The British Sailor – A Social History of the Lower Deck*, Dent, 1970.
—, *Oxford Companion to Ships and the Sea*, Oxford University Press, 1976.
Kennedy, Ludovic, *Sub Lieutenant*, Batsford, 1942.
Kent, Captain Barrie M., *Signal! A History of Signalling in the Royal Navy*, Hyden House, 1993.
Kerr, J. Lennox and Granville, Wilfred, *The RNVR*, Harrap, 1957.
Kerr, Admiral Mark, *The Navy in My Time*, Rich and Cowan, 1933.
—, *Prince Louis of Battenburg*, Longman's Green, 1934.
Keyes, Admiral of the Fleet Sir Roger, *Adventures Ashore and Afloat*, Harrap, 1939.
Kilbracken, Lord, *Bring Back my Stringbag*, Peter Davies, 1929.
King-Hall, L., *Sea Saga – Naval Diaries of four generations of King-Hall family*, Gollanz, 1935.
Kipling, Rudyard, *A Fleet in Being*, MacMillan, 1898.
Knock, Sydney, *Clear Lower Deck*, Philip Alan, 1932.

'Knocker', Clinker, *Aye Aye, Sir – The Autobiography of a Stoker*, Rich and Cowan, 1938.
Laffin, John, *Jack Tar*, Cassell, 1969.
Lamb, Charles, *War in a String Bag*, Cassell, 1977.
Lawrence, Ivor D., *A Naval Schoolmaster Looks Back*, 1986.
Le Bailly, Vice-Admiral Sir Louis, *The Man Around the Engine*, Kenneth Mason, 1990.
—, *From Fisher to the Falklands*, Marine Management Holdings, 1991.
Lewis, Michael, *England's Sea Officers*, Allen and Unwin, 1939.
—, *The Navy in Transition – A Social History 1814–1864*, Hodder and Stoughton, 1965.
Liddle, Peter, *The Sailors' War 1914–1918*, Blandford Press, 1985.
Lipscombe, Commander F.W., *The British Submarine*, Conway Maritime Press, 1975.
Lloyd, Christopher, *The British Seaman 1200–1860*, Collins, 1968.
Lombard Hobson, Captain Sam, *A Sailor's War*, Orbis, 1983.
Lowis, Commander Geoffrey L., *Fabulous Admirals*, Putnam, 1957.
Lyne, Rear Admiral Sir Thomas, *Something about a Sailor*, Jarrolds, 1940.
Macdonald, John D., Staff Surgeon, *On Ship Ventilation as a Department of Naval Hygiene*, *USM*, May 1895.
Mack, George, *HMS* Intrepid, Kimber, 1980.
Mackay, Rudolf F., *Fisher of Kilverstone*, Clarendon Press, 1973.
Mallalieu, J.P.W., *Very Ordinary Seaman*, Gollancz, 1944.
Marder, Arthur J., *Fear God and Dread Nought*, 3 vols, Jonathan Cape, 1952–9.
—, *From the Dreadnought to Scapa Flow: the Royal Navy in the Fisher era*, 5 vols, Oxford University Press, 1973.
—, *From the Dardanelles to Oran*, Oxford University Press, 1974.
'Martello Tower', (F.C. Norman), *At School and at Sea*, John Murray, 1899.
Martin, Pay Rear Admiral W.E.R., *Adventures of a Naval Paymaster*, Herbert Jenkins, 1924.
Mathew, David, *The Naval Heritage*, Collins, 1945.
Matson, John, *Dear Osborne*, Hamish Hamilton, 1978.
May, Commander W.E., Karman, W.Y. and Turner, John, *Badges and Insignia of the British Armed Services*, A. & C. Black, 1974.
Messer, H.J., *Able Seaman RNVR*, Merlin Books, 1989.
Middlebrook, Martin, *Convoy: the battles for Convoys SC 122 and 45X229*, Allen Lane, 1976.
Monsarrat, Nicholas, *Three Corvettes*, Cassell, 1943, and now published by Pan Books.
Moran, Lord, *The Anatomy of Courage*, Constable, 1945.
Moresby, Admiral John, *Two Admirals*, John Murray, 1909.
Morgan, K.O., *The Oxford Illustrated History of Britain*, Oxford University Press, 1991.
Morris, James, 'A View of the Royal Navy', *Encounter*, March 1973.
Musson, Surgeon Rear Admiral R.W., *The story of a Naval Doctor*, 1983.
Noble, Sam, A.B., *'Tween decks in the Seventies*, Sampson Low, 1925.
Owen, Charles, *No More Heroes: The Royal Navy in the Twentieth Century*, Allen and Unwin, 1975.
Pack, Captain James, *Nelson's Blood*, Kenneth Mason, 1982.
Pack, Captain S.W.E., *Britannia at Dartmouth*, Alvin Redman, 1968.
Padfield, Peter, *Aim Straight: a Biography of Admiral Sir Percy Scott*, Hodder and Stoughton, 1966.
—, *The Battleship Era*, Hart-Davis, 1972.

—, *Rule Britannia*, Routledge and Kegan Paul, 1981.
Paget, Admiral Lord Clarence, *Autobiography and Journals*, Chapman and Hall, 1896.
Paxton, Lieutenant P.J., *The Story of HMS* Fisgard, Truran Publications, 1983.
Paynter, Lieutenant Commander H., *Battleship Life in the early Eighties*, *JRUSI*, 1929.
Penn, Commander Geoffrey, *Up Funnel, Down Screw*, Hollis and Carter, 1955.
—, *Snotty: the Story of the Midshipman*, Hollis and Carter, 1957.
—, *HMS* Thunderer, Kenneth Mason, 1984.
Poland, Rear Admiral E.N., *The Torpedomen: HMS* Vernon*'s story 1872–1986*, Kenneth Mason, 1993.
Poolman, Kenneth, *The British Sailor*, Arms and Armour, 1989.
Popham, Hugh, *Into the Wind*, Hamish Hamilton, 1969.
Pugsley, Rear Admiral Anthony, *Destroyer Man*, Weidenfeld and Nicholson, 1957.
Pursey, Commander Harry, *From Petitions to Reviews*, Brassey's Annual, 1937.
—, *Lower Deck to Quarterdeck*, Brassey's Annual, 1930.
—, *The Making of a Seaman*, Brassey's Annual, 1939.
Putt, S. Gorley, *Men Dressed as Seamen*, Christophers, 1943.
Quigley, Dave J., *Under the Jolly Roger: British Submarines at War*, Conifer Press, Fareham, 1988.
Rasor, Eugene L., *Reform in the Royal Navy: A Social History of the Lower Deck 1850 to 1880*, Archon Books, 1976.
Reynolds, L.C., *Gunboat 658*, Kimber, 1955.
Reynolds, Stephen, *The Lower Deck and the Nation*, J.M. Dent, 1912.
Riley, Patrick, *Memoirs of a Bluejacket*, Sampson Low Marston, 1931.
Robinson, Commander C.N., *The British Tar in Fact and Fiction*, Harpers, 1911.
Rodger, N.A.M., *Naval Records for Genealogists*, HMSO, 1988.
—, *The Admiralty*, Dalton, 1979.
—, *The Wooden World: An Anatomy of the Georgian Navy*, Collins, 1986.
Roskill, Captain S.W., *HMS* Warspite, Collins, 1957.
—, *The Navy at War 1939–1945*, Collins, 1960.
—, *The Art of Leadership*, 1964.
—, *Naval Policy between the Wars*, Collins, 1968.
Russell, W. Clark, *Sailors' Language*, Sampson Low Marston, 1883.
Schofield, Vice-Admiral B.B., *The Story of HMS Dryad*, Kenneth Mason, 1977.
Scott, Admiral Sir Percy, *Fifty Years in the Royal Navy*, John Murray, 1919.
Scott, Lieutenant Commander Peter, *The Battle of the Narrow Seas*, Country Life, 1945.
Seymour, Admiral of the Fleet Sir Edward, *My Naval Career*, Smith Elder, 1911.
Sherwood, Martyn, *Coston Gun*, G. Bles, 1954.
Simpson, Rear Admiral C.W.G., *Periscope View*, MacMillan, 1972.
Sloane-Stanley, Captain Cecil, *Reminiscences of a Midshipman's Life*, 2 vols, Eden, 1893.
Smith, Vice-Admiral Humphrey H., *A Yellow Admiral Remembers*, Arnold, 1932.
Smith, Stan, *Sea of Memories*, 1985.
Smith, Waldo E.L., *The Navy Chaplain and his Parish*, 1967.
Smyth, Admiral W.H., *The Sailor's Word Book*, Blackie, 1867.
Stephen, Adrian, *The Dreadnought Hoax*, Chatto and Windus, 1983.

Stevens, Captain J.S., *Never Volunteer: A Submariner's Scrapbook*, 1971.

Stuart, H., *The Novice or Young Seaman's Catechism*, Whithorn, 1860.

Sturdee, Lieutenant Commander B.V., *Five Minutes to One Bell: a Few Hints to Junior Watchkeepers together with some Remarks of the Duties of a Destroyer First Lieutenant*, Gieves, 1914.

Taprell Dorling, Captain H., ('Taffrail'), *Adventures of an Officer's Steward, NR* vol. 23 (1935).

Taylor, Gordon, *The Sea Chaplains*, Oxford Illustrated Press, 1978.

—, *London's Navy: a Story of the RNVR*, Quiller Press, 1983.

Thompson, Paul, *Close to the Wind: The Early Memoirs of Admiral Sir William Cresswell*, Heineman, 1965.

Trendell, John, *Operation Music Master: The Story of Royal Marines Bands*, RM Musuem, Eastney, 1982.

Trevelyan, G.M., *English Social History*, Longmans Green, 1944.

Trotter, Wilfred Pym, *The Royal Navy in Old Photographs*, J.M. Dent, 1975.

Turner, E.S., *Gallant Gentlemen*, Michael Joseph, 1956.

Tute, Warren, *The True Glory*, McDonald, 1983.

Tweedie, Admiral Sir Hugh, *Story of my Naval Life*, Rich and Cowan, 1939.

Underwood, Geoffrey, *Our Falklands War*, Maritime Books, 1983.

'Undistinguished Naval Officer' (H.J.B. Montgomery), *The British Navy in the Present Year of Grace*, Hamilton and Adams, 1884.

'Vanderdecken', *The Modern Officer of the Watch*, Griffin, 1904.

Vian, Admiral of the Fleet Sir Philip, *Action this Day*, Muller, 1960.

Walker, Sir Charles, *Thirty-six Years at the Admiralty*, Lincoln Williams, 1933.

Walker, Lieutenant Commander C.F., *Young Gentlemen*, Longmans Green, 1938.

Wallis, Ransome, *Two Red Stripes*, Ian Allan, 1955.

Wardroom Officers of *Formidable*, *A Formidable Commission*, Seeley Service, 1948.

Warlow, Lieutenant Commander Ben, *The Pusser and his Men: A Short History of the Supply and Secretariat Branch*, 1984.

Warner, Derek, *A Steward's Life in the Royal Navy 1943–1961*, Stockwell, 1990.

Wells, Rear Admiral Gerard A., *Naval Customs and Traditions*, Philip Allan, 1930.

Wells, Captain J.G., *Whaley*, HMSO, 1980.

—, *The Immortal* Warrior, Kenneth Mason, 1987.

Wester Wemyss, Lady, *Life and Letters of Lord Wester Wemyss, Admiral of the Fleet*, Eyre and Spottiswoode, 1935.

Weston, Agnes, *My Life amongst the Bluejackets*, Nisbet, 1911.

Wettern, Desmond, *Decline of British Sea Power*, Janes, 1982.

Wigby, Frederick, *Stoker Royal Navy*, Blackwood, 1967.

Williams, Mark, *Gilbert Roberts RN*, Cassell, 1979.

Willis, Pay Captain G.H.A., *The Royal Navy as I saw it*, John Murray, 1924.

Wincott, E.N., *Invergordon Mutineer*, Weidenfeld and Nicholson.

Winn, Godfrey, *Home from the Sea*, Hutchinson, 1944.

Winton, John, *We joined the Navy*, Michael Joseph, 1959.

—, *Hurrah for the Life of a Sailor: Life on the Lower Deck of the Victorian Navy*, Michael Joseph, 1977.

—, *The War at Sea: An Anthology of Personal Experience*, Hutchinson, 1967.

Woods, Gerard A., *Wings at sea: A Fleet Air Arm Observer's War 1940–1945*, Conway Maritime, 1985.
Woodward, Admiral Sir Sandy, with Patrick Robinson, *One Hundred Days*, Harper Collins, 1992.
Wright, Rear Admiral (S.) Noel, *Sun of Memory*, Benn, 1947.
Yexley, Lionel, *The Inner Life of the Navy*, Pitman, 1908.
—, *Our Fighting Seamen*, Stanley Paul, 1911.
—, ed., *The Bluejacket*, 1898–1902.
—, ed., *The Fleet* .
Young, G.M., *Early Victorian England*, 2 vols, Oxford University Press, 1934.
Young, Commander Edward, RNVR, *One of our Submarines*, Hart-Davis, 1952.
Young, Filson, *With the Battle Cruisers*, Cassell, 1921.
Ziegler, Philip, *Mountbatten: The Official Biography*, Collins, 1985.

Index